GOLDEN AGE R'S MARGIN

Golden Ages at The Fenner's Margin

Edited by A. P. A. Wykes

(or A Generous Theorem of Enjoyment, Wickets and Strokes)

*Contains diary entries attributable to John Neville Keynes
and other writings attributable to John Maynard Keynes*

SERENDIPITY

Copyright © A. P. A. Wykes, 2005

First published in 2005 by
Serendipity
Suite 530
37 Store Street
Bloomsbury
London

All rights reserved
Unauthorised duplication
contravenes existing laws
British Library Cataloguing-in-Publication data
A catalogue record for this book is available from the British Library
ISBN 1-84394-099-X
Printed and bound by The Alden Press, Oxford

To the memory of Lesley Butcher, an un-Wodehouselike Cambridge aunt, who, like J.M.K., died far too early at 62, with a fresh vitality intact.

For Fiona, Stella and Lydie, who haven't read it and don't need to, and George W. Bush, who should read it (the right way up).

Adrian Wykes, as Percy Pavilion, with David Gower, trying to promote the *Gower Power* single in 1984. Adrian also put out *The Cricket E.P.* (1983, with Captain Sensible and Dolly Mixture), *Pay Later* (a 1986 L.P. with his collective, named do it now!), The Cricket C.D. (1994) and *World Cup Anthems 1999* (a cassette E.P.). When playing with Cambridgeshire in the Natwest Trophy (1987–9; 2 for 14 against Derbyshire, and 3 for 36 at Edgbaston) Ralph Dellor and *The Daily Telegraph* aptly used to refer to him as a 'failed pop star' in the paragraph where they would also talk about cricketing goldfish and llama farmers.

Adrian lived in London until he was fifteen, attending St. Paul's School, but spent the holidays with his grandparents in central Cambridge. The family moved to Glisson Road near Fenner's entailing study at Cambridgeshire High School (which rapidly turned into Hill's Road Sixth Form College) and then The Leys, where Adrian discovered Economics (achieving an A grade in one year). He then read, notionally, Geography at University College, London, living in Taviton Street and Woburn Square in the heart of Keynesian Bloomsbury, but only got a 2.1 since he captained both his college and the University of London at cricket while simultaneously wrestling with the History of the Philosophy of Science and The West Indies.

After several years finding out how impossible it was to become a fusion of Garry Sobers and Jimi Hendrix, Adrian went to St. Catharine's College, Cambridge to study education, and has worked since 1985 in the public sector teaching Economics, Business, Accounting, History, Geography, P.E., and Cricket in the U.K., New Zealand, and Luxembourg. This has left time for six cricket tours of the Caribbean, the setting-up of a recording studio whose proudest sons were The Stupids, and the aforementioned (futile) attempts to counter the soccer supremacy in modern global culture. He has already settled down with his wife, twin daughters, and a rose garden on the assumption that this latest attempt will also fail. His greatest achievement has been as the Luxembourg contributor to the 2000 *Wisden Cricketers Almanack* in getting the top item in the 'Index of Unusual Occurences'. He would like, finally, to thank Dr. Rob Iliffe and Giles Ecclestone for holding onto catches from Messrs. Waugh (1985) and Atherton (1989) off two of the worst balls ever delivered in the history of Cambridge cricket.

Contents

Acknowledgements	ix
Preface by David Frith	xi
Editor's Introduction	1

PART ONE
J.N.K.'s Cricket Diaries, With Commentary …

April 1896	12
May	35
June	70
July	103
August	127

PART TWO
J.M.K.'s Cricket Articles

An Article Compiled During September 1905	145
A Second Article Compiled During September 1905	163
An Article Compiled During May 1909	175
An Article Compiled During October 1915	187
An Article Compiled During April 1935	201
An Article Compiled During July 1937	219
An Article Compiled During February 1946	227
A Second Article Compiled During February 1946	235
An Article Compiled During April 1946	247
Appendix: The Luxembourg Visitations	255
Literary References	303
Video and Film References	308
Musical References	308
Endnotes	309

A Fenner's scene from the early 1960s that wouldn't have been out of place eighty years earlier. In 2003 only some of the trees remain.

Acknowledgements

People: thanks to David Frith for exhaustive, detailed responses when under duress and twenty years of encouragement at the right moments; to Lord Skidelsky and his son Edward at Tilton for information, inspiration, honest criticism, and taking so much trouble in marshalling the lower order; to Duncan Bush for showing great tolerance, interest and enthusiasm, and robust intervention; to Geoff Harcourt for being so open, young at heart, and encouraging; to Milo Keynes for solidity, for understanding, for hospitality, and for my licence to explore; to Matthew Engel for the processes of confidence-giving generosity and honest reflection; to Chris Jakes for his patience at the Lion Yard; to the late Pierre Werner for the interview (October 1999) and his support for cricket in Luxembourg; to Robert Mundell for permission to film the Luxembourg lecture (March 2000); to Hans Tietmeyer and the Banque Centrale De Luxembourg for permission to film the first Pierre Werner Lecture in October 2003; to Eddy Edwards, Ian Graham, Rob Iliffe, and Andy Hibbert for encouragement, constructive criticism, and proof-reading; to all who have helped Apple Computers remain innovative and independent enough to allow this writing process (it could not have been done in any previous era). And Joe, of course.

Places: thanks to all at the Moulin de Chemin, Poitou, for the perfect ambience for my writing holiday (and my wife's riding holiday), Easter 2000; to Coastguards Cottages, Sidmouth, for the August Bank Holiday week at the seaside later in the year; to all involved in Cambridgeshire, Luxembourg, and Barbadian cricket a special acknowledgement of debt, particularly the communities at Holder's Hill and Camden C.C., Cambridge. Mostly thanks to the route de Longwy (Luxembourg, 2000–1) and the Schuman farmhouse (Évrange, 2001–3) for year-round inspiration, never blocked, always wanting to do more rather than less.

Sources: the lists at the back are in effect a tribute to the authors and composers of the books, films, and music that were referred to to try to make an informed criticism of the texts in the endnotes and footnotes. These are the just the ones that I consulted over the last three years and do not represent a comprehensive list of recommended sources. Thanks to the friendly and efficient staff at King's College Library, Cambridge University Library, Lord's Cricket Ground, and The Cambridgeshire Collection.

Many thanks to the memory of Harold Macmillan for the stylistic precedent of not having to have an index (see *The Middle Way*, Macmillan, 1938).

The views expressed in this book do not represent the views of the Optimists Cricket Club, the Luxembourg Cricket Federation, the European School in Luxembourg, the D.f.E.S. in the U.K., the European Parliament, or the European Commission.

Any errata, corrections, comments etc. should be passed to:
adrian.wykes@ci.educ.lu

Geoffrey, Maynard and Margaret Keynes in 1895.

5, 6, 7 and 8, Harvey Road in 2000; at the end of the road on the extreme left in 1896 one would have encountered the Fenner's Pavilion designed by W.M. Fawcett.

Preface

by David Frith

We met to discuss this under the Bradman painting in the Long Room at Lord's. Adrian Wykes had already made his mark on me. Years earlier, in the guise of his alter ego Percy Pavilion, he had sent me some of his idiosyncratic musical compositions to review in *Wisden Cricket Monthly*. Later, under extreme pressure, he revealed that he had once captured the wicket of Steve Waugh. I was won over completely.

Not that it was an easy decision on my part to accept his invitation to contribute this preface. What he could not have known, and what I continued to withhold from him, was that I failed Economics in my matriculation half a century ago. Nor have I taken any serious interest in the subject since, apart from what is force-fed us by the media. The limit of my involvement in the study of Economics is the checking of the (tumbling) interest rates to ensure that my savings are doing no worse than is unavoidable. What, I find myself wondering, would John Maynard Keynes be doing with his hard-earned cash in these difficult times? I did at least share certain knowledge with J.M.K. insofar as I understood that the three functions of money are [a] as a medium of exchange; [b] as a standard of value; and [c] ... You see? I can't remember the third purpose for the life of me.

Perhaps Adrian felt that his highly imaginative literary creation, built on a meshing of spirits of two brilliant men of Cambridge – Keynes and Jack Hobbs – might be satisfactorily introduced by somebody who at least seemed to know what he was talking about when it came to cricket. In all modesty, I'll pay that one. Back in 1953 I failed Economics because I neglected my homework on the subject. I neglected it for three reasons (and this time I can remember them all): [a] I had four other major curriculum subjects to pursue which were much to my liking and would assure me of that matriculation so long as I achieved A passes in all of them; [b] I'll make no pretence: Economics was boring; and [c] I was up late most nights listening to the radio commentary through five Test matches being played 12,000 miles away as Len Hutton, Alec Bedser, Trevor Bailey *et al* worked England into an Ashes-winning position. Suffering such sleep-loss, it was quite beyond me next day to function mentally in the classroom much before lunchtime.

So, yes, I would be interested in what Keynes might have made of Jack Hobbs, and *vice versa*. The early remark that both came from a happy home environment and went on, each in his own *milieu*, to create pleasure to millions was an attractive one. Then came the equally pleasing prospect of being taken by the author through these pages on a guided tour of Cambridge, and finding that so much of it still stands as it was in the time of J. M. Keynes and J. B. Hobbs.

GOLDEN AGES AT THE FENNER'S MARGIN

The outline of Hobbs's emergence from a humble background to a premier position in the world of cricket is inspiring, and the touchpoint in these pages where it is supposed that both these men may have been watching the same match at Fenner's in 1893 (Cambridge University *versus* The Australians) is delightful. Certainly 10-year-old Jack was there. Keynes? The vision of the two boys, unknown to each other, on that distant June day jointly watching Ranji and F.S. Jackson competing against Giffen and Turner and Trumble makes the imagination tingle. Two great worlds meeting, just as they did when Don Bradman bumped into Winston Churchill on Victoria railway station in 1934.

My anxiety came gusting back. What is Adrian's view on Europe? Is he a staunch Europhile, and if so, did he expect me, a believer in the Commonwealth, to feel just as keenly that the United Kingdom should tumble unconditionally into the bosom of mainland, administrative, decision-enforcing Europe? I could only shelter behind the conviction that Jack Hobbs – or W. G. Grace, for that matter – would not have liked that idea at all.

The coaxing for the preface reached a climax with an ingenious ruse by the author. Would I care to pen something up front along similar lines to the foreword J. B. Priestley wrote in the late 1970s for my own book *The Golden Age Of Cricket 1890–1914* – around the time, as it happens, that young Wykes was to stumble upon (allegedly) the unpublished Keynes papers? Mr Priestley's acceptance of my challenge to him was made with characteristic grumpiness, and he suggested payment in the form of a box of Havana cigars, which were to be left on his doorstep. I don't smoke.

I recall too that J.B.P.'s theme throughout the foreword was that although the period under review was precious in his memory, he really ought to have been doing something more useful now, like earning a living, rather than reading through my proofs and constructing a foreword in his mind and on his battered old typewriter.

* * * * *

If it's ideas and opinions that matter, this volume is packed tight with them: Lord Keynes's retrieved and supposed ideas and the ideas of Adrian Wykes himself and others. They fly everywhere, like so many Trescothick fours and sixes. And when we pause to reflect on the volume of ideological chatter that must have been aired over the years around the boundary at the lovely Fenner's ('the smoothest ground in England') and other Cambridge cricket fields, the impression is quite literally stunning.

Here we have the humorous and rather clever device of going back in order to look forward pseudo-conjecturally, foreseeing what we, of course, now know became fact. Artificial surfaces, speculates Keynes's father, 'and umbrellas to protect new grass development'. 'Perhaps in fifty years,' he (allegedly) writes in 1896, to judge from the current speed of development in photography and telegraphy, 'we may be able to follow a series in Australia.' Too right.

Father and son continue to debate cricket as Economics. The similarities can certainly be drawn in abundance. When I caught sight of the liquidity preference theory as seen

PREFACE

in a batsman's choice of either facing the bowling or sheltering at the non-striker's end, I began to wonder if it might be worth having a belated crack at my Economics exam after all. Then there is J.M.K.'s dissection of the Bodyline rumpus, and the author's proposition that Monnet and Schuman rate comparison with Benaud and Worrell, the captains who gave cricket a pronounced and much-needed shot in the arm in 1960–61. He also tenders the very plausible observation that cricket's expansion in the late nineteenth century was not solely because of WG, as is generally accepted.

Poignantly, he has Keynes musing on cricket's virtues – its absence of meanness and sharp practice, and compliance with the laws of the game – knowing full well that in the hundred years since then cricket has changed, in step with society, from a pursuit based on honour into a mongrelised high-pressure entertainment where winning is all. Presciently he brands the truncated form of the game as 'Fricket' (an interesting variation on Bill O'Reilly's assertion to me in the late 1980s that limited-overs cricket ought to be called 'Crackit'). But just when the reader might feel a little depression coming on he/she will be uplifted by a reference to *Mary Poppins*, albeit framed in a socialist context. And among the other rays of sunlight is the comparison posed between the French franc of 1926 and a sticky wicket.

This is a restless, earnest, probing exercise by Adrian Wykes, and I thank him for giving me an early look at it. It would have been as boring as a three-year Economics course had I agreed with everything he had written/ghosted, or, by the same token, had I disagreed with everything. Yet how persuasive it must be for anyone who has ever gone out to bat to read here of a batsman's 'unequal struggle, a true metaphor for labour in its struggle in the factor market'. This had me nodding vigorously, and somehow reminded me of the Saturday morning in 1960 when I was forced to sell my Morris Minor. I went straight to the cricket ground after the transaction and utilised the wad of notes (£125) as a thighpad.

A final thought on the mental legacy of reading this imaginative book: might it not be true that from time to time English cricket has yearned for a batsman of Hobbs's rare quality? And equally, in this neurotic age of global boom and bust, how reassuring it would be if we had somebody as wise as J. M. Keynes to act as an influential government adviser who might just get us out of this mess.

1 July 2003

David Frith, former editor of *The Cricketer* and mentor of *Wisden Cricket Monthly* for seventeen years after he founded it in 1979, is perhaps the world's leading cricket historian. His commited views have been expressed in books as popular as *The Fast Men* and as esoteric as *Silence of the Heart* (an analysis of cricket suicides). His biographies include John Edrich, Jeff Thomson, A.E. Stoddart and Archie Jackson, and at the time of writing this preface he had just published *Bodyline Autopsy* (the most comprehensive work ever on the subject). His associations with John Arlott and (through his *Golden Age* book) with J.B. Priestley takes us back to the world of J.B. Hobbs and the cricket of pre-Great War England.

6, Harvey Road, the home of the Keynes family, in 2000.

Like Conan Doyle's dog that didn't bark, the garden of 6 Harvey Road was conspicuous by its abscence from J.N.K.'s Diary, especially when compared to the frequent mentions of Fenner's

Introduction

My account of the acquisition of John Neville Keynes's (hereinafter J.N.K.) lost cricket diary and the several new manuscripts attributable to his son, John Maynard Keynes (hereinafter J.M.K.), has aroused sceptical responses from the chosen few who have heard it. I can only recount the events as I recall them, and plead that if there is any question about reliability there are greater scholars than I who have been similarly duped by fate in recent years.

It was in the summer of 1979 that a late Saturday night saw the players of Camden Cricket Club carousing in a curry house on Regent Street in Cambridge. This was not only near the house where England opening batsman Tom Hayward had lived after retirement over sixty years earlier, but also just around the corner from Camden House, an impressive building facing Parker's Piece, which gave the club its name in 1881. The restaurant may have been the Mumtaz, it may have been the Taj, I can't recall. Pleased with the day's work I may have indulged in the odd drink as well as a spectacle-fogging Bangalore phall. Soon it was time to wend wearily home across the empty cricket pitches on Parker's Piece. Drifting slightly astray, I rounded the lamp post in the centre of the twenty acres (known as Reality Checkpoint) clockwise rather than to the right, although 'homewards' implied heading course for Gresham Road, not the indoor swimming pool. I then became convinced that I had reached my bed, and, since I was weary, settled down to doze. A light drizzle some time later disabused me of this conviction, and it was revealed that I was still fifty yards short of crossing Gonville Place. The precipitation also gave me the distinct impression that I didn't require any sleep at all.

The next thing I knew I was waking up under the steps up to the front door in the front area of number 6, Harvey Road, around the corner from my home at 34, Glisson Road. It had been a pleasant sleep and this was attributable to a package that I had picked up and used as a pillow, having dislodged a stone that secured it in a hiding-place under the steps. The writing on the outside said, 'Not to be opened before Easter 1996', and, having no reason to think it significant at the time, I put it away in the attic.

Following university, travelling, and work, I was offered a job in Luxembourg on Maundy Thursday, 1996. In the packing-up that ensued after tidying the attic in our new home much later in January 1999, I at last opened the mystery package from nearly twenty years earlier and apprehended with wonder the lost cricket diary of John Neville Keynes, dating from the spring of 1896, and nine other manuscripts bearing the name of John Maynard Keynes.

The covering letter made it clear why the articles had been hidden:

GOLDEN AGES AT THE FENNER'S MARGIN

April 1946

Dear Mother,

Can I trust that your diligent and sober regard for the work of two generations of this family will enable you to find a suitable cache for these papers, which are capable, if released too early (I suggest a fifty year moratorium) of destroying any small public recognition that I may have built up during my lifetime? The flimsy and puerile basis in experience for the ideas intuited and expressed herein would only be meat and drink to hostile forces such as Schumpeter and Hayek. Imagine the effect on Roy Harrod, for example, if he were to be asked to take the field of the cloth of cream seriously!

It is especially important that these papers remain a mystery to all in the United States, for much as I would welcome plaudits from the puritan republic of the old guard, it is the power of the new gaudy empire that I fear, and its opinion will carry all before it for the remainder of this century. If my economic revolution is to carry any long-term resonance throughout the world, it will have to bear the heavy accent of Congress and the Federal Reserve rather than the playing fields of Eton and Fenner's Pavilion.

Success through distortion is preferable to failure through purity, so I beg you to carry out this request on behalf of all of us,

Your loving son,
Ever,
Maynard

The date was indeed the month of his death at the age of 62 (both his parents lived past the age of ninety) but could the parcel really have lain dormant for half a century? At an early stage after deciphering the collection of handwritten papers and typescripts I contacted experts. Matthew Engel, then editor of the *Wisden Almanack*, was uncertain of the provenance, but thought that, whoever it was, the author

might have written a cult classic.

Lord Skidelsky, at the time completing the third volume of his magisterial biography of J. M. Keynes, was quite clear about why the manuscript (even if it proved to be genuine) would have been hidden:

> Strange and original. Technically it is very interesting, in substance difficult and confusing. I'm not sure that the attempt to fuse cricket and economics (or should it be using cricket as a metaphor for economics?) really works. Economics, even Keynesian economics, is difficult enough without being translated into cricketing terms; and the cricketing romance is overburdened with economic concepts. In short there are too many things going on to make the book an artistic or intellectual success. At the same time it is wonderful in its way.

INTRODUCTION

J.N.K., the great man's father, has found renewed fame in Cambridge circles for the longevity and completeness of his Diary, which enabled Phyllis Deane to publish her excellent recent biography. He also (like fellow-economists Ricardo and Jevons) won the posthumous award of a single entry in the *Oxford Dictionary of Quotations*. Although overwhelmed by Smith's eleven and his son's twelve entries, and narrowly overtaken by Malthus's two, he beat the ducks registered by Marshall, Pigou, Menger, Walras, Fisher, Friedman, and Lucas. Surely, in view of his solid position and approaching middle age, the 1896 cricket diary was superfluous? But this would not have been the first time that he kept a second diary; back in the period 1868–73, under the heady influence of leaving home and entering eligible bachelordom, he had also run a parallel line of thought, of which the official Diary seems to have contained edited highlights.

What may have prompted the cricket diary was the certainty that for J.M.K., the beloved firstborn, 1896 would be the last summer as a carefree child of Harvey Road; from September he would be studying hard to get an Eton scholarship, and then he would leave home in September 1897. True, he had been away for a term in Bedford earlier in 1893 owing to sickness, but this time it really was the end of an era, which J.N.K. was determined to mark, and enjoy. Cricket-mania nationally had reached a peak the summer before, when Dr W.G. Grace, nearing fifty years of age, became the first batsman ever to score a thousand runs in May. This fascination with Fenner's Cricket Ground, just sixty yards from the Keynes's front door, was despite the fact that (according to Deane's analysis of the Diary) 1895–96 was the busiest period of J.N.K.'s career, resulting in over 2,200 hours of work each year. Given the pattern of university terms and vacations he would have regularly worked twelve hours a day in the month of May 1896.

Was J.M.K.'s 1905 article both a response to his father's diary and the start of a series on cricket that he hoped to bequeath to a future son of his own? If so, at what point did he give up hope that that son would ever appear? The articles dwindle in size as the years go on, and become less and less oriented towards cricket. Indeed by the end the collection seems to be made up of the unpublishable scraps he couldn't face throwing away, chiefly because they tied him to his father and so they were chiefly concerned with his own origins. Even days before death he seems to be searching out wisdom from his father's teachings of half a century earlier. The relationship between the doting, anxious father and the brilliant, questing son is both fascinating and attractive, and yet ultimately we are faced by the nonagenarian parent outliving the offspring who faced the tragic trade-off between hoarding his health at Tilton and what Skidelsky called 'fighting for Britain' in a transatlantic frenzy.

The renewed English interest in ballet in the years following 1909 temporarily (and curiously) enhanced rather than eclipsed J.M.K.'s cricket writing, as can be seen from the tribute to Dr W. G. Grace in 1915. His friend A. L. Haskell shrewdly observed that the cricket-lover and the *balletomane* share many symptoms: studying finesses, respecting traditions, making heroes of exponents. The actual participants also share the experiences of going through many years of overwork for a small wage, getting a generous share of applause from a small public, and retiring with a few press cuttings to the

GOLDEN AGES AT THE FENNER'S MARGIN

agony of the school of grind all over again, this time vicariously. The 1915 essay looks back, not only to the writings of his father, but to the lessons of Fenner's for the monetary economist. W. G. Grace, a great cricketer, seems to pave the way for J.M.K. to Lydia Lopokova, a pre-eminent ballerina; the sparkle of the Lilac Fairy lured the Master Economist away from cricket for twenty years until memory was re-stimulated by the retirement of his contemporary Cambridge hero, the Master Cricketer, John Berry Hobbs.

Intriguingly J.M.K. seems gradually to have realised that the rather fanciful J.N.K. survey of the 1896 cricket season at Fenner's was in fact a work of genuine prophesy, and this clearly amused and delighted him. To what extent, therefore, did some of the 'rebellion' become self-fulfilling as J.M.K. reconsidered the path his father had intuited in the youthful cricket enthusiast? Beyond this is revealed a parochial, non-conformist, triumphalist spirit (particularly with regard to the pre-eminent 1860s Cambridgeshire side) which one either finds endearing or irritating. It is also clear that a lot of research remains to be done to flesh out the characters of those cricketers like Tarrant, Carpenter, and Hayward who were at that time Cambridgeshire names of world renown.

For in Edwardian days cricket's influence in terms of nuance and detail were universal and can even be found in another contemporary of Cambridge's Keynes and Hobbs: Arthur Ransome, who had no manifest interest in cricket. Born shortly after J.M.K. in 1884 and equally inept at ballgames, Ransome, like J.M.K., found his soulmate and life partner in a Russian. In his case, however, Evgenia was (as befitted Trotsky's secretary) a tireless and lifelong critic of his writing. But she was as devoted to Ransome as the ballerina Lydia Lopokova was to J.M.K. in providing unstinting material and spiritual support for a sickly and easily-tired partner. In 1922 Ransome, as the expert for the *Manchester Guardian* on Soviet Russia, helped Keynes to produce the Russian section in a series of twelve *Reconstruction Supplements* for the *Manchester Guardian Commercial*. In addition to (loosely) liberal principles (which in both their cases led to fierce criticism of the recently-failed western, Churchill-supported, policy of Intervention) Keynes and Ransome shared an erudite yet iconoclastic style of writing. They were of the generation that included P. G. Wodehouse (born 1881), and as David Frith points out, that fellow-imp named his most famous character, a manservant and therefore a *professional*, after an abundantly-promising Warwickshire all-round cricketer who was killed during the Great War. It is a marketing trick that they have not yet thought of at Edgbaston; a life-size model of Jeeves in the executive suite might increase American patronage and endowments no end, for the library if nothing else.

In the world of Ransome sailing, fishing, birdwatching, and exploring all came way above cricket in importance, despite his Ipswich family's name being an everyday word at all the first-class grounds thanks to their revolutionary grasscutting machines. Even those who have never read one of his books register the name subconsciously whenever they pass Ipswich on the A14/A12 with its roadsigns for 'Ransome's Europark'. But he couldn't escape mentioning cricket once in his twelve books for children. In *Winter Holiday*, with thick snow surrounding the freezing lakes of north-west England, he

INTRODUCTION

needed to conjure up a sound and a picture that was universally accessible at that time, and only cricket would do. Approaching a rough stone hut, newly covered with snow, which Nancy and John were turning into an igloo, Dick and Dorothea Callum came up the path through the wood.

> Presently they heard a noise as if someone were beating the ground with a cricket bat ... there were John and Nancy hard at work with spades, piling more snow on the mound and beating it firmly together.

On the opposite page is an illustration, 'The igloo in the snow', showing Captain Nancy of the Amazons as the spitting image of Alec Stewart forcing a medium-pacer through the covers off the front foot with a spade.

The irony is that even a cricket-loving youngster would be lost with this simile today in these days of covered wickets (which are like tarmac) and artificial pitches. We have to go back to the days of Sobers and Arlott in 1966 to remember that the bat was partly for hitting the ball with, but was also crucial for repairing the uncovered and rain-affected wicket: 'doing a spot of gardening', as Arlott would call flattening out divots. The impressionable youngster (such as I) practised this as carefully as the Sobers stance, in the hope that it would make one a better batsman. In the present age which sees cricket as a method of harking back to manufacturing rather than agriculture the bare-headed youngster practises fiddling with an imaginary helmet's chinstrap instead. J.M.K. might say that Capital is now of more concern than Land, but the delusion that this imitation will help the scoring of runs remains as deep in the soul as ever.

The J.N.K. diary and the J.M.K. articles recount for us along the way the popular success of cricket in the late-Victorian era, the rise of the professional in the Edwardian period, and the importance of Cambridge in these processes. They hypothesise that cricket was a central metaphor for economists and suggest how it may have influenced Keynes's later theories of probability and money. They swim against the current tide of published opinion with great confidence in both Englishness and Europeanness. What does the Italian tourist or the British toddler take in when they see the Hobbs Pavilion on Parker's Piece? It is somewhere to get refreshments, nothing more. What do they see when they walk past The Leys School cricket nets? Nothing, because they are too far away from the tourist track for them to be there in the first place, and anyway there is a high wooden fence. I know. I used to hurt my hands pulling myself up to have a look over it in the early 1970s. But even I, a fanatic, only knew of Freddy Brown practising there. I had no idea about Ranjitsinhji and John Maynard Keynes possibly entering the frame.

Take also the Sphere publication *Philby* by Page, Leitch, and Knightley (1968). Arising from investigations for the *Sunday Times* it reads now like a dreary catalogue of detail, and gives no illumination at all about Cambridge. Chapter 4, 'The Cambridge Marxists', is candyfloss:

> Cambridge's beauty and freedom were intoxicating

5

and Keynes is briefly mentioned as an old mother hen being spurned by the young turks (so to speak). Spying and watching paint dry are not among the highest of artistic endeavours, yet this book must have sold in droves at airports, and millions of people seem to be captivated by the mere mention of the SIS. The 2003 series on B.B.C. TV *Cambridge Spies* has merely reinforced a stereotypical and easy view of Cambridge history.

Surely this can now be seen as unhistorical? The baby-boom generation was shaped by orange juice, Clean Air Acts, and growth in the E.U,. not Le Carré, Dubcek, and Nagy (pronounced, apparently, 'nodge' although the school texts don't usually mention this). Cambridge was not some autonomous backcloth whose function was to provide camouflage for Marxians; it was a real testing ground of ideas and practices, where the influence of Keynes outwitted the crisis of capitalism without resorting to Philby's prescription. Yet it is the name of Philby that is more closely linked to Cambridge in the modern popular mind, while Keynes came some way from knocking Shakespeare and Churchill off their perches as Radio 4's *Man of the Millennium* and B.B.C. TV's *Greatest Briton* recently. This lack of popular feeling baffles, irritates, and diminishes the British understanding of self-worth; why are Keynes and Beveridge accorded such low status compared to Bobby Moore and Cliff Richard?

Taking stock at the turn of the millennium it seemed there were no realistic or properly historical explanations offered by academics and media hacks in the *fin de siècle* rash of books about 'modern' Europe and 'Englishness'. They all assumed that Europe was something dark and that English people had lost the light and were groping around in search of something to get a grip on, clutching on in hope to all things American. This was the opposite of the experiences of my family and friends, and books like Paxman's, Mazower's, and Ferguson's were therefore intensely annoying and virtually unreadable. They did not connect at all with the dilemma of being secure in both Englishness and Europeanness, but not being sure how one had got into that state. As soon as I read the J.N.K. diary and the J.M.K. articles I felt truly enlightened about where the century's journey had begun and the direction in which it ought to go at the start of a new one.

Why is 'Fenner's' in the title? It is, surely, becoming accepted as commonplace that local environments will affect the development of ideas through effects on the makers of those ideas. A recent example is the research on W. H. Auden which has illuminated the peculiar influence on his work of lead mines and the Pennine landscape in which those mines are located. Alan Myers and Robert Forsythe have delivered a challenge to metropolitan critics, who at the mention of the word 'mine' conjured up a picture of a West Yorkshire colliery, although this would be as far from the reality of Nenthead as a Fenland drainage channel.

With regard to J.M.K., it is clear that Harvey Road and Cambridge have not been ignored; Lord Skidelsky has determinedly reinforced the importance of the 'presuppositions' of 6, Harvey Road as signified in Sir Roy Harrod's official biography of J.M.K. It is Fenner's itself that has been dismissed, because economists tend to see cricket as an insignificant diversion if they understand it at all. Cambridge University, however,

INTRODUCTION

owned a cricket ground with one of the best pavilions in the world long before it got Schools in Botany, Law, Medicine, Archaeology, and Ethnology. There wasn't a separate Economics Tripos until the twentieth century. Natural Sciences as a subject didn't even exist in 1882, when Studd's University side was playing the Australian XI at Fenner's watched by thousands of spectators from both Town and Gown. The greatness of C. L. R. James is that he attacked historians in the citadel to show how the Victorian period cannot be understood without understanding the phenomenon of W. G. Grace and the explosive growth of organised mass leisure pursuits with which he was associated. That he succeeded can be seen in the writings of authors like Professors Hilary Beckles, Brian Stoddart, Neil Lazarus, and Helen Tiffin.

But these are Professors of History, English, Cultural Studies, Media, and Communication, not Economics. There may be *some* economists (for example Geoffrey Harcourt, the cricketing Australian, of Cambridge University) who have subconsciously made some allowance for Fenner's, but this seems highly unlikely in the case of most U.S. practitioners. However, an explicit journey of discovery has not, as far as I am aware, been made until now, and it is appropriate that it is the hand of the Master Economist that guides us on our travels.

It can further be contested that the lack of appreciation until now of what took place at Fenner's (in 1896 in particular) has impaired public understanding of Keynes as an economist, and the structures and processes that he strove to set up in defence of the common weal. The dismissal of cricket, or rather the *lack of apprehension of a need to appreciate it,* is a symptom of the economist's retreat into technical obscurantism, linguistic and conceptual inaccessibility, and myopia about the development of the 'dismal science'.

Having said that, this is a happy book. Its subject matter centres on happy people, trying to be constructive in a pleasant environment, in which endeavour they generally succeeded. Maynard Keynes and Jack Hobbs (as Cambridge contemporaries and Masters in their own fields their stories are bound up together to some degree) were indisputably products of happy environments and gave pleasure to millions of people. They had their roots in the small locality surrounding Fenner's Cambridge University Cricket Ground in Cambridge and provided many (including, I find, me) with both inspiration and a framework for life. It's often only after half that life has gone, and most people have become indifferent to or discounted the dominant influences upon that life, that their importance becomes clear.

The heroes' doings can also be tracked in the real world with the use of the maps and an hour or two on a sunny afternoon in Cambridge. Many of the buildings and streets where the action took place can be seen much as they were a century ago. True, the old Fenner's pavilion has gone, but the future of the ground has been secured in a recognisable form. Brewhouse Lane has mercifully disappeared with the rest of the East Road slums. However, Harvey Road is intact, although the trees have grown a lot. Also Belvoir Terrace, Bateman Street, Parker's Piece, Jesus Close, and Rivar Place haven't altered much. These, rather than King's College and the Senate House, make up the

'Fenner's Margin' that produced not only a master economist, but also (concurrently) 'The Master', in the cricketer John Berry Hobbs. Indeed, a generation later round the corner from Fenner's in Glisson Road came the son of a pathologist, 'Syd' Barrett, who revolutionised English music in 1967 and helped bring G. E. Moore's philosophy to the masses in a way Keynes never could.

The composer Sir Michael Tippett discussed artistic metaphor extensively with that long-lived Bloomsbury figure E. M. Forster when both were staying with Benjamin Britten and Peter Pears in 1948. Tippett was recovering from hepatitis and Forster was writing the libretto for *Billy Budd*. They were exploring why metaphor may be successful. Why do we accept Wilfred Owen recasting the Great War as a latter-day version of the story of Abraham and Isaac? Why do audiences feel moved to cry rather than snigger during *A Child of Our Time*, a piece about Nazi persecution of Czech Jews, when instead of Bach-like chorales Tippett uses negro spirituals? What price to have been a third party stirring it by asserting that the cricket at Fenner's in 1896 was also a suitable metaphor for the political economy being nurtured on its margin by Marshall, Pigou, and Keynes?

Tippett knew that *A Child of Our Time* was a major turning point, a major work, and in 1935 he knew that *War Ramp*, an agit-prop play about the relations between war and banking, was an important step along the way. This very realistic, literal, and unsuccessful drama was based on the political economy of C. B. Douglas, particularly the idea of 'social credit'. If war is built on the ramp of credit which the survivors have to pay off, 'where is the real enemy?' Over half a century later Stereolab's drummer, reflecting on two recessions and the wars in the South Atlantic and the Gulf, made a similar point in the song *Ping Pong*:

> It's alright 'cos the historical factor has shown how the economical cycle tends to revolve.
> In around a decade three stages stand out in a loop
> Slump and war then peel back to square one back for more
> Bigger slump and bigger war and a smaller recovery
> Huger slump and greater war and a shallower recovery
> ... There's only millions that lose their their homes their jobs and sometimes their sense
> There's only millions that die in their bloody wars it's alright
> It's only their lives and the lives of their next of kin that they are losing
> ... It's alright recovery always comes round again there's nothing to worry [about]
> Things can only get better
> ... Don't worry shut up sit down things'll get better naturally

War Ramp and *Ping Pong* are both little-known, if interesting, pieces of art; *A Child of Our Time* is a monstrous success, hitting on the right metaphor at the right time. Can one contend that Keynes could not try to publish his works on cricket as a serious metaphor for political economy because the world that could appreciate such connections was dwindling continuously and at an ever-increasing rate as his own life progressed?

His work requires us to register substantial general links in the psyche between Cricket and Economics, links that help explain the popularity of such a difficult game in late-Victorian society, and specifically with academics of Cambridge University such as Keynes and Pigou (the young Edwardian successor to Alfred Marshall as Professor of Economics). Cricket was the first sport to take off in terms of mass spectatorship and organisation in the late 1860s and was far more organised and popular in Cambridge than soccer when J.M.K. was growing up.

There are, of course, a plethora of casual or coincidental links between cricket and Keynesianism. An immediate example arises with an initial run-through of the fun pieces in *Wisden Almanack* of 2000. On page 1483, a dentist tells how he put a six through his own car window. The bowling side was Horsted Keynes, the village where, Lord Skidelsky tells us, the Count of Mortain gave William de Cahagnes hundreds of acres of Sussex in return for services rendered at the battle of Hastings. Thus the faithful servant from Calvados was prosperous enough to go forth and multiply many Keyneses, amongst whom we can number J.N.K. and J.M.K. But casual coincidences aren't the sort of scholarship that will convince sceptics.

However, what if a disinterested yet discerning reader could not tell whether a piece was written by Joan Robinson or by R. C. Robertson-Glasgow? Experts on each side of the divide blink. One, the beloved 'Crusoe', was a distinguished player, and then a respected writer about cricket throughout his retirement at Pangbourne; the other was a member of Keynes's 'Cambridge Circus' who ranks as one of the greatest economists of the last two centuries (disgracefully ignored by the Nobel Prize committee), and is still the only woman economist of world reputation. Surely this is a jest? Here goes then.

> Prudence is something akin to virtue and needs the exercise of self-command. The concept of *waiting* as a sacrifice is connected with the view that any batsman is under a constant temptation to hit out in 'present gratifications', and the spotlight at the crease is the 'reward' that leads him to refrain.

and

> Note that these crude plans for so much revenue increase and so much output per month are concerned entirely with consumption. They are framed on the postulate of standard market structures, standard rates of investment, and standard productive efficiency. Note too that they attribute high profits to the households' willingness to spend, never to the excellence of the firms' output.

One sounds like a classical description of the tensions in a batsman's approach at the wicket, the other sounds like an attack on crude business models that merely extrapolate current trends. Yet the truth is that the first is from *Economic Philosophy* (Robinson, 1962) and the second is from the 1945 *Wisden Almanack*. I have merely followed the example of the articles attributable to J.M.K. and the diary (to J.N.K.) and translated

GOLDEN AGES AT THE FENNER'S MARGIN

certain words from Cricket into Economics (and *vice versa*).

Here is Sir John Hicks, writing about liquidity in *The Crisis of Keynesian Economics* (1974); or is he?

> An innings [liquidity] is not a matter of a single choice; it is a matter of a sequence of choices, a related sequence. It is concerned with the passage from the unknown to the known – with the knowledge that if we wait we can have more knowledge.

Or get accustomed to the conditions? This, I would argue, goes deeper than mere coincidence and potted whimsy. In fact it is arguable that the late Joan Robinson was an expert on the psychology of batting whether she knew it or not. Even Steve Waugh would probably learn a lot from her second-hand if he popped in to Cambridge for a conversation with her friend Geoffrey Harcourt (the only direct Robinson-Australia connection I am aware of). But then Robinson also had Piero Sraffa on hand to connect reality with concepts like investment in fixed, working, and human capital. He wrote to her in October 1936:

> If you ask your gardener how many people he's got, the farmer how many people he's employing, and how much land he's got, he'll understand and answer in terms of hours or heads or acres. But if you say, 'how much capital have you got?', he'll think you're dotty.

The same might have been true at Fenner's in 1896 if you had asked the groundsman, Walter Watts, if his horses were capital.

Joan Robinson was also an expert on 'disguised unemployment' (the classic interwar example being the Strand matchseller during a recession). This is often to be found in cricket where player(s) may be chosen just on the basis of their fielding, or their 'bits and pieces' batting/bowling because the foundations of the side are so sound. I found myself in this position in the successful 1988 Cambridgeshire side, when I was quite contentedly quoted in the *Cambridge Evening News* as being happy just to be 12th man for the rest of the season; how winning helps your outlook! As London University captain I learnt to be wary of freshmen who claimed to be regular members of Lancashire League sides; they invariably went in number 10 to prop up things as non-striker for the professional batsman at the other end, and never bowled. Good for morale in the nets, though.

An intriguing supplementary point about Cricket is that the model is very weak when one looks at the distribution of income, and in particular the rewards to labour (for there is a vacuum once we have assigned wickets to the role of interest) and this is precisely the area where J.M.K. showed very little theoretical interest. He was seemingly happy to let the neo-classical marginal productivity theory sit in the textbooks as long as it wasn't doing any real harm. To overturn the macro orthodoxy he had to show that the system was different *given* the micro assumptions of the Marshall school. Social and institutional factors (like the merit rating given to many professional service sector workers) would perhaps obviate marginal productivity theory, but one didn't point out to a

INTRODUCTION

Duchess that her gown and accessories didn't match.

This is not to say that spectators did not empathise with the batsman as a metaphor for the worker; they clearly did, for the batsman was an individual facing an overwhelming (monopsonistic) power in the fielding side (or employer) and faced terminal oblivion if one mistake was made (the fall of a wicket seen as redundancy in a world without a welfare state). Cricket, however, was much simpler than the economy, having just one transactionary market-place between the stumps, rather than many (the product market, the factor market, the financial market, and the international market).

Ironies abound as this volume progresses. The long western European peace since 1945 has rested crucially upon a Keynesian framework of managed markets rather than *laisser faire*, although Monnet, Schuman, and Adenauer would not be generally have regarded themselves as 'Keynesians'. The economic Golden Age following 1948 encouraged the U.K. to participate in the E.U., but without fully confronting the myth of the possibility of continued Empire. In turn the E.U. embraced the legacies of the Golden Age of London's underground movement in the 1960s and thus, at second hand, the philosophy of Cambridge's G. E. Moore and his disciple, Maynard Keynes. By 2003 core continental society, it can be argued, is formed more fully in the image of Keynes than much of U.K. society. English liberal pluralism has been truly pooled and is widely appreciated throughout the E.U.

This book may be a challenging read for a variety of reasons, but as Wilfred Rhodes was wont to point out when he was coaching the Harrow boys out of playing the cut (or 'coot'):

> Cricket's not meant to be foon!

Perhaps by the end of the opus one should have a feeling that liquidity preference is improperly apprehended until one has been the nervous non-striker joining an established batsman in a vital partnership; that the Bretton Woods system of international stabilisation cannot be understood without a sound grasp of the County Championship results of the 1890s; and that the approach of Keynes (rather than the Keynesian approach) to inflation requires a knowledge of the 'Cricket Reform' chapter of the 1888 Badminton Book, as well as an intimate appreciation of the batting of W.G. Grace and Kumar Shri Ranjitsinhji. There is certainly much to ponder on.

Adrian Wykes,
Évrange,
September 2003

PART ONE

Cambridge University Cricket Club's Progress Through the Season of 1896

J.N.K. was a fellow of Pembroke College, Cambridge, and a lecturer in Logic and Political Economy. His wife Florence was the daughter of the Reverend John Brown, for thirty years minister of Bunyan's chapel at Bedford. She was one of the first female students to go up to Cambridge, attending Newnham College. The couple had three children: Maynard (born in 1883), Margaret (1885), and Geoffrey (1887). The transition from provincial trade and Nonconformism to 'thinking' middle class with Establishment connections came about through the efforts of the parents. They created a stable and self-confident atmosphere in which hard work and playfulness were both valued. J.M.K. never felt the need to rebel against a cradle that provided this combination of variety and continuity.

Rebellion would be directed at darker, external forces.

THE DIARY ENTRIES

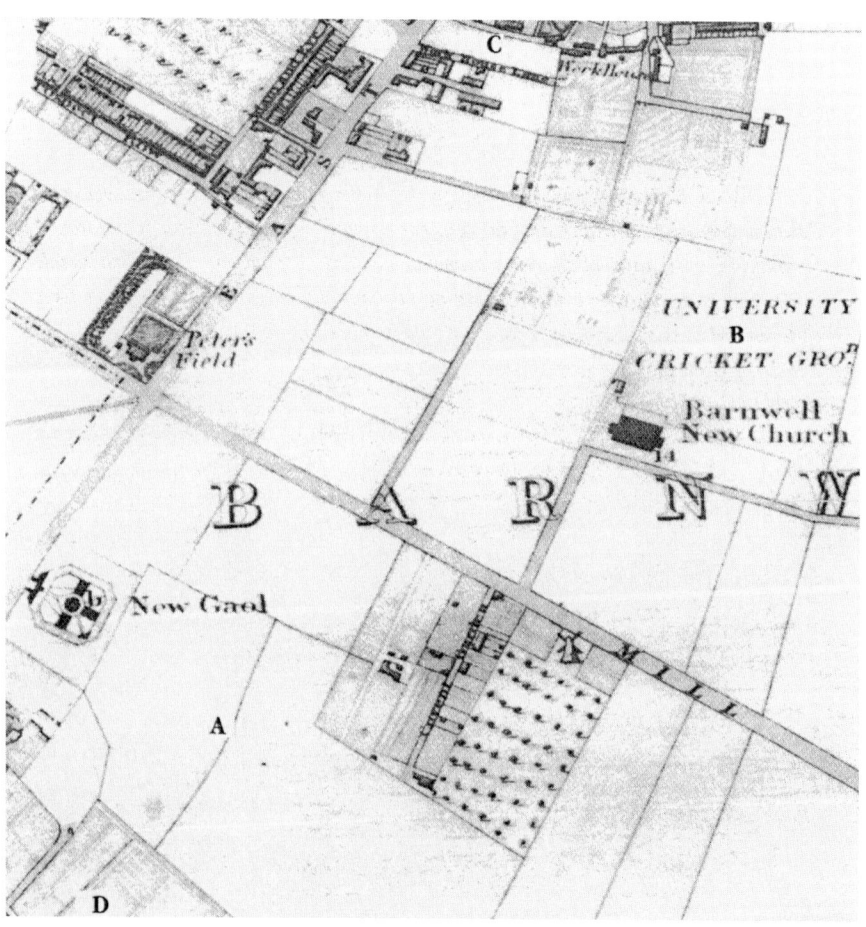

The 1889 25-inch Ordnance Survey compared with Baker's map of Cambridge (1830). The latter shows open fields to the south east of the new Gaol (A) where Fenner relocated the University ground. The old ground (B) became a cemetery. Brewhouse Lane (C), birthplace of Jack Hobbs, led to an old workhouse, and there was another just north of it. Only one generation later the Cambridge Chronicle could describe Gas Lane (the intervening road) as the 'receptacle of all the physical dross of Cambridge'; 'all is poverty, and barren dreariness' (1853). Hobbs was born in 1882. Harvey Road (D) would not appear in the bottom left hand corner until the early 1880's

GOLDEN AGES AT THE FENNER'S MARGIN

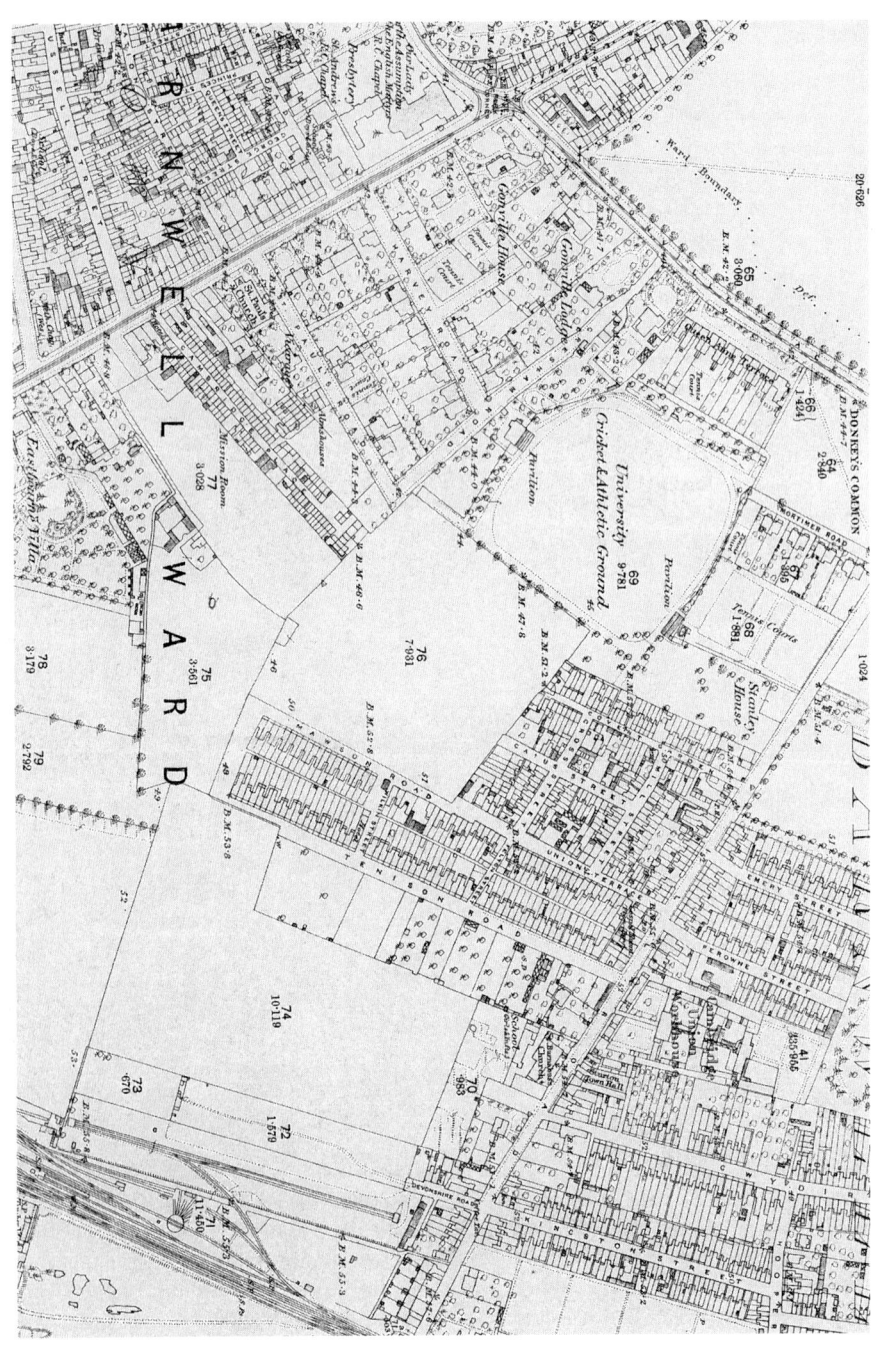

THE DIARY ENTRIES

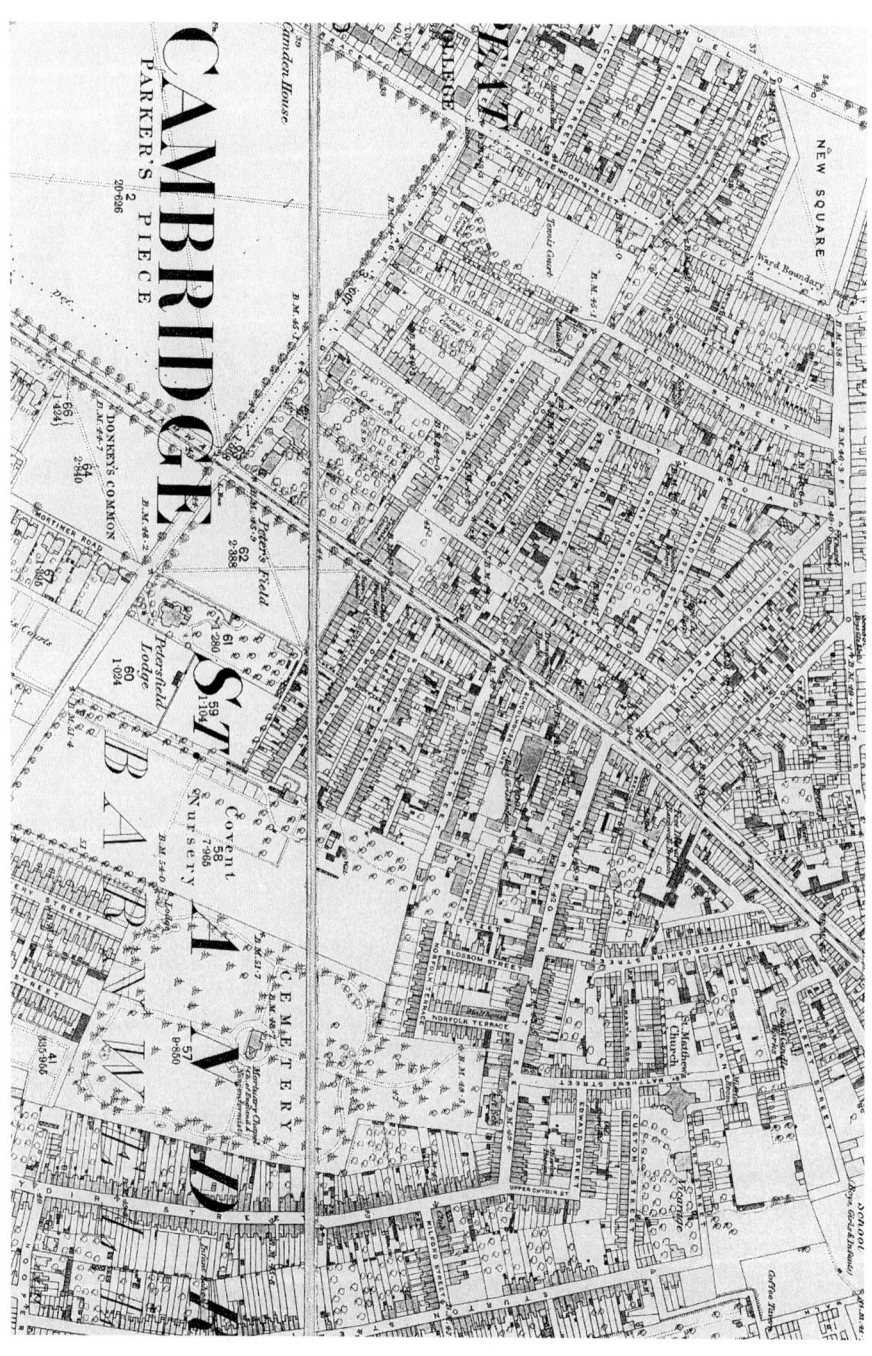

GOLDEN AGES AT THE FENNER'S MARGIN

Inspirations; Fisher, J.N.K., Marshall and Sidgwick.

THE DIARY ENTRIES

Grace, King, Ranji and Spofforth.

GOLDEN AGES AT THE FENNER'S MARGIN

The second 'old' pavilion at Fenner's was, of course, very new in 1896, and was at the opposite side of the ground to the current one. Romanesque arches and sash windows give it the look of baby brother to the railway station further down Hill's Road, yet there are also Greek tops to the windows and a Dutch roof gable that make this building a European union of the late-Victorian age that in addition reflected the sources of Cambridge values. W.M. Fawcett also designed the 1895 wing of the Guildhall in Guildhall Street which J.M.K.'s mother strove to replace in the 1930s. The windows of the building behind (top right) belong to 8, Harvey Road, just two doors along from J.M. Keynes's lifelong family home.

THE DIARY ENTRIES

Early Season
Wednesday, April 1st, 1896

When we removed to Harvey Road following our wedding[1] we knew we were very fortunate in the matter of the location of our home; this is also true of Maynard's disposition. With Parker's Piece at the end of Gresham Road and Fenner's sports ground at the end of Harvey Road there are purposeful public areas of recreation nearby. The town's margin is close; we used to be at the *very* edge,[2] and fruit trees and paddocks still proliferate beyond the noise and business of building work.

Glisson Road is being completed for the staff of Gonville and Caius, so we will soon lose the pastoral scene of the Perse School sports ground. Mawson Road, running parallel behind Glisson Road already displays terraces of more modest houses for the domestic servants of the college.

---

[1] 11th November 1882

[2] It is important to note that the energy and vibrancy brought to the house by J.N.K.'s high-flying academic career was in harmony with the pace of speculative development taking place in the surrounding area; perhaps too semi-rural, too static an impression of the Harvey Road ambience during the 1880s and 1890s is usually given in books about Keynes's Cambridge. The quotation on which strangers to the city usually base this view is from Florence Ada Keynes's *By-Ways*;

> My children looked from their nursery window across 'Bulman's field', where the drovers kept their cattle over the week-end, ready for the Monday market, and the lowing of cows was a familiar sound. With the exception of the houses in Station Road there was indeed little or nothing between us and the Gogs.

Visiting nowadays it does still seem to be a surprisingly spacious and stately area of Cambridge, but at the time there would in reality have been constant noise both from construction and the traffic serving that construction. In particular the noisy building-over of the Perse School playing fields around 1895–6 as Glisson Road was extended south-west towards Hills Road would have been noticed daily.

THE DIARY ENTRIES

We are fortunate that M. has become fond of cricket; he jokes that for a similar expenditure of energy he could have become an expert on the Latin Mass or the Great Eastern Railway.[3]

Maynard's school[4] is quite near the house, although not as close as the C.U.C.C. ground.

---

[3] This refers to the proximity of 6, Harvey Road to the 1890 Catholic Church at Hyde Park Corner, and to the railway station, a considerably longer walk away to the south-east. Mathematician (and atheist) G. H. Hardy was an ardent fan of cricket, and left us the best quotation with reference to the geography of Fenner's:

> It's rather unfortunate that some of the happiest hours of my life should have been spent within the sound of a Roman Catholic Church.

[4] The Leys School's preparatory feeder is currently on a sizeable site down Trumpington Road from the senior school and is officially called St. Faith's. But in 1896 as a very small independent set-up it was just known as 'Goody's'. J.M.K. would have been attending the original foundation set up in a wooden garden shed at 1, Belvoir Terrace, set slightly back from the west side of Trumpington Road. The headmaster, R. S. Goodchild, and his charges were able to observe the use of The Leys playing fields just over the fence. This is where pupils older than thirteen still have their nets, and is where (some five years before these diary entries) Goodchild took an interest in a rather older pupil, Kumar Shri Ranjitsinhji. The latter was living in Chaucer Road while working towards entry to Trinity College and was a regular practitioner at the nets next to Goody's.

THE DIARY ENTRIES

Early Season
Friday, April 3rd, 1896

Maynard takes a diversion to school down Bateman Street, passing his grandmother's house, over Hobson's Conduit near Brookside then crossing Trumpington Road. This means he avoids the slums of Coronation Street and Saxon Street. Florence[5] keeps abreast of the incidence of scarlet fever and diphtheria in the environs, and is concerned that this pocket of recent origin is far more neglected than Pound Hill, Nine Pins Court, or the beery alleys between East Road and Norfolk Street.[6]

---

[5] J.M.K.'s mother, Florence Ada Keynes (née Brown), was a classic example of the non-conformist liberal who got things done with disregard for the popular view of this period as an age of 'doubt'. She was Secretary of the Charity Organisation Society, and later became involved with Sir Pendrill Varrier-Jones and the Papworth Settlement. This started in 1916 as a Hospital and Sanatorium for 340 tuberculosis sufferers, industry for their employment, and a village for their residence. It grew to be the prestigious heart centre of today. The C.O.S. was inaugurated by Sidgwick at 82, Regent Street (just along from number 74 where Newnham's first students took residence) as a gateway/database for those seeking relief. This brought Mrs. Keynes into contact with every sector of Cambridge society; for example a collaboration with Alfred Marshall's wife, Mary Paley Marshall, and one of Charles Darwin's twenty eight grandchildren, Eglantyne Jebb, led to the 1906 *Cambridge: A Brief Study In Social Questions*, which necessitated exploration of all the recesses of poverty and disease mentioned in note 6. Keynes's descriptions of Mrs. Marshall and her protégés may have given Virginia Woolf the copy for Mrs. Ramsey at the start of *To the Lighthouse*, elucidating the social problem. The first woman councillor in Cambridge, Florence Ada Keynes, became Mayor, and Lord Skidelsky quotes a 1916 reporter describing her as being 'the busiest woman in Cambridge'.

[6] The first of these was near the mediaeval origins of the port near Magdalene Bridge and the fabric deteriorated with its social reputation right up to the 1980s. The second was known for notoriously poor housing situated on top of the King's Ditch, which brought water into the town from the Nine Wells springs in the chalky downlands south of the town, *via* Hobson's Conduit and the open drains along Trumpington Street. Nine Pins Court was partially demolished in 1911, with one dwelling turned into a wash-house, and the others improved. It became the site for the town synagogue in 1936. But generally clearance in the old centre was carried out carelessly, wholesale, and in fits (*e.g.* St. John's College's 1932 Lutyens project, the 1961 Park Street car park, the 1971 Lion Yard project). The phrase 'beery alleys' refers to places like Brewhouse Lane (Hobb's's birthplace) off East Road. Saxon Street, to the west of Hills Road, was rebuilt in the 1980s.

THE DIARY ENTRIES

But I think M. is happy to avoid the children as much as the squalor because he is artless when it comes to deflecting verbal or physical abuse; in fact his verbal responses, he says, merely provoke increased enemy action, so he has ruled out a career in the Foreign Office.

David Gower *et al* in the mid-1980s little contemplated the commercial frenzy that accompanied the development of Covent Garden and Glisson Road behind them nearly a century earlier.

THE DIARY ENTRIES

The facade of Goodchild's house that hides behind the trees on Trumpington Rd.

This view of New Town from St. Paul's Church next to Harvey Road shows the rough area on the route to school that JMK would have been so earnest to avoid. The main artery he should have used resonates to modern ears as it is called Coronation Street.

GOLDEN AGES AT THE FENNER'S MARGIN

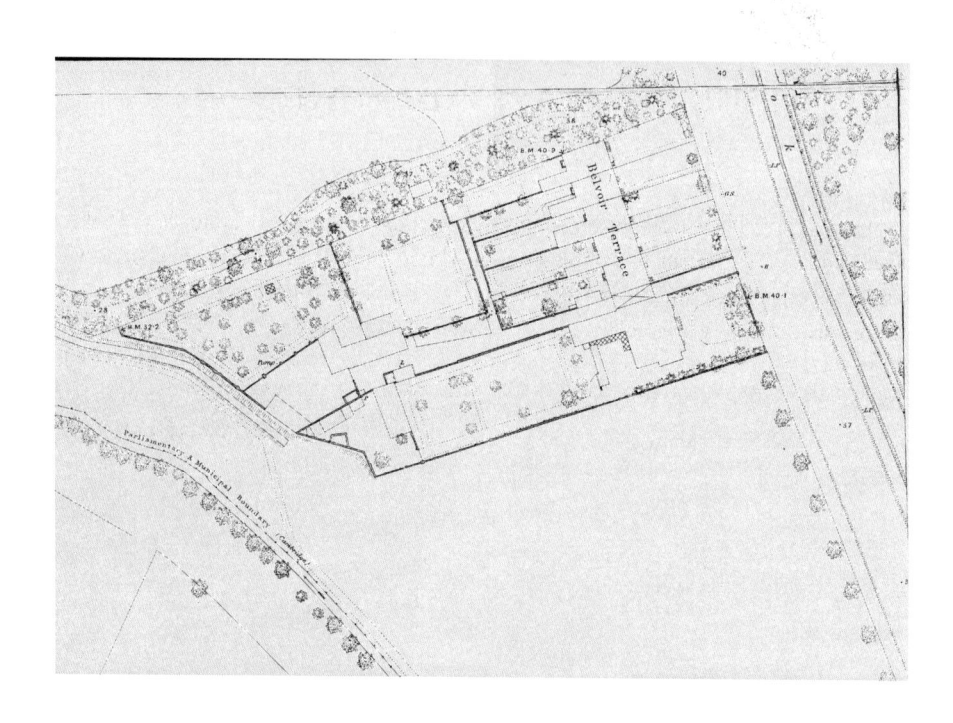

The original site of 'Goody's' school at 1, Belvoir Terrace (the top property on this plan) where J.M.K studied for his Eton entrance.

THE DIARY ENTRIES

Early Season
Easter Sunday, April 5th, 1896

There is a very keen delight for us in the household as April arrives, for both Parker's Piece and Fenner's seem to awaken from a winter slumber of underemployment with an air of expectancy and fecundity that Henry[7] says should never fail to bring out the pagan beneath every dog-collar. For those who live on the west side of the town this experience might arrive earlier, when they see the bulbs in bloom behind Clare College, but for me that is a sinister display of treachery that is more likely than not to be followed by a fortnight of biting easterly snow flurries and a renewed risk of pneumonia or worse. Give us Fenner's in April, and we Keyneses are happy!

---

[7] Henry Sidgwick, doughty fighter for women's rights at Cambridge University and doubty academic who made social science a respected area of the curriculum. He lives on not least in a road name. He was a golfing partner of the Keyneses and died four years after these entries in 1900.

THE DIARY ENTRIES

This seasonal flow continues with a sense of loss when the Varsity match is concluded at the start of July, and a deeper sense of grief as September rolls on, made keener by the apprehension that the rainfall records show that month of year to be the driest in Cambridge. It is the darkening evenings and chill around the boundary that foretell winter's advance. In between we may have the allure of a series of Test Matches[8] against a touring side, and during winters there are tours overseas that may or may not engage our attention, depending on whether the opposition are Philadelphia or Victoria.[9]

---

8 The June Test of 1896 against Australia was only the fiftieth one ever played, and was still being conducted according to the five ball over; in the 1880s four ball overs had been the norm in England.

9 The pattern of tours was not restricted to Australia and South Africa. In September 1897 ex-Oxonian 'Plum' Warner was to take a team to Philadelphia including Cantabrigian Jessop, the third of five major tours there in the 1890s, and only a few weeks after the Philadelphians had finished a tour of England. The chief American attraction was the great swerve bowler J. Barton King, who many say invented controlled swing bowling. He became a friend of Ranji, playing in a lot of his Edwardian 'pick-up' sides, and was included in many players' imaginary world XIs for decades (right up to 1967, in the case of Arthur Mailey, who also put Douglas Jardine in his team to play Mars). The traffic was not restricted to the English crossing the North Atlantic; the Australians followed up their 1896 tour to England with a three-match series against the Gentlemen of Philadelphia on their way home in the autumn, winning two and losing one of the big games.

THE DIARY ENTRIES

Early Season
Saturday, April 11th, 1896

Maynard feels that these seasonal expectations[10] are so strong that they must also affect the players, except perhaps the most hard-bitten and experienced professional who may not care if he is playing at Edinburgh in August or Dunedin in February.[11] He feels there may also be longer cycles of expectation to do with injury[12] and skills. I said he should compare this to the economic world, for it sounded to me like talk of depreciation of capital (we had covered the straight-line method some years before) and the life-cycle of a product (to borrow a biological analogy) with the overall theme being obsolescence. Maynard dismissed this with a cursory mention that we had looked at this childish stuff before, and that this season he meant to go much deeper into the game of cricket and its relations to life.

'After all, father, I am never going to have a better opportunity than this summer to study "cigalles"[13] during the whole of the rest of my life-cycle!'

---

[10] The summer was to prove to be an exceptional one for the weather, the bat in general and Cambridge graduate K. S. Ranjitsinhji in particular. He broke W. G. Grace's 1871 record for the greatest number of runs scored in a first class season, and was given centre place in the photograph of Wisden's Five Cricketers of the Year.

[11] A neat geographical and cultural juxtaposition. When the editor visited Otago University in 1992 he remarked on the statue of the poet Burns in the centre of The Octagon (Dunedin's equivalent of the Arc de Triomphe). To the question 'why was it put up?' the reply was given: 'Jeez, didn't he live here?'

[12] A prophetic comment, for Cambridge were to be hampered throughout the season by Jessop, their fast bowler, suffering a toe injury which also led to him having a disappointing time with Gloucestershire later on.

[13] A childish pun on the French for crickets.

THE DIARY ENTRIES

Early Season
Monday, April 13th, 1896

I've been trying to remember when this interest in cricket started and can trace it back to very early days when Maynard first noted with astonishment that there were two batsmen at the wicket, and that there were eleven on the fielding side. Like many young boys he thought cricket was played at one end with one batsman, and two alternating in the field. A wall had to be played against, for a stumper and backstop[14] were unthinkable luxuries. On this first occasion at Fenner's I had to explain every basic detail (he was very excited by the concept of the men in white coats sitting as judges, and asked if Henry Sidgwick was an umpire!).

We then saw a wicket fall, a short, a rather slow head-ball pulled straight into the hands of long leg down towards the 'fruit market'.[15] M. was struck by the fact that if the fielder had left the ball it would have been six and yet, in the event, a wicket had fallen. I said yes, the batsman will be very crestfallen thinking that he had come so close to glory.

I remarked that the bowler would have felt the same the over before when the ball had cut from leg on a good length and taken the edge through wide short-slip. But there was no wide short slip and the third man had failed to cut off the boundary.[16]

'So any ball can take a wicket, and any ball can go for four,' murmured Maynard.

---

14 J.N.K. seems to be recalling his own youth. *The Badminton Book* of 1888 notes that backstop had already become almost redundant in top flight cricket, as the wicketkeeping techniques and the outfields had improved. Interestingly, as the mechanical mower replaced the scythe, slow bowling became more common than fast owing to the need for more accuracy in length and line.

15 This must refer to the short *cul-de-sac* named Covent Garden, now a very quaint corner of Victorian Cambridge, but at the centre of considerable development around this time. New shops sprouted up between Mortimer Road and Covent Garden, and the south side of Mill Road was renumbered in the mid-1890s. Caius College prevented the mains sewer (and hence Union Terrace, later Mawson Road) developing southwards in the 1860s by acquiring the three acres next to that corner of Fenner's at enormous expense from speculative builders in 1865. This enabled them to have a clear run to Hill's Road with Glisson Road (for teaching staff) and the Mawson Road extension (for college servants) in the 1890s.

16 This indicates a much shorter hit for four than one sees now at Fenner's. There was, of course, the athletics cinder track around the ground's perimeter taking up a lot of space. Only after the 1972 C.S. Smith pavilion replaced the 1877 Fawcett design did the Gresham Road end become the very long boundary it is today.

THE DIARY ENTRIES

Early Season
Tuesday, April 14th, 1896

It must be way back in '91 that I let Maynard borrow a *Wisden Almanack* for the long winter evenings when he was feeling too poorly to do any mathematics homework,[17] and my little ruse worked because in a moment he came back to me brandishing a sheaf of papers with figures on. Apparently he had decided to see which county had the best aggregates of runs for (maximum) and against (minimum). When he summed the entire contents he found that the total number of fors equalled the total number of againsts, hence his excitement. He saw no tangled knots in the logic of the situation, and did not start spouting nonsense about how there was no point trying to score runs at all if the against column would go up by as much as the for column, but he did make seize on some rather magnificent points with regard to the results.

---

17   J.M.K. was not yet eight years old, J.N.K. had not yet discovered golf, and the Golden Age of cricket was dawning.

THE DIARY ENTRIES

Firstly he said it was like looking in a looking-glass (and I introduced the word 'symmetry' to him);[18] then he said it wasn't really like a mirror because the details differed, and it was more like a bank who borrowed from and lent to different people, which pleased me greatly; but thirdly he said that the only way to help the counties performing worst would be to curtail the ones doing best, and it was pointless criticising or cajoling the worst if the best were much better and the symmetry was cast in iron.[19]

This I did not like, but since it was only cricket I let it pass.

---

18 Symmetry and logic were certainly not strangers to J.N.K. working away in his study (after 1905 this was to be moved to be adjacent to the dining room of number 6 in 5, Harvey Road). *The Scope and Method of Political Economy* was published in January 1891 seven years after *Studies and Exercises in Formal Logic*, each being a characteristically painful effort that both exhausted J.N.K. and resulted in a minor classic. Besant, his Mathematics tutor, had teased him that he had

> too good powers of reasoning logically to be in my proper element as a logician.

Edgeworth said he relied on 'ingenuity and happy conjecture' rather than method. With three children to look after, however, he relinquished academic ambition in the 1890s for a less stressful administrative career in the university.

19 This sounds curiously like J.M.K.'s approach at the Bretton Woods conference in 1944 when he tried to argue for a world currency (Bancor) and an international lender of last resort to ensure that payments, surpluses and deficits could be corrected without weakening the deficit nation's position further. It is the first indication of how an understanding of cricket may have influenced his understanding the economist's work.

THE
DIARY ENTRIES

Early Season
Wednesday, April 15th, 1896

Maynard has spent a lot of odd moments at Fenner's watching Walter Watts[20] and his team preparing the ground for the new athletics and cricket seasons, and has decided that the pitch and the outfield are in receipt of investment expenditure! Playing him at his own game, I probed him about the team toiling in the net practice under the April showers. Surely they were expending just as much energy as the groundsmen? He thought for a moment and said that training was an extension of education and does indeed constitute investment, but in the acquisition of *productive* skills;[21] the

---

20 J.N.K. seems to have been clear in his own mind although there is often some confusion about the groundsmen in Cambridge owing to a plethora of Haywards, Hobbses, and Wattses. Maverick author F.T. Unwin further muddied the waters by naming the 1866–1953 Dan 'Mr Haylock'. More recent visitors to Corpus Christi College would have known groundsman Mick Hayward, and those at The Leys School in the 1990s would have been familiar with yet another Tom. Millions of tourists also know the name Hayward; they would have subconsciously picked it up from the signs above Ben Hayward's cycle shop in Trumpington Street.

21 What we now call human or social capital, expounded on by J.N.K. on page 99 of his book *The Scope and Method of Political Economy*.

THE DIARY ENTRIES

groundsmen are making the site fit for potential gods, and are concerned with *fixed* capital. This was a very pleasing answer off the cuff, and showed that he really appreciates the art of Druce[22] and company. I later more pessimistically wondered if he was watching the groundsmen 'invest' because he apprehends so fully his own lack of skill on the playing field, and realises his rate of return at Eton[23] is likely to be very low?

---

22 Norman Druce was arguably the most successful Varsity batsman of all time, and the surname was used by Wodehouse in his 1904 classic *Mike*. In 1895 he had twice been left stranded on 199 not out at Fenner's (Perambulators *versus* Etceteras, and the University *versus* M.C.C.. The Perambulators were drawn from Harrow, Eton, Westminster, Charterhouse and Rugby, the Etceteras from the rest. This was a big annual fixture at this time, but not first class). 1896 was his least impressive Fenner's season, however.

23 There were fewer than ten schools that mattered in 1896 when it came to providing players of a calibre suitable for the Varsity, and Eton was numerically head and shoulders above the others. J.D. Betham's *Oxford and Cambridge Cricket Scores and Biographies* (1905, Jacksons, Sedbergh) produced figures for all the Blues who played between 1827 and 1904; Eton 144, Harrow 106, Winchester 78, Rugby 64, with the next offering being a mere 32. J.M.K. would have been keenly aware that no other stable in the world was more apt for a cricket-mad adolescent, but also that few of his fellow pupils would be less likely to do well at the game than he.

CHESTERTON RURAL DISTRICT COUNCIL.

The fortnightly meeting of the Chesterton Rural District Council took place in the Board-room, at the Workhouse, Old Chesterton, yesterday (Thursday) morning, under the presidency of the Chairman (Mr. A. M. Robinson). Present—Messrs. F. Parsons (vice-chairman), H. H. Wiles, B. J. Chaplin, J. Layton, W. A. Payne, J. L. Rutter, R. Osborn, E. Few, A. E. Tollemache, F. B. Money, Rowley, H. W. Holben, Swann, W. Heffer, Whitechurch, T. Chivers, T. Ivatt, Pamplin, G. Bland, G. K. Ambrose, H. F. Cook, J. Bester, Doggett, Raymont, J. Foster, R. A. Benton, and the Rev. A. J. Micklethwaite.

NUMBER IN THE HOUSE.

The MASTER reported that the number in the House during the past week had been 148, as against 160 in the corresponding week last year.

VACCINATION RETURNS.

The VICE-CHAIRMAN, in asking for copies of the vaccination returns last sent to the Local Government Board, said he thought no words of his were needed to commend to them the advisability of inquiring into the subject, in view of the terrible epidemic raging in Gloucester. He was very sorry to see the action taken by the Cambridge Board of Guardians with regard to the same matter on the previous day, and he hoped they would not get in the same drift. One of the Cambridge Guardians proposed that they should wait for the report of the Royal Commission before going into details. When one saw it in print that there were about 200 children unvaccinated in Cambridge, he thought it was time for the Cambridge Board of Guardians to pass over the Royal Commission and act at once.

Cambridge Chronicle 1/5/96

THE DIARY ENTRIES

Early Season
Wednesday, April 22nd, 1896

The investment mix seems to be a good idea of Maynard's in that the application of technology can improve the utility gained by a batsman. The ball may run for four on a well-cut outfield instead of dribbling for two, as we have seen in the nineties, courtesy of Ransome and Rapier's Ipswich mowers.[24]

A fast, well-rolled pitch will yield more utility to the batsman than an uncovered pudding of dandelions. Similarly, time spent in the nets may yield up the secrets of the late-cut which will scarcely emerge from learning by heart a page of Thucydides.

---

24 The firm's founder was the great-grandfather of author Arthur Ransome, who, it is often forgotten, set four of the first ten of his bestselling books for children in East Anglia.

THE DIARY ENTRIES

Microeconomics
Sunday, May 3rd 1896

Maynard has been happily using the season openers to distinguish total, average, and marginal quantities,[25] using the batsmens' scores, scoring rates, and bowlers' analyses with the incremental passage of overs. I have negotiated entry for him to the seating at the front of the University pavilion, the news of which he received with a look of surprise, as if he hadn't realised how important I was up to that point.[26] I pointed out with amusement to him that some of those (to him) gods were rather shaky administrative intruders to me, and were more than happy to grant me the occasional favour!

---

25   These ideas and their successors are all very clearly explained in modern microeconomics texts, but these days it is their defence as a valid pursuit for young business students that is at issue. They are charged with being 'unrealistic' and 'irrelevant', but, interestingly, rarely as 'static'. This is curious. The weakest spot, arguably, is the assumption of diminishing marginal utility, whereby the goldminer in the desert is willing to offer fewer and fewer grains of gold in exchange for litres of water from a passing merchant. One litre too many (and a stomach upset) would lead to negative marginal utility. This is the origin of the demand curve, which describes how the lower the price is, the more of a commodity will be demanded by purchasers. The drawback with this assumption is that from the merchant's point of view it doesn't hold. He is as interested in the last grains of gold traded as in the first. This seems to be true of the trappings of wealth as well, as Veblen showed in theory and Imelda Marcos showed in practice with her shoes. If the basis of micro theory, in particular the downward-sloping demand curve, is not a valid assumption for the wider picture, where does this leave the *laisser faire* school?

26   J.N.K. was appointed Secretary of the Local Examination Syndicate in 1892, and was elected to the Council of the Senate in the same year, soon becoming its Honorary Secretary. It was unlikely that he would feel inadequate standing next to F. Mitchell, the University captain, even though he was just five foot four inches tall. With the examination season upon him, J.N.K. would have been glad to see J.M.K. occupied at Fenner's. Brother Geoffrey's preference was the study of *flora* and *fauna*.

ENTERTAINMENT AT ST. MATTHEW'S SCHOOL.

Last (Thursday) evening a penny popular entertainment was given by the teachers of St. Martin's Sunday School, in St. Matthew's Schoolroom, Norfolk Street. The Rev. J. H. Richards presided, and there was a well-filled room. The programme opened with a pianoforte duet, "Ivanhoe March," played with great spirit, after which Miss Johnson sang "Sunshine and Rain" very sweetly. The "Tableaux Vivants" were admirably carried out, and afforded a pleasant variety to the entertainment. A musical tableau, entitled "Where are you going," illustrating the wide difference between the young ladies of the 17th and 19th centuries, was capitally acted and thoroughly appreciated. The comic songs of Mr. Gray gave great satisfaction, and the efforts of "Le Rouge et Noir Mandoline Quartette," which formed one of the principle items on the programme, were loudly applauded. A most successful concert concluded with the singing of "God Save the Queen." The programme was as follows:—

PART I.

Pianoforte duet..."Ivanhoe March"...
    Miss Watts and Miss E. Jackson
Song... ..."Sunshine and Rain" ... Miss Johnson
Tableau..."As Good as New"...Misses Baldry,
    Atkin, Bradbury, Dockerill, and M. Pryor
    With Recitation by Miss Watts.
Flag drill ... ... Choir Girls
Song... ..."Songs and Sense" ... Mr. S. G. Gray
Musical Tableau..."Where are you going?"...
(17th Century)... Nellie Trinn and Hilda Miller
(19th Century) _ Miss Baldry and Mr. Pryor
Mandoline Quartet...Miss Seymour, Miss Brown,
    Mr. Panchaud and Mr. Braid
Tableau..."You Dirty Boy"...Miss Atkin and
    W. Malthy
Song ... ... "Tit for Tat"... Miss L. Webb
Tableau..."Crowning of Sloper"...Mr. Gray and
    Misses Atkin, Elliott, Slack, Bradbury, Martin,
    Prior, Watts, Baldry, Dockerill and Fange

PART II.

Violin Solo ... ... Mr. J. Stearn
Recitation ... ... Mr. J. P. Gallron
Tableau..."Past"... ... ... Miss Slack
    "Present" ... Miss Watts and Mr. Pryor
    "Future" _ Miss Fange and Mr. Gray
Song... ... "Our Johnnie"... Mr. H. Hornsby
Mandoline quartet...Miss Seymour, Miss Brown,
    Mr. Panchaud and Mr. Braid
Song ... ... "All alone" _ Mr. S. G. Gray
Tableau..."The Wedding Morn" _ Misses Watts,
    Atkin, Baldry, Bradbury, Dockerill, Elliott,
    Fange, Slack and L. Dockerill.
    With Song by Miss Johnson.
Song... "In Old Madrid" ... Mr. Cozzins
Toy Symphony "Pantomania" Sloper and his Court
    God Save the Queen.

There were three main causes for the success of the Conservative and Unionist party; they were, firstly, the merits of the three candidates, secondly the good hard work done by all the local associations, and thirdly, the fact that the agricultural labourers were beginning to find out the hollowness and the sham of the promises made by the late Radical Government. [Applause.]

Mr. G. F. Whitmore proposed "Kindred Clubs." It was not necessary for him to enlarge upon the importance of the outside Clubs. It was to a large extent due to the work of these Clubs that Mr. FitzGerald was returned with so substantial a majority. [Hear, hear.] They gave the working men, who lived where votes lay thickest, an opportunity of discussing political questions and refuting errors. [Cheers.] He coupled with the toast the names of Mr. Stanton, Mr. Coulson and Ald. Kett.

Mr. S. Stanton, President of the Beaconsfield Club, assured the assembly that the members of that Club would not rest on their oars, would not go to sleep, but would continue to do their level best to promote the interests of the Party in the Borough.

Mr. Coulson, President of the Salisbury Club, said they had not relaxed their efforts. They had obtained 60 new members since the last election. [Cheers.]

Mr. Ald. Kett, President of the New Town Conservative Club, also responded. He referred to the retirement of their President, Mr. C. A. Vinter, remarking that it was a loss to the town politically. The Club began in a bad way; it began with nothing [laughter], and he was afraid they now stood with something less than nothing. [Renewed laughter.] But they were doing a very good work at that end of the town, the Club numbering at the present time something like 250 members, which, he thought, considering the short time that the Club had been established, was a fair number. [Hear, hear.]

This concluded the toast list, and after the singing of the National Anthem, the company separated.

The toasts were interspersed with songs by Messrs. Parker and Bowers, whose good bass and tenor voices were much appreciated.

Cambridge Chronicle 1/5/96

SPORTS AND PASTIMES.

CRICKET.

TRINITY COLLEGE FRESHMEN'S MATCH.

The initial fixture of any importance was commenced on the Trinity ground on Monday, when teams captained by Messrs. E. H. Bray and E. Garnett, and composed of freshmen, played in a trial game. The teams included prominent public school cricketers in F. H. Clay, of Charterhouse, and H. W. Barrett, of Bath. Both batted well for M, and G. E. Winter, of Winchester, and C. R. Wills, of Marlborough, also shaped creditably. C. A. Anderson, of Charterhouse, punished the bowling freely until a change produced the desired effect, his score being the highest of the day. J. S. Richardson, of Charterhouse, showed to advantage behind the wicket. Tuesday also produced some interesting play. Score:—

MR. R. GARNETT' XI.

J. H. Stogdon (Harrow), b Gowers 17	A. W. Cecil (Winchester), b Cumberlege ... 4
G. E. Winter (Winchester), st Bray, b De Zoete 34	H. W. Barrett (Bath), b Cumberlege ... 36
H. H. B. Hawkins (Whitgift), b De Zoete ... 10	J. S. Richardson (Charterhouse), b Gowers ... 5
C. R. Wills (Marlborough), c Hughes, b Cumberlege 81	E. Garnett (capt.), not out 20
F. H. Clay (Charterhouse), c and b Cumberlege ... 16	Extras 16
W. F. Faulkes (Uppingham), b De Zoete ... 2	214

Second Innings.—Stogdon, b De Zoete, 18; Winter, c Bray, b De Zoete, 5; Hawkins, not out, 103; Wills, c Druce, b De Zoete, 14; Clay, b De Zoete, 3; Faulkes, c Druce, b De Zoete, 0; Cecil, b De Zoete, 0; Barrett, not out, 25; extras, 18; total for six wickets, 181.

MR. BRAY'S XI.

R. F. Cumberlege (Durham), c Richardson, b Stogdon 20	G. B. Winch (Charterhouse), b Stogdon 0
H. W. De Zoete (Eton), c Richardson, b Hawkins 6	W. H. Barry (Winchester), b Hawkins ... 6
C. A. Anderson (Charterhouse), b Hawkins ... 89	H. Gibson-Watt (Eton), b Clay 5
W. F. Gowers (Rugby), c Cecil, b Stogdon ... 19	Prince Eric of Thurn-Taxis, b Clay ... 1
E. A. C. Druce (Marlborough), b Hawkins ... 81	E. H. Bray, not out ... 9
W. E. Hughes (Tonbridge), c sub, b Hawkins 23	Extras 8
	172

Second Innings.—Cumberlege, not out, 35; De Zoete, b Stogdon, 1; Anderson, b Clay, 2; Gowers, b Cecil, 8; Druce, not out, 10; extras, 4; total for three wickets, 65.

THE DIARY ENTRIES

Microeconomics
Monday, May 4th, 1896

Maynard is now in a sort of heaven with his pencil and his pad at the ground for the Seniors match, saying very little and shyly looking sideways at the players and spectators when they become proximal. He has to sit in the open seating; the covered area is reserved for life members. It seems he may be joined by ladies this season, although none have yet presented themselves for admission (perhaps for fear they might be labelled '*débutantes*'?). He is still over-awed at this early stage and hasn't yet learned how bored, curious, and friendly the assembled grandees can be.[27] It is a delightful *entente cordiale* and the company, although rather light on the grey matter, is one that I am happy for him to explore at this stage in his education.[28]

---

[27] The spectators would have been full of expert analysis as they had the chance to see the best players in the world regularly, and would have witnessed in just thirty years astonishing changes to the ground and the game (*e.g.* the demise of underarm lob bowling, the rise of the pad, and new technology such as rubber bat handle covers).

[28] The identification of cricket as a game associated with an approach to life has been made in an unmatchable way by C.L.R. James in *Beyond A Boundary*, but it is well worth going back to one of C.L.R.'s bibles, *The Badminton Book* of 1888, to feel the force of this cultural wave. Largely written by Cambridge men A.G. Steel and the Hon. R.H. Lyttelton, with two chapters by W.G. Grace, it is well worth looking at just for the print on page 143 of 'A pokey batsman dealing with a high dropping full pitch'.

THE UNIVERSITY FRESHMEN'S MATCH.

Three hours proved sufficient to bring this match to a close on Saturday, Mr. Druce's side winning by nine wickets. When stumps were drawn on Friday, Mr. Mitchell's team, who followed on in a minority of 184, had lost five batsmen for 132. Mr Stogdon, who was not out 42, hit well for a little while, until Mr. Jessop found out the weak point in his defence. The total eventually reached 264. Mr. De Zoete, who played for Eton against Winchester last season and was 12th man for the Harrow match, bowled with great effect. Mr. Druce's side had 82 to get for victory, and this number they found little difficulty in obtaining, as shown by the complete score attached:—

N. F. DRUCE'S SIDE.

A. C. Miller, b Hawkins ... 0	W. Campbell, c Mitchell, b Lee ... 23
G. G. Ellett, b Hawkins ... 12	H. W. de Zoete, b Lee ... 13
G. L. Jessop, c Makie, b Hawkins ... 107	A. E. Eastwood, c Stogdon, b de Gex ... 52
A. T. Coode, b Hawkins ... 4	N. F. Druce (capt.), not out ... 3
R. F. Cumberlege, run out 23	Extras ... 9
W. F. Gowers, b Lee ... 68	
C. S. Franklyn, b Lee ... 0	
S. R. Worthington, c and b Lee ... 66	
	371

Second Innings.—A. C. Miller, not out, 15; G. G. Ellett, c Cargeaven, b Hawkins, 17; G. L. Jessop, c Mackie, b Cargeaven, 23; A. T. Coode, not out, 21; extras, 4; total, 82.

F. MITCHELL'S SIDE.

H. H. B. Jeffrey, c Miller, b Jessop ... 28	b De Zoete ... 10
O. G. Mackie, c Druce, b Jessop ... 2	b Eastwood ... 29
J. H. Stogdon, c Druce, b Gowers ... 33	b Jessop ... 62
H. H. R. Hawkins, run out ... 2	b De Zoete ... 6
W. H. Maundrell, b Jessop ... 29	b De Zoete ... 12
R. L. Harke, c and b Franklyn 11	not out ... 43
H. G. Cargeaven, b Franklyn... 12	b De Zoete ... 10
R. O. De Gex, b Jessop ... 34	b Eastwood ... 14
E. B. L. Lee, st Cumberlege, b Franklyn ... 8	c Cumberlege, b De Zoete... 11
C. R. Peacock, c Miller, b Franklyn ... 2	b Jessop ... 0
G. Apthorp, b Jessop ... 6	c Franklyn, b De Zoete ... 27
F. Mitchell (captain), not out 2	c Jessop, b De Zoete 15
Extras ... 22	Extras ... 25
188	264

Cambridge Chronicle 8/5/96

GOLDEN AGES AT THE FENNER'S MARGIN

THE SENIORS' MATCH.

The usual trial game between two elevens of Seniors was commenced at Fenner's Ground on Monday. There were twelve a-side, captained by Mr. C. J. Burnup and Mr. E. H. Bray. The latter's side batted first, and compiled 249, F. J. S. Moore being the chief contributor with a sound innings. At the call of time the other side had made 170 for the loss of five wickets. Mr. Burnup's side played lucky cricket and on Tuesday completed a first innings for 195, of which the captain contributed a fine innings of 91. To this the opposition replied with 405, every batsman but one securing double figures. Mr. Richardson was top scorer; his total was obtained by sound cricket. The match was brought to a conclusion on Wednesday, when after no fewer than 1,210 runs had been registered in the four innings, Mr. Bray's side proved victors by 98 runs.

MR. E. H. BRAY'S SIDE.

F. J. S. Moore (St. John's), c De Linde, b Dyne	74	c Dyne, b Alexander	48
W. Outram (Pembroke), b Simpson	0	b Crocker	21
W. Clarke (St. John's), b Alexander	14	c Crocker, b Simpson	19
A. G. Richardson (Corpus), run out	12	c Robinson, b Alexander	65
H. T. C. Weatherhead (Emmanuel), b Dyne	0	l b w, b Crocker	22
A. S. Farnfield (Queens'), b Crocker	1	c Dyne, b Garnett	37
W. Mortimer (Trinity), c Burnup, b Simpson	21	c Crocker, b Alexander	19
E. H. Bray (Trinity), c Taylor, b Dyne	22	b Crocker	29
P. W. Cobbold (Trinity) run out	21	run out	44
A. W. Watson (Magdalene), not out	20	b Simpson	8
R. Boucher (Pembroke), b Burnup	0	st Robinson, b Simpson	29
E. B. Shine (Selwyn), c Crocker, b Dyne	46	not out	48
Extras	16	Extras	16
	249		405

MR. C. J. BURNUP'S SIDE.

C. D. Robinson (St. John's), c and b Shine	16	c Farnfield, b Boucher	23
C. J. Burnup (Clare), b Shine	96	c Farnfield, b Shine	27
H. B. J. Taylor (Jesus), b Shine	22	c Shine, b Cobbold	21
W. L. Bunting (Trinity Hall), c Shine, b Boucher	1	c Bray, b Shine	25
J. M. Brydone (Jesus), b Shine	3	c Outram, b Clarke	34
G. H. Simpson (Clare), c Clarke, b Boucher	14	c Richardson, b Moore	210
E. Garnett (Trinity), b Shine	24	c Bray, b Boucher	2
C. L. Alexander (Trinity), b Shine	3	b Moore	33
V. F. De Linde (Peterhouse), b Shine	0	not out	23
J. F. Strimshire (St. John's), b Cobbold	1	b Cobbold	26
J. A. Crocker (Trinity), b Cobbold	0	c Cobbold, b Moore	4
J. E. Dyne (King's), not out	0	b Cobbold	9
Extras	17	Extras	25
	195		361

Cambridge Chronicle 8/5/96

THE DIARY ENTRIES

Microeconomics
Saturday, May 9th, 1896

From his analysis of batsmen, Maynard has built up a statistical picture of how a batsman constructs an enterprise, almost like the builders on the edge of town down Hill's Road. Nothing seems to happen for a long period of play and just when you think they are going to disappear for good into a hole of their own making, a scaffolding seems to emerge, followed by a more certain structure and then the edifice starts to take shape at an ever-gathering pace until some coherent whole can be discerned. At least, that is the aim. Tragic collapses of scaffolding have been as frequent as complete architectural artefacts for the Varsity in recent seasons.[29]

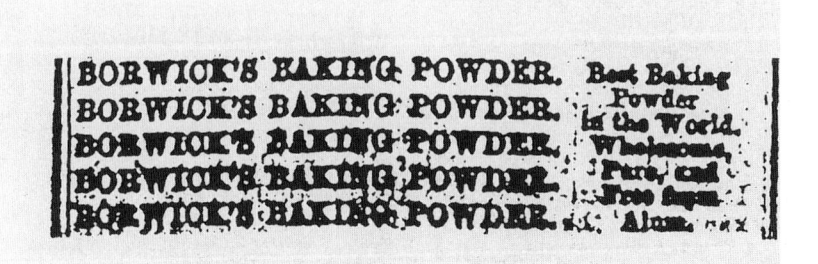

---

29 At his best J.N.K. could be a very persuasive writer conveying ideas with that certainty and lightness that made his textbooks so longlasting. A good example can be found on page 326 of *The Scope and Method of Political Economy*, where he tries to point out, more gently than his son perhaps, that in the long run we are all dead:

> To postpone considerations of theory until an indefinite number of facts have already been collected is, even from the historical point of view, a mistake.

His humour tended to be self-depracating and somewhat in line with his gently fatalistic view of life, with all his agonising over material and health-related matters. It is fitting that with such a track record of concern he should live to be nearly a hundred.

CAMBRIDGE UNIVERSITY V. MR. C. I. THORNTON'S ELEVEN.

Played at CAMBRIDGE, *Thursday, Friday, Saturday, May* 7, 8, 9.—The wicket was up to the best standard reached on Fenner's ground, and after three full days' cricket, the game was left drawn. At the finish, the powerful England eleven got together by Mr. Thornton held a strong advantage, but considering that the Cambridge men had nothing to play for in their last innings but to avert defeat, the performance reflected a great deal of credit upon them. The University did well in dismissing their opponents for 219, and thanks largely to Burnup and Marriott, they gained a lead of 70 runs on the first innings. On going in a second time, Mr. Thornton's team fared infinitely better than before, some splendid batting being shown by Captain Wynyard, Shrewsbury, Alec Hearne and Albert Trott. Cambridge were left with 371 to get to win, but no time in which remained to make such a number. The England team seldom looked like winning, Druce, Marriott, Burnup and several of the others playing good and correct cricket.

MR. C. I. THORNTON'S ELEVEN.

A. Shrewsbury run out	0	— c Mitchell b Lowe	62
Mr. C. I. Thornton b Jessop	10	— st Robinson b Jessop	16
Alec Hearne c Druce b Jessop	0	— c Mitchell b Jessop	37
G. Davidson c Robinson b Wilson	6	— c Druce b Jessop	26
Mr. C. W. Wright c Mitchell b Wilson	7	— b Shine	12
Mr. A. J. Webbe c Marriott b Wilson	8	— retired hurt	31
Mr. G. J. V. Weigall b Lowe	75	— b Burnup	0
Mr. F. W. Maude c Shine b Lowe	60	— b Lowe	37
Captain E. G. Wynyard not out	26	— c Shine b Wilson	121
A. E. Trott c Jessop b Wilson	15	— b Shine	58
W. Mead b Shine	0	— not out	0
B 11, l-b 1	12	B 31, l-b 4, w 3, n-b 2	40
	219		440

CAMBRIDGE UNIVERSITY.

Mr. F. Mitchell c Wright b Mead	23	— b Trott	25
Mr. C. J. Burnup lbw, b Trott	92	— c Webbe b Trott	35
Mr. W. M'G. Hemingway b Davidson	17	— b Mead	3
Mr. N. F. Druce c Weigall b Davidson	0	— b Hearne	63
Mr. H. H. Marriott b Mead	76	— c Hearne b Mead	39
Mr. J. H. Stogdon run out	29	— c Thornton b Mead	2
Mr. G. L. Jessop c Wynyard b Davidson	25	— c Weigall b Mead	1
Mr. C. E. M. Wilson b Mead	1	— b Davidson	26
Mr. W. W. Lowe b Mead	4	— lbw b Hearne	21
Mr. C. D. Robinson c Trott b Davidson	5	— not out	7
Mr. E. B. Shine not out	0		
B 11, l-b 5, n-b 1	17	B 5, l-b 4	9
	289		231

CAMBRIDGE UNIVERSITY BOWLING.

	Overs	Mdns.	Runs	Wkts.	Overs	Mdns.	Runs	Wkts.
Jessop	20	2	58	2	41	10	117	3
Wilson	22	5	61	4	34	11	85	1
Burnup	6	2	23	0	23	10	45	1
Lowe	12	2	42	2	28	6	95	2
Shine	11.4	4	23	1	28.2	11	52	2
Druce					4	2	6	0

MR. THORNTON'S ELEVEN'S BOWLING.

	Overs	Mdns.	Runs	Wkts.	Overs	Mdns.	Runs	Wkts.
Mead	42	12	101	4	50	19	70	4
Trott	19	2	76	1	38	12	88	2
Davidson	26.3	6	68	4	16	6	34	1
Hearne	5	1	12	0	16	7	14	2
Maude	3	0	15	0				
Wynyard					2	0	16	0

Umpires: R. Carpenter and G. Watts.

THE DIARY ENTRIES

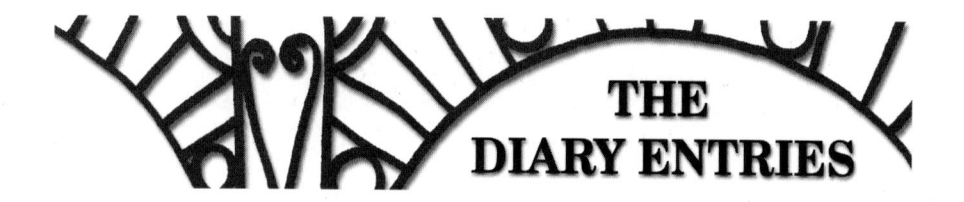

Microeconomics
Monday, May 11th, 1896

Foxwell came to lunch, and M. seems to be enjoying our hebdomodary discussions that include cricket in the summer in so far as it can provide food for thought in logic and mathematics. Foxwell said that in the U.S.A. the evangelical mind of the 'fundamentalist' writers is becoming part of the undergraduate economists' approach in their worship of the post-graduate researchers.

'They trawl the campuses promising that they can bring economic salvation by making Fishers of men!'[30]

We all roared, and M., quick as a flash, grabbed one of the candlesticks on the sideboard and pointed to the charred top end, saying

'But in Cambridge we prefer Singe-wick!'

---

30 'Fundamentalism' as a term did not originate in the Islamic world, but with the back-to-the-bible evangelism of the United States in the 1890s.

Irving Fisher was nearly thirty years old, but had only moved into the economics department at Yale the previous year. His startlingly original PhD thesis of 1892 had provided the bridge from his Mathematics studies. In January 1895 J.N.K. had been offered the professorship of Economics at Chicago, a move which would have been very interesting; what price Friedman and the new monetarists if J.M.K. had been raised in Chicago?

THE DIARY ENTRIES

Microeconomics
Wednesday, May 13th, 1896

Thanks to the fine weather Maynard has now enough data to identify what he calls 'bad trots' and 'purple patches', and is puzzled by the patterns. He had always been sceptical about the notion of 'form' in cricket, assuming ability to be a concrete substance that had been perfected with practice and could be used in any circumstance to build an innings.[31] He has had to rethink this in a psychological context and has come up with a concept of habituality, which I said sounded barbaric; he then started talking about tendencies, but I said that gave an impression of instinctiveness which went against the need to describe a situation of feedback where the habit could be self-perpetuating, spiralling down or up through feeding on itself. Maynard was disappointed by this, as he had earmarked the word *tendenz* in German to try to distinguish the batting aspect of human behaviour.

---

31 This is a popular fallacy amongst those who are not adept at cricket, those supremely adept at cricket, and those without sympathy or imagination. The view is that with practice, as at darts or billiards or even whist, the expert will know what to do and how to do it in each situation. But these other three games pose largely static challenges, or at most only partially dynamic ones. The feedback loop between performance and psychological state has been explored in many cricket and economics books. In the *Jubilee Book* Ranji showed how Hon. E. Lyttelton (he affectionately calls him 'Ed') disproved that a cricketer could become 'stale' in the sense of monotony leading to a failure of nerve power. He called a bad trot 'the Dumps' and felt it was mental rather than physiological. This was dubbed 'reflexivity' by George Soros in his 1998 book. Ernst Gombrich preferred the term 'mutual reinforcement' in his books on the apprehension of art. The most extreme examples of negative mutual reinforcement in the Golden Age were Shrewsbury, Trott, and Stoddart, demigods who ended up taking their own lives.

THE DIARY ENTRIES

In the context of 'bad trots' I remarked that it was a pity the word 'pejorative' had become so abused in English as to lose its original Latin sense.[32] I then suggested the French word *propension* which might be applied in a way that would not be baffling because he could settle its connotation from the outset.[33] All this sent Maynard hurrying off to the dictionaries and I later saw him carrying a copy of *Robert*[34] down to Fenner's which must have been the catalyst for some interesting conversation with the pavilion elders!

---

32 *i.e.* going from bad to worse.

33 This translates as 'propensity', and the idea of a measurable tendency or habit became a key part of the Keynesians' analysis of economic dynamics some forty years later. The events on 22 June suggest we were quite fortunate to receive the legacy of this concept, given the Keyneses bias against French in favour of German.

34 Rather an adolescent display of showmanship; this implies a French dictionary in French rather than a French-English lexicon.

GOLDEN AGES AT THE FENNER'S MARGIN

THE DIARY ENTRIES

Microeconomics
Thursday, May 14th, 1896

Maynard has been anthropomorphising the bowler's art this week. He has decided, not unreasonably, that lob bowlers represent the primary industries as portrayed in his Frye's Geography textbook,[35] while pace is more suitable as a parable of manufacturing. Swerve and spin 'proximate to the service industries, such as finance and retailing.

Where this leaves the supply side of the Varsity side is open to question, as even Jessop's steel production is wont to transform itself into a milliner's shop front after a heavy Fenner's lunch. In considering an application for Dunlop shares I have had some levity from Maynard, who has been researching the most pneumatic bowlers in the county championship, even to the point of asking Mrs Watts which visiting team eats the heartiest teas!

Eton College

35 This 1895 United States publication, *Complete Geography*, contains fearsome little line drawings of Sheffield roofscapes and claustrophobic mining scenes, contrasted with plucky fishing smacks ('Herring boats running into Lowestoft') and pastoral farming. Now as then popular sympathy lies with the latter two, but the better wages and modern temper lay in the former. Sheffield Smoke is pictured four pages before Eton College.

In 1898 the book was reworked for Britain by Andrew J. Herbertson with the same drawings; it is typically avant-garde of the Keynes family to have had the early version of what became a standard Edwardian text.

THE DIARY ENTRIES

Sheffield smoke.

Canal, Stoke-upon-Trent.

Flax Plant.

Herring boats running into Lowestoft.

The orchestra, occupied by a large number of little juveniles prettily attired, presented a bright and pleasing sight. The chorus, "The Kazoo Band," given by a number of little boys with trumpets, was encored, and so also was, "Eight Little Mothers," by the eight little girls with their dolls, while "The Merry Shoeblack," by the Shoeblack Brigade, was much applauded. The costumes selected for the various performances had evidently been carefully chosen, and must have taken considerable time to prepare.

At the conclusion of the programme, the Holy Trinity Boys' Brigade, the 3rd Cambridge Company, were marched into a cleared space in the centre of the hall, and put through a number of drills before the Inspecting Officer, Lieut. Cartwright, of the C.U.R.V.

Lieut. CARTWRIGHT, in addressing the boys afterwards, said he felt that the work of a Boys' Brigade was very necessary in a place like Cambridge. Besides training them physically, it taught them to be smart and obedient and amenable to discipline. They were improving every time he visited them. Of course there were faults he could pick out, but they were mainly due to some boys not having regularly attended the drills. They would soon be one of the most efficient companies in the whole Brigade.

The Right Rev. CHAIRMAN then distributed the following prizes amongst the members of the Brigade:—

Efficiency and Attendance Prizes:
(Full Marks: Bible Class 18, Drill 21; total 39).
Corp. Gilkes ...18-21 39   Pte. Haggis ...18-20 38
Corp. Start ...18-21 39   Pte. Williams ...18-20 38
Pte. Start ...18-21 39   Pte. Cutting ...17-20 37
Recruit's Prize: Pte. Cutting.
Squad Challenge Medal:
Squad II : Corp. Gilkes.
Good Conduct Stripes:
Awarded to those who have not missed more than three attendances at Bible Class and Drill:
Corp. Gilkes, Corp. Start, Lce.-Corp. Rooke, Ptes. Bullock, Cutting, Challis, Fuller, Haggis, Start, and Williams.

It was now the turn of the Girls' Club to display the results of their efforts during the winter, and as they marched into the hall, led by Miss Edith Hunnybun, they created a highly favourable impression. Their dresses, which were of various shades of blue with red sashes and trimmings, formed a pleasing combination of colour and blended with very pretty effect in many of the marches. The calisthenic, dumb bell and wand exercises were most gracefully performed by many of the girls, and the general effect quite charmed the spectators.

THE DIARY ENTRIES

TRINITY COLLEGE v. JESUS COLLEGE.

The annual two days' encounter between the above colleges was commenced on Trinity Ground on Monday. The home team batted first, and were not dismissed until 357 had been scored. Towards this total the secretary of the C.U.C.C., N. F. Druce, contributed 158 in fine style. His chief strokes were eighteen fours, fourteen threes, and eleven twos. Jesus lost two wickets for 40. The game was concluded on Tuesday, the visitors being easily defeated. Score:—

TRINITY COLLEGE.

J. H. Stogdon, b Gray	11	C. L. Alexander, c Brydone, b Snell	10
H. J. Davenport, c Fichardt, b Snell	12	E. B. Bray, not out	17
E. Garnett, b Lee	20	F. J. Peers, b Snell	12
N. F. Druce, b Coode	158	C. J. L. Rudd (retired)	26
C. E. M. Wilson, b Gray	30	Extras	36
W. Mortimer, b Sangster	7		
H. H. B. Hawkins, b Snell	3		357

JESUS COLLEGE.

H. Gray, b Peers	11	b Peers	6
K. D. Thorburn, c Druce, b Peers	36	b Wilson	15
A. T. Coode, a and b Wilson	25	b Rudd	13
H. B. J. Taylor, b Peers	0	c Bray, b Rudd	14
A. H. More, c Bray, b Peers	5	c Bray, b Wilson	15
J. M. Brydone, not out	13	c Mortimer, b Rudd	36
G. M. Hill, c Stogdon, b Wilson	2	b Rudd	4
H. T. Wallis, b Peers	0	c Mortimer, b Peers	14
R. Snell, c Druce, b Wilson	2	c Hawkins, b Wilson	18
E. B. L. Lee, c Alexander, b Wilson	10	c Mortimer, b Alexander	19
P. H. Sangster, b Peers	0	not out	0
Extras	10	Extras	11
	114		165

Cambridge Chronicle 5/5/96

THE DIARY ENTRIES

Microeconomics
Friday, May 15th, 1896

The classification of bowlers has continued apace with some proving to be easy (Kortright, Richardson) while others provoke tendentiousness and doubt (A.G.Steel, C.G.Lyttelton). This reintroduced the question about changes in the structure of bowling attacks through history, and enabled me to discuss the Agrarian, the Industrial, and the Transport Revolutions[36] with Maynard.

---

36 The general view would be that the agricultural revolution occurred in the mid-eighteenth century, the industrial revolution before and just after the turn of the nineteenth century, and the transport revolution during the second quarter of the nineteenth century. It is very difficult to know how helpful these descriptions are in the twenty first century when one is conditioned to think of an ever-increasing pace of change.

The idea of long waves of innovation had, however, already emerged in the writings of Kondratieff, and J.N.K. would have seen for himself the difference steel had made in the later part of the century to ships, as well as other innovations like gas, electricity, refrigeration, and chemicals. He would also have been aware of the white collar revolution, as the quantity of service sector workers rose quicker than the numbers of manufacturing blue collar workers. The official figures do not make this point clearly enough and overstated the extent of deindustrialisation in the U.K. in the 1970s and 1980s, as did the experience of privatisation (from the time of the Heath government hiving-off industries onwards). How many of the employees at John Dickinson's and Company, for example, were accountants, supervisors, typists, sales representatives, managers, drivers, caterers, medical/social/library/educational staff rather than producers of Basildon Bond paper? Yet the small Nash Mills at Hemel Hempstead would have been seen as providing secondary employment since its inception in 1809, five years after Dickinson had invented his machine.

THE DIARY ENTRIES

He rapidly assimilated the concept that one generation of the Field family might have been yeoman, the next two might have been labourers in a factory mill, and thereafter they might have been pulling dray carts or driving public service vehicles with a subsequent flourish to their surnames (Field-Buss, perhaps?). It seems the repeal of the Red Flag Act is now unstoppable, and the thought of urban traffic moving at over 12 m.p.h. seems to suggest another revolution is under way.[37]

---

37 By a freak of fate, one of the best known names on the county 2nd XI circuit in the 1980s was a Field-Buss (of Essex) known as Mousey to his colleagues. The revolution in speed was *not* to come as we now know, although steam-driven horseless carriages were being released from over three decades of inhibition. Average urban speeds have barely changed even with the internal combustion engine, and the ability to go over 14 m.p.h. on rural roads merely led to the substitution of the car for the train; Cambridge is no nearer London in 2004 than it was in 1904.

THE DIARY ENTRIES

Microeconomics
Saturday, May 16th, 1896

Maynard had hitherto had a bit of trouble trying to work out the nature of the motivation of the bowler, and I feel it is this season that is showing him what the fielding side is trying to do. Like all young boys he would love to run up all in a rush and hurl projectiles like thunderbolts from Zeus, shattering stumps and being offered ambrosia afterwards by adoring comrades in the pavilion reserved for heroes. He might also be bewitched by the serpentine approach and hypnotic menace of a slow bowler imparting great break on the ball, fascinated by the repetitive ritual and seeming torture on the batsman carried out with such minimal physical effort. But the vast majority of what most bowlers are capable of and what their strategy is seems to leave most youngsters behind. Perhaps it is because they do not appreciate the desperate balance, the tiny margin for error, the risk involved in any ambition to be more than averagely effective?

But this May I can see he perceives in the professional bowlers visiting us a steely pride in the way they minimise the Varsity's opportunity to score, the savage nature with which they pluck a wicket with a change of pitch speed, or break having lulled the batsman to become accustomed to what they assumed to be the full repertoire of the deliveries on offer. The vital importance of the field placings and the way they give rise to certain expectations in the batsmen, which lead to his undoing as temptation of a subtle kind works at his mind along with the perception of how slowly the telegraph-board is moving. He can see wonder in the way a leg break can take a wicket with a catch to wide mid-on when there are seven men on the off-side from a ball that has seemingly slipped out of the hand in careless fashion. He sees the extent to which distrust can be aroused, almost independent of intelligence or knowledge, and whether moral restraint can prevent them from giving way to panic.

THE DIARY ENTRIES

Maynard concluded that these labourers, professional bowlers, regarded runs as losses, maidens as profit, and the ball which is not scored off as revenue or income.[38] In fact, the common parlance of 'trying to turn a shilling'[39] became associated for us with the concept of bowling maiden overs. And M. has perceived that the ball which is not scored off may be a reward for a job well done, a ball precisely pitched, but in the hands of the professional it may be a confidence trick or trinket, given respect only because of who produced it or the manner in which it was produced. This trick would depend on the gullibility or, dare one say it, stupidity and cowardice of the batsman, the supply of which the Varsity seems to have a greater quantity than Yorkshire or Australia. How to convince the consumer that some worthless item will generate utility for them? As we would go round the cattle market near the station, or the main market in the centre of the town he would rummage through various items on the stalls, then put them back saying:

'Just maiden overs, father, nothing to buy here today!'

---

38 This loosely identifies the bowler as labour, and J.M.K. had also formed a view of the captain as entrepreneur, so he then had to find a satisfactory measure of their performance in economic equivalents. Capital and land are neutral, however, provided by the authorities, so he focuses on general flows of income rather than rent, dividends, wages, although he does make a special effort to allow interest into the picture, as we shall see later.

39 *i.e.* searching out casual jobs, no matter how menial, to generate income.

Those readers born in the late 1960s or after should note that a shilling became 5 pence in February 1971 as the U.K. geared up for a decimal world. The E.E.C. was planning to have a single decimal currency by 1980, following the Solemn Declaration at The Hague in 1969 and the *Werner Report* of 1970.

Interestingly Pierre Werner, the chairman of that committee (which included a young Hans Tietmeyer, later in charge of the Bundesbank) became the main champion for cricket in Luxembourg during a brief period when he wasn't Prime Minister in the mid 1970s.

As President of the Optimists Cricket Club and also an icon who could attract Professors Mundell, Kindleberger, Cooper, and Portes, Vaclav Klaus, Lord Skidelsky, and about sixty others to a conference on the euro in December 1998, he presents an interesting case of the Tebbit Test. His interest in cricket stemmed from a visit to London in 1930 to improve his fourth language, English. This, in fact, predated his economic education, which he identified as the currency shocks imposed on his country by the Belgians in the turbulent years that followed. He would have heard of Bradman before he had heard of Bradbury.

CAMBRIDGE UNIVERSITY V. MR. A. J. WEBBE'S ELEVEN.

Played at CAMBRIDGE, *Thursday, Friday, Saturday, May* 14, 15, 16.—Following his usual custom, Mr. A. J. Webbe took down a powerful team of amateurs to oppose the Light Blues, and in this instance he had the assistance of Albert Trott, the Australian. Cambridge, though they made a plucky uphill fight in the second innings, were far from sustaining the capital form they had shown against Mr. Thornton's team, and the side got together by Mr. Webbe had the best of the game all through, winning easily in the end by eight wickets. On a beautiful wicket it was nothing extraordinary for Mr. Webbe's team to score a first innings of 422, but no one could have been prepared to see the Cambridge men dismissed, as they were for 136. Trott and Bromley-Davenport bowled unchanged throughout this first innings of Cambridge, their capital performance contributing very largely to the success ultimately achieved. For Mr. Webbe's team, C. W. Wright played very fine cricket, and for Cambridge, Mitchell, Hemingway, Wilson and Marriott, greatly distinguished themselves.

MR. A. J. WEBBE'S ELEVEN.

Mr. A. E. Stoddart c Druce b Wilson	5	— c and b Wilson	17
Mr. H. B. Hayman b Lowe	27	— not out	35
Mr. J. R. Mason c Wilson b Jessop	54	— b Shine	0
Mr. C. W. Wright lbw b Shine	114		
Mr. F. E. Lacey b Burnup	50		
Mr. G. J. V. Weigall b Shine	34	— not out	14
Mr. A. J. Webbe b Shine	12		
A. E. Trott b Lowe	0		
Mr. H. R. Bromley-Davenport not out	73		
Mr. C. A. Beldam c Robinson b Shine	15		
Mr. L. C. V. Bathurst b Jessop	17		
B 9, l-b 7, n-b 5	21	B 4, l-b 4, n-b 1	9
	422		75

CAMBRIDGE UNIVERSITY.

Mr. F. Mitchell b Trott	6	— c Davenport b Trott	84
M. C. J. Burnup lbw b Trott	18	— run out	8
Mr. W. M'G. Hemingway b Bromley-Davenport	7	— lbw b Trott	72
Mr. N. F. Druce c Webbe b Bromley-Davenport	0	— b Beldam	30
Mr. H. H. Marriott lbw b Bromley-Davenport	16	— c Mason b Beldam	46
Mr. G. H. Simpson c Mason b Trott	0	— b Beldam	0
Mr. G. L. Jessop c Webbe b Bromley-Davenport	13	— b Trott	1
Mr. C. E. M. Wilson b Trott	19	— c Stoddart b Beldam	63
Mr. W. W. Lowe not out	16	— lbw b Beldam	0
Mr. C. D. Robinson c Beldam b Bromley-Davenport	19	— c Wright b Trott	19
Mr. E. B. Shine c and b Bromley-Davenport	1	— not out	5
B 11, l-b 4, w 1 n-b 5	21	B 23, l-b 8, n-b 1	32
	136		360

CAMBRIDGE UNIVERSITY BOWLING.

	Overs	Mdns.	Runs	Wkts.	Overs	Mdns.	Runs	Wkts.
Jessop	37.4	9	96	2	2	1	8	0
Wilson	48	17	87	1	8	2	16	1
Lowe	21	7	66	2				
Burnup	10	3	26	1	2.1	1	9	0
Shine	26	4	84	4	9	2	33	1
Simpson	11	1	42	0				

MR. A. J. WEBBE'S ELEVEN'S BOWLING.

	Overs	Mdns.	Runs	Wkts.	Overs	Mdns.	Runs	Wkts.
Trott	27	6	54	4	35.4	8	120	4
Bromley-Davenp't	26.1	11	61	6	6	0	41	0
Beldam					29	7	97	5
Mason					11	3	32	0
Stoddart					7	2	23	0
Bathurst					6	0	15	0

Umpires: G. Watts and J. O'Connor.

THE DIARY ENTRIES

Microeconomics
Monday, May 18th, 1896

The reasons for structural change in our great game seemed to be simple to Maynard; permanent alterations in the attitude of pitches and of the climate offer ample scope for thought. The seasonal variability seems to go in cycles[40] so that some periods of years seem to favour the round-arm quick, while others favour the spinner from the off. Of course the possibility of permanent unemployment exists (lobs are never seen delivered underarm these days) but I hardly like to introduce this dangerous line of thought to Maynard.[41]

---

40 The Keynes household would have been well aware of the sunspot theory of the trade cycle put forward by W.S. Jevons which had agriculture as the transmission mechanism between climatic variation and the level of business activity. Jevons was sure that a cycle of 15.2 years was produced by sunspot fluctuation, but concentrated on research into prices rather than meteorology because as a true deductivist he did not want to fall prey to the temptation of looking for the evidence he needed to support his hypothesis.

41 Dangerous because in the Cambridge or Lausanne or Austria of the 1890s permanent unemployment was a possibility that could be entertained only if rigidities in the market existed, such as monopolistic unions. Wage changes would direct workers to change their skills; the corollary is that bowlers can change style, but (as Malcolm Nash found out when he tried to bowl with a new slow action to Sobers and got taken for six sixes) this can have its problems. 'Unemployment' had only entered the dictionary in 1888.

THE DIARY ENTRIES

He has been preoccupied with the latest pictures from Pompeii, with the 'Dancing Faun' particularly preoccupying him because it patently isn't what it seems. A faun, M. says, should not have human legs, and a dancer should be more contorted. His theory is that it is in reality a right-armed slow bowler coming around the wicket in front of the umpire, just before the delivery stride. Looking at the likeness in the newspaper I must admit this seems to be a capital theory, and much more like it than any 'dancing faun'.

The Dancing Faun of Pompeii, or the slow right-armer round the wicket?

THE DIARY ENTRIES

Microeconomics
Tuesday, May 19th, 1896

Too late! I saw M. looking grave the other day, and on being pressed he recounted how he had developed a line of thought based on the premise that if batsmen found all types of bowling too easy on the scientifically-improved pitches of the future the imbalance in the game might lead to crowd ennui, diminution of all the records we have seen built up this century, and the end of the game as we know it – permanent unemployment and the collapse of the edifice!

Imagine, he said, a Test batsman who averaged 100, and a side batting for all three days of a Test. I chastised and comforted him in equal measure, and wondered how he could dream up such unlikely possibilities.[42] I gather that this penumbra of concern was prompted today by the young Gloucestershire freshman Gilbert Jessop, who made 212 not out in under two hours out of Christ's 281 against Clare; thought-provoking indeed.[43]

Bridge is much more soothing and less stressful than cricket; at least there isn't the threat that someone will one day introduce a fifth suit.

---

42 This seems a strange reaction. Perhaps the changes had crept up on J.N.K., or perhaps he hadn't read his *Wisden Almanack*, as J.M.K. had. The scores and rates of scoring had climbed steeply since the 1870s, and were largely ascribed to the technological changes in ground care, the increase in the number of fixtures, and the weather. Batsmen made 1,000 runs in the season 53 times in the years 1893–6, compared to just 7 in the years 1873–6.

   The new premium placed on accuracy in medium pace bowling derived from the reduced returns from pace bowling on truer pitches and the lack of technique in swing bowling. There seems to be a conflict here, however, since accuracy was a response to scoring rates, yet pace and spin were the surest ways to curtail batsmen. Of course, despite Grace's scoring, nobody had envisaged a Test career such as Bradman's.

43 This innings would not have taken place at either of the current grounds, which are a long way out of Cambridge to the north in the case of Christ's and the south in the case of Clare. It is possible that J.M.K. actually witnessed this innings on Parker's Piece the previous day; the Clare reply of 239–9 was shaped by the Blue H.Marriott who made 68 and an unlikely draw was achieved.

THE DIARY ENTRIES

Microeconomics
Wednesday, May 20th, 1896

Maynard has been watching F. Mitchell[44] closely as a captain during the last two matches, and can scarcely believe that just a few years ago he was also a callow thirteen year old, on the verge of his career at St. Peter's, York. The captain, he feels, acts like the entrepreneur in some great financial enterprise, dispensing his resources in a variety of purposeful directions, trying to maintain the cohesion of the disparate parts in the pursuit of an attainable aim, and grasping any opportunities lent by the opposition to further the cause of the team.[45] Crucial to this are the visible signs that M. sees as a spectator: the decisions about who should bowl and who should field where, which lend themselves very well to the concept of productive efficiency and least-cost operation. Maynard became rather free with criticism of the handling of Jessop, Wilson, Shine and Burnup, so I had to point out that Mitchell would be reacting to many unseen factors as well as the current state of the game. There might be potential injuries to consider, the trend of the form of his players; even the social temper of the participants has to be considered. M. understood, and added a further thought, that this match, though in itself important, was but one part of the long preparation for the culminating burst of activity on July 2nd at Lord's against the Dark Blues. I was pleased to see that he had widened his vision of Mitchell's little enterprise.

---

44 Born in Market Weighton, Yorkshire, Mitchell became captain of South Africa and also played Test Matches for England. He was used as a model in some of George Beldam's most interesting photographs during the Edwardian period, but in 1896 his upright stance in combination with Jessop's crouch caused much amusement for the spectators.

45 Ranji makes a similar point in his captaincy chapter in the *Jubilee Book*, 'it is the commonest occurrence in the world for captains to have their fields placed without any reference to the variations of conditions.' How often are entrepreneurs equally blind to macroeconomic reality?

CAMBRIDGE COUNTY TWELVE v. TWENTY-TWO COLTS.

The Cambridge County Cricket Club opened their 1896 season on Tuesday in the picturesque grounds of Cheveley Park—by kind invitation of the President of the Club, Mr. H. McCalmont, M.P.—with a match, the County XII. v. Twenty-two Colts. The day was beautifully fine, and the game, which took place on the Park Club ground, was watched by a large number of local enthusiasts. Mr. F. W. Jarvis, who was in charge of the Colts, winning the toss, sent in E. W. Thornton and Hitch, who were opposed by Messrs. O'Connor and Bellamy. In a good light and on a hard wicket runs came very freely. Mr. Thornton retired after a useful 18, knocked up in a few minutes. A little later J. P. M. Robins, who had joined in the interval, ran himself out in endeavouring to steal a run. Runs came at a great pace, the batsmen treating the bowling with great severity. When the total had reached 56, H. A. Ellis was also run out. G. F. Pigott partnered Hitch, but the March man only stayed a few minutes, giving place to F. Chennell, who had barely taken his bearings before the pro. was sent to the pavilion through a catch by Winter off O'Connor. P. N. Gray arrived only to see the downfall of the Newmarket representative, who fell a victim to the Cambs. wicket-keeper. Messrs. Stubbs and Phillips were both clean bowled by the Irishman before scoring. Shortly before the adjournment for luncheon "the captain" succumbed to a catch in the slips, and the game simply turned itself into a ludicrous procession passing to and fro between the pavilion and the wickets, until W. S. Halford joined N. G. Jackson. Directly the men partnered it was evident that they meant business, and the total innings realised exactly 200. Mr. Jackson's 46 included seven boundary hits.

The Twelve started badly, Mr. Winter losing his wicket in the first over from the Cheveley pro. The Rector joined, but shared the same fate as his predecessor. F. W. French partnered with the old county batsman, but only stayed a couple of overs. With the advent of the old Surrey wicket-keeper, matters improved considerably, and a splendid stand was made. Both men played first-class cricket, and as the result of 50 minutes' play, the half-century was signalled, followed soon by 60. At last the useful partnership came to a termination, the professional being splendidly taken in the long field by Mr. F. E. Morgan off Halford, after knocking up 22. Sixty-two runs had been put on for the fourth wicket. V. F. de Lisle partnered the Ely crack and kept his wicket intact while the other did the run-getting. With the score at 91, Mr. Roberson was captured by Mr. Jarvis at mid-on, off Gray. He had been batting just an hour and thirty-five minutes for his 51, which was the result of careful, pretty cricket. The union of de Lisle and Bellamy produced slow cricket. When stumps were drawn, seven wickets had fallen for 180. Just previous to the adjournment Mr. Dalton played a ball on to his face, receiving a severe blow in the region of the right eye, which obliged him to retire.

The game was considerably marred on Wednesday by the rain. Play was resumed at 11.15, and the twelve completed their innings, the aggregate coming out 186—14 below that run up by the Colts. At luncheon time the Colts had lost three wickets for 45. No play was possible afterwards. The scores stood as follows:—

59

```
                    TWENTY-TWO COLTS.
Hitch (Cambridge), c G. S. Winter, b O'Connor       ...  23
E. W. Thornton (Hildersham), c sub., b O'Connor     ...  18
G. P. M. Robins (Moulton), run out    ...    ...    ...   6
H. A. Ellis (Cambridge), run out      ...    ...    ...  18
G. F. Piggott (March), b Covell       ...    ...    ...   3
F. Chennell (Newmarket), st Watts, b O'Connor       ...   2
P. W. Gray (Cambridge), c de Lisle, b O'Connor      ...  25
A. Stubbs (Ely), b O'Connor           ...    ...    ...   0
F. T. Phillips (March), b O'Connor    ...    ...    ...   0
F. E. Morgan (Cambridge), b Bellamy   ...    ...    ...   7
F. W. Jarvis (capt.) (Newmarket), c F. A. Dalton, b
    O'Connor    ...    ...    ...    ...    ...    ...   8
J. Robins (Isleham), b O'Connor       ...    ...    ...   0
R. Robins (Isleham), lbw, b O'Connor  ...    ...    ...   0
E. S. Saunderson (Stetchworth), b O'Connor          ...   0
R. Lush (Cambridge), c Watts, b Bellamy...   ...    ...   0
H. Gardner (Fulbourn), b Bellamy      ...    ...    ...   0
P. Mooey (Landbeach), c Rev. E. R. Douglas, b
    O'Connor    ...    ...    ...    ...    ...    ...   0
Hurry (Newmarket), b Bellamy          ...    ...    ...   0
N. G. Jackson (Wisbech), not out      ...    ...    ...  46
W. Cobb (Ely), c Roberson, b Bellamy  ...    ...    ...   1
A. W. Cook (Cambridge), b Bellamy     ...    ...    ...   0
W. S. Halford (West Wratting), run out ...   ...    ...  34
        Extras  ...    ...    ...    ...    ...    ...  14
                                                        ———
                                                        200
Colts' second innings—Hitch, b O'Connor, 7 ; Thornton,
c Dalton, b O'Connor, 0 ; P. M. Robins, not out, 15 ; H. A.
Ellis, b Bellamy, 2 ; W. S. Halford, not out, 12 ; extras, 9 ;
total, 45.
                    CAMBS. COUNTY XII.
F. Roberson (Ely), c Jarvis, b Gray   ...    ...    ...  51
G. S. Winter (Trinity College, Cambridge), b Hitch  ...   0
Rev. E. R. Douglas (Cheveley), b Hitch              ...   6
F. W. French (Cambridge), b Gardner                 ...   0
Watts (Cambridge), c F. E. Morgan, b Halford        ...  28
V. F. de Lisle (Peterhouse, Cambridge), c Hitch, b F. E.
    Morgan      ...    ...    ...    ...    ...    ...   5
Bellamy (Stetchworth), not out        ...    ...    ...  45
W. E. Warren (Cambridge), c Jackson, b Halford      ...  18
F. A. Dalton (Chesterton), b Hitch    ...    ...    ...   4
H. S. French (Cambridge), c Morgan, b Gardner       ...  15
O'Connor (Cambridge), c Hitch, b Lush               ...  10
Covell (Cambridge), lbw, b Lush       ...    ...    ...   0
        Extras                                            9
                                                        ———
                                                        186
```

THE DIARY ENTRIES

Microeconomics
Friday, May 22nd, 1896

Maynard said today that he wishes he could be as good at cricket as at golf.[46] I chaffed him and said I didn't know he was any good at golf, but he straight-facedly agreed that he wasn't but that wasn't what he meant. It seems that he feels golf is a totally solitary game, similar to athletics or rowing, even if you are in a combination of players. Cricket, however, is based on transactions of a dynamic nature between batsman, bowler, and fielders, and that there are huge demands made on the player to subordinate himself to others at crucial moments, to take the lead as an individual, or at some junctures to be neutrally vacuous and determined by the ritual and others' actions. He feels occasionally to be in control of the skills but in a team match he generally feels either ineffective, out of place, self conscious, ignorant, slow, or even ugly.

This made a most compelling case, and I tried to reassure him that all young boys who learn cricket go through phases of not establishing the decorum, or correctness of place, for their behaviour. He shook his head and said it was more than this. Those key transactions at the wicket between bowler and batsman were beyond him. He could perfect the strokes in a mirror, he could copy a run-up and delivery in the garden, but to react dynamically in the full theatre of the middle left him all at sea, and full of wonder that anybody could be accomplished at this game at all. I did my best to console him and suggested that he might spend as many moments observing at Fenner's as he could, because he might learn and gain confidence from this transactionary model. He left me deep in thought.

---

46 This was the sports day for Goody's, and was held at Fenner's. It was a moment of truth for J.M.K.; both his sister and his brother won prizes, but he did not. J.N.K.'s official diary proudly records the triumph of the younger siblings, and the absence of J.M.K. from the winner's rostrum speaks volumes.

THE DIARY ENTRIES

Microeconomics
Saturday, May 23rd, 1896

Maynard has been considering the nature of transactions between bowler as firm and batsman as household and found some useful points of paradox that seem to be not so much metaphors of cricket in economics as identities!

Perhaps a Marxian would say conflict rather than paradox? For a particular firm tries to minimise its wage costs and the individual household tries to maximise its purchasing power in the same way that a bowler tries to bowl maiden overs and a batsman wants to hit a four.[47]

In the overall situation, however, it is clear that there must be a symmetry between runs scored and runs given away, or costs paid out and incomes earned.[48]

It is a pleasing pattern that makes me glad to have helped the thing on; M. is taking a closer interest in cricket despite his lack of success on the field.

---

47 J.M.K.'s attitude to microeconomics (or lack of attitude considering he thought of himself as a heretic with regard to macroeconomics) puzzles many students. They trawl through marginal utility analysis, indifference curves, revealed preference theory, then supply and demand curves, factor rewards, economies of scale, returns to scale, and the theory of the firm all without seeing Keynes's name mentioned. He was content to let Joan Robinson and others mine these veins while he went opencast for the richer pickings. It was perhaps a vote of confidence in his fellow professionals' ability to advance in these areas rather than in the existing theories themselves.

More importantly, he felt he had to defeat the neo-classicist view of macro theory using their micro assumptions to avoid charges of prestidigitation.

48 Marginal productivity theory is a particularly weak spot where the market cannot be allowed full play in even model capitalist economies. There are public sector jobs that have merit rating in the public eye, there are private sector jobs that have no clear output to measure, and the arguments are clouded by the variety of timespans involved. Furthermore there has long been much argument about labour's justification in setting up a countervailing monopoly (through combining into a union) to oppose the employer's monopsony position. This action creates a zone of indeterminacy for wages, and perhaps unions were resented more for spoiling the elegance of marginal productivity theory than any potential class threat.

THE DIARY ENTRIES

Say's Law
Sunday, May 24th, 1896

Maynard and I were sad to learn of the death of F.P.F.[49] two days ago. Without his vision, and the co operation of Gonville and Caius, Reverend Ward would not have had the chance to develop the University ground as it is now. Perhaps prompted by thoughts *in memoriam* of the creator of the smoothest ground in England, M. has developed his transactionary model of cricket in an unusual way.

What if the firms succeed in cutting costs and invest in ways that lead to the impossibility of scoring runs (*e.g.* very long boundaries, outfields full of dandelions in flower, wet pitches that will not bounce, and two accurate medium pacers of deadening pace)?

M. says that there will be unemployment of many types of bowler, the best fielders, the attacking bats, and that the arrested development of the game as a spectacle will lead people to other pastimes. This was quite a shocking prognosis, and marked a great change in his analysis of the game. I advised him to dismantle this chain of events he had created and to observe and test out each portion of it before he became sure that such a scenario was a real possibility.

---

49 This is the great Cambridge Town bowler Francis P. Fenner, who acquired the lease of the orchards south of the gaol overlooking Parker's Piece in 1846 and turned the ground over to the cricketers fully two years later. Between 1861 and 1873 there was acrimony between C.U.C.C. and Fenner. He later hit hard times in Bath and was granted a £10 *douceur* some years before this entry.

GOLDEN AGES AT THE FENNER'S MARGIN

THE DIARY ENTRIES

Say's Law
Tuesday, May 26th, 1896

Maynard has been anticipating Yorkshire's professional bowlers delivering their wares to our amateur batsmen at Fenner's[50] and has decided that the fielding side are definitely the supply side of the game.[51] They initiate, decide, constrain, liberate, and, on occasions, dictate in the manner of firms to a household. He is even developing a view that fielding represents the production of capital goods, but I am not sure how useful that line of imagination will prove to be.

He has also been musing on a line from Wilde's recent play[52] and has concluded that it should be reversed to make any sense. Someone who knows the 'price of everything and the value of nothing' is not a cynic, he says, but an *innocent*, because they lack a crucial dimension in which to judge life's economic decisions; the *economic* dimension.[53]

---

50 The gap in fixtures between the end of the warm-up matches on 16 May and the first county match on 4 June must have been very frustrating for a cricket-mad teenager.

51 This setting of the pieces in their context before analysing them in detail explains why 'Say's Law' comes into the picture between 'Microeconomics' and 'Marginal Utility'. The sense of there being a system, in which there must always be sufficient purchasing power to consume output because the value of that output must equal output's value and have been paid out prior to the output going to the marketplace, owes less to Say, in fact, than James Mill writing in 1808, three years after Say.

52 This refers to *Lady Windermere's Fan*, 1892.

53 Silvio Gesell used this point in his demolition of the theory of value, saying that value in business is context-specific, and is actually price as determined by supply and demand. A separate theory of value is superfluous and in commerce alone nothing is known of the principal theory of the science with which it is connected. Marx and the neo-Ricardians were making everyone victims of the mythology of gold.

THE DIARY ENTRIES

Say's Law
Wednesday, May 27th, 1896

I am pleased to note that Maynard has pleasure as the main overarching aim of the game of cricket, but it does raise the question of where this leaves the professional. Or it did. I have been able to use the distinction between amateur and professional to introduce him to the niceties of company law, whereby the private limited company is likely to be a family concern with aims of sustainability, longevity, stability, and incrementality, while the public listed company has an aim of maximising shareholder value to a singular extent. He seemed to pick this up (albeit with incredulity) very quickly, and was wondering at the case of the South Sea Company's greedy eyeing-up of the potential profits in the Spanish slave market when I last left him with the E.B.[54]

> **NEW SEASON'S**
> SPARKLING AMERICAN
> # CYDER.
> Champagne Pints, 3s. 3d. per Doz.
> ,, Quarts, 5s. 6d. ,,
> 6d. less for Bottles when Returned.
>
> **LINCOLNE & SON,**
> BOTTLERS,
> 35, SIDNEY STREET, CAMBRIDGE

---

54 *Encyclopaedia Britannica.*

THE DIARY ENTRIES

Say's Law
Thursday, May 28th, 1896

Maynard has concluded from his analysis of yesterday that batting is the demand side of the economy, and so has to work out some form of utility theory to please Marshall the next occasion he sees him. He feels comfortable with the concept of the batsman being at home at the wicket, trying not to lose his castle, and having a potential to feed off the bowling, to attempt the occasional luxurious shot, or merely subsist on a series of meanly eked-out singles. I warned him that he will have to hone this a bit for Robert Giffen's[55] visit at the weekend, because he will want to know how the Middlesex stroke-makers resemble his Irish peasants of many years ago! This left M. with much food for thought.

---

55 Giffen is well-known to students as the investigator of goods which seemed to have an upward-sloping demand curve. If there is a subsistence diet of rice and fish and the price of rice goes up, an increase in price of rice, the basic necessity, means a greater proportion of income will go on rice and the amount left for the luxury becomes much less significant; better to spend even more on that rice, and besides the price may go up again in future.

SPORTS AND PASTIMES.

CRICKET.

TETWORTH v. WARESLEY.
Played between Tetworth and Waresley at Tetworth, on Saturday, May 23rd. Score: — Tetworth, 48—5; Waresley, 10—41.

TRUMPINGTON CRICKET CLUB.

The Parish Council having seen its way to provide a recreation ground for the village, advantage has been taken to start a Village Cricket Club, which opened its season on Whit Monday by a match between the Married and Single members. The ground was visited during the afternoon by a large number of villagers and many expressions were heard approving highly of the work of the Parish Council in securing so favourable a piece of land for recreation. The following is the score, which shows that the veterans were rather superior to the younger players:—

MARRIED.

F. Hatcher, b Hutt ... 0	Wm. Steggles, b Hutt ...	0
D. Gentle, b Short ... 0	C. Forbes, not out ...	1
G. Pamplin, b Short ... 1	Wm. Kefford, c Peters, b	
A. Gentle, c Hutt, b Peters 19	Hutt	11
G. Rayner, b Hutt ... 3		
C. Salmon, b Seekings ... 9	Extras	15
G. Read, c and b Peters 3		—
D. Cowell, hit wicket ... 16		78

SINGLE.

H. White, b Cowel ... 4	C. Harradine, c and b	
A. Stallan, c and b Rayner 5	Cowel	1
Wm. Careless, b Cowel ... 0	C. Seekings, b Gentle ...	4
F. Peters, c Kefford, b	A. Forbes, not out ...	4
Rayner 2	P. Whiting, b Cowel ...	0
S. G. Hutt, b Hatcher ... 9	Extras	6
H. Short, run out ... 9		—
E. Peters, c and b Gentle 6		50

GREAT SHELFORD v. THE IDLERS.
Played at Great Shelford on Monday. Score:—

GREAT SHELFORD.

A. Pearce, b Hartland ... 16	T. Flack, l b w, b Safford	6
F. H. Aves, c Marsden, b	C. H. Topham, b Safford	0
Phillips 0	A. G. Bate, b Safford ...	0
T. C. Charnley, b Vickers 30	E. A. Pearce, not out ...	1
T. Hayes, b Hartland ... 8		
H. W. Clarke, st Harkness,		
b Hartland 19		
P. Whitechurch, b Safford 17	Extras	8
J. Maris, c Burdett, b		—
Safford 5		116

THE IDLERS.

H. J. Burdett, c A. Pearce,	H. Vickers, b Topham ...	19
b Clarke 15	E. Sumner, b Topham ...	2
W. H. Hartland, b Clarke 4	E. H. Marsden, c Pearce,	
T. Phillips, b T. Flack ... 6	b Flack	9
E. L. Hartland, c Aves, b	R. A. Clapham, b Flack...	0
Whitechurch 18	J. F. F. Tate, b Flack ...	0
F. C. H. Safford, b Top-	Extras	10
ham 8		—
E. L. Harkness, not out 8		89

Cambridge Chronicle 29/5/96

67

THE DIARY ENTRIES

Marginal Analysis
Friday, May 29th, 1896

Maynard has been thinking seriously about the problem of utility and has decided that utils cannot exist but runs necessarily do, because they are accounted for in the scorer's book. I am somewhat apprehensive that Marshall or Edgeworth may come into contact with us this week since the idea is so fresh in M.'s mind that if he sees either of them he is likely to badger them to redraft their marginal theories along the lines of cricket.

Saturday, May 30th, 1896

Much to my irritation, Maynard's cock-eyed theorising about batsmen achieving what the French would call *parallelisme* with households in their marginal utility (or runs) has seeped its way into my general consciousness over the last few days. The taste of the potatoes at lunch yesterday seemed to suggest a soft turning of the ball in front of square leg for a single, while the raspberries with cream brought to mind an HB-pencilled '4' in the scorebook from a sumptuous front foot cover drive. Ridiculous.

THE DIARY ENTRIES

Marginal Analysis
Sunday, May 31st, 1896

The concepts of total and marginal utility seem to be covered by M.'s little theory but yesterday I was able to exorcise its recent perpetual haunting of my imagination when the coalman was delivering and M. was inquiring about why the horse had been changed this week. He was sad to hear that the previous incumbent had died, and as the coalman broke off his story and interrupted the filling of his pipe with a coughing fit of the worst, hacking kind, I found the chink in M.'s armour. A few minutes after the wagon had left I chaffed M. with my thought. 'Quite a bad cough that fellow has got from his smoking; I wonder how *dis*utility is measured in the scorebook?'

I don't know which upset him more, the horse's demise or my little triumph.

```
NEW CHESTERTON JUNIORS v. PITT PRESS
2ND XI — Played on Parker's Piece on Saturday.
French did the hat trick for the Juniors, taking
four wickets for twelve runs. Scores:—
         NEW CHESTERTON JUNIORS.
  J Butler, b Howlett ................  8
  W. Stubbens, b Howlett ............  0
  W Rayment, b Howlett ............. 12
  E. A. French, b Kirkup............  1
  T. Soole, b Howlett................  1
  W. Evans, not out ................. 46
  E. Hills, b Howlett................  2
  R. Manns, b Howlett ..............  0
  T. Kirkup, c Juler, b Howlett .....  5
  E. A. hall, c Franklin, b Kirkup ..  9
  A. H. Sargent, b Howlett .........  0
         Extras.....................  6
                                     --
                                     90
         PITT PRESS 2ND XI.
  G. Kirkup, c Evans, b French......  0
  H. Juler, b Butler ................  3
  A. F. Dent, b French .............  0
  Franklin, b French................  9
  J. G. Gillingham, b French........  7
  Howlett, b Butler  ................  4
  S. Bavey, b Butler ...............  0
  E. Ludman, b Butler ..............  2
  A. J. Kent, run out ...............  0
  H. Whittaker, c Hills, b Butler ...  0
  H. Slater, not out ................  0
        Extras.....................  5
                                     --
                                     30
```

Cambridge Chronicle 26/6/96

THE DIARY ENTRIES

Trade
Monday, June 1st, 1896

Maynard has moved on to explore another identity in cricket, that of the number of wins and losses. It is a truism that the number of results in a given period must divide equally between wins and losses, and that it therefore seems perverse to him that the supporters of the Varsity are concerned in a partisan way about the balance of results during a particular season. When I appeared to be astonished at this (M. is fanatical when the Varsity match is approaching) he explained that a wonderful record like that of the 1878 team was probably worse news for cricket as a whole than the more mixed season of last year. When I asked why he said that if Cambridge, a mere nursery for cricketers, could not be beaten by the cream of England's professional bowlers and amateur batsmen then the standard in the country must be pretty poor, and the Cambridge supporters must in their hearts realise this. It is equally perverse to hope that every match will be a draw, in the knowledge that that will guarantee that there can be no defeats, for the game would die.

SOMERSET DAIRY BUTTER,
1s. per lb.
TITLEY'S BEST HAMS,
9½d. per lb.
HUGON'S REFINED BEEF SUET,
8d. per lb.
SOLD BY
LINCOLNE & SON,
35, SIDNEY STREET, CAMBRIDGE

THE DIARY ENTRIES

With such reasoning results are something to reflect on *a posteriori* in a detached manner, not to be fervently hoped for *a priori* to the detriment of the passage of the game.[56] He seems to suggest that objective knowledge must invalidate normative passions.[57]

---

[56] This is the astonishing conclusion that generations of cricket enthusiasts have come to, from the Golden Age, through the late 20s of the Chapman era, to the Worrell/Benaud series, and the Botham miracles. Spectator numbers are more easily swayed by entertaining cricket then winning cricket, logically, since there must always be the same number of wins as losses in any season. It is equally astonishing that J.M.K. related results to the macro sphere of international trade. A golfer or soccer devotee would surely picture competition between businesses; indeed, we now have league tables provided for schools, hospitals, and police forces, which cause much heartache to the professionals involved because a low position doesn't have the same significance as it does in soccer.

[57] Perhaps J.M.K.'s opinion was coloured by the way competition was being conducted in Cambridge's transport system that spring and summer. The Cambridge Street Tramway had lost its monopoly and the Cambridge Omnibus Company had prompted fares to drop from 2*d.* to 1*d.*, but for four years there was wasteful duplication of services that nearly forced both companies out of business. Eighty horses were needed rather than forty, yet there were no great increases in use. Public complaints to the four weekly papers in the town were clear; the companies should amalgamate, and the buses should only operate where the trams didn't. It is impossible to believe that similar sentiments weren't constantly on the lips of the Keynes family during the late 1890s, and that competition seemed more like lumbering trench warfare than efficient cut and thrust, especially considering the fact that a child could easily outpace the trams in the busy streets.

THE DIARY ENTRIES

Trade
Wednesday, June 3rd, 1896

Maynard has altered his position somewhat on results. He has got it into his head that they are a simile for trade, or more generally the flows of income derived from the trade in goods and services between nations together with the incomes derived from overseas for your factors of production. In this more sophisticated approach it is clear that it is in each team's interest to attempt to win as many matches as possible from the outset,[58] but it is necessary to appreciate that anyone's win is someone else's loss, and that the symmetry which gives us a whitewashed team cannot be met merely with criticism of the losers. Without the loser losing, however good they might be, the greatness of the winners could not be appreciated. The surplus of wins is therefore a positive signal about the current state of trading, not the achievement of some final unchanging state. These surpluses should therefore be seen as temporary and a delusion of permanence should be as unthinkable as the fundamental disequilibrium on the part of deficits.

---

58   The identification of exchange rate systems as the correct instrument for managing trade balances has had a more torrid history than the average student is led to believe. The changes in the composition of trade (from visible to invisible) plus the increased flows of incomes across national borders led to concentration on the current account in general rather than merely flows of goods. A distinction came to be made between temporary (cyclical) and fundamental (implying permanent) deficits. The much-vaunted Gold Standard (which in truth only predominated in the sterling area during the twenty years leading up to the Great War) was followed by dirty floating and then the movable peg with bands system of Bretton Woods from 1944 to 1971. The theoretical correction of deficits worked in the case of pegs by a reduction in the money supply as reserves dwindled away overseas which would lead on to price reductions and a recovery in competitiveness. The peg would lead to settled business expectations in the trading sector. Under floating conditions this certainty would disappear, but so would deficits; the rate would adjust immediately to any imbalance in trade through changes in supply of and demand for the currency. Thus, for example, in the case of a surplus, the appreciating currency (in excess demand) would immediately raise the price of exports and lead back to a balance. The compromise positions of Bretton Woods and the Exchange Rate Mechanism (E.R.M) of the European Monetary System (E.M.S.) in the years after 1979 seems to work much better than a doctrinaire approach from either of the extreme ends of the spectrum.

THE DIARY ENTRIES

Trade
Thursday, June 4th, 1896

I reconsidered our thoughts of a few days ago on trade while walking round the Fenner's boundary today, and realised how shockingly perverse we seem to get when we approach economics through cricket. We have abandoned the concept that adjustment of prices and quantities to correct trade comes through the Gold Standard *for the benefit of the deficit country.*[59] I must have a word with M. about this.

> **THE RISING IN MASHONALAND.**
>
> A body of 50 men of the Natal column have met and defeated 2,000 insurgents on the Upper Umfuli. There was a hot fight across bad country as far as the Beatrice Mine. Several of the patrol were wounded. The whole country round Salisbury is reported to be in a state of revolt, and relief is anxiously looked for. The stations along the Salisbury and Umtali road have been attacked, and several murders are reported—among them that of a whole party of Ayrshiremen, nine in number. There is strong feeling in Cape Town, and nearly all the members of Assembly have signed a petition to the Government urging that the colony should offer aid to the Imperial authorities in the suppression of the revolt, especially in the form of volunteers accustomed to native warfare.—An American scout reports that he has killed the native " god," M'Limo in a cave in the Matoppo Hills 15 miles from Buluwayo.
> Official telegrams from Sir F. Carrington report further fighting in Mashonaland, and state that among the killed is Lieutenant Bremner, of the 20th Hussars. Fort Charter is surrounded by the insurgents, who captured at Marandella's 25,000 rounds of ammunition left there because the rinderpest had killed all the transport oxen.

Cambridge Chronicle 26/6/96

---

59 A consistent thread of Keynes's criticism of international adjustment practices was that it was the deficit country that was treated with a dose of deflation to reduce prices and increase competitiveness, although this would reduce the resources and the psychological climate available for investment (both private and public). The surplus countries would not be penalised directly, however, even if their surplus derived not from price competition but from an imperfectly-competitive or even monopoly situation.

73

THE DIARY ENTRIES

Trade
Saturday, June 6th, 1896

Maynard has celebrated his thirteenth birthday[60] by digging in his heels on trade. He says the symmetry of the win/lose situation makes it impossible to distinguish between the surplus and the deficit nation/team. I countered by asking him about Say's Law and the doctrine that supply creates demand and has precedence although there must be a symmetry there as well, but he dismissed this. Results are a two-way outcome of the match process, he claims, with nowhere else to go. Yesterday's win against Yorkshire bolsters his views, he believes; it reflected a particular set of match conditions (fortuitously for the home side) rather than a fundamental disequilibrium of advantage.

'You cannot save some of your wins for next year's County Championship, father.'

Whether he is right or wrong, it all goes to illustrate that this is a far greater sport than cycling, although I dare not point this out to Florence or Margaret at present.[61]

---

60 The previous day, in fact.

61 The official J.N.K. diary reports that they were suffering 'bicycle mania' at this time.

THE UNIVERSITY AND YORKSHIRE CRICKET MATCH.

Following a fifteen days' interval, the Cambridge eleven were again engaged yesterday, when they received a visit from the famous Yorkshire team. The latter, however, was not quite representative, as, in view of impending Championship engagements, it was deemed advisable to give a rest to F. W. Milligan, Peel, Hirst, and Hunter, whose places were filled by Moussey, Haigh, Earnshaw, and Shaw, the latter making his first appearance for the county. On the University side H. Gray, W. W. Lowe, W. G. Grace, jun., C. D. Robinson, and G. H. Simpson were, from various causes, unable to play, and places were found for F. J. S. Moore, E. H. Bray, and H. H. B. Hawkins. The attendance was excellent, and although a storm threatened after lunch, it happily held off. F. Mitchell won the toss, and taking first innings his side made excellent use of their good fortune. For four hours they kept the Yorkshiremen in the field, and totalled 309. Burnup, Druce, and Moore were the principal scorers. The first pair mentioned added 80 for the third wicket. Burnup was then caught and bowled, after batting in excellent style for an hour and fifty minutes. His 53 included six fours. Druce, who hit eleven fours, left shortly after, but was lucky, however, as he should have been caught at the wicket after scoring only three. When Moore and Jessop were associated, runs came at a terrific pace, as may be gathered from the fact that the 47 of the last-named included no fewer than ten hits to the boundary. Moore's innings, if not so lively, was certainly a very stylish one. It extended over an hour and three-quarters, and included five fours and four threes. Yorkshire, who had one hour left for batting, fared very badly indeed. With three scored Tunnicliffe was caught, Jackson and Brown both left at 20, and Moorhouse was dismissed a run later. Denton and Wainwright played out time, when Yorkshire, with six wickets to fall, were 255 runs behind.

A good company visited the ground this morning on the re-opening of the match at half-past eleven o'clock. The not-outs—Denton, whose score stood at 26, and Wainwright, who had made eight—went to the wickets to play the bowling of Jessop and Wilson, and Jessop took Denton's wicket with his first ball. A complete collapse of the Yorks. team followed. Mounsey was splendidly caught in the long field by Hemingway, and Lord Hawke was taken behind the wicket for three, while Haigh and Shaw were clean bowled without scoring, and the innings closed for 85. Yorkshire followed on, Tunnicliffe and Mr. Jackson, the old Blue, making another start. They played confidently, but at 27 Jackson was caught by Wilson at point, the ball unexpectedly "kicking." Brown took his place, and the score rose to 101 before Tuncliffe, after a fine innings, was caught for 40. Moorhouse was shortly afterwards caught by Shine, and at the adjournment for luncheon the score was 119 for three wickets. After luncheon, Denton, Brown, Lord Hawke, and Haigh were all dismissed within a little over half-an-hour. Score at 3.30 p.m. :—

Cambridge Chronicle 5/6/96

Cambridge Chronicle
12/6/96

THE UNIVERSITY v. SOMERSETSHIRE CRICKET MATCH.

The University, who last week defeated Yorkshire by an innings and 35 runs, yesterday commenced their annual match against Somersetshire at Fenner's. The weather was fine and bright, but the heavy rains of Wednesday had left the ground in a state favourable to the bowlers. Somersetshire were without the services of the Palairets, W. U. Roe, G. Fowler, V. Hill, Rev. A. P. Wickham and Capt. Hedley, whilst G. L. Jessop and W. W. Lowe were the most prominent absentees from the home eleven. The visitors won the toss and batted first. Woods and Tyler opened the innings and were opposed by Shine and Cobbold. Runs came freely for some time, Woods in particular making some fine hits. With the score at 27 he was caught and bowled by Shine, and Tyler was shortly afterwards dismissed with a fine catch by Grace. The next few batsmen were easily disposed of, with the exception of Trask, who knocked up 22 before he was bowled by Gray. The only remaining batsmen who offered any resistance to the bowling were Smith and Maclean who made a short stand for the last wicket. Of the bowlers, Gray, who took four wickets for 15 runs, was by far the most successful. Shine took two for 23 and Cobbold three for 66. Cambridge opened in an unpromising manner, Burnup being caught in the slips without scoring and Marriott dismissed with the score at 10. Druce was clean bowled by Woods after making a couple and Grace, who had been playing a good game, was dismissed with the score at only 29. Hemingway and Wilson made the best stand of the day for the fifth wicket. With the score at 69 Woods bowled Hemingway. Wilson continued to play a sound game, although he was not well supported, and was still not out when stumps were drawn with the score standing at 89 for nine wickets.

Play was resumed in beautiful weather at 11.37 a.m. to-day, and the not-outs added nine runs to the overnight score, when Cobbold played on a ball from Nicholls. Somerset in the second innings made but a poor show against the bowling of Wilson and Gray, and were all out by 2 o'clock for 68, leaving the 'Varsity 80 to get to win. Play was again resumed at 2.45, and the score at 3.30 was as under:

SOMERSETSHIRE.

S. M. J. Woods, c and b Shine ... 31	c Grace, b Cobbold	9
Tyler, c Grace, b Cobbold ... 12	b Wilson	4
Robson, c Marriott, b Cobbold ... 3	c Druce, b Wilson	0
W. Trask, b Gray ... 22	c Druce, b Wilson	11
M. A. S. Sturt, c Bray, b Shine ... 0	b Wilson	6
D. Smith, b Gray ... 5	b Gray	10
Nichols, b Gray ... 8	c Druce, b Gray	1
A. G. Barrett, b Gray ... 6	b Gray	0
L. H. McDonald, run out ... 0	not out	21
W. Smith, c Burnup, b Cobbold 15	c Gray, b Wilson	0
D. H. Maclean, not out ... 9	b Gray	4
Extras ... 5	Extras	1
109		**68**

THE UNIVERSITY.

W. G. Grace, b Woods ... 17	E. H. Bray, c Macdonald, b Woods	4
C. J. Burnup, c D. Smith, b Woods ... 0	E. B. Shine, c Macdonald, b Woods	2
C. H. Marriott, b Woods ... 4	H. Gray, b Nicholls	2
N. F. Druce, b Woods ... 2	F. W. Cobbold, b Nicholls	8
C. E. M. Wilson, not out 29	Extras	3
W. McG. Hemingway, b Woods ... 29		**93**
F. Mitchell, b Nicholls ... 3		

Second Innings.

W. G. Grace, not out ...	19
C. J. Burnup, not out ...	7
Extras ...	2

Cambridge Chronicle 12/6/96

77

THE DIARY ENTRIES

Trade
Monday, June 8th, 1896

Dining at Marshall's tonight, we concluded that Maynard's thoughts on fanaticism with regards to results gave rise to a moral (or dare one say psychological?) problem for the successful sides. If the 'surplus' they enjoy is presented as permanent (with a seemingly endless positive feeding back of fixed investment and investment in human capital) then what is the incentive for the deficit side to engage in the transaction market (*i.e.* play the game at all)? Further, if the unsuccessful decline to play, then the surplus sides will have no fixtures and will *ergo* have no surplus in future. The retreat to protectionism is a dangerous concept to introduce to M. at such a politically-sensitive juncture, but I fear he will be working it out for himself and may come up with some very combustible proposals for the world of cricket which if translated into the national political arena would make Mr Chamberlain[62] splutter with indignation.

What can you give the boy who lives so near Fenner's for his birthday in June?[63]

---

62 This connotes Joseph, who produced two future Chancellors of the Exchequer in Austen and Neville.

63 In fact J.N.K. took J.M.K. to London to see *The Prisoner of Zenda* the next day.

THE DIARY ENTRIES

Contexts of Laisser Faire & Intervention
Friday, June 12th, 1896

Maynard was very struck by a comment we heard passed between two of the old boys sat in the pavilion yesterday.[64] It was before lunch and they had walked around in an anti clockwise fashion as usual to take the sun as they approached the tennis, then accept the propulsion of the wind as they headed off en route to Mill Road, turning again to feel the sun on their backs as they minded themselves around the bowling-screen at the far end. The long walk back into the wind past deep cover or square leg would be put up with through heated diversions about the old pavilion's vast superiority over the new, tales of the old gaol yard, and suspicions about the new spire of the Catholic Church with its seeming pretensions towards college or even cathedral status. Maynard could interpret every step of this walk, but on this occasion he overheard as they returned

'Yes, he'll return that one with interest.'

This really foxed him, and it took him some moments to work out that they meant the batsman who had just been dismissed by a viciously spinning off break on the drying pitch. The prediction was that the Varsity was doomed to bat on an equally bad surface and the dismissed batsman would be the cause of their downfall as a *bowler*.[65]

---

64 J.N.K. managed to unwind watching the cricket after invigilating exams in June.

65 This may refer to Gray's dismissal of Nicholls in the Somerset first innings; in the event Burnup and Grace knocked off the 80 runs in the final sessions without loss, so the experts' pessimism was unjustified. Somerset, desperately short of regulars away from home, seem to have been allowed to try out a substitute player, Mold of Lancashire, in that final innings, unless the 1897 *Wisden Almanack* has a misprint. He was almost a local by birth (Northamptonshire) and, like Richardson, was one of many professionals who worked in the nets for the University. Although a Test player and highly rated by players like Spofforth, Mold was later branded a chucker, and his career petered out.

THE DIARY ENTRIES

M. found that a missing element of his economic simile had been revealed. The fielders view the wickets as interest received for the emplacement of their efforts, or rather the actualisation into one particular course of all the different possibilities of energy denoted as action open to them. Equally, batsmen view a wicket as interest that must be paid as a result of minutes, or liberties, taken at the wicket. The tendency for greed or ambition to require payment of more interest is matched on the bowler's part by more thrift, or more efficiency to generate more interest. It is a pleasing and neat piece of symmetry for him, and he has gone off to search out any potential pitfalls inherent in this mode of thinking.

CRICKET FIXTURES.

CAMBRIDGE VICTORIA CLUB.

Monday, June 29, v. Ely, at Ely.
Tuesday, June 30, v. Leys 2nd XI, at The Leys.
Tuesday, July 7, v. The Leys, at The Leys.
Monday, July 13, v. Papworth, at Papworth.
Monday, July 20, v. Old Leysians, at Parker's Piece
Wednesday, July 2, v. Bedford, at Parker's Piece.
Tuesday, July 21, v. Persians, at Parker's Piece.
Friday, August 21, v. Ely, at Parker's Piece.
Monday, August 31, v. Papworth, at Papworth.

CAMDEN CLUB.

July 2, v. Liberals, on Parker's Piece.
July 9, v. Newmarket, at Newmarket.
July 16, v. Old Higher Grade, on Parker's Piece.
July 23, v. College Servants, on Parker's Piece.
July 30, v. St. Giles, on Parker's Piece.
August 3, v. Tavistock C.C., London, on Parker's Piece.
August 6, v. Little Shelford, at Little Shelford.
August 13, v. Old Perseans, on Parker's Piece.
August 20, v. Newmarket, on Parker's Piece.
August 27, v. Old Higher Grade, on Parker's Piece
September 3, v. Cassandra, on Parker's Piece.
September 10, v. Liberals, on Parker's Piece.
September 17, v. Chesterton District, on Parker's Piece.
September 24, v. College Servants, on Parker's Piece.

Cambridge Chronicle 26/6/96

THE DIARY ENTRIES

Contexts of Laisser Faire & Intervention
Tuesday, June 16th, 1896

A chap Maynard bumped into at Fenner's yesterday said he intends to write a history of the Varsity match one day, there is so much life in it. He played in 1873, he said, and made a fifty in the first innings. Mr. Ford, it must be, judging from my *Wisden Almanack*.[66] M. eagerly asked him to share the most interesting thing he had found out. Curiously, it was a very modern incident of which M. had not heard which subsequently provoked a change in the laws of the game. During the '93 match the Cambridge side were convinced that Oxford were going to get out deliberately in order to follow on. Quite why they would wish to do this baffled the pundits afterwards, and equally at that moment they were unaware of the motivation. They merely saw Oxford at 95 for 9 with Wells bowling eponymously. But he then proceeded to bowl a no-ball and four wides. Oxford got over the hundred and Cambridge batted again, F.S. Jackson scoring fifty, and Oxford finally succumbing for 64. The point was that a high-profile occasion and a level of uncertainty felt universally and impartially led to a feeling that something had to be done; the law was changed so that the follow-on would occur with arrears of 120 rather than 80.

---

66 W.J. Ford had played his last major match for M.C.C. at Lord's against Leicestershire just a month before, retiring hurt in the second innings. He wrote the Public Schools Cricket section of *Wisden* for the 1896 season, and a history of the C.U.C.C. for Ranji's *Jubilee Book* of 1898, which he later developed it into a full volume. Did he come to Fenner's for a valedictory perambulation knowing his time was up? Or was he just in Cambridge to investigate The Leys School all-rounder W.S.A. Brown, who went on to play for Gloucestershire and top their bowling averages after the school term ended? This wasn't the end of the line for the Ford family in first class cricket. Brother F.G.J. Ford, known as 'Stork', was a legendary smiter of the ball, and played 5 county matches for Middlesex in 1896.

THE DIARY ENTRIES

This concept of intervention by M.C.C. stupefied Maynard who had never considered that the laws of the game were anything other than a natural code handed down from ages immemorial. He has since found out about five ball overs, the genesis of leg before wicket, the middle stump, and overarm bowling. The constant question of the last twenty four hours has been 'can you think of any other changes, father?' My worry is, of course, that having learnt about the past he will now be projecting interventions onto the present game, and potential ones onto its future.

And what a future! Today we marvelled at the old torchbearer passing on the flame of revolution to the new.[67] We will never forget the significance of today's play.

Wednesday, June 17th, 1896

Maynard had another very exciting day at Fenner's yesterday, which set him thinking further about the administration of both the game of cricket and of an economy. He saw an unfamiliar figure of interest in his mid-forties walking around the boundary and managed to strike up a conversation with him. It turned out that he had been a blue in '79, and had made a hideous wreck of Oxford at Lord's with the ball. His chief memories were that each side's captain had faced the first delivery in each innings, which is fairly unusual, and that he had been a change bowler in the first innings but opened in the second. He had no idea why, and after he had bowled nearly forty overs he forgot to ask.

'Webbe wouldn't have done it, but Lyttelton saw something in the situation, and it won the match ahead of the rain for us. I just did what I thought was normal.'[68]

---

[67] The official J.N.K. diary confirms he watched M.C.C. including W.G. Grace and Ranji at Fenner's that afternoon. W.G. was out early to a good slip catch by Druce off Jessop, but Ranji and Albert Trott then put on 99 for the second wicket sending the former on his way to his fourth century of the summer.

[68] This must be A.F.J. Ford; was he in town to meet his younger brother, who had engaged J.M.K. in conversation the previous day? The news seemed to have got out that Ranjitsinhji was in on a good wicket. One hopes C.U.C.C. bowler Shine did not play for M.C.C. against his own team to avoid damage to his bowling average.

THE DIARY ENTRIES

Contexts of Laisser Faire & Intervention
Thursday, June 18th, 1896

Henry, Maynard, and I had a very successful game of golf at the Heath today.[69] While we rested after the round we observed the Royston cricketers playing in the bowl of a ground that never seems to get wet even in the foulest weather. It was a scene that spoke of an unbroken rhythm of over a hundred years,[70] and we mused about how it might look in 1996.

Henry wondered if the advances in manufacturing may lead to changes in the machinery at the wicket; he has in mind siege towers and mechanical accelerators that might lead to a faster, more exciting spectacle. I felt that there might be reversion to curved bats and underarm bowling, perhaps even period dress, as people sought a pagan continuity with their forebears in an age of aspiration to time travel. M. was very sceptical about the pace of change, and said that Royston would stay the same but man's recreational hours would become so precious that it would be the pitch that would change, with artificial surfaces that would resist the rain, and umbrellas to protect new grass development. He said he also thought the ideas would change more than the appearance, but looking around the scene we all agreed we couldn't predict how.

---

69 The pioneer of university golf, W.T.Linskill, had championed the practicality of creating a course at Royston in 1890, but left Cambridge in 1896 for St. Andrews twenty three years after bringing the game to Coe Fen, within the town boundary behind 'Goody's' school. Lord Dunedin was dismissive of Linskill's importance, claiming to have played on Midsummer Common in 1869. But with the departure of Linskill's enthusiasm the adverse conditions of the course he bequeathed on Coldham's Common led to neglect and its slow further deterioration. It was abandoned by university players in 1902 for the Gog Magogs and Royston. Over seventy years later Cambridgeshire High School pupils were still making the journey by train and foot to play golf at Royston to avoid the exigencies of rugby football at Luard Road.

70 Royston C.C. celebrated its bicentenary with a match against M.C.C. (for whom the editor played) in 1990. It is where a twenty year old John Berry Hobbs was first paid for playing a game of cricket (Royston versus Hertfordshire Club and Ground, 1903).

GOLDEN AGES AT THE FENNER'S MARGIN

THE DIARY ENTRIES

It seemed to us to be a normal landscape: a lob bowler setting up his field with a long stop and two others deep behind square on the leg side, the batsman dispensing with his gloves for the new bowler, and the deep man straight shooing off a few sheep who dared to ignore the boundary marker.

```
         PANTON HOUSE, CAMBRIDGE.
          Head Mistress—MISS STREET.
                    MANAGERS.
       PROF. E. C. CLARK, LL.D., Chairman.
    Rev. Dr. MOULTON, J.P.    | Mrs. BURN.
    Rev. Prof. RYLE, D.D.     | Mrs. LATHAM.
    A. W. W. DALE, Esq., M.A  | Mrs. PRILE,
    Mr. Alderman DECK.        | Mrs. SHUCKBURGH,
    E. H. PARKER, Esq.,       |           Secretary.
            Treasurer.
    FEES from £3 3s. to £5 per Term, according to
       age. Pupils prepared for Cambridge Local
    Examinations.
              KINDERGARTEN:
    Mistresses hold 1st Class Certificates from the
    Froebel Society. Fees from £2 to £3 per Term,
    according to age.
```

Cambridge Chronicle 26/6/96

THE DIARY ENTRIES

Contexts of Laisser Faire & Intervention
Friday, June 19th, 1896

M. has been thinking about the future of cricket again and has changed his mind. He says that the exploitation of new materials and fundamental evolution *will* occur, leading to implements derived from oil and metal. He also considers that some adaptation of electronics may happen quite quickly as well (he is particularly struck by the possibilities in Herz's development of James Clark Maxwell's theories regarding remote effects.[71]) The greatest consequence of using this as a means of communication will be the opening up of the game to illiterate peoples arising from the transmission of matches. This assumes that the speed of development in photography and telegraphy match the transition from the canal of the eighteenth century to the railway of the nineteenth. Perhaps in fifty years, I ventured, we may be able to follow a series in Australia? M. was insistent however that it is in India that this will have greatest effect. Using population projections and the canal-railway model of technological step changes he has decided that India will be beating everyone else by 1930, and that seven hundred and fifty million people will be able to hear and see them do it, a number greater than the total population that has ever seen a cricket match thus far![72]

---

71 Marconi arrived that spring in Britain to seek a patent (granted on 2 June 1896) for his 'system of telegraphy using Herzian waves'. Maxwell had predicted the possibility of electrical disturbance producing a remote effect by electro-magnetic propagation using mathematical models in 1864 in Cambridge.

72 A trifle early, but on the right lines. This in fact came to pass with the 1987 World Cup in the sub-continent, with positive repercussions half a generation later in Brussels, Athens, Luxembourg, and anywhere else in the world that runs a cricket league and needs new players.

THE DIARY ENTRIES

Contexts of Laisser Faire & Intervention
Saturday, June 20th, 1896

Maynard commented that technology was in cricket as in economics a strangely neutral factor that altered the context and the dynamics of a situation rather than the intrinsic activity. He has in mind a comparison of two examples. The blacksmith may, firstly, feel that the bicycle and the car may present a threat to his traditional mode of employment (although not the way the Keynes family use them!) and try to prepare to alter his skills and use of time accordingly to avoid unemployment. In the same way an off break bowler who comes into his own on a quickly-drying pitch may find that he has to alter his flight and speed, and his role in the overall attack if technology does lead to non-turf surface or protection of the grass from rain. This has a neat aspect to it, and displays a positive view towards unemployment. I think it is safe to let Marshall and Maynard come into contact with each other again.

Sunday, June 21st, 1896

Maynard is very struck by the way that seemingly intelligent and educated people seem to have no concept of what investment is. I have tried to explain that he has had a special upbringing through which he is more likely to confuse pâté and caviar than savings and investment, but he still squirms when he hears high-ranking colleagues pompously discussing the secondary markets and financial assets as if they were real railways and factories. I suggested that perhaps he should explore this through his cricket metaphor and see if he could use Fenner's at the dinner table as a Trojan horse to do good works amongst the mighty! He took to this idea with alacrity.

THE DIARY ENTRIES

Savings & Investment
Monday, June 22nd, 1896

M., under the influence of Fraulein Rotmann,[73] has decided that the Germans have a much more sensible nomenclature for savings and is using the term *sparen* at all hours of the day, but in such a broad accent that it comes out as 'spearing'! Marshall was struck by this and suggested that the French, *placement*, would be even better, but M. and I demurred; this seemed to be another example of Alfred's romantic (and wrong) *tendenz*.[74]

Its equivalence on the cricket field is the manner in which bowlers deliver; the more speculative the effort or the more guileful the 'spearing', he says, (or the placement, says Marshall) the more possible is spectacular reward through a wicket (or interest). This distinguishes the 'saver' from the batsman who is making decisions about the available resources (minutes at the wicket) and attempting to invest to produce commodities that will bring utility when he feels the interest rate environment is suitable (*i.e.* when there is little risk of losing his wicket). This, I said, makes another French saying seem sensible although it stems from a common mistranslation; friends often say that one context is more 'interesting' for a business than another when they really mean profitable in English.

---

73 With intensive coaching available from a German *au pair* (if such a concept is acceptable) J.N.K. managed to persuade Goodchild that J.M.K. should be examined in German rather than French during the summer term school exams.

74 It is not surprising that the Keyneses were much more taken with Germany (represented in the media as the new economic powerhouse) than France (the sclerotic and backward-looking lumberer). But it did colour their judgement on occasion, as with this perfectly valid point by Marshall who seems to have been often treated as old before his time on account of his whiskers, delicate health, and intensely sad appearance. These combined to make him seem even more like a biblical prophet than the golf-playing Henry Sidgwick.

THE DIARY ENTRIES

Savings & Investment
Tuesday, June 23rd, 1896

I then recalled that M. had decided that fixed capital investment took place through the ground authorities, and human capital investment was conducted by the players. How could he deny that bowlers (savers) were conducting investments when they practised their skills just as much as batsmen? I really thought he'd ended up in cleft stick on this one. However, without a moment's hesitation Maynard's riposte disabused me of any superior notions. Yes, it is the groundsman and M.C.C. (the law makers) who determine the level and type of fixed investment, and yes, batsmen in the nets may hone their strokes and be said to be investing in the sense that such practice means that in a match situation they are more likely than otherwise to be able to attempt a run-scoring stroke rather than defend or try to avoid the strike. But the bowlers in the nets? Well, like the pompous pundit fussing around the prices of shares or property in the newspapers, they certainly *think* they are investing, but when you look at a net situation in fact they are merely placing balls for the batsmen to practise against. Who is always wanting to go in the nets? The batsmen! Who is always being reluctantly persuaded to bowl? Anyone who isn't going to get tired from bowling properly in the middle and anyone who is artless enough not to need to conceal the intangible and fleeting quality of their wicket-taking deliveries. Let's face facts, says Maynard, most of the great bowlers say to me that they don't really know why they take wickets rather than their colleagues, while the batsmen are all convinced that it is technique that brings them success. Bowlers are made or broken in the middle, batsmen can construct a basic keep in the nets; but both, M. thinks, ultimately sink or swim with their minds.

SUSSEX v. THE UNIVERSITY.

Considering the many capital things in batting accomplished this season by the Sussex eleven, Monday's cricket at Brighton was of a surprising character, and it is difficult to account for the failure of the county team. Apparently the ground at Hove was in its usual excellent condition, this being emphasised by the easy manner in which the Light Blues made their runs towards the close of the afternoon, but the fact remains that though Sussex won the toss, and had the advantage of going in first, they were dismissed in a little over two hours and a half for the very meagre total of 129. On going in to bat Cambridge rendered a very different account of themselves to what their opponents had done, and scored with such freedom from the Sussex bowlers that they were able to finish up the day with a great advantage, scoring 217 for five wickets, and being thus 98 ahead with half their batsmen to be got rid of. On Tuesday the Cambridge eleven were seen to great advantage. Two of their number ran into three figures, while the innings produced 514. The finest piece of hitting was Mr. Jessop's 93, which was made out of 142 in 75 minutes, and in which were 19 fours. Mr. Hemingway obtained his first 100 in important cricket; he got his runs in an hour and three-quarters, and hit 15 fours and seven threes. Mr. Mitchell scarcely played so freely as he used to do; but he contributed eight fours, eight threes, and ten twos in his 110. Sussex, in their second innings, had to face odds of 385. There was some fine play by K. S. Ranjitsinhji, Marlow and Mr. Murdoch; but at the close, with four men out for 130, the county were still in a bad way. The match terminated on Wednesday in favour of the University by an innings and 136 runs. Score and analysis:—

SUSSEX.

Bean, c Cobbold, b Wilson	5	b Wilson	0
Marlow, b Jessop	1	c Bray, b Wilson	59
K. S. Ranjitsinhji, b Jessop	0	c Bray, b Burnup	37
W. L. Murdoch, c Wilson, b Jessop	4	c Jessop, b Cobbold	55
W. Newham, l b w, b Wilson	31	c Marriott, b Jessop	23
G. H. Arlington, b Jessop	9	st Bray, b Cobbold	12
Killick, c Burnup, b Shine	49	not out	26
Parris, c Jessop, b Wilson	8	c Shine, b Cobbold	15
Butt, c Mitchell, b Wilson	5	c Shine, b Wilson	1
Tate, c Druce, b Shine	1	st Bray, b Cobbold	2
Humphreys, not out	10	c Jessop, b Cobbold	3
Extras	5	Extras	16
	129		249

THE UNIVERSITY.

W. G. Grace, jun., c Butt, b Parris	27	P. W. Cobbold, c Ranjitsinhji, b Parris		8
C. J. Burnup, c Ranjitsinhji, b Parris	44	F. Mitchell (capt.), st Butt, b Humphreys		110
H. H. Marriott, b Parris	71	G L Jessop, b Arlington		93
N. F. Druce, c Arlington, b Tate	0	E H Bray, c Butt, b Humphreys		37
C. E. M. Wilson, st Butt, b Tate	4	E B Shine, not out		6
W. McG. Hemingway, c Arlington, b Killick	104	Extras		10
				514

ANALYSIS OF THE BOWLING.
Sussex.—First Innings.

	o.	m.	r.	w.		o.	m.	r.	w
Jessop	28	8	77	4	Shine	7.3	4	11	2
Wilson	32	16	25	4	Cobbold	3	2	1	0

Wilson bowled two no-balls.

Second Innings.

	o.	m.	r.	w.		o.	m.	r.	w
Shine	19	2	72	0	Burnup	5	3	7	1
Wilson	30	12	55	3	Jessop	10	0	20	1
Cobbold	25.2	3	67	5	Mitchell	4	2	2	0
Grace	4	1	10	0					

Burnup bowled one wide.

THE UNIVERSITY.

	o.	m.	r.	w.		o.	m.	r.	w
Tate	56	17	147	2	Killick	14	2	51	1
Murdoch	5	1	12	0	Bean	2	2	0	0
Humphreys	29.1	7	85	2	Ranjitsinhji	13	2	49	0
Parris	49	11	147	4	Arlington	8	2	13	1

Umpires: Lillywhite and Carpenter.

THE DIARY ENTRIES

Money & Prices
Wednesday, June 24th 1896

I have suggested to Maynard that there is at present a large flaw in his Fenner's model of 'cricket as economics', and that is the absence of a theory of money and the stability of prices. He immediately saw the seriousness of this challenge and I can congratulate myself that either I have set up an insurmountable obstacle that will lead him to lose interest in what is after all a trivial pursuit, or he will learn very quickly the nuances of the recent development of monetary theory and add a new layer of sophistication to his knowledge of cricket. The father in me hopes for the latter, of course, and I suggested that he talks to Marshall about this on the next occasion they meet, as this knot requires the best in consultancy circles. I fear however that he will have a difficult job in turning round the facer I have left him as I head off for Victoria.[75]

> EMPLOYMENT FOR THOSE OUT OF WORK. GOOD FOOD, GOOD CLOTHES, GOOD LODGINGS, and MONEY to SPEND every day, are offered to Active and Steady Young Men between the ages of 18 and 25.—Apply for all information to Recruiting Sergeants at Cambridge, Wisbech, March, and Royston, or any Sergeant-Instructor of Volunteers. A pamphlet, "The Advantages of the Army," can be had free at any Post Office.

Cambridge Chronicle 26/6/96

---

75 Not the cricketing state in Australia, but the University in the city of Manchester, where examinations business beckoned.

CRICKET.

PARK RANGERS v. CAMBRIDGE ELECTRIC SUPPLY COMPANY.—Played on Parker's Piece on Saturday. Holden did the hat trick. Scores:—

PARK RANGERS.

Finding, b Mickle	14
Carter, c Randall, b Holden	2
Martin, c and b Holden	0
Bailey, c and b Holden	0
Barker, c Randall, b Holden	10
Everitt, b Holden	8
Brook, c Holden, b Morgan	26
Hunt, c Holden, b Mickle	6
Smith, l b w, b Holden	9
Pilgrim, not out	8
Kent, b Mickle	13
Extras	7
	98

ELECTRIC SUPPLY COMPANY.

Holden, b Carter	0
Taylor, b Carter	8
Arnott, b Barker	5
Randall, b Barker	0
Chillison, run out	4
Mickle, b Barker	0
Morgan, b Carter	3
Guyton, b Carter	0
Barr, b Carter	0
Anker, b Barker	0
Farrier, not out	0
Extras	2
	22

LEYS SCHOOL v. FELSTEAD SCHOOL.—Played on the Leys ground on Saturday, and resulted in a victory for the home team. Scores:—

LEYS SCHOOL.

W. S. A. Brown, not out	102
A. B. Horsley, c McEwen, b Denson	6
H. D. Wyatt, b Denson	15
L. Walker, c Partridge, b Morrell	2
J. T. Tullock, c Denson, b Morrell	2
J. K. Walker, c Dann, b Morrell	32
N. Spicer, l b w, b Howell	8
H. D. Brown, c Partridge, b Morrell	7
W. H. C. Kidston, c Chapman, b Mullins	10
L. T. Willis, c Partridge, b Chapman	4
W. B. Beckett, b Howell	10
Extras	7
	200

FELSTEAD SCHOOL.

K. G. McEwen, c H. D. Brown, b Spicer	50
R. G. D. Howell, c and b L. Walker	75
E. W. Dann, b J. E. Walker	0
P. W. Partridge, b W. S. A. Brown	7
G. E. Morrell, b W. S. A. Brown	0
E. A. Prout, b W. S. A. Brown	0
R. A. W. Archer, c H. D. Brown, b W. Brown	0
H. W. Gwyther, b W. S. A. Brown	2
P. G. Denson, b Spicer	0
H. L. Mullins, b Spicer	0
A. H. Chapman, not out	0
Extras	7
	141

Both Cambridge and Oxford University elevens are going strongly, and it becomes more and more apparent that the contest of 1896 will be a battle of giants. Each has taken another scalp this week, Cambridge beating Sussex and Oxford beating Surrey. Our team put on the magnificent total of 514, which included two centuries, 110 by Mitchell and 104 by Hemingway, whilst Jessop came well within sight of three figures, being out for 93. The last-mentioned player had the satisfaction of dismissing Ranjitsinhji for a duck, a fate which the Indian has not had to endure for many a day. Shine obtained a good bowling average in the first innings of Sussex, taking two wickets for eleven runs in 7.3 overs. Gray stood out of this match, being desirous of taking his degree whilst his mathematical honours were still thick upon him.

Oxford's match was also, as I have said, a notable one, and the University obliged Surrey to follow on. Of course, it has to be said for the County that they were deprived of the services of four of their best players, who were doing duty for England, but the University still had a strong team to meet, and their success was highly meritorious. Waddy was 107 not out, Bardwell obtained 97, and Foster made 67.

I am both pleased and sorry with the position of affairs in relation to the Cambs. Cricket Association's Cup Competition this season, pleased to see the Liberals again competing, and sorry to find only six Clubs entered for the contest. What has come over the County Clubs? Nothing seems capable of tempting them out of their ordinary groove of silly little matches, in which there is very little credit in being the winner. Sawston is the only village organisation in the whole of the County which has the courage to face a Cambridge Club, either at cricket or football. Yet there are several village clubs which, by repute, occupy a prominent position in the County, and amongst them may be mentioned near at home the Histon and Impington Club, and farther afield Soham, whilst at other places promising clubs are upspringing. Then at Ely, March, and Wisbech, they surely have teams capable of making a good show in this competition.

The principal local fixtures for next week are the following:—
Saturday, Old Higher Grade v. University Press.
Monday, Victoria v. Ely at Ely.
Tuesday, Victoria (2nd XI.) v. Leys (2nd XI.).
Thursday, Camden v. Liberals.

Abel was still at the head of the batting averages on Monday, his average being 65·81, and K. S. Ranjitsinhji was second with 52·73. Both of these players completed their first thousand runs of the season on Friday last. Hayward's place at third was taken by Gunn, whilst the Surrey-Cambridge player fell into the seventh place. The matches of the last fortnight brought Cambridge men into the averages, and Burnup was on Monday scored eleventh with 44.50, N. F. Druce thirty-seventh, F. Mitchell forty-fifth, and W. M. Hemingway fifty-first. Diver stood at forty-first at the commencement of the week.

In the bowling averages, J. T. Hearne remains cock of the tree, his average being 10·62. His nearest rival is the Australian, Trumble, whose average was 10·9s. Hayward was fourth and Lohmann fifth, E. B. Shine thirteenth, C. E. M. Wilson twenty-seventh, and G. L. Jessop thirty-first.

Cambridge Chronicle, 26/6/96

GOLDEN AGES AT THE FENNER'S MARGIN

M.C.C. AND GROUND BATTING AVERAGES.— FIRST CLASS MATCHES.

	Matches	Innings	Runs	Most in an innings	Times not out	Average
W. Gunn	3	5	283	138	2	94.1
G. Bean	3	5	230	20	0	46
Mr. C. E. de Trafford	2	4	165	60	0	41.1
H. Carpenter	4	7	246	161	1	41
K. S. Ranjitsinhji	3	5	187	146	0	37.2
Mr. H. B. Hayman	2	4	108	70	1	36
Mr. A. E. Stoddart	4	7	249	61	0	35.4
W. Chatterton	3	4	132	66	0	33
J. H. Board	3	5	142	45	0	28.2
Mr. R. W. Nichols	2	4	84	59	0	21
A. E. Trott	7	13	246	67*	1	20.6
J. Harry	3	6	106	56	0	18.1
W. Storer	4	6	69	50*	2	17.1
Mr. C. C. Stone	2	4	50	35	1	16.2
Dr. G. Thornton	2	4	50	25*	1	16.2
W. Mead	7	12	158	46*	2	15.8
Mr. W. G. Grace	3	5	73	33	0	14.8

A consolation for young Carpenter in a disappointing 1896 season was finishing above Ranji and W.G. in the M.C.C. batting averages. Perhaps he needed to get one of the contraptions below, advertised in the 1897 Wisden, to get fitter.

GYMNASTICS FOR EVERYBODY.
HEATH & GEORGE'S FAMILY EXERCISER.

Price Thirty Shillings.

This invaluable little Apparatus should be a feature in every household where Health is cultivated. The youngest can use it with the same facility as the Athlete, the weights being adjustable to suit the requirements of each. Everybody whose occupation is of a sedentary nature will find immediate relief and freedom of lung action after a few minutes' use.

Is sent out complete and ready for fixing without trouble, in bed, or bath-room, office or study.

JOHN WISDEN & Co.,
INVENTORS AND PATENTEES OF
THE CATAPULTA,
The most effective substitute for the Professional Bowler, and only Bowling Machine now in use.

"Your patent Catapulta continues to work well, and is a capital invention." "I consider it invaluable to Clubs who cannot keep a Professional." "It certainly has improved the batting here, which is much straighter." "We quite agree that it is more likely to tire the batsman than exhaust itself."

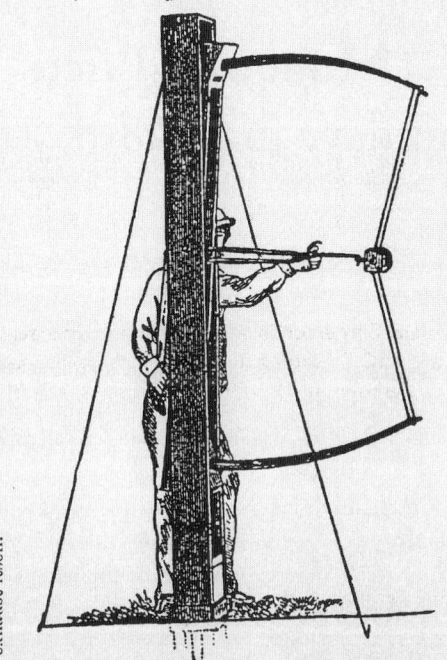

The principle of working it will be shewn at 21, Cranbourn Street, Leicester Square, London, W.C., where alone it can be purchased. Printed instructions accompany each Catapulta, but if necessary, Noblemen or Gentlemen can be waited upon at their seats.

To Colleges, Schools, Clubs (particularly foreign), or for Gentlemen's private practice, where there is scarcely employment for a Professional Bowler or a good one cannot be obtained, this invention is not to be over-estimated, for the most inexperienced can bowl as good pitch, pace and straight a ball as the best of bowlers, and which can easily and without the batsman's knowledge be varied or set, so that a weak point may be perfected.

Price complete, 12 Guineas.

Bowling machines have a suprisingly long history, dating back to Felix in the mid-nineteenth century. This model, also advertised in Wisden, would not have simulated the subtleties of swing or spin .

THE DIARY ENTRIES

Money & Prices
Sunday, June 28th, 1896

What a pleasing outcome to the question of money! Maynard did indeed carry out his researches at the summit and produced the following analysis during our long journey to London and back. A batsman may receive many balls at the wicket, some of which he defends and some of which he attacks. But he is also attendant as a non-striker while his partner is receiving, a nice noting of detail that produces the following options. The resources a batsman has at his disposal may be used for convenience (non-striking) which may be very useful at the start of his innings or if he is a junior partner or clearly incompetent. One might indeed share in a productive stand without ever facing a ball. The second, or defensive use of resources is clearly designed to protect the wicket, to abjure risk for the future. The batsman may thirdly use resources for the production of commodities that will produce utility (runs), and this is offensive play.[76]

---

76 This reads like a forerunner of liquidity preference theory, with its transactionary, precautionary, and speculative motives for holding money rather than less liquid assets.

THE DIARY ENTRIES

In this picture M. has depicted money as the range of strokes available in the textbook. Those coloured plates of posed strokes almost remind one of banknotes, as the artist usually cannot tell between a Flemish groat and a backward defensive push.[77]

These pictures do have an empty feel to them, suggesting that there is some value in being able to mimic the shot independently of a ball being propelled towards one and of the result of playing the stroke. The concept of money as strokes also has a nice appropriateness as one is then begged to ask 'what is a stroke exactly, and what is not?', especially when you see some of the leg byes taken at Fenner's these days that seem to produce returns from no sort of stroke at all.[78]

I must have a word with R.H. Bond to see if he will take some photographs at Fenner's; after all, he did call that one he took of the Cambridgeshire farm hands taking snuff 'How's That'!

M. has discovered the trade-off between liquidity and profitability, and believes it to hold for cricket as well! He says that during a period which the batsman is hard-pressed there will be a lot of defensive shots attempted with many maiden overs. So stonewalling is profitable for the bowler in M.'s system. But in a context in which the batsman will try a number of offensive strokes the bowler is supplying liquidity in the hope of interest (or wickets, in M.'s system). The batsman will be drawn into investment of resources

---

[77] J.N.K. is being rude, presumably, about not just lesser practitioners but also Spy (until Chevallier Tayler the doyen of cricket print producers). But anyone who loves the dynamics of cricket must find even the latter disappointing, although the works were closely based on George Beldam's action photographs (as his son's posthumous book clearly proved in 2000). To modern eyes the astonishing work of Charles Ambrose and the more recent and formal John Hawkins are preferable. The editor's favourite is Caribbean artist David Skinner who combines the two approaches, and achieves in his Sobers portraits some of the accidental but dramatic effects of Blitz hose water seen on Beldam's photograph of Fry.

George Beldam jnr.'s chaotic 368-page collection of his father's masterpieces contains the well-known but riveting picture of Barton King resembling Malcolm Marshall, the leaping Alan Marshal, and finishes with a glorious, mirthful ensemble at Shillinglee in 1908. The overall, if unintentional, theme seems to be that passing of the torch between Grace, the 19th century, and Ranji, the 20th century. Although 1914–60 seemed to be post-'Golden Age', Worrell, Benaud, one-day cricket, Sobers, Warne and the Asian explosion seemed to confirm that Ranji was indeed the spiritual primogenitor of late twentieth century cricket.

There is a lot of speculative ruminating in the book on past virtues *versus* present which becomes tiresome, but as a reference collection it is outstanding. The jujutsu photographs and Tuke paintings are particularly revelatory.

[78] The law at this stage did not specify that a stroke had to be attempted for a leg bye to count.

THE DIARY ENTRIES

(*i.e.* attacking strokes go up in circulation) by the improved conditions, even though it means abandoning a defensive option (*i.e.* there is a greater possibility of losing your wicket). I was quick to show I understood that it is the interest-bearing conditions of trade that induce the degree of offence or defence in the attitude of both lender (bowler) and investor (batsman); it is not that the attitude leads to the change in conditions.

M. listened to this nodding with agreement and then added that it was important to admit the possibility that the batsman's strategy to risk could, if it proved to be fortunate, have a feedback effect on the bowler which would lead to a lessening of the risk of losing a wicket.[79] This spectacle is unusual, and much loved by spectators because it leads to general uncertainty in the spectacle, although it derives from firm conviction on each playing side. However, it rarely comes about because players are experienced in many different situations of play, and have the imagination generally to deal with circumstances as they arise (*e.g.* a left hander who is strong square on the off on the back foot). M. says he hears one phrase repeated *ad nauseam* by Cambridge spectators as they walk round Fenner's watching undergraduates tempted into making elementary errors by the experienced opposition; 'I've seen it *all* now!' [80]

A theory of interest, of sorts, has therefore emerged, with general expectations about changes in the trade context taking precedent in determining the rate of interest which then determines the various behaviour of placers and borrowers of savings. Unforeseen changes in the conditions of supply of and demand for funds (being very much more unlikely because they are unconventional and uncommon) constitute very much more a secondary mechanism in determining the rate. This is an interesting variation by M. on the classical loanable funds theory [81] which stresses the second relationship, and I am interested to see if it leads him anywhere. I confess it still seems a bit general at present.

---

79 *e.g.* hitting the bowler off his length, as Smith was to do to Jessop in the Varsity match, or grinding out a bowler to the end of his stamina, as Leveson Gower was to do to Cobbold at the other end.

80 An expression heard even in the mid-1970s from the lips of the old Camden and Cambs. wicket-keeper Bill Cockell. Another nineteenth century affectation still handed down in Cambs. C.C. is the Rev. Ward pronunciation of 'bowl' as a rhyme of 'howl'.

81 In the laisser faire system savings from households are recycled as loans to firms by the financial institutions through the balancing mechanism of the interest rate; a market-clearing rate must be constantly changed to effect equilibrium, and government must balance its own budget so as not to crowd out private firms competing for the limited pot of loanable funds.

   Keynes later said that this is all wrong, because a stronger equilibrating force is involved between savings (a leakage) and investment (an injection); that force is income.

THE DIARY ENTRIES

What then could Maynard do to link his concept of money as strokes to the idea of prices and develop a coherent general approach to the effects of changes in the monetary system? He made a good beginning by concentrating on the individual situation. For example, a defensive stroke might luckily produce a return (an edge) but the probability of this would vary with the playing conditions, so that W. G. Grace jnr. as an opener might expect to get more return this way than Jessop. The batsman might choose to play defensively because the expected rate of return on the offensive strokes would be very low in certain conditions (*e.g.* the drive against an off break bowler on a sticky, where the correct approach is to let the sun dry it out while you defend).

This produced in M. a conviction that the velocity of circulation of strokes varies with the type of bowling on offer and the state of the game as well as the physical environment. So at the start of the innings you would expect a lot of use of the straight dead bat and the leave. But furthermore he felt able to quantify a general identity that might contain predictive as well as descriptive elements.

He has gone on from his understanding of the velocity of circulation and the total stock of strokes to venture that the average rate of scoring per ball will vary inversely with the fraction represented by the ratio of balls played with defensive strokes as numerator and the quantity of strokes in the manual as denominator. This is a very neat move which has Marshall's cash balances view at its root.[82] I like the way he has identified strokes as high-powered money, but wonder if this elaboration will lead him up cul-de-

---

82   $MV=PT$, or the quantity of money times the velocity of circulation must be equivalent to the price level times the number of transactions. The student usually gets fed the Fisher identity with the injunction that since V is fixed by institutional arrangements and T is determined by the growth rate, any increase of M above that growth rate will raise prices. The weight of transmission does not fall on quantity changes in this view, and the possibility of P rises leading to a rise in M is also discounted. Such simplistic assumptions, or 'premisses' as J.N.K. called them, are clouded in the real world by events. The new monetarist explanation of the early 1970s 'falling purchasing power' posited a time-lag of two years between cause and effect (Lord Rees-Mogg's infamous 'hose') in which attempts to change output and habits of velocity might be made but would be unable to persist, the price effects winning out in the end. The main problem with the elegant theory was that no sooner had the relationship been identified than it, and the instruments by which it was meant to be controlled, broke down.

THE DIARY ENTRIES

sacs as he extrapolates from his fantasy-world of cricket to the real world of affairs? Can he now identify and explain price changes in cricket?[83]

Maynard has glimpsed the possible controversies that can arise from identifying an identity in the system where some significance seems to be apportioned to the stock of money in circulation. He has looked at his defensive strokes (or cash balance) explanation of the scoring rate and seen that various interpretations, some mischievous, may be made of it. Clearly, he says, the total number of batsmen times the average score each makes will equal the total number of balls scored off times the average runs per ball. If the number of balls scored off is conditioned by Maynard's concept of strokes as money (the cash balance fraction mentioned in the last page) then the range of strokes might be held to determine the rate of scoring, and hence the sort of totals we might expect to see in a game of cricket, and also the averages of the batsmen and bowlers. So a loss of one or two strokes from the repertoire of the players due to lack of practice or opportunity might lead to rates of scoring of perhaps only forty per hour, totals regularly under a hundred,

---

83 Creativity, imagination, and problem-solving are rarely encouraged in school-level Economics. One symptom is that, sadly, few students are encouraged to look at the contra-quantity theory of Thomas Tooke, who held that indeed it was changes in P that led to changes in M, or the work of Knut Wicksell linking the classical theory to the new world of macroeconomics (or what J.N.K. referred to as 'general conditions') which predicted different effects on prices from changes in expenditure. Most interesting, perhaps, are the writings of Silvio Gesell, a link between Irving Fisher (*Stamp Scrip*) and J.M.K. (*The General Theory*) who both admired the ingenuity of his approach to the highly-variable velocity of money, V. The translations of his works further help a cricketer realise how accessible is Keynes's language.

Eisler (1933) is very sniffy about Keynes, Gesell, Kenworthy, Douglas, and all other 'heretics'; he manages to condemn taxation as deflationary and inflationary spirals as the wrong way to eliminate deficits and slump, so can only plump lamely for a dual currency in a massive sterling area with credit as 'current' money and a complex indexation for 'actual' money. The effect of the idea on the reader, after a knowledgeable and painstaking setting-up of the problem, is like treating a broken back with ralgex spray; he basically says that Paris's carnet of metro tickets was the solution to the Great Depression.

This shows how very hard it must have been for the 'Cambridge Circus' to convince the orthodox schools that they had a different and convincing view on matters. There were allies in unexpected quarters, however; in 1933 a bill was introduced in the US House of Representatives to introduce Gesell/Fisher stamping of money to speed up its circulation.

The more passionate Gesell is the only economist mentioned in the final chapter of *The General Theory*, and his inclusion led many to demean it, because of his low standing. But people should remember how right Gesell was when it comes to phone cards, discount vouchers, books of stamps, and canteen tickets; whenever you try to use them you find they've expired, and neither Lucas nor Friedman predicted that.

THE DIARY ENTRIES

and batting averages around twenty and bowling averages around ten. This would have serious and direct consequences for the estimation of the worth of those performances. How would one be able to judge the value of a century, or the making of a hat trick in such variable circumstances? How would we discern the expert from the journeyman?

Reading the scores in the newspaper we find our Cambridge Town heroes. But the lesser one[84] has been eclipsed by the Gown faction in a frenzy of price instability at Lord's! How the brood is protected by the mother hen; it is all the talk of Cambridge that Perkins asked for Trott to be taken off after bowling at a fearsome pace. This rather takes some of the shine off a remarkable victory.

> **CAMBRIDGE YOUNG MEN'S CHRISTIAN ASSOCIATION CLUB.**
>
> **FIRST ELEVEN MATCHES.**
>
> Thursday, July 2, v. St. Giles' C.C., on Parker's Piece.
> Thursday, July 9, v. Old Higher Grade C.C., on Parker's Piece.
> Thursday, July 16, v. Liberals C.C., on Parker's Piece.
> Thursday, July 23, v. Willingham C.C., at Willingham.
> Thursday, July 30, v. Willingham C.C., on Parker's Piece.
> Monday, August 3, v. London Central Y.M.C.A., on Leys Ground.
> Thursday, August 6, v. C.E.Y.M.S. C.C., on Parker's Piece.
> Thursday, August 13, v. Rodney C.C., on Parker's Piece.
> Thursday, August 20, v. Old Higher Grade C.C., on Parker's Piece.
> Thursday, August 27, v. Liberals C.C., on Parker's Piece.
> Thursday, Sept. 3, v. Chesterton District C.C., on Parker's Piece.
> Thursday, Sept. 10, v. Rodney C.C., on Parker's Piece.
> Thursday, Sept. 17, v. St. Giles' C.C., on Parker's Piece.

---

84 Carpenter made 161 in M.C.C.'s second innings, but was on the losing side. Some reports said that Mitchell the captain complained about Trott bowling too fast, others point the finger at M.C.C. Secretary Henry Perkins (a three-time Blue and member of the great 1860s Cambridgeshire side) intervening. Their reasoning was that this was only a trial match to see who should play in the Varsity Match and it was ridiculous that injury should be risked at such a critical stage of the season. One can easily imagine Trott's reaction and the effect on his team's morale.

GOLDEN AGES AT THE FENNER'S MARGIN

THE DIARY ENTRIES

Money & Prices
Monday, June 29th, 1896

Maynard has done miracles; he has taken up my challenge to incorporate a theory of money into his Fenner's system and shown up the danger of how variability in prices may ruin the game. He loves to use the word 'debauch',[85] almost as a cross between a curse and an almost bodily onomatopoeia. Now he is going on to show how there might be different kinds of changes in prices and how there is a constant pressure of factors held in some sort of delicate balance over time, disturbed occasionally by some sort of shock to which the system has to adjust. He has already opined that the biggest shock of the current century has been monetary, so to speak, in the giant form of W.G. Grace snr. This amused Marshall when Foxwell told him about it, and they both agreed that the good doctor was far more imposing, effective, and ultimately memorable than the Old Lady of Threadneedle Street.

When pushed on how W.G. had caused an adjustment of prices, M. was very serious and said that it had been a benign rather than a retrogressive step in that a revolution had occurred in batting with a huge expansion in the number of strokes made possible to any particular ball in any particular situation and an increase in the absolute number of strokes in existence. The doctor's example had made a change of behaviour possible for others. Marshall said after this incident that he was glad Maynard had discovered increases in liquidity could benefit mankind even in grim Kennington and sooty Trafford! He even postulated that the relief on taxation given by Hicks Beach in this year's budget speech will not be neutral in either monetary effects or in terms of household appetites for wares.[86]

---

85 Presumably a reference to the currency becoming devalued through over-supply.

86 Indeed, this was a classic case of cutting tax during a boom; Lord Jenkins tells us that this particular Chancellor had a very easy ride until his fifth budget speech when the downturn was really showing its effects. The orthodox economists of the time thought Hicks Beach was right to aim for a balanced budget, of course, and wouldn't have connected the actions of looser fiscal policy with the consequences.

In the midst of the Great Depression a letter to *The Times* (20 August 1932) from G.A.H. Samuel drew attention to the unintentional inflationary effect of the 1896 budget, and contrasted it with the effects of the orthodox advice of '*Geddes axes*', economy drives, and raised taxation to deal with the public deficits during the current slump.

THE DIARY ENTRIES

I am delighted with the way he has come out of this challenge unscathed with a very Cambridge view[87] of falling purchasing power. It would have been quite possible that he would have found no resolution to the problem of money in cricket and, further, that if he had come up with an idea it would have been simply deterministic in its accommodation of causation. Instead he has emerged from the problem with enhanced understanding of psychological factors, the role of probability, judgement of actions by outcome, and not least the vital role played by W.G. in the history of the English-speaking peoples!

I can now leave for Scotland with Florence certain that Maynard will keep me informed about the Varsity match and other important developments.

> CORNS! DO YOU SUFFER? IF SO USE A. SIDNEY CAMPKIN's Corn Solvent (a special preparation), used according to the directions, will speedily relieve and effect a cure. In Bottles -/7½ and 1/1½ each.
> For Perspiring or Tender Feet use the CAMBRIDGE FOOT POWDER. It is Cooling and Antiseptic, Unequalled as a Dusting Powder. Sold in Tins and Packets 1d., 3d., 6d., and 1s. each.

---

87 Backhouse claims that the changed formulation between the Fisher equation and the Cambridge equation led proponents of the latter to

> ... stress changes in expectations and confidence as an important cause of changes in the value of money.

It was regarded as a framework

> ... within which to analyse the various effects on the value of money, not as the expression of a rigid quantity theory.

Hicks, in *Classics and Moderns* (p.128), sums up the flexible approach that cricket presented to J.M.K.:

Circumstances are possible in which an increase in the supply of money [range of strokes] does not increase Liquidity [innings' length].

GOLDEN AGES AT THE FENNER'S MARGIN

THE DIARY ENTRIES

Money & Prices
Tuesday, June 30th, 1896

Maynard has expanded his analysis of falling purchasing power and has divided these further sources into two categories. There are a number of ways in which the scoring rate may be pushed up by the fielding side, some of which are passive like misfields and dropped catches, some of which are active like overthrows and extras (no balls, wides). He separates these from ways that a scoring rate may be actively drawn up *e.g.* the aforementioned invention of new strokes for given situations (the W.G. thesis), a change of laws or playing regulations that alters expectations (*e.g.* 8 ball overs increases the likelihood of fatigue and scoring opportunities late in the over), an intervention by the groundsman either in the form of the Fenner's workshop (mowing the outfield), or the atelier in the atmosphere (showers over the lunch break).[88]

[88] This most clearly shows how the complexity of cricket saved Keynes from dogged monetarist views; there are a plethora of supply and demand side factors that can raise the score, and a reductionist explanation will never satisfactorily explain all situations of high or low scoring.

THE DIARY ENTRIES

Money & Prices
Thursday, July 2nd, 1896

There is amusement to be had also from our cricket as well as pain. A group of logicians visited us from Oxford for some reason, I recall, and while at the house one of the younger ones picked up the London paper and scrutinised a new acrostic word game that was on the back page. While his elders were discussing probability and the weather in a light-hearted way this blood flourished a pencil and pointedly filled in several of the spaces on the sheet. When the moment came for the group to depart I saw Maynard sidle up to the paper to take a look at the pipsqueak's progress. He said nothing and came to the front door as we were saying our farewells, then just as I was about to shake hands with our young friend, Maynard crept behind him, pointed vigorously at his head, and mouthed extravagantly with that charming smile of his, 'maiden overs, father, maiden overs!'

He also developed a habit at this time for essaying a bowling action in the hallway of the house whilst crying, 'Everyone is afraid of Jessop, but Jessop is afraid of me!', referring to Jessop's fast bowling rather than his furious batting. This delighted me because I could introduce formal logic to him to prove that, if true, this meant he was, himself, Jessop! We moved on to prove that a false proposition could imply any proposition, so that the cry changed to, 'Two plus two equals five, so I'm Jessop!'[89] From there it was a short step to, 'If this sentence is true, then I am Jessop!' A bit harder was the idea that the following statements were actually saying the same thing: 'If Grace is turning the ball, so is Gray,' and 'either Grace is turning the ball or Gray isn't.'

---

[89] If 2+2=5, then 2+2 −3=5−3, and so 1=2. Since 2 is 1, then Jessop and J.M.K. must have been one, so J.M.K. *was* Jessop. This device was later used by Russell to make fun of the Pope.

M.C.C. AND GROUND v. THE UNIVERSITY.

Some very rapid scoring was witnessed at Lord's last Friday, 489 runs being obtained in less than six hours, and only nine batsmen being dismissed. The honours of the day rested almost entirely with the M.C.C. eleven, who in four hours scored 391 runs, raising their overnight score in the second innings of 92 for two wickets to 481. A fine innings was played by Carpenter, who increased his score of 48 to 151. Cambridge were set the exceptional number of 507 to get to win, and in the last hour and 50 minutes they scored 98 for the loss of two wickets. Mr. Norman Druce played in good style, and was 50 not out at the close. On Saturday the Cambridge eleven established a record that even in these days of heavy scoring will probably stand long. As we have said, they were set 537 to win and they got them at the cost of seven wickets in six hours and a half. This performance eclipses anything in the way of scoring ever done in important cricket in the fourth innings of a game. Its nearest approach perhaps was last year at Lord's, when Sussex going in to get 405 against the M.C.C. made 385. There was an incident on Friday evening at Lord's which should be mentioned, as it may have had something to do with the success of the Light Blues. Albert Trott, the Australian, was bowling very fast and well when a ball got up and struck Mr. Marriott, who retired in consequence. Then, apparently on the protest of Mr. Mitchell, the Cambridge captain, Trott was not allowed to go on again that day. This was rather an unusual occurrence in serious cricket, and may have taken some of the earnestness out of the match. When Trott was off Cambridge found runs easier to get, and Mr. Norman Druce and Mr. Wilson rapidly took the score to 93. From this point the game was renewed on Saturday, when the M.C.C. laboured under the disadvantage of having no proper wicket-keeper owing to an injury to Davenport. The Wilson and Druce partnership lasted until 289, and realised altogether 240 as the result of three-and-a-quarter hours' cricket. Mr. Druce, who was then out, played very finely, his driving being especially good. He hit 17 fours, five threes, and nine twos. Four more wickets fell for the addition of 109 runs, seven being down for 462. Mr. Wilson, who was fourth out at 296, played very pretty cricket, and his best hits were seven fours and four threes. Mr. Marriott had sufficiently recovered from his overnight injury to resume his batting when Mr. Druce left. He played a strong forcing game, and when only three wickets remained he and Mr. Bray hit off the last 117 runs of the Cambridge task in 75 minutes. Mr. Marriott's 146 on Saturday were made in two-and-a-half hours, and included a five, 20 fours, and five threes. The Cambridge rate of scoring on Saturday was between 80 and 90 an hour.

Score :—

M.C.C.

Carpenter, b Gray ... 37	c Gray, b Grace	151
A. Hearne, c Marriott, b Gray 3	b Gray	5
Trott, b Gray ... 5	b Shine	14
Davenport, b Shine ... 18	absent, hurt	0
C. H. Hulls, b Shine ... 0	b Druce	30
B. W. Nicholls, c Bray, b Gray 10	c Burnup, b Marriott	59
H. E. Symes Thompson, c & b Shine ... 6	b Marriott	0
R. J. Burrell, c Stogdon, b Shine 16	c Stogdon, b Marriott	19
Mead, c Bray, b Burnup ... 12	not out	46
Martin, not out ... 14	c Bray, b Marriott	36
F. A. Phillips, c Stogdon, b Gray ... 2	c Shine, b Mitchell	74
Extras ... 10	Extras	39
134		**483**

CAMBRIDGE.

C. J. Burnup, b Trott ... 26	c Phillips, b Martin	96
W. G. Grace, jun., b Martin 28	b Trott	0
H. H. Marriott, b Martin ... 0	not out	146
N. F. Druce, c Carpenter, b Trott ... 13	b Mead	146
C. E. M. Wilson, b Martin ... 6	c and b Martin	81
W. McG. Hemingway, b Trott 4	b Trott	12
F. Mitchell, b Trott ... 4	c Hulls, b Martin	7
J. H. Stogdon, b Trott ... 15	c Nicholls, b Hearne	8
E. H. Bray, c Martin, b Trott 3	not out	32
E. B. Shine, c Nicholls, b Martin ... 14		
H. Gray, not out ... 0		
Extras ... 1	Extras	65
111		**507**

THE DIARY ENTRIES

GRANTCHESTER v. TRUMPINGTON.

Played at Trumpington on Monday. Score:—

TRUMPINGTON.

H. Short, b Ling	39	R. S. Goodchild, not out	12
W. Robinson, c and b Ling	6	C. Peck, b Ling	2
A. Gentle, c Chapman, b Pearce	2	R. Ambeton, b Pearce	10
E. Northrup, b Pearce	0	H. White, b Pearce	0
E. Cowel, c Whitaker, b Pearce	13	G. Pamplin, b Gordon	0
S. G. Hutt, b Gordon	13	Extras	12
			108

GRANTCHESTER.

J. Chapman, b Gentle	2	b Hutt	0
G. Tolliday, b Short	2	b Hutt	0
R. Whitaker, c Cowel, b Gentle	10	run out	1
C. Ling, b Short	2	b Hutt	32
B. Willers, b Short	2	c Cowel, b Hutt	1
H. Robinson, b Short	3		
N. Pearce, b Gentle	0	b Cowel	3
W. Gordon, not out	5	not out	17
H. Wagstaff, b Short	1		
W. Bard, b Short	0		
W. Brammet, b Gentle	4	c and b Hutt	0
Extra	1	Extras	3
	30		57

LILLEY'S C.C. v. R. SAYLE & CO.,'S C.C.

Played on Trinity Ground on June 25th and won by Lilley's. Score:—

LILLEY'S

B. Garner, c Parnell, b Spinks	1	C. R. Wright, b Kent	2
S. C. Gray, b Spinks	19	F. Graves, b Barwood	0
J. Haigh, c Parnell, b Spinks	0	R. Leech, c Hayes, b Barwood	2
E. C. Smith, c and b Kent	21	R. Tebbutt, b Barwood	0
G. W. Gray, c Parnell, b Kent	9	J. Baldwin, not out	1
F. Bullock, c Barwood, b Kent	0	Extras	9
			64

R. SAYLE AND CO.

A. G. Kent, b E. Smith	15	F. Hayes, c Baldwin, b Haigh	5
P. Parnell, c Wright, b Haigh	2	A. J. Holiday, b E. Smith	2
L. Geard, c Wright, b Haigh	2	R. Spinks, b Haigh	2
H. Thurkettle, c Wright, b Haigh	3	E. Pearson, b E. Smith	4
S. F. Williams, b E. Smith	0	E. Harradine, not out	0
A. Barwood, c and b Haigh	3	Extras	6
			44

Cambridge Chronicle 3/7/96

THE GIRTON B.A.

To the editor of the Cambridge Chronicle

Sir, – The world is coming to a pretty pass. Women with university degrees! What next? Women are not equal to men. The Almighty never intended that they should be. Women possess their individual qualities and charms, putting poor man into the shade, and we admire them for such nobel traits of nature – then let them be contented. The "New Woman" is, to a sensible man and woman, a disgusting creature – a parasite of obliquity. What is more objectionable than a female doctor, who has to leave her husband in bed to mind the babies while she attends to duty's call? The nurse, for which she is admirably qualified, is better than the doctor, and the lawyer, the M.P., or even to be on the suffrage list? or a woman who rides bicycles in the streets of London – plays cricket or football! or the other positions only fitted for the man. There is no objection to literature, for some women surpass men in this. It is to be fervently hoped that the University will not grant them a degree equal to men.

EDGAR ATHELING.

Primrose Club, St. James',
19th June, 1896

SLEEPING OUT AT NIGHT.

To the Editor of the Cambridge Chronicle.

Sir,—Will you allow me to call attention to the extreme absurdity of the Magistrates sending people to prison who prefer the open air to the dirty casual ward of some union, on the usual charge of having no visible means of subsistence, as if that were a crime rather than a misfortune. The same sort of wrong-headedness both in county and borough magistrates causes them to let off with a fine some violent ruffian guilty of some cowardly and brutal unprovoked assault, instead of giving three months or six months hard labour. Such a mode of administering justice, or rather injustice, is a way of manufacturing criminals.

Yours, &c.,
JUSTITIA.

It is a matter of great regret to Cambridge cricketers that H. Gray should have had to retire from the 'Varsity eleven in the eleventh hour, as it were, the more so because there is a strong opinion prevalent in the Borough that a dead set was made against him right through the term. Gray, however, possesses the entire confidence of his captain, who has a great appreciation of his powers of attack. The Old Persean has been much troubled with his shoulder this season, and his retirement on that account is quite reasonable.

It is useless for me to allude in this column to the match, as it will have reached its critical stage, and may even be decided before any remarks I might make could be read by my readers. I, therefore, content myself by stating that I believe the match will be found to have been one of the most interesting on record, and that either Cambridge will win or a draw will be made.

Much good feeling is created by the carrying out of spirited cricket matches between the young people employed by rival business houses. Messrs. Lilley and Co's. young men and those employed by Messrs. Sayle and Co. have a standing dish in this respect, meeting, I believe, every year. The cricket, perhaps, is not of the highest class, but it is thoroughly earnest, and every player does his very level best to secure a win for his side. The match was played last Thursday, and Lilley's were the proud victors. One could wish to see more of these matches, which are helpful to the game and also to the esprit de corps of the houses concerned.

The meeting between the Cassandra and the Camden on the same day was a most interesting one, and the win by the former by two runs was a very great stroke of luck. One thing seems to be clear, and that is that the Cassandra of to-day is not the Cassandra of two years ago. I wonder what club is destined to take its place in the headship of local cricket.

Hayward has shown top form again this week. In the second innings of Surrey against Hampshire he got set, and had made 108 when his captain decided to close the innings. This not out century score will be very helpful to "Tom," who was sliding very rapidly towards the bottom of the batting averages.

The Australians are continuing their victorious career, having beaten Notts and Yorkshire since I last recorded their positions. They have won nine out of fifteen matches.

Yorkshire are still at the head of county cricket on the new reckoning by comparison of finished games:—

	P.	W.	L.	D.	Pts. in Games.	Finishd Games.
Yorkshire	12	8	0	4	8	8
Surrey	16	12	2	1	10	6
Middlesex	7	5	1	1	4	6
Lancashire	10	8	2	0	6	10
Essex	4	2	2	0	0	4
Notts	6	2	2	2	0	6
Hampshire	5	1	3	1	—2	4
Sussex	6	1	3	2	—2	4
Derbyshire	8	2	4	2	—2	6
Gloucestershire	9	2	5	2	—3	7
Somerset	8	1	5	2	—4	6
Warwickshire	8	1	5	0	—4	6
Leicestershire	6	1	6	0	—5	7
Kent	7	0	6	1	—6	6

SPORT AND PLAY.

GOSSIP UPON CURRENT SPORTS AND PASTIMES.

Whether we win the Inter-University cricket match or not, the Cambridge team of 1896 has obtained fame which will cause it to be long held in remembrance, a record having been set up by the beating of the M.C.C. and Ground by three wickets, after having been set 507 runs to win. Saturday morning's cricket news was thick with head-lines, "Hopeless position of Cambridge," but the team never lost heart, and by a splendid batting performance converted this assumed "certain defeat" into a "glorious victory," so that everyone was singing their praises on Saturday evening. Druce, Marriott, and Wilson showed splendid form. The credit of winning the match largely rested with Marriott and Bray, the two not outs, who came together when the score stood at seven for 369, and hit with the greatest freedom. Marriott had a let off when he had scored 99, the only conspicuous fault of his innings, which was an ideal one for the crowd. The memorable second innings lasted six hours and-a-half.

The Cambridge bowling was a little weak on the second day, which partly enabled the M.C.C. to make the big score of 453, and threaten the Cantabs' prospects. I am very pleased to notice that Carpenter contributed 161 to this total. The Cambridge boy has played so poorly this season that I believe I have not previously had the opportunity of alluding to his performances, and I am heartily glad to see him "on song" again.

Marriott got rather badly hurt from Trott's bowling on Friday, and Mr. Perkins, the secretary of the M.C.C, was so indiscreet as to enter the field and advise the captain to take Trott "off," which was done at once. Much comment has arisen from this act, and the Cambridge batsmen have, incidentally, had a large amount of ridicule turned upon them in consequence. There are some lines in *Sport* which are amusing, but which are a little severe on the Cantabs. I quote a few of them :—

> I'd like, oh! Mr. Perkins,
>   To be a batsman bold,
> To have my deeds in "Wisden"
>   And other records told ;
> But I never will be able
>   To make a decent show,
> Unless you'll interfere, sir,
>   To have the bowling slow.
>
> Then prithee, Mr. Perkins,
>   Go out and tell them now,
> That bowling which is speedy
>   You really can't allow.
> Yes, please, go out and tell 'em
>   I'm very fond of lobs,
> Which do not rap your fingers,
>   And do not bring you "blobs."
>
> For I'm nervous, Mr. Perkins,
>   I'm afraid that I'll be hurt,
> For there isn't much protection
>   In a flannel cricket shirt.
> I'd rather not go batting,
>   But I'll risk it, don't you know,
> If you'll stop that fellow bowling,
>   And make them bowl 'em slow.

The times for lighting cycle lamps next week are as follow :—Saturday, 9.17 ; Monday, Tuesday, and Wednesday, 9.16 ; Thursday and Friday, 9.14.

The Cambridge Cycling Club has a run on Thursday through Trumpington and Newton to Pampisford.

The Rovers on Thursday go to Bottisham, and on the following Saturday to Royston.

Cambridge won the cycle races, in competition against Oxford, which were held at Wood Green on Friday. Cambridge won all three events.

The daring of lady riders is beyond the conception of mere male persons. On Tuesday one of these heroines met the Volunteers marching for the Market-hill on their return from drill and encompassed by the thick fringe of the general public. A man a-wheel would have dismounted and waited until the crowd had passed, but the lady rider was above yielding this point to the majesty of crowds. She stuck out most tenaciously for the claims of her sex, *place aux dames*, and triumphantly rode past the column. I admired her temerity, but I trembled for her safety. She, apparently, never thought that any male thing dare bar her path. Cheek (I can scarcely call it pluck) succeeded on this occasion, but I should not advise other ladies to copy the example. The lady in question was undoubtedly right. She was entitled to her fair half of the roadway, but crowds are unreasonable, and in the strength of numbers are quite indifferent to the obligations of the law. The daring of the lady carried her through where a man would most assuredly have been shouldered off his machine. It will not do, however, to carry these experiments to too great a length. I am certain that some of our lady riders are foredoomed ere long to unpleasant experiences.

VIM.

The principal local cricket fixtures for this week are the following :—
Saturday—Old Higher Grade v. Sawston Institute.
Tuesday—Victoria v. Leys.
Thursday—Old Higher Grade v. Y.M.C.A. Camden v. Newmarket.

The Histon and Impington Cricket Club meet the Cambridge Rodney C.C. on Parker's Piece to-day (Saturday). On Tuesday next they play Grantchester, and on Wednesday next they meet Waterbeach and Landbeach. Both of these matches are to be played on the home ground.

GOLDEN AGES AT THE FENNER'S MARGIN

THE DIARY ENTRIES

Unemployment
Sunday, July 5th, 1896

The Varsity match is over for another year and I for one am not displeased, for I find it hard to stand up to such excitement at my stage of life. Set the largest total of the match to win, it seemed impossible that Oxford had won by four wickets when Maynard first heard the news filter through from the public library. Maynard is inconsolable, but I will remind him constantly in my letters of the result last year and the imminent departures of Warner and Leveson Gower from Oxford. These things go in cycles and this triumph will assuredly be a short one for them. The shock was made greater as the thought of defeat only entered our minds after lunch on the third day, Cambridge having posted over three hundred on July 2nd. But M. really began to get involved during the second day when he discovered there had been another controversy about the follow-on, similar to the '93 one but on this occasion received with hostility rather than confusion. M. got very cross about this, feeling that it was within the laws and that unlike the '93 example there was a clear reason here for the tactic of bowling deliberate wides and no balls. M. said that if he had been captain he would have taken the stumper's gloves and stood at mid-off to give away the runs in bigger tranches! Whether the reaction upset Cambridge or not is a moot point, but by the evening of the 3rd we were rocking at 154 for 8, the damage done by Cunliffe, who was totally toothless last year. M. had humorously contrasted the opening attacks in '95, opining that Wilson & Gray sounded like an armaments manufacturer, while Cunliffe & Arkwright was more appropriate for a high street baker. I doubt he will ever look on anyone named Cunliffe again with an unjaundiced eye.[90]

---

[90] Prophetic words; one of the self-righteous 'Heavenly Twins' at the Versailles negotiations, Lord Cunliffe, compounded his malevolent influence in Keynes's eyes with his 1919 report affirming the self-adjusting nature of the gold standard and the desirability of the balancing of the public sector budget. The immediate results of the post-war budgets were a massive recession in 1921 and high unemployment unaffected by Pigou's 'doldrums' years (1923–8) of low growth. That set the backdrop for the *Treatise* and the *General Theory*. Pigou, Marshall's successor as Professor at Cambridge, was a member of the Cunliffe Committee, and would not have seen fiscal tightening and overvaluation of the currency as anything other than desirable.

Major Sir F. H. E. Cunliffe was in the Rifle Brigade and died of wounds on 10 July 1916, twenty years after the Oxford team's moments of glory at Lord's against Cambridge.

108

The Varsity Match at Lord's,

July 2nd–4th, 1896

Oxford won by 4 wickets.

CAMBRIDGE: Batting	First Innings		Second Innings	
C. J. Burnup	ct. Mordaunt b. Hartley	80	ct. & b. Hartley	11
W. G. Grace jnr.	b. Hartley	0	b. Cunliffe	0
H. H. Marriott	ct. Warner b. Hartley	16	b. Cunliffe	1
N. F. Druce	ct. smith b. Cunliffe	14	ct. Pilkington b. Waddy	72
C. E. M. Wilson	ct. Cunliffe b. Hartley	80	ct. Lewis b. Hartley	2
W. McG. Hemingway	ct. & b. Hartley	26	b. Cunliffe	12
F. Mitchell(c.)	ct. Leveson Gower b. Hartley	26	b. Cunliffe	4
G. L. Jessop	ct. Mordaunt b. Hartley	0	st. Lewis b. Hartley	19
E. H. Bray (w-k)	ct. Pilkington b. Cunliffe	49	ct. Lewis b. Waddy	41
P. W. Cobbold	b. Hartley	10	not out	23
E. B. Shine	not out	10	ct. Hartley b. Waddy	16
EXTRAS	B 4, L-B 1, W 2, N-B 1	8	B 5, W 1, N-B 5	11
	TOTAL	319	**TOTAL**	212

OXFORD: Batting	First Innings		Second Innings	
P. F. Warner	run out	10	run out	17
G. J. Mordaunt	b. Jessop	26	b. Jessop	9
H. K. Foster	b. Wilson	11	ct. & b. Cobbold	34
G. O. Smith	ct. Bray b. Wilson	37	ct. Mitchell b. Cobbold	132
C. C. Pilkington	b. Jessop	4	ct. & b. Jessop	44
H. D. G. Leveson Gower(c.)	b. Jessop		26	ct.
Bray b. shine	41			
G. R. Bardswell	ct & b. Cobbold	9	not out	33
P. S. Waddy	st. Bray b. Cobbold	0	not out	1
J. C. Hartley	ct. Marriott b. Wilson	43		
F. H. E. Cunliffe	b. Shine	12		
R. P. Lewis(w-k)	not out	0		
EXTRAS	B 12, L-B 4, N-B 8	24	B 6, L-B 6, W 6, N-B 1	19
	TOTAL	202	**TOTAL (6 wickets)**	330

OXFORD: Bowling	Overs	Runs	Wickets	Overs	Runs	Wickets
Cunliffe	55	87	2	33	93	4
Hartley	59.3	161	8	30	78	3
Waddy	24	35	0	11	28	3
Pilkington	29	24	0	3	2	0
Leveson Gower	2	4	0			

CAMBRIDGE: Bowling	Overs	Runs	Wickets	Overs	Runs	Wickets
Jessop	37	75	3	30	98	2
Wilson	37	48	3	42	50	0
Shine	12.3	29	1	20	41	1
Cobbold	11	26	2	44.4	96	2
Burnup				2	3	0
Druce				7	11	0
Mitchell				2	12	0

GOLDEN AGES AT THE FENNER'S MARGIN

THE DIARY ENTRIES

Unemployment
Tuesday, July 7th, 1896

The Varsity debacle has prompted new thoughts from Maynard on the nature of unemployment. The card shows that our opener, W.G. Grace jnr., bagged a pair, did not bowl or keep, and didn't take any catches. We feel it is very unlikely that he ran out Warner in either innings, and he was on the losing side. Could anyone, says M., be a clearer case of unemployment? I wish to point out that until three quarters of the match had gone Grace would have thought he was going to be on the winning side, but M. will probably feel that such expectations merely led to a sense of greater uselessness and guilt after the event. I can point to Grace's role last year,[91] but M. might raise the same objection, and claim it adds to his case!

He now has a new metaphor for employment, and it is an engagingly simple linguistic trick; it is enjoyment.[92] This has a neat encapsulating simplicity. If Grace had also misfielded every ball in the Oxford innings, and given away overthrows, and dropped catches, then it is likely he would have had a miserable game and detracted from his team's enjoyment. He might have been part of the undeserving poor. But if he received two excellent deliveries (at least we know they were straight), fielded well, and didn't receive any chances, then for most of the match he would have been happy, and his captain could not be accused of misallocating his resources. Very often you feel there is severe unemployment in these games as only two bowlers will share a tremendous number of overs and a fifth bowler is, typically, rarely used.[93] What about Pilkington? Bowling more overs than he conceded runs!

---

91 Grace scored 40 and 28 as an opener, bowled in each innings, and took the wicket of the Oxford captain Mordaunt. Cambridge beat Oxford by 134 runs. He died less than a decade later following an appendectomy.

92 J.M.K. much later paid tribute to the 1881 publication of *Mathematical Psychics* in his essay on Edgeworth, in which he developed his 'calculus of *feeling*, of pleasure'. Pupils who now struggle with the move from marginal utility theory to indifference curve analysis may be unaware that it all began with poetic phrases like

   We cannot count the golden sands of life; we cannot number the innumerable smiles of love.

93 In the 1937 *Wisden Almanack* the Oxford captain described this match in some detail, and remembers how he only included Smith on the morning of the match in favour of a fifth bowler (Raikes). Leveson Gower concluded:

   You can never have too much batting in a 'Varsity match.

THE DIARY ENTRIES

Unemployment
Thursday, July 9th, 1896

M. has come up with two ideas since our last letters. One is that within the rules of the publicly quoted commercial sector (which he feels are daftly wide open to abuse) a small number of companies will come to dominate ownership, but not as Marx predicted in an open, tyrannical way. He feels that by maintaining links with the appearance of the company engulfed the new parent will be able to hide its growing power from the households. Well-known names of items will be traded to and fro with the general public hardly realising what is happening, fondly imagining that their favourite firms are enjoying the sort of deserved (even natural?) longevity that only arises through wholesome tradition and conservative habit. This scenario pleases his growing sense of irony.[94]

---

[94] This is a point routinely made now in G.C.S.E. Business Studies textbooks, with tables showing how brands like Kodak, Del Monte, and Wrigley's were as dominant in the 1990s as they were in the 1920s. During television business bulletins these facts are confusingly used to stress both the continuity and the dynamism of the corporate world.

While J.M.K. might have been further amused by this, J.N.K.'s sense of logic would have produced in him a state of tension, if not stress, for which J.M.K. might have teasingly prescribed a remedy by Beecham, perhaps?

GOLDEN AGES AT THE FENNER'S MARGIN

The Dark Blues entered upon their second innings at 12.25, Mordaunt and Warner being the first pair of batsmen. Jessop and Wilson shared the bowling. The first-named proved very difficult to get away. The batsmen, too, came in for some nasty knocks, Jessop's deliveries getting up very awkwardly. A four to either batsmen was the only hit for some time, and the figures had only been advanced to 16 when Mordaunt was beaten by Jessop. Foster came in and made some splendid cuts, while he also despatched the fast bowler prettily to leg. As the pair looked like making a stand, a change was deemed necessary in the attack, Cobbold at 46, and Shine at 49, being requisitioned. The half century was reached after 55 minutes' play, but a disaster was near at hand, as directly afterwards Foster foolishly called Warner for a short run, and the batsman paid the penalty. Warner had been at the wickets an hour and five minutes for 17. Foster signalled the arrival of G. O. Smith by driving Shine to the off for four, but with another run added the old Malvern captain tamely returned the ball to Cobbold, and retired caught and bowled for 84, made in 50 minutes. With Pilkington in, Jessop resumed bowling at 62, but the batsmen played a steady game, and scored slowly. Smith twice got Jessop to leg for four, while the Etonian put on runs by lesser hits. At lunch time these two were still together, having taken the figures to 89, Smith having made 18, and his confrere 16.

On resuming after the interval the batsmen gave a lot of trouble. Despite frequent changes in the attack, they carried the total to 144 ere Pilkington, who was missed by N. F. Druce in the slips when 19, tamely returned the ball to Jessop. The partnership had yielded 84 runs. Pilkington at one period hit Jessop three times to the boundary from successive deliveries. The Oxford captain filled the vacancy, and a most serviceable stand was instituted. Despite frequent changes in the attack, the pair scored at a steady rate. Two hundred appeared shortly before five o'clock, and when 230 had been made two hours remained for play.

Cambridge Weekly News 10/7/96

112

THE DIARY ENTRIES

Mitchell tried his hand for a couple of overs, and Druce also had a turn, while the others changed about very frequently, but with no good result. When 97 had been added the desired separation was brought about by Shine, who after bowling three wides in succession, got the Oxford captain caught at the wicket, with the total 241 for five wickets, leaving only 89 for the second half of the team to obtain. Bardswell opened with a four, but his partner did most of the run-getting, and by a snick for four made his total 100, a performance that earned for him well-merited applause from fielders and spectators alike. Slowly but surely the goal was being reached, and just when it seemed certain the runs would be obtained without farther loss, Smith let out at one from Cobbold, and was caught in the slips. Waddy came in, and Mitchell and confreres strained every nerve to lessen their defeat. The new-comer opened with a single, but Bardswell let out at the next delivery, which he sent straight to Burnup in the deep-field, but the Light Blue failed to bring off the catch, and Oxford had won a remarkable game by four wickets, the match ending at 6.20. There was much cheering at the finish, the Dark Blues meeting with a great ovation, especially G. O. Smith.

The match will always be remembered for wonderfully good fielding, but on Saturday afternoon the Light Blues did not accept all the chances, otherwise it might have been an even more exciting game.

The innings of 182 is the third highest in Inter-Varsity matches, K. J. Key having made 143, and M. R. Jardine 140, both Oxonians. G. O. Smith is the 20th batsman to contribute a three-figure innings. Last year, it will be remembered, H. K. Foster scored 121, but his effort did not meet with success.

Going in to get 330 in the last innings, is the heaviest task that has been set a team, which makes the Dark Blues' success all the more meritorious.

So much has been written concerning the follow on business that I need not enlarge upon it. I witnessed the incident, and have talked with some of the greatest judges of the game, who think with me, that in suggesting the course Mitchell did, he ran a great risk, with the result known. If he, in the interests of his 'Varsity thought it advisable, surely he acted within his rights, and it is with very bad grace that Cambridge people complain of his action.

Cambridge Weekly News 10/7/96

113

RANSOMES' LAWN MOWERS.

The best for Cricket Grounds, Large Lawns, &c.

**ONLY GOLD MEDAL AWARDED,
INDIA & CEYLON EXHIBITION, 1896.
HIGHEST AND ONLY AWARD,
FORESTRY EXHIBITION, 1893.**

At the Jubilee Meeting of the R.A.S.E., Windsor, 1889, HER MAJESTY THE QUEEN and H.R.H. the Princess Victoria of Prussia each purchased one of RANSOMES' LAWN MOWERS.

RANSOMES' HORSE-POWER LAWN MOWERS
ARE IN USE AT THE
University Cricket Grounds of Oxford, Cambridge, and Edinburgh.
ALSO AT
Royal Military Academy, Woolwich; Royal Indian Engineering College; The Wellington College; Haileybury College; Dulwich College; Harrow School; Most of the London Parks. &c.

These Machines are manufactured from new designs, embodying many improvements, and are recommended as the best Machines yet introduced.

PRICES:
Pony Machines—26in., £14; 30in., £18.
Horse-Power—30in., £20; 36in., £24; 42in., £28; 48in., £32.
Leather Boots for Pony, 25s.; Horse, 30s. per set.

This shows another Wisden advertisement for Ransomes' mowers, which did so much, in the long term, to account for the wealth of Cambridge University's batting averages and the poverty of the bowling.

CAMBRIDGE UNIVERSITY BATTING AVERAGES.

	Matches	Innings	Runs	Most in an innings	Times not out	Average
C. J. Burnup	9	16	666	95	1	44.6
H. H. Marriott	8	13	503	146*	1	41.11
C. E. M. Wilson	8	13	424	82	1	35.4
N. F. Druce	9	15	518	146	0	34.8
W. M'G. Hemingway	9	15	391	104	1	27.13
E. H. Bray	6	8	184	49	1	26.2
F. Mitchell	9	14	367	110	0	26.3
W. G. Grace, junr.	6	11	188	68*	2	20.8
G. L. Jessop	7	11	225	93	0	20.5
J. H. Stogdon	3	6	96	32	0	16
E. B. Shine	7	9	56	16	5	14
C. D. Robinson	3	6	69	19	1	13.4
W. W. Lowe	3	6	59	21	1	11.4
P. W. Cobbold	5	7	44	23*	1	7.2

The following also batted:—H. Gray, *8, 2, 2, *0 and *0; G. H. Simpson 0 and 0; H. H. B. Hawkins 9, and F. J. S. Moore 61.

The following made scores of over 100:—146*, H. H. Marriott, v. M.C.C. and Ground; 146, N. F. Druce, v. M.C.C. and Ground; 110, F. Mitchell, v. Sussex; 104, W. M'G. Hemingway, v. Sussex.

*Signifies not out.

CAMBRIDGE UNIVERSITY BOWLING AVERAGES.

	Matches	Overs	Maidens	Runs	Wickets	Average
F. Mitchell	4	28	13	55	3	18.1
P. W. Cobbold	5	209·3	48	470	24	19.14
H. Gray	4	120·2	28	334	16	20.14
C. E. M. Wilson	8	356	137	654	31	21.3
E. B. Shine	7	203·2	69	512	23	22.6
G. L. Jessop	7	323·1	80	889	34	26.5
W. W. Lowe	3	74	21	231	8	28.7
C. J. Burnup	6	67·1	20	185	4	46.1
N. F. Druce	5	34	7	93	2	46.1
W. G. Grace, junr.	4	44	8	121	1	121

The following bowled in one innings only:—H. H. Marriott, 20·1, 1, 60, 4; G. H. Simpson, 11, 1, 42, 0; and H. H. B. Hawkins, 2, 0, 19, 0.

CAMBRIDGE UNIVERSITY WICKET-KEEPING.

E. H. Bray caught 13 and stumped 3.
C. D. Robinson caught 3 and stumped 1.

CRICKET.
(Continued from page 7.)
LIVERPOOL AND DISTRICT v. CAMBRIDGE UNIVERSITY.

In their annual match with Liverpool and District, which commenced at Aigburth yesterday, Cambridge University made a very poor show, for, after getting their opponents out for 127, they lost nine wickets for 67 runs before a thunderstorm broke over the ground and stopped play. The Liverpool combination was a strong one, Frank Sugg and P. J. Henery, the old Middlesex player, being the only absentees of note, while Cambridge, with the exception of N. F. Druce and P. W. Cobbold, were up to full strength. The District team batted first, and were in two hours and ten minutes for their 127 runs, the chief credit of the innings attaching to C. F. Hutton, who, going in second wicket down, carried out his bat for 65, but during his stay he gave two chances, a difficult one at 6, and another to Marriott in the slips when he had made 62. The Cantabs collapsed in a most remarkable manner. Ringrose, a fast right-hand bowler, and Price, capturing eight wickets for 47 runs, but by spirited hitting Bray took the total on to 67 for nine. Present score and analysis:—

WHAT SHALL WE EAT THIS HOT WEATHER?
To the Editor of the Cambridge Chronicle.

SIR,—During this and ensuing hot weather the appetites of those who eat such things revolt against hot, greasy, highly-seasoned made dishes or joints, and the thoughts turn longingly towards summer salads, cool stewed fruits, cold shapes of blanc-mange, gooseberry fool, custards, home made ices. Numbers of people are unaware, however, of the infinite variety of recipes from which these and other equally dainty and appetising dishes may be prepared. We shall be pleased to send some economical recipes by means of which people may enjoy a diet of sweetness and light, and give their long-suffering bodies a slight respite from masses of fleshy foods.

FLORENCE L. NICHOLSON,
Secretary.
London Vegetarian Society,
Memorial Hall, Farringdon Street, E.C.

Cambridge Chronicle 10/7/96

SIDNEY SUSSEX TERCENTENARY.

To the Editor of the Cambridge Chronicle.

SIR,—Since you have done me the honour to publish my poem, written apropos of the recent celebration of the Sidney Tercentenary, may I ask you to kindly print a few almost impromptu lines, which were not inserted until the last moment, but which I should be sorry to have omitted from the Poem, owing to the fact that they not only refer to a late distinguished man, viz., George Butler, a Senior Wrangler and quondam Head Master of Harrow and Dean of Peterborough, but also to his not less distinguished son, the present Master of Trinity, who has presented his father's portrait to Sidney College. Giving the said lines below, and only adding that they ought to follow the line

  A loyal Master fills the Master's chair,

   I am, yours faithfully,
    E. GILBERT HIGHTON.

The Owls' Nest, Soho Square, London, W.,
 July 7, 1896.

Another name we must not here forget,
A link between the present and the past,
George Butler, Sidney's pride in days gone by,
Her Senior Wrangler just a century since.
His portrait doth on yonder wainscoat hang
The gracious present of a grateful son,
While graven on the hearts of Sidney men
His memory in golden letters dwells.

THE DIARY ENTRIES

Unemployment
Friday July 10th, 1896

As far as professional cricket goes, M. believes that the enjoyment (or employment) level goes up with the pay, but this ultimately depends on general performance, and not just the measurement of wickets and runs. The context of the stage of the game and the make-up of the team also matter here. An opener will have a different role from a lower order hitter, and may be measured in terms of overs or minutes rather than runs for his effectiveness. A specialist short slip in a side with a leg break bowler and a slow orthodox left armer may be given much latitude with the bat if he goes in at number six, say. He has actually become convinced that using the correct mix of indicators may lead one to conclude that all cricketers should be professionals, or be measured on the professional plane, since there is a constant incentive to give of one's best whatever the situation; M. is unconvinced that honour can be a sufficient constraint on underperformance. He came up with a very curious illustration of this idea, by

---

95 The false dichotomy between public and private, interventionist and free market, is most clearly shown when policies to lower unemployment are suggested. The traditional free marketeer invokes wage flexibility, the Keynesian invokes government projects. But free migration and unrestricted markets for arms and drugs are more usually opposed by self-styled marketeers. A free market for housing seems to inhibit geographical mobility, whereas a bigger public rented sector would lead to smoother working of the labour market. Imaginative solutions require action in the market; higher benefits and pensions can smooth out shortages of expenditure and instability in the securities market. The establishment of a common currency can lead to greater product market competition, lower costs, and therefore an extension of employment. Gesell's plan for Free-Land was one such creative attempt to solve the problem of labour mobility, involving the nationalisation of all terrain in an attempt to save the market mechanism from itself.

J.N.K. was clear about public economic factors being intrinsically bound up with private on page 68 of *The Scope and Method of Political Economy*, where he said:

it is far from being the case that political economy always presupposes the absence of government interference.

He listed duties, monopolies, poor relief, currency convertibility, and the exchange rate system as areas where governments inevitably exercise control.

THE DIARY ENTRIES

indicating how little 'honour' was putting in F.'s COS coffers, and that professional charity organised by the government authorities would do the job better. Marshall would shiver if he heard this attack on his 'Economic Chivalry';[95] I had better invite Johnson[96] to lunch when we return instead, and hope he moves M. on to another topic quickly.

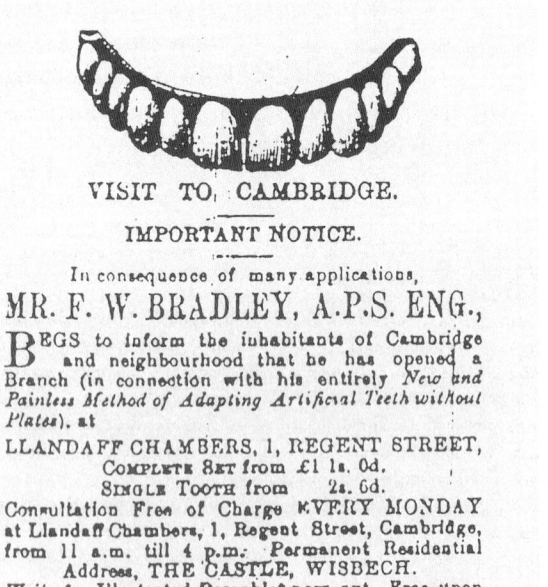

VISIT TO CAMBRIDGE.

IMPORTANT NOTICE.

In consequence of many applications,

MR. F. W. BRADLEY, A.P.S. ENG.,

BEGS to inform the inhabitants of Cambridge and neighbourhood that he has opened a Branch (in connection with his entirely *New and Painless Method of Adapting Artificial Teeth without Plates*), at

LLANDAFF CHAMBERS, 1, REGENT STREET,
COMPLETE SET from £1 1s. 0d.
SINGLE TOOTH from 2s. 6d.
Consultation Free of Charge EVERY MONDAY at Llandaff Chambers, 1, Regent Street, Cambridge, from 11 a.m. till 4 p.m. Permanent Residential Address, THE CASTLE, WISBECH.
Write for Illustrated Pamphlet now out, Free upon

---

96 W.E. Johnson the logician was a close friend who enthused Bertrand Russell as much as J.M.K. He was a regular diner at 6, Harvey Road.

THE DIARY ENTRIES

Policy Requirements
Thursday, July 16th, 1896

On our return to Cambridge I have been pushing Maynard to give me examples of how the central authorities might intervene in cricket[97] and it has been quite illuminating.

He suggested limiting the number of fielders in certain positions; controlling the length of run ups; a system of penalty runs that could leak away from the batsmen and be injected to the fielding side's score; these are standard static changes that could be changed by the season.[98] But he has a number of dynamic changes that could be triggered by various thresholds within the game, so that as a team gains ascendancy the nature of the challenge they face grows greater. As a batsman's score increases, for example, the number of consecutive balls he is allowed to face might diminish but the value of any boundaries he manages might be increased. If a bowler takes wickets at an accelerating rate the bowler's crease might be taken back progressively beyond twenty

---

97   Hicks held that the story of the Keynesian view of the 'instability of capitalism' really began with Hawtrey in 1919. The system has to be stabilised by policy, but appropriate policy would change (e.g. it would be different in 1935 from 1919). Cricket reformers were accustomed to similar swings of analysis as bat gained ascendancy over ball and vice versa.

98   This bears the legacy of Lyttelton's famous Chapter XVI on Cricket Reform, the grand finale of *The Badminton Book*. Like Liberals railing at Unionists, the progressives of Cambridge University called upon the old guard at M.C.C. for law changes to maintain equilibrium between the bat and ball. Apart from the issue of the follow-on, the most widely canvassed idea was to tire out the batsmen more to stem the inexorable rise in scores and draws. The most popular lobby demanded a net to be placed around the boundary, which would mean that for shots near ground level the batsman would have to keep running, simulating the lack of a rope in the 1860s.

In early 1900 M.C.C. indeed tried this out at Lord's, and during one match a ball went for 10 runs, including overthrows. This was hit off the Cambridge University bowler Burnup by the Derbyshire captain Wood, who later assumed the name Hill-Wood, became Chairman of Arsenal F.C. and (ironically for one involved in such revolutionary action) a Conservative M.P. Burnup was, of course, primarily a batsman for Kent after the University term ended, and on 7 August 1896 reached a century against the Australians out of 196 at Canterbury.

A free market solution to the high scoring emerged eventually, as mentioned above, with King's development of swing bowling, and Bosanquet's revolution in spin bowling. There was also the seasonal cycle of weather which had a major impact on uncovered pitches.

THE DIARY ENTRIES

two yards, and he might have to bowl longer overs. Maynard refers to this as variable geometry, and has applied it to the request to carry out various household duties, to the amusement of his parents and exasperation of his brother and sister. The feelings were reversed, however, when he declared that going out to buy the local newspaper in the rain should excuse him from keeping his room tidy as much as when the weather is fine

Friday, July 17th, 1896

We have had great fun with Maynard's concept of variable geometry[99] and the intervention of the central authorities. What if W.G. decided that he had a surplus of runs in 1895 and that he would like to sell some of those this summer to the Varsity in return for some of Jessop's wickets?

We developed this to the championship arena, and thought that Yorkshire might start specialising in slow left armers and trade maiden overs for some of Somerset's faster scoring sessions with the bat. M. even suggested that teams could manage their results; they might decide to lose, but at a very fast rate, to quite an inferior team each season so that at a crucial stage in a match against a top team they could swap some of their defensive streaky runs for some of the earlier fast scoring total.

We might even be going back in this model to the halcyon days of cricket in the mid eighteenth century when betting on cricket was a normal pastime from the aristocracy down to the meanest labourer in the shire!

---

[99] This seems to be the equivalent of J.M.K.'s automatic stabilisers. The free market orthodoxy called for tax increases in a recession to claw back the public sector borrowing requirement which would open up as a result of lower revenue. Keynes may not have gone as far as advocating counter-cyclical fiscal policy (*e.g. cutting* taxes in a recession), but he argued that leaving the system alone was a better idea than the 'Treasury view'. As income goes down the consumption of domestic output reduces, making more available for export, the demand for imports goes down, the lower amount of tax and the increases in the numbers receiving benefits taken together lead to higher injections into and lower leakages from the circular flow.

In Britain the clearest example of inappropriate fiscal policy and most intriguing major recession of the twentieth century was the 1919–21 period of boom and bust.

THE DIARY ENTRIES

Policy Requirements
Saturday, July 18th, 1896

Maynard has been thinking again about the extent to which variable geometry can be put into cricket. A Fenner's venerable told him today about the story of William Lambert and how M.C.C. banned him and the practice of betting from the game. That such an eminent player should be treated in this way shook M. somewhat, and he is now very confused about why the similar practices adopted with regard to the stock market and horse racing are not similarly dealt with.[100] I fear I must come up with a convincing explanation or he might resort to concluding that the vested interests of the propertied classes are better represented through the Jockey Club and the merchant banks than the professional cricketer is through M.C.C.. We can't have anarchism and Marxian tendencies triumphing at this early stage in Maynard's development! I am sure his mother can promote a more durable social philosophy than the utilitarian idealists could manage. Since Maynard came up with his system of a secondary market of options and futures for runs and wickets I have often wished that I had squashed his early notion of symmetry a bit more effectively.

---

[100] Percy Pigott's chaotic 1936 reminiscences (he did not need tight editing, as he owned the Alexandra Street press) includes the words of a resolution passed by the C.U.C.C. committee in 1876 to curtail the entrance of a local town bookmaker and moneylender who was plying his trade at Fenner's. Characteristically the letter that was sent to him did not directly inflame the scandal, referring only to the 'right of refusing admittance to any person whose presence may be thought inexpedient'.

Rev. Ward had method in his madness. Similarly his legendary banning of umbrellas and walking sticks was not because he was superstitious. Rather, it was through fear that damage would be done by members pointing at the gilt-painted names of the Blues on the new (and expensive) panelling. These have been retained from the old Fawcett pavilion, and another example, in its charming original context, can be found in the St. John's College Pavilion.

SPORTS AND PASTIMES.

CRICKET.
CAMBRIDGE UNIVERSITY v. LIVERPOOL AND DISTRICT.

Last Friday, at Liverpool, the local side played the better cricket, and aided by the effective bowling of Ringrose, they beat Cambridge by 115 runs. Score:—

LIVERPOOL AND DISTRICT.

Sugg, b Wilson 21	c Mitchell, b Jessop	0
W. Hilton, c Bray, b Jessop ... 6	b Jessop	5
T. Ainscough, b Jessop 0	c Stogdon, b Burnup	33
O. F. Hutton, not out 65	c Mitchell, b Wilson	4
W. P. Barnes, c Stogdon, b Wilson 2	c Marriott, b Jessop	85
C. Holden, b Shine 15	c Marriott, b Mitchell	63
W. B. Stoddart, c Bray, b Shine 0	b Jessop	3
A. T. Kemble, c Bray, b Grace 4	b Jessop	3
Price, b Grace 0	c Jessop, b Shine ...	2
L. Ainsworth, c Mitchell, b Grace 1	c Jessop, b Shine ...	10
Ringrose, b Jessop 7	not out	3
Extras 6	Extras	15
127		**236**

CAMBRIDGE UNIVERSITY.

W. G. Grace, jun., c Kemble, b Ringrose 1	run out	12
C. J. Burnup, c Barnes, b Ringrose 8	b Ringrose ...	10
H. H. Marriott, b Ringrose ... 12	b Ringrose ...	21
G. L. Jessop, b Price 4	st Kemble, b Ringrose	0
J. H. Stogdon, b Ringrose ... 5	b Ringrose ...	1
F. Mitchell, c Kemble, b Price 0	c Barnes, b Ringrose	21
C. E. M. Wilson, not out ... 12	c Kemble, b Ainsworth	0
W. M'G. Hemingway, c Hutton, b Ringrose 10	c Sugg, b Ringrose	0
E. Garnett, b Ringrose 0	c Kemble, b Ringrose	79
E. H. Bray, b Ringrose 13	b Sugg, b Ringrose	21
R. B. Shine, b Ringrose 0	not out	20
Extras 6	Extras	2
71		**137**

M.C.C. AND GROUND v. CAMBRIDGESHIRE.

The County, yesterday, sent a thoroughly representative team to Lord's for this two day engagement, and the M.C.C. paid the visitors the compliment of organising an eleven that included Flowers, G. Bean, Rawlin, Martin, and H. B. Champain. Unfortunately but little progress could be made, rain confining play to something less than an hour and a half, during which the M.C.C. put on 60 for the loss of four wickets. Score:—

M.C.C.

J. A. Gibbs, not out ... 26	O. C. Stone, c Winter,	
Flowers, b O'Connor ... 0	b Hayward	12
G. Bean, c Hayward, b O'Connor 6	H. B. Champain not out Extras	5 / 8
Rawlin, c Coulson, b O'Connor 19		
		60

C. H. M. Taring, Martin, Rev. E. A. Villiers, W. C. C. Ash, and Pike to bat.

Cambridgeshire: F. Roberson, H. Gray, W. N. Cobbold, H. S. French, W. B. L. Hayter, V. F. de Lisle, G. K. Winter, Hayward (D.), Watts, O'Connor, and Coulson.

GREAT EASTERN RAILWAY COMPANY'S STEAMSHIPS.
TRIAL OF THE "ESSEX"

The Great Eastern Railway Company's new steamship *Essex*, built for the Ipswich, Harwich and Felixstowe traffic, had, her trial trip on Monday, when, thanks to the cordial invitation of the Chairman and Directors of the Company, a numerous party of guests embarked at Parkeston Quay, shortly before one o'clock.

The *Essex* is a double-ended paddle saloon steamer, 90 tons gross, and 600 indicated horse-power. Built of steel, rigged as a fore and aft schooner, and from her fine lines has a very smart appearance. The principal dimensions are—175 feet long, 23 feet beam, and 7 feet 3 inches depth from main deck, drawing 4 feet 6 inches of water. The *Essex* carries two life boats, and is provided with buoyant deck seats, life buoys, and life belts for 317 passengers, in accordance with Board of Trade Regulations.

The first class accommodation, which includes two saloons, are handsomely fitted with oak and birds eye maple, upholstered with olive green velvet backs and cushions. The second class cabins are neatly pannelled in polished pine, with sparred wood seats along the sides and at the ends.

The machinery of the *Essex* comprises a compound engine on the direct acting diagonal system, having cylinders 24 inches and 48 inches in diameter, by a stroke of 42 inches, operating on a paddle shaft with wheels having feathering floats. Steam is supplied by two single-ended cylindrical boilers with two furnaces in each boiler, with a working pressure of 110 pounds per square inch. The speed of the vessel is 14 knots per hour. The steamer is fitted throughout with electric light. She has the usual Board of Trade Certificates for this class of vessel, viz.: 3, 4 and 5. The vessel was built and engined by Messrs. Earl's Shipbuilding Company, of Hull.

The *Essex*—like the sister ship *Suffolk*—has been specially designed, not only with the view to provide every accommodation for the convenience and pleasure of passengers travelling on the River Orwell, but also with a view of affording a comfortable and a safe boat for making occasional trips out to sea. The trips to sea are a popular feature with visitors to Dovercourt and Harwich, and with the residents in Ipswich.

Cambridge Chronicle 17/7/96

THE CLIMATE.

Registered by W. E. Pain, 18, Sidney Street, Cambridge.
All readings except the Barometer and the Degree of Humidity refer to the 24 hours previous to 9 a.m. of the day of observation.

1896.	Barometer Corrected.	Degree of Humidity. Saturation equal 100.	Thermometer. Maximum.	Thermometer. Minimum.	Mean Velocity of wind in Miles per hour.	Amount of Rainfall in inches.
July 10	30.090	88	85	64	6	0.—
" 11	30.352	63	70	50	5	0.—
" 12	30.296	66	78	58	3	0.—
" 13	30.270	55	84	59	3	0.—
" 14	30.222	50	88	61	4	0.—
" 15	30.018	65	89	62	5	0.—
" 16	30.128	93	72	54	9	0.04

These observations being taken in the centre of the town necessarily differ from those taken in the country.

TRAFFIC RECEIPTS.

Railways Week ending July 12.	Passengers. £	Merchandise. £	Total. 1896. £	1895. £
Great Eastern	57,722	33,615	91,337	85,534
Great Northern	41,525	52,081	94,606	89,928
Midland	62,185	118,808	180,993	171,928

THE DIARY ENTRIES

Policy Requirements
Sunday, July 19th, 1896

In line with Maynard's view that fanatical as opposed to partial support for individual teams is irrational, considering the identity between wins and losses inherent in the system, he has tried to expound the way in which the authorities may intervene to enhance short run incentives for the losing teams so that they might improve in the long run. This goes beyond the idea of a Gold Standard, whereby points for a win help bring on general strategy changes to correct the balance of performance. This idea of intervention has led to some interesting mealtime discussions with visitors. Foxwell was most diverted today watching Walter Watts with the thought of the Fenner's groundsman acting as a sort of independent central bank, deciding whether to lower the discount rate by scarifying the square during the autumn![101]

Marshall did not approve at all when Maynard suggested there might be circumstances in which M.C.C. might have to issue directives to groundsmen about the course of action they should take, until Maynard posed the example of the recent phylloxera disaster in Spain.[102] What if, he posited, a similar disaster should occur through the actions of the country's groundstaff, based on the conventional wisdom, and the root stock of all the cricket grounds in England became destroyed, rendering mass

---

101 Foxwell must have been invited to watch the Goody's pupils take on the Paters, or Fathers', XI. One can be pretty certain that Marshall was not; he was not even an occasional formal dinner guest at Harvey Road, let alone a social butterfly. People were summoned to visit him. The first time J.N.K. visited him in 1874 he 'found him in his tub', implying he stood on rather less dignity before his spells in Bristol and Oxford. Foxwell moved to 1, Harvey Road in 1901, following which J.N.K. found increasingly that his role was as an intermediary between Foxwell and Marshall. This was especially true when the latter was due to retire in 1908, and the youthful Pigou rather than the insider Foxwell became hot favourite to succeed him. Lobbying became intense.

102 The Jerez vineyards were devastated in 1894, and the future of sherry seemed to be full of uncertainty until A.G. Sandeman persuaded Don Antonio Bernaldo de Quirós to sell him 800 casks of añadas. This restored confidence of continuity within the Bodega; indeed it caused a sensation that was commented on in *The Times*. Sandeman had already been judged to be one of the shrewdest businessmen in Britain and was appointed Governor of the Bank of England the following year, just a year before the above discussion between J.M.K. and Marshall.

THE DIARY ENTRIES

unemployment to English cricketers? Surely that would require central decision-making to co ordinate the investment that would be required to get the game back on its feet. Marshall admitted this (as who could not given the dire effect of the French disaster on everyday life in Cambridge?) but then added a warning that this was a special case, and that in general the game should be left to find its own equilibrium once the authorities had made the laws clear to the players, and the groundsman had done his best within the constraints the cycle of sunspots imposed on the weather patterns. He and I were very pleased with this neat *précis* of the economic world expressed in the language of game so beloved at present by M. He generously joined in the laughter as we celebrated our little victory at his own game with a further passing of the sherry.

> More than 170 Grand Prizes, Diplomas of Honour and Gold Medals have been awarded J. S. Fry and Sons Ltd., for "Excellence of Quality" of their Pure Concentrated Cocoa and other productions.
>
> **FITS OR EPILEPSY.** Giddiness, Sensations Faints.—I will demonstrate to the whole world how that most dreadful of all complaints, "*Epilepsy*," which has been hitherto considered incurable, can be permanently cured (*without the chance of failure*). Write to the "Secretary," Burwood House, Burwood Place, Hyde Park, London, he will send you, "Gratis," full instructions for cure.

THE DIARY ENTRIES

The Revolution of Keynes
Tuesday, July 21st, 1896

Maynard has broken with Marshall!

Not to his face, I have talked him out of that, but effectively Alfred has diminished in M.'s eyes, which was always a danger once he'd started responding to M.'s Fenner's system in kind.

It happened at Fenner's today; he blurted out his feelings after witnessing that blunderer Porter[103] provoke another crisis with his new dog. The trauma of seeing a helpless animal being passed from pillar to post at the mercy of impersonal regulators like Porter, and the knowledge that I had earlier been a key contributor to an increasingly entangled imbroglio with said pompous elder of the University, seems to have spurred M. into a rebellion of his own. Never can Sugar have produced such bitterness!

Maynard says that Alfred is right in general, that the authorities will perpetually have to change the short-run incentives for losers to make any impression on the long-run pattern, and that is an improvement on laisser faire. But, he goes on, it is what he has called Marshall's full employment equilibrium which is the special case. I was astonished with his certainty and asked him how he had concluded this.

His response was based on logic and the rather negative situation of Marshall's understanding being limited to a world where Oxford and Cambridge were the only teams of any significance, and the Varsity Match was the perpetual mechanism whereby long-term and short-term incentives to change existed. But in a trading system of many teams rather than the bipolar picture this sort of Gold Standard would be insufficient. Imagine Royston or Camden playing Australia; plenty of unemployment to solve there!

I am well aware that what is under consideration here is the whole justification for liberal, laisser faire economics, but M.'s mother has tried to ease my nagging worries on this by pointing out that Maynard must investigate these different traditions sometime. If he is to look at anarchism, Bismarckianism, or Marxianism he is as likely to see their logical and structural faults as be seduced by the impulsion towards change.

---

[103] Master of Peterhouse; see the first 1905 article. Generally mild-mannered, J.N.K. could be provoked to anger on odd occasions, as in May 1882 when he had a huge open row with the Master of Pembroke, Searle, about Gladstone.

THE DIARY ENTRIES

The Revolution of Keynes
Saturday, August 1st, 1896

Somewhat to my shame I succumbed to taking a sideways glance at Maynard's log of the season while he lay ill in bed. Never again! I saw such a release of emotion and torrent of heresy as I wish never to witness again. His quest for a new thinking approach to cricket and the constant proximity of the ultra-orthodox spectators of Fenner's has produced a powder-keg of revolt and loathing cloaked ever so effectively by the adolescent 'innocence' and apparent receptiveness of M.'s manner. To me it is clear that many of these old boys are delighted to have the rare opportunity of an audience that will put up with their endless musings; but does that invalidate M.'s rejection of their analysis? Surely he should not do it in these terms, however?

It is the riposte to this exposition and the conclusion that really caught my eye.

> These are unthinking barbarians, fools dressed in the clothing of their masters. To cling on in faith to such trivialities! To limit the scope of all that's wonderful to simpletons' constraints! To tyrannise over those with real potential who defer to what? To their august appearance? Their homespun tales of the old pavilion, hits into the gaol yard, how you shouldn't trust overarmers? The grandeur of their delusions makes mockery of Jessop; they would dress him up like a monkey and put him on a leash while they grind each other's organs and order him about. Would they ask him how he would play his own bowling? They would have to ban him from imagining that or he might break their spell!
>
> Fools!
>
> If they bowl every ball a daisy-cutter I'll play the ramp shot to them. If they try every ball as a short riser I'll invent the reverse ramp.[104]

---

[104] This has been popularised by Australia's Adam Gilchrist at the start of the twenty-first century, although the editor took part in a formation reverse-ramping display at Trinity College in 1989 when four successive ramp shots were played before the ball's momentum was finally lost.

THE DIARY ENTRIES

I will accept no limits in my mind's eye, and if it can be seen in imagination, then with investment it can be made into reality. Any ball can be hit for four, it must be possible to hit every ball for four; but equally every ball can yield a wicket.[105]

CAMBRIDGE BOROUGH.

MONDAY.

(Before C. J. Clay, Esq., presiding; and A. Macintosh, Esq.)

BAD BOYS.—Two small boys, named George Richardson and Arthur Aylett, were charged with sleeping in the open air and not giving a good account of themselves, on the 12th inst.—The boys pleaded guilty.—P.-c. Lee said he saw the boys asleep in the front garden of 7, Maids' Causeway, at 4.30 a.m. He awakened them and asked them the purpose for which they were there. The boys said they had not been going to school and were sleeping out. Aylett had 9d. upon him and Richardson was found to be in possession of a hymn book. — Both boys admitted previous convictions and the Bench sentenced them to be detained in a Reformatory School for five years.

---

105 An echo of Ranji's 'enigma' on page 177 of *The Jubilee Book*:

No yorker is ever bowled which by proper timing might not be turned into a full pitch.

A yorker must bowl you; if you hit it, it can't be a yorker – the length becomes relative, even immaterial, rather than objective, although there is a length at which a yorker will have a higher probability of success because of the batsman's pattern of expectations.

THE DIARY ENTRIES

The Revolution of Keynes
Sunday, August 2nd, 1896

Stamping gave us time for a good discussion. Maynard's basic argument is against the old idea that it is the quality of the bowling which determines the response of the batsmen, constraining or allowing strokeplay and therefore becoming the main focus for praise or criticism. Like any orthodoxy this seems to make common sense which covers all cases, until someone like Maynard dishes up special case after special case and you realise that the conventional wisdom is in itself a special case.

The thrust of these cases was that the game should end up in a *cul-de-sac* if the old view is correct. By practising and improving his pitch, spin, and speed the bowler should make scoring progressively more difficult, until it dries up altogether. M. divides the traditional view of the pitch of the ball into two aspects, the line and the length, intimating that different vectors might be required to strangle particular styles of batting. He then goes through different players and shows how the old boys would choose to stifle them effectively, and seems to present a pretty solid case for the orthodoxy to most eyes.

But it is demolished if one thinks of anything but an even contest between batsman and bowler. Imagine a village player facing Richardson.[106] The 'even' contest is a special case that we have come to think of as ordinary because of the activities of fixture secretaries! M. says a bad over from a skilled bowler with a badly-set field demonstrates the lowest type of productive efficiency yet may yield profit (in this case the 'interest' of wickets) if the batsman is extremely inept. Equally an abominable bowler may bowl

---

[106] Richardson the star Surrey bowler, who was one of *Wisden Almanack's* Five cricketers of 1896, but succumbed quickly to the setbacks and temptations of retirement and died aged 41, a heavy smoker and drinker.

THE DIARY ENTRIES

a tidy over to a capital batsman and be rewarded with maiden overs if the latter is just getting his eye in. Next over, the same deliveries might go for boundaries.

Context and psychology are all, and a sequence of results may produce a fad or fashion. The old guard's acceptance, for example, of deadening medium pace bowling to combat the runscoring revolution of Grace and Ranjitsinhji is not a sign of inevitability. Innovation will out! A tall bowler of pace, perhaps, or a spinner with new guiles will emerge, says M., beyond the imagination of the crowd.[107]

I wonder if Marshall in fact would be sympathetic to this view, at least in cricket if not in Economics?

> **TUESDAY.**
> (Before Dr. Cooper, presiding, the Mayor, the Master of Corpus Christi College, A. S. Campkin, G. Smith, and J. Burford, Esqs.)
>
> DISCHARGED. — Priscilla Mizzledine, 60, hawker, was charged with being drunk and disorderly, on East Road, on the previous day.—Prisoner was discharged with a caution.
>
> ADJOURNMENT.—Alfred Richard Gray, porter, Wheeler Street, was summoned for driving a handcart on the footpath, in Senate House Passage, on July 1.—On the application of the Chief Constable, the case was adjourned until October 20th.

---

[107] As mentioned in a footnote above: 'King's development of swing bowling, and Bosanquet's revolution in spin bowling' were about to impact on Edwardian cricket. In 1896, however, Bosanquet was purveying fast bowling for Eton in school matches.

THE DIARY ENTRIES

Nemesis
Monday, August 3rd, 1896

I remarked to Maynard that I had thought of a further teaser for him to incorporate into what we are now calling his 'Fenner's system'. He had dealt superbly with my queries about money and prices, and had come up with many concepts off his own bat, so to speak. But his patterns of trade between the counties depended on results (wins representing exports, defeats imports). These resembled flows of income earned from goods, services, profits, &c. Where, I asked, did the corresponding *capital* flows fit into this picture? He asked me to explain how exactly I meant this to be a challenge, since he had already taken up the idea of the Gold Standard and produced his expanded model of a managed system, with the authorities able to intervene through the laws of the game and the playing conditions of the competitions. I quickly sketched out how capital flowed in a global pattern, and he went off confident that this new problem was as soluble as all the others.[108]

---

[108] Students of Economics tend to have a very clear idea that the balance of payments must balance, and that the current account is where trade in goods and services come into the equation. They are less clear, however, about the capital account, particularly the distinction between earnings flows on the current account (like interest, profits, and dividends) and foreign direct investment, portfolio investment, and 'hot' money. It is generally a step too far for them to bear in mind additionally that the exchange rate is also involved in equilibrating these ever-changing flows. The situation has been far more complex since the U.K. abolished exchange controls in 1979 leading to a 'globalisation' similar to the international context in which J.M.K. was growing up.

THE DIARY ENTRIES

Nemesis
Tuesday, August 4th, 1896

Alas! The flood has burst, and, through my own fault, too soon has Maynard cast cricket aside to join the other detritus of juvenilia that once entertained and informed him. The final concept[109] that broke the spell seemed to me to be no more beyond his powers of imagination and assimilation than any other I had given him, but after exhaustive research, discussion, and analysis, M. has concluded that his Fenner's system cannot be made to accommodate the notion of a capital account on the balance of payments.

Worse, his exploration showed him that this drawback fundamentally undermined the usefulness of the whole project of creating a harmonious identity between cricket and economics for him.

---

[109] The realisation that changes in the capital account (*e.g.* a removal of 'hot' money or even portfolio investment, which is notionally 'long term') could, if the exchange rate couldn't take the strain, lead to constraints on trade and affect employment, seemed to knock the stuffing out of J.M.K. It seemed to negate the point of trying to improve competitiveness and to erode the possibility of trust between the factors of production and the government. The sorts of crises we have seen in Russia, Asia, Mexico, Brazil, the Exchange Rate Mechanism, etc., have all served to justify Keynes's view at Bretton Woods that fixed pegs with bands need some capital controls, support for deficit nations, and curtailment of surplus nations, in order to provide a stable international context for growth. It was not only simply *unfair* to leave the market-place totally open, but it would lead to unfavourable results for those who proposed it.

The disastrous events in Europe between 1945 and 1947 along with the speedy response of Marshall Aid (camouflaged through the free market Congress as an anti-communist measure) suggest that the U.S. quickly realised this, and Keynes's ghost would thoroughly have approved of the general developments in most of western Europe during the ensuing quarter-century.

THE DIARY ENTRIES

Nemesis
Wednesday, August 5th, 1896

Although at various moments this year I have become anxious and wished that the Fenner's system had not engulfed his attention to such a degree, I am at this moment heartbroken that it has ended this way. M. is consumed with a deep bitterness, almost hatred for the game now, as if it had deliberately toyed with his affections and jilted him.

I hope this will be temporary, and that he will retain an affection for this innocent, if slight, diversion in future years. There are, it seems to me, few better ways of maintaining a sense of direction and perspective in life wherever you might be in the world than comparing the real world with that you can perceive on the field of the cloth of cream.

We must now move on to the pressing concern of gaining the scholarship to Eton College for ourselves in 1897, and then Cambridge will be able to look after itself.[110]

Today, thank goodness, we left Cambridge for our holiday at Lealholm.

---

[110] As Keynes *père et fils* were turning their minds towards Eton, John Berry Hobbs, almost of an age with J.M.K., had just finished his formal schooling, and found employment as a servant at Jesus College.

HOW KUMAR SHREI RANJITSINHJI BECAME A CRICKETER.

How many people know the story of how Kumar Shrei Ranjitsinhji became a cricketer? It is barely seven years since the young Gozerati Prince—then only seventeen—first held a bat. He had just come over with two other students of the high caste to go through an English course of education, and Mr. W. Campbell Partridge describes in the *Birmingham Gazette* his first appearance as a spectator at a great English cricket match. Curiously enough, it was a match at the Oval against the Australians. Mr. Partridge says:—

As to their athletics, they were nil. The first visit to a gymnasium was absolutely ludicrous. The first racket was acquired at the same time, and "Ranjit" at once, as if to the manner born, began to display that wonderful wrist-play which, with a development of frame and strength, has become magnificent and made his name a household word throughout the civilised world. As to his knowledge of cricket, his first bat was not yet purchased nor had he yet seen a game, in England at all events. It was left for a visit to the Oval at the Surrey v. Australians match to kindle the enthusiasm which has had such remarkable results. A small club was in process of formation at Wormwood Scrubbs, for the Kumars and a few Indian students reading at a celebrated London crammer's, and things progressed very quietly for a few weeks, until a game was played in London, which was to alter the whole tenour of Ranjy's life, and the following are the facts, which the writer vouches for from personal participation in the circumstances, and concerning which he was talking to the Australian captain no longer than three weeks ago. During the 1889 Australian tour, one of the earliest matches was against Surrey, and the Kumars' tutor suggested a visit which was eagerly acquiesced in. By the courtesy of the Surrey secretary, to whom the incognito was privately explained, seats were given to the party on the top of the pavilion, and, very considerately, Mr. Allcock brought up some of the prominent members of the Australian team to chat with them, amongst whom were especially McDonnell, Scott, and G. H. S. Trott, the present captain. It was a glorious cricketing day, the Surreyites bowling and fielding superbly; while C. T. B. Turner made 105 runs and defied all attacks, so that it was a battle of giants and caused unbounded enthusiasm. None could be more delighted than the Indians, despite their native stolidity, and from that day dates Ranjy's determination to be a cricketer. It was for him actually the commencement. How well he has succeeded we all know. His name has been a foremost one for, it seems, several years: yet also it seems but the other day he learnt to hold a bat. The writer at all events bought his first and that was barely seven years ago.

It surely adds a chapter to the romance of cricket that this Indian stripling, seven years ago an alien and a stranger to our national game, should last week have been the hero of the English team in a great international encounter—knocking all over the field the bowling of the very Australian captain who, in 1889, kindly explained to him on the grand stand at the Oval the rudiments of the game!

First class cricket is going apace now, and since the Colonials have shown us what they can do with a representative English team pitted against them, the interest in the rest of the tour is assured. The hero of the hour is, without doubt, K. S. Ranjitsinhji, for not only does he lead the way in the batting averages, but he has the honour of being the first cricketer to score a century against the Australian team of 1896. And it was an innings too! George Giffen and his merry men strained every nerve to displace him, but the young Indian, whom we in Cambridge know so well, played some of his finest strokes, and when all his *confreres* received their quietus, his wicket still remained intact, with 154 standing to his credit —a truly magnificent performance, when it is considered that the cream of the bowling which is to be found in Australia was pitted against him. Another Cambridge cricketer who has been doing well lately is E. J. Diver, and on Saturday he scored his first century in intercounty cricket, although he has been playing first class cricket for many years. On the other hand, it is not his first 100 in a first class match, for whilst playing for Surrey he compiled 145 against Oxford University. Of Hayward's doings I have written many times and oft, and I am one of those who think that he should have played instead of A. C. Maclaren in the Manchester test match. Just notice the improvement. He is a good bat, and to put with that one of the best change bowlers of the day. Appended will be found the averages of Cambridge men in first class cricket:—

BATTING.

	No. of Inns.	Times not out.	Total runs.	Most in an Inns.	Avge.
K S Ranjitsinhji	32	4	1,703	171*	61·00
T Hayward	30	7	1,000	229*	43·47
S M J Woods	23	2	869	158*	41·38
C J Burnup	19	1	733	95	40·72
F S Jackson	26	3	925	117	40·21
O H M Wilson	15	2	456	82	35·07
H H Marriott	17	1	553	146*	34·56
H G Owen	15	4	379	82	34·45
E J Diver	22	1	707	112*	33·66
N F Druce	16	0	526	146	32·87
G J V Weigall	19	2	515	79	30·29
F Marchant	20	0	563	128	28·15
A O Jones	27	3	674	98	28·08
F Mitchell	15	0	391	110	26·06
W M Hemingway	21	1	493	104	24·65
Lord Hawke	26	4	529	166	24·04
H W Bainbridge	28	0	648	89	23·14
H Carpenter	25	1	528	161	22·00
C W Wright	22	1	438	114	20·85

BOWLING.

	Overs.	Mdns.	Runs.	Wkts.	Avg.
T Hayward	382·1	127	855	51	16·76
E B Shine	344·4	113	895	43	20·60
O E M Wilson	361	140	663	31	21·38
S M J Woods	316·3	109	763	35	21·80
F S Jackson	449	155	872	38	22·94
G L Jessop	409·1	110	1,125	44	25·56

Cambridge Chronicle 24/7/96
(Article syndicated throughout the U.K.)

Yesterday's Cricket.

M.C.C. AND GROUND v. ROYSTON DISTRICT.

This, which was to have been a two days' match, began and ended yesterday on Royston Heath. The home side were unable to get some of the players expected, and had to include a majority of the eleven from the Town Club. Gray, the old Cambridge bowler, and C. Pepper, of the Three Counties' Asylum team, did good service for the home team with the bat, and D. Hayward, O'Connor, and Gray with the ball, and Watts at the wicket proved useful. The bowling of Rawling and Richardson was, however, too strong. The home team made 73, and the visitors 113. With 40 to the bad, the home team could do nothing with the bowling of Rawling and Richardson, and, with the exception of Pepper, there was a regular collapse, which ended in a score of 36, or four less than required to save a single innings defeat. The visitors were therefore victorious by an innings and four runs, and the match ended just at the time for drawing stumps. The following is the score :—

ROYSTON AND DISTRICT.

H Gray, b Richardson ... 29	c Richardson, b Rawlin ... 8
D Hayward, b Richardson ... 4	c Richardson, b Rawlin ... 0
C Pepper, c Percy, b Rawlin .. 21	not out ... 22
Watts, b Richardson ... 0	c Carlin, b Rawlin ... 0
A T Titchmarsh, c C Warren, b Richardson ... 4	b Richardson ... 1
S Camps, c O Warren, b Rawlin ... 5	c Carlin, b Rawlin ... 0
R G Lush, c Warren, b Rawlin ... 3	c Carlin, b Rawlin ... 1
W O Titchmarsh, b Rawlin ... 2	b Richardson ... 0
O'Connor, b Richardson ... 0	c Flowers, b Richardson ... 0
E Shepherd, c Warren, b Rawlin ... 0	c Dr Murray, b Richardson ... 2
G Pickett, not out ... 0	c Flowers, b Rawlin ... 0
Extras ... 5	Extras ... 2
Total ... 73	Total ... 36

M.C.C. AND GROUND.

H M Barnes, st Watts, b Hayward	2
Rawlin, b O'Connor	10
Flowers, b Gray	46
T Attewell, b Hayward	0
Bean, b Hayward	0
Major Montresor, c A T Titchm'r'h, b O'C'nn'r	8
Carlin, b Gray	33
Dr. Murray, b Gray	3
Richardson, b Gray	5
C Warren, c Watts, b O'Connor	1
J Percy, not out	0
Extras	5
Total	113

HISTON v. GREAT ST. MARY'S.

Played on Parker's Piece last Saturday, when the first-named club won by 21 runs. Score :—

HISTON.		GREAT ST. MARY'S.	
W Sidney Gandy, b Richford	27	H Tebb, b F Saunders	17
Rev C A Barnes, c Sk's, b Richford	13	H Skoyles, c Willson, b F Saunders	4
J P Willson, c King, b Richford	1	P King, lbw, b W Saunders	7
F W Saunders, b Langly	0	H Richford, c & b F Saunders	13
W Saunders, c Pratt, b Langley	6	O Shanks, c Ingle, b W Saunders	1
W Ingle, not out	28	Langley, st Gandy, b W Saunders	4
F Peck, b Langley	2	J Pratt, b Saunders	4
E Toller, b Pratt	6	W Wells, not out	31
A E Saunders, c King, b Shanks	0	Wright, b J Willson	5
S Mowlam, run out	7	Allen, run out	0
G Tolliday, c Langley, b Shanks	9	Hemmings, c Gandy, b J Willson	0
Extras	18	Extras	4
Total	117	Total	96

VICTORIA v. OLD LEYSIANS.

These teams met on Parker's Piece on Monday in a match with 12 a side. The match was left a draw greatly in favour of the Victoria, for, with 256 to win, the Old Leysians only had one wicket to fall. Score :—

VICTORIA.		OLD LEYSIANS.	
H S French, c Dell, b Hayes	105	W E Walker, b Bryan	7
R Stearn, c Holden, b Willis	21	W R Bell, c O'Connor, b Bryan	4
H Gray, c G'll, b Gur'n	87	D Hayward, b O'Connor	0
V F de Lisle, c Holden, b Walker	16	J H Holden, c and b O'Connor	0
W E Warren, c & b P'ko	21	W O Willis, b Gray	5
H A Ellis, b Parke	0	M H Horsley, lbw, b H Gray	22
P W Gray, c Gurteen, b Hayes	40	L Walker, b H Gray	3
W Bryan, not out	25	J H Hayes, b O'Connor	7
R G Lush, b Hayes	0	T S Hill, c Fr'ch, b H Gr'y	7
W C Holt, b Hayward	0	H Thorpe, b O'Connor	0
J O'Connor, not out	10	A E Parke, not out	0
Extras	11	F W Gurteen, not out	0
		Extras	27
*Total (9 wks)	238	Total (10 wks)	82

*Innings declared closed. S French (captain) did not bat.

A good deal of nonsense has been written lately with reference to the inclusion of Ranjitsinhji in the English team, and the Lancashire Executive has had all sorts of accusations made against it. I place myself on the side of those who think that, after the decision arrived at by the Marylebone Club (which, after all, is the supreme head of the summer game), the Lancastrians committed an impolitic act by selecting the Indian ; but, at the same time, when a body is placed in authority to do a certain thing it seems a thousand pities that carping critics should indiscriminately throw out insinuations which are as groundless as they are foolish. Of course we in Cambridge have a distinct local feeling in the matter with reference to the non-inclusion of Hayward, but I am sure we are sportsmen enough not to seriously question the action of a body which undoubtedly is prompted by the purest of motives. If all goes well, young Tom will be seen in the third match, to be played at the Oval, and may he be a "shining light."

CRICKET.

M.C.C. AND GROUND v. CAMBRIDGESHIRE.

Pretty strong elevens were organised for this two days' fixture, which opened at Lord's on Thursday, July 16th. Rain sadly interfered with play, which was impossible after half-past one in the day. The M.C.C. batted first, and although Flowers was dismissed when only a single had been scored, they totalled 60 for the loss of four wickets before cricket had to be given up for the day. On Friday, a full day's play was witnessed. The Club only only added 59 to their previous day's total, being got rid of for 119. The county could only reply with 103. At the second attempt Marylebone did better, and after scoring 187 for the loss of two wickets, declared their innings closed. Cambridgeshire, wanting 204 runs to win, were got rid of a second time in just over two hours for 121, the last wicket falling a few minutes after the usual time for drawing of stumps (seven o'clock). The home club were, therefore, left victorious by 82 runs. Full score and analysis :—

M.C.C.

J. A. Gibbs, c Hayward, b O'Connor	26	b Gray 11
Flowers, b O'Connor	0	
Bean, G., c Hayward, b O'Connor	6	c Watts, b Hayward 46
Rawlin, c Coulson, b O'Connor	2	
O. C. Stone, c Winter, b Hayward	18	not out 41
H. B. Champain, b Gray	21	not out 77
C. H. M. Thring, b O'Connor	0	
Martin, b Gray	13	
Rev. E. A. Villiers, not out	15	
W. O. O. Ash, b Gray	0	
Pike, b O'Connor	1	
Extras	22	Extras 12
	119	*187

* Innings declared closed.

CAMBRIDGESHIRE.

W. N. Cobbold, b Martin	8	b Rawlin 4
W. L. B. Hayter, b Rawlin	14	c and b Rawlin 0
G. E. Winter, c Rawlin, b Martin	13	b Martin 16
F. Roberson, b Martin	2	st. Pike, b Bean 11
H. S. French, b Rawlin	30	b Rawlin 31
Hayward, D., b Martin	25	c Pike, b Rawlin 16
Coulson, b Rawlin	0	st. Pike, b Rawlin 3
Watts, l b w, b Martin	2	b Rawlin 11
V. F. de Lisle, b Rawlin	1	not out 5
H. Gray, not out	0	b Martin 0
O'Connor, c Ash, b Rawlin	0	c Rawlin, b Martin 14
Extras	8	Extras 10
	103	121

BOWLING ANALYSIS.

M.C.C.—First Innings.

	O.	M.	R.	W.
O'Connor	19.3	6	30	6
Hayter	12	2	44	1
Gray	7	2	23	3

Second Innings.

O'Connor	10	0	45	0
Gray	7	0	42	1
Coulson	12	0	46	0
Hayward	5	0	21	1
Hayter	4	0	21	0

CAMBRIDGESHIRE.—First Innings.

Rawlin	23.3	7	42	5
Martin	23	7	50	5
Bean	2	1	3	0

Second Innings.

Martin	23.3	4	41	3
Rawlin	26	10	58	6
Bean	6	2	12	1

CAMBS. CRICKET ASSOCIATION CUP.

OLD PERSEANS v. SAWSTON.

This match was played at Sawston on Saturday, and resulted in a win for the visitors by 16 runs. Scores :—

OLD PERSEANS.

R. Swann Mason, c Riddle, b Stubbings	4
H. Gray, b Stubbings	9
V. F. de Lisle, b Falkner	1
W. E. Warren, c and b Falkner	0
F. K. Robinson, b Falkner	11
J. H. Widdicombe, b Edwards	33
H. A. Hancock, b Riddle	12
W. R. Gurley, b Riddle	2
A. N. Mason, b Stubbings	1
R. J. Fuller, b Stubbings	0
G. Roper, not out	1
Extras	6
	80

SAWSTON.

J. C. Falkner, b Gray	9
O. Riddle, c Warren, b Widdicombe	14
G. Freestone, b Gray	0
H. G. Edwards, c Fuller, b Gray	3
J. J. Bailey, b Gray	3
A. F. Beagle, b Swann Mason	26
J. J. Curtis, run out	2
J. Ward, b Swann Mason	2
F. Stubbings, b Gray	0
S. K. Hughes, b Gray	0
G. Churchman, not out	3
Extras	2
	64

HINTON C.C. v. GREAT ST. MARY'S C.C.—This match was decided on Parker's Piece last Saturday, when the first named club came off victorious by 21 runs. The country club had the services of Mr. W. Sidney Gaudy, the well-known society entertainer, of London, and formerly a resident of Hinton. Mr. Gandy not only distinguished himself behind the wickets, as he so frequently used to when playing for his old club, but contributed a most useful and faultless score of 27. Mr. W. Ingle also played a useful innings for his 28 not out. For the losers, Mr. Wells carried out his bat for a creditable 31. Scores :—

HINTON C.C.

W. Sidney Gandy, b Richford	27
Rev. C. A. Barnes, c Skoyles, b Richford	13
J. P. Willson, c King, b Richford	1
F. Saunders, b Langley	0
W. Saunders, c Pratt, b Langley	6
W. Ingle, not out	28
F. Peck, b Langley	2
K. Toller, b Pratt	6
A Saunders, c King, b Shanks	0
S. Mowlam, run out	7
G. Tolliday, c Langley, b Shanks	9
Extras	18
	117

GREAT ST. MARY'S C.C.

H. Tobb, b F. Saunders	17
H. Skoyles, c J. Willson, b F. Saunders	4
P King, lbw, b W. Saunders	7
H. Richford, c and b F. Saunders	13
O. Shanks, c Ingle, b W. Saunders	1
S. Langley, st Gandy, b W Saunders	4
J. Pratt, b F. Saunders	0
W. Wells, not out	31
Wright, b J. Willson	5
Allen, run out	6
Hemmings, c Gandy, b Willson	0
Extras	4
	96

Cambridge Express 25/7/96

CAMBRIDGE DIVISION PETTY SESSIONS

SATURDAY:—Before Mr. H. W. Pemberton (chairman), Dr. MacAlister, and Messrs. A. Gee, W. W. Olear and J. Beater.

"THE RIVER KING."

Thomas Rickwood, Water-street, Chesterton, was summoned for taking eels from the river Cam, over which the Cambridge and Ely Angling Society had a private right of fishing, at Chesterton, on July 6.—He pleaded guilty.—Mr S. J. Miller prosecuted on behalf of the Society..—P.s. Dean said he saw the prisoner take four eels from the river. When questioned, Rickwood said he was getting a few "reptiles." Mr. Carmichael, of Ely, and Dr. Cooper had given him permission. He (P.s. Dean) replied that he knew Dr. Cooper had christened him "the River King," but he did not give him permission to take eels.—The man was fined 10s. and costs, or in default 14 days' hard labour. He was next charged with stealing a tame duck, value 2s. 6d., the property of Thomas Banyard, farmer, at Ditton, on July 14. Mrs Peachey, said she saw Rickwood pass her house at 5 15 a.m.—Sergeant Warren said he saw the man go into a public-house. Suspecting that something was wrong he went after him. He said "You brought something into the house with you, Rickwood." Defendant replied "It's a lie." On searching the taproom, however, he found a sack with the duck in it, under a settle. When charged defendant said "You'll have to find an owner for it." —Mr. Banyard identified the duck.—Rickwood said he caught the bird on the river.—On the charge being read over the prisoner said, "You might as well hang me at once." He was committed for trial at the Quarter Sessions.

CHESTERTON YOUTHS.

William Chapman, Arthur Masters, George Coxall, Walter Stanford, William Barton and Samuel Fordham, all of Chesterton, were summoned for damaging grass, the property of Mr. J. S. Few, of the value of 1s., at Chesterton, on Sunday, July 5.—Mr. S. J. Miller appeared for complainant.—P s. Warren said he watched the field in consequence of complaints from Mr. Few. He saw the lads playing banker there. He went after them and got possession of some cards and money. A considerable space had been quite stripped of herbage.—Chapman had been convicted twelve times before, and several of the others had also been convicted three for gaming.—Chapman was fined £2, Stanford 10s., Masters, Coxall and Barton 5s, and Fordham 2s. 6d, with costs.

ELY PETTY SESSIONS.

THURSDAY.—Before O Bidwell, A J Pell, Esqs, and Colonel Baldwin.

DRUNKENNESS.—Absolom Taylor, of Littleport, was charged with being drunk at that place on 23rd of June, also with assaulting Samuel Heffer, of Downham, at the same time; ordered to pay 5s. for the first offence, and 6d. fine and 11s. costs for the assault.

SCHOOL CASES.—For neglecting to send their children to school the following persons were summoned:—Littleport, Walter Cragg, adjourned for three months; Elijah Somerlee, paid 5s; Samuel Durham, medical certificate produced, case dismissed. Phœbe Smith, 5s; Jacob King, adjourned for three months; Herbert Malt, 5s. In the case of Newell, of the Adelaide, which had been adjourned, it was stated that the child regularly attended school, which was satisfactory.

PERSE SCHOOL v. C.E.Y.M.S. — Played Parker's Piece on Thursday. Scores :—

PERSE SCHOOL.

Mr. Swann Mason, b Plumb	22
Mr. Widdicombe, c Wootten, b Church	37
H. A. Hancock, b Bevis	24
S. L. Porter, b Lawson	15
Mr. Gurley, b Church	0
G. Wiles, b Bevis	1
Whiteley, b Bevis	13
G. Lambert, b Bevis	0
Sherlock, c Plumb, b Lawson	14
Skelton, b Bevis	3
James, not out	1
Extras	7
	147

C.E.Y.M.S.

S. A. Wootten, c and b Swann Mason	0
A. Bevis, b Swann Mason	18
F. Miesen, b Wiles	21
E. H. Church, c Hancock, b Wiles	75
G. Roper, b Wiles	0
G. W. Lawson, c Porter, b Swann Mason	23
E. Plumb, b Wiles	0
G. H. Barnsdale, c Skelton, b Wiles	2
W. Betteridge, b Swann Mason	0
H. W. Marfleet, c Hancock, b Swann Mason	4
H. Pratt, not out	4
Extras	0
	147

M.C.C. AND GROUND v. ROYSTON AND DISTRICT. Played on Royston Heath on Thursday. The home team were short of some of their expected players. Scores :—

M.C.C. AND GROUND.

H. M. Barnes, st Watts, b Hayward	2
Rawlin, b O'Connor	10
Flowers, b Gray	46
T. Attewell, b Hayward	0
Bean, b Hayward	0
Major Montresor, c A. T. Titchmarsh, b O'Connor	8
Carling, b Gray	33
Dr. Murray, b Gray	3
Richardson, b Gray	5
C. Warren, c Watts, b O'Connor	1
T. Percy, not out	0
Extras	6
	113

VICTORIA v. OLD LEYSIANS.—This was a twelve-a-side match played on Parker's Piece on Monday and drawn very much in favour of Victoria, who having scored 338, declared their innings closed at twenty minutes past four. Scores :—

VICTORIA.

H. S. French, c Bell, b Hayes	105
R. Stearn, c Holden, b Willis	21
H. Gray, c Bell, b Gurteen	67
V. F. de Lisle, c Holden, b Walker	16
W. E. Warren, c and b Parke	21
H. A. Ellis, b Parke	0
P. W. Gray, c Gurteen, b Hayes	40
W. Bryan, not out	25
R. G. Lush, b Hayes	40
W. O. Holt, b Hayward	2
J. O'Connor, not out	10
Extras	11
*Total (9 wkts)	338

*Innings declared closed.
S. French (capt.) did not bat.

OLD LEYSIANS.

W. E. Walker, b Bryan	7
W. R. Bell, c O'Connor, b Bryan	4
D. Hayward, b O'Connor	0
J. H. Holden, c and b O'Connor	0
W. O. Willis, b Gray	5
M. H. Horsley, l b w, b H. Gray	22
L. Walker, b H. Gray	3
J. H. Hayes, b O'Connor	7
T. S. Hill, c Sid. French, b H. Gray	7
H. Thorpe, b O'Connor	0
A. E. Parker, not out	0
F. W. Gurteen, not out	0
Extras	27
	82

CAMBRIDGE BOROUGH POLICE v. CORPORATION EMPLOYES.—Played on Trinity College ground on Saturday. Scores:—
Corporation Employes.—W. Wisbey, c Lilley, b Rackham, 12; R. Walls, b Rackham, 6; W. Baker, b Rackham, 0; S. Newbold, b Rackham, 10; O. J. Gray, b Simmonds, 3; A. Barham, c Rackham, b Williamson, 17; W. Hoyl, b Rackham, 5; W. McCarthy, c Simmonds, b Rackham, 0; W. Edwards, not out, 7; P. Cole, b Rackham, 0; G. Ellis, st Hurst, b Rackham, 0; extras, 2; total, 62.
Police.—Simmonds, run out, 6; Sharman, c and b Newbold, 0; Williamson, c Wisbey, b Gray, 21; Lilley, b McCarthy, 4; Simmons, run out, 4; Hurst, b Gray, 10; Doggett, l b w, b Newbold, 6; Rackham, c and b Newbold, 8; Savidge, c Baker, b Newbold, 0; Caswell, not out, 0; Cook, b Newbold, 0; extras, 9; total, 68.

OLD BRITISH BOYS v Y M C.A. 2ND XI.—Played on Parker's Piece on Thursday, and won by the Y.M.C.A. by four runs, the scores being Y.M.C.A. 70, Old British Boys 66.

LEYS SCHOOL v. BEDFORD MODERN SCHOOL.—Played on Saturday. Scores:—
LEYS SCHOOL.
W. S. A. Brown, c Knox, b Foulkes .. 52
A. B. Horsley, c Bull, b Groves 18
L. Walker, b Groves 0
H. D. Wyatt, c Owen, b Groves 49
J. E. Walker, b Foulkes 9
J. T. Tulloch, b Foulkes 0
H. D. Brown, l b w, b Foulkes 4
H. A. Morgan, b Foulkes 33
W. Spicer, c Bull, b Foulkes 39
F. O. Trapnell, c Groves, b, Foulkes .. 7
W. B. Beckett, not out 8
Extras 15
—
214

BEDFORD MODERN SCHOOL.
R. D. Richmond, c and b W. S. A. Brown 24
E. H. Philbrick, b Beckett 19
P. Foulkes, l b w, b Beckett 0
E. C. Knox, c Morgan, b W. S. A. Brown 6
F. C. Evans, run out 15
F. H. Bull, c Horsley, b J. E. Walker 6
G. G. Warder, c Brown, b J. E. Walker 1
W. Owen, not out 23
J. H. Cantrell, b W. S. A. Brown 1
K. J. C. Groves, b W. S. A. Brown.... 0
O. L. Fullinson, b L. Walker 1
Extras 17
—
113
Second Innings—91 for two wickets (P. Foulkes not out 46, Owen 32).

BEDFORD v. VICTORIA.—Played on Parker Piece on Wednesday. Scores:—
BEDFORD.
A. S. Richardson, c Thomas, b O'Connor 6
J. E. Willett, b Bryan 3
H. Tebb, b Bryan 0
W. P. Bensley, b Bryan 0
G. F. Tendall, b O'Connor 0
A. J. Green, c Gray, b Bryan 21
T. G. Devitt, b Gray 13
G. Edwards, b Bryan 31
A. W. Sale, not out 8
E. N. Vipan, c O'Connor, b Gray 4
H. Wyatt Smith, c Whibley, b Gray .. 13
Extras 11
—
112

VICTORIA.
H. S. French, c Wyatt Smith, b Green 24
R. Stearn, b Sale 78
H. Gray, c Tebb, b Sale 105
R. Swann-Mason, c Sale, b Tendall .. 21
A. B. Whibley, c Bensley, b Tendall.. 55
P. Gray, l b w, b Green 9
W. Bryan, c Tebb, b Tendall 3
C. H. Parish, not out 12
J. O'Connor, c Bensley, b Tendall ... 16
Extras 29
—
Total for 8 wickets.. 351
W. Thomas and R. G. Lush absent.

SPORT AND PLAY

GOSSIP UPON CURRENT SPORTS AND PASTIMES.

The Australians showed in the second test match last week that they do not deserve to be spoken of so slightingly as has been done on several occasions during their tour. In the first match they were decidedly off colour. Some of their players were beginning to feel the effect of a change of climate and others had been hurt, so they were far from being up to their average form. Since that defeat they have improved wonderfully, and the second England team did not prove equal to holding them. It is rather strange that the home players should have failed as they did at the wicket, for Manchester, wet place as it usually is, altogether escaped the rain, and the conditions were, therefore, favourable to good batting.

The Australians, who won the toss, soon shewed that the wicket was in a satisfactory state. Iredale, rising Phoenix-like from the ashes of his misfortunes, made 108, and with the exception of Hills and Jones, all the players made double figures, including "Mr. Byes," the total reached by the Colonials being the magnificent one of 412. They fairly broke the hearts of our bowlers, seven of whom were tried against them; the best record was obtained by Richardson, who took seven wickets at an average cost of 24 runs.

England made a wretched start, W. G. Grace and A. E. Stoddart both being stumped for very few runs. Ranjitsinhji and Abel improved matters, but the Indian Prince and Lilley alone did themselves justice, and the side collapsed for 231, after batting nearly three hours and a half, of course obliging a follow on. Going in again, 181 to the bad, England lost four wickets for 109 runs, so that a severe task was left them for Saturday.

The match concluded on Saturday in very exciting fashion. The Australians won, but only by three wickets, and thanks, firstly, to the magnificent batting of Ranjitsinhji and, secondly, to some superb bowling by Richardson, at one time victory looked quite likely to slip away from their grasp. The winning stroke was only made twenty-five minutes before the time fixed for the drawing of stumps, and the flight of time all added to the interest provoked by the encounter.

The popularity of Ranjitsinhji is beyond question, and if any doubt about it existed the reception he received from the Lancashire crowd on going to the wicket shewed how widely esteemed he is by cricket loving people, and was also convincing evidence of the approval of the crowd of the action of the Selection Committee in giving him a place in an England team. Ranjitsinhji, fortunately, came off in both innings.

Cambridgeshire lost to the M.C.C. and Ground, and very much through ill-luck, more than a fair quantity of which seems to dog the footsteps of the county players. They held their own very well in the first innings, being only 16 runs behind, but Bean, C. O. Stone, and H. B. Champain fairly collared the bowling in the second, which was closed at 187 for a loss of two wickets. Cambridgeshire tried hard to save defeat, but they lost by 82 runs. I am very sorry for it, for it is very discouraging that so good a team as was sent up—nearly the full strength of the county—should have been beaten in this way. May better fortune attend the next venture.

In local cricket matches the Victoria has been compiling big scores. H. Saunders French has done remarkably well with the bat, and his success has been followed by others. H. Gray has lately developed into a run getter. He, with Bryan and O'Connor, has lately been bowling with effect, but the Old Persean's chief success during the week has been with the willow. Connoisseurs of the sport have been delighted with a couple of fine innings, Gray having on Monday run up 87, eclipsing the performance on Wednesday with 105 against Bedford.

Who's going to have the *Express* £5 note next week? is a question a good many people have asked themselves and their friends lately. Next Friday night our readers will be aware of the name of the fortunate possessor who will get the note by post on Saturday morning, August 1st. Hurry up with your collections, everybody! I see Wednesday next is the last day for sending in coupons.

The old boys of the Perse and Higher Grade Schools have beaten Sawston and the Camden, and qualify for the semi-finals. The success of both teams was only what was expected, but neither team achieved victory without affording plenty of excitement to onlookers. The final is likely to be contested between the first-named two clubs, but cricket, as I have often remarked before, is such a glorious uncertain game, that one may be prepared for surprises.

Quite one of the best school boys Cambridge has developed is W. S. A. Brown, of the Leys. In the School matches, this young gentleman has totalled over 1,000 runs, and has compiled innings of 128 not out, 102, 102 not out, 109 not out, 178, and 154 not out. It falls to the lot of very few cricketers to make a hundred half dozen times in one season. Brown is not only a very wonderful batsman for a school boy, but is an excellent bowler, and is not unlikely to occupy a very conspicuous place in future cricket, whether he finally decides to play for Gloucestershire or Cambridgeshire.

Our champion cricketer, W. G. Grace, reached his 48th birthday on Saturday.

Diver made a very good innings on Friday against Essex, playing very merry cricket for 67, one of his strokes lifting the ball clean over the pavilion.

In the County Championship the following are the relative positions up to date:—

	P.	W.	L.	D.	Pts.	Finshd in Games.
Yorkshire	18	11	2	5	9	18
Surrey	17	13	3	1	10	16
Lancashire	12	9	3	0	6	12
Middlesex	8	5	2	1	8	6
Notts	9	4	3	2	1	7
Essex	7	3	3	1	0	5
Hampshire	9	3	4	2	—1	7
Derbyshire	11	3	5	3	—2	8
Sussex	9	2	5	2	—3	7
Kent	9	2	5	1	—4	8
Somerset	10	2	5	2	—4	8
Leicestershire	8	1	6	1	—5	7
Gloucestershire	11	2	7	2	—5	9
Warwickshire	12	2	7	3	—5	9

The 'bus competition has introduced a new form of pleasure and recreation to Cambridge people, which they have been by no means slow to avail themselves of. For a penny one can now get a ride from the Town to Chesterton or to the Railway Station, and many there are who now enjoy this new form of carriage exercise. I may be wrong, but it seems to me that these 1d. rides have given quite an impetus to vehicular travelling in Cambridge. The tops of the trams seem to be fuller than they used to be, and certainly the Tram 'buses cannot complain of want of patronage. It really looks as if both Companies (the Tramways and the Omnibus) might live and pay a dividend.

A friend of mine sent me a paper the other day, and though I may be infringing the rights of your "Sport and Play" column, I cannot help quoting the following opinion of Prince Ranjitsinhji, which was evoked by his play in the second test match against the Australians. "When the time comes to chronicle Ranji's feats," says the *Morning Leader*, " he will want a book all to himself, for another like him never has been, and, probably enough, never again will be. Mr. Grace is greater, and his power of placing a ball has never been approached by anyone, certainly it is not by the Indian Prince; but Mr. Grace's play is not elegance, and it is the combination of elegance and skill which so specially distinguishes the agile Asiatic amongst cricketers as to make him the single representative of his class."

Sports and Pastimes.

Notes by "The Wanderer."

Next week will be busy for the Cambs. County Cricket Club, and, given fine weather, three enjoyable matches against the Marylebone Club, Norfolk, and Oxfordshire should be played. The return match against the Metropolitans opens the ball, and if the team sent down is not too strong, our men should render a good account of themselves, as I understand that the Executive has been fortunate enough to secure an excellent side. F. Roberson, H. S. French, H. Gray, E. M Butler, P. Cornell, P. Hattersley-Smith, G. E Winter, with Dan Hayward, Watts, O'Connor, and Coulson are expected to play during the week, and partisans of coun'y cricket will be disappointed if an eleven picked from those do not distinguish themselves in one or another department of the game. Several other useful cricke'ers are available, amongst them being G. Diver, whose fast bowling, whilst he resided in Cambridge, caused destruction in many camps, but this particular branch is well represented by Horace Gray and Cornell. Urgent professional duties will, in all probability, prevent raunders French taking part in all the fixtures, but he is likely to figure against Oxford. It seems that all that is wanted is the support of the Cambridge public (for two out of the three matches will be played on the University Cricket Ground), and I hope that, for once in a way, sportsmen (and I am sure there are many) will rally round their old county, and see what can be done to pull it out of a position which, to say the least, is unenviable.

Four clubs are left in for the Cambs. Cricket Association Cup Tie, viz, Old Higher Grade, Liberals, Old Perseans, and Y.M.C.A, and as the semi-finals are to be played off by August 15th, the clubs interested are busy preparing for the fray. The old Perse boys should have no difficulty in disposing of the representatives from Alexandra-street, but the game between the Old Higher Grade and the Liberals should be a hard struggle. Various dates have been suggested, but the difficulty which now exists is the clashing with the county fixtures. It is rumoured that the politicians will have a strong side, including E. Briggs (who is playing in fine form at Northampton just now), H. Edwards, H. Tebb, G. Woodcock, T. M. Phillips, F. Brinkley, S. Newbold, and H. Skoyles, but with this average local talent pitted against them, the Old Boys are not to be treated lightly. R Stearn and his *confreres* have shown supporters of Parker's Piece cricket what they can do, and it would not at all surprise me if, in spite of the team that the Old Perseans are capable of putting in the field, the cup once more found its way into the possession of the Old Higher Grade. I think I have previously written that it is on the cards that Dan Hayward and George Watts are likely to appear for the O.H.G.'s.

Cambridge Independent Press 31/7/96

The Leys School cricket season of 1896 will long be remembered as W. S. A. Brown's senr, and I very much doubt whether any public school cricketer has equalled his performances. To score over a thousand runs in 16 innings does not fall to the lot of many first class cricketers, and it is a performance of which he may feel justly proud. He also stands at the top of the bowling averages, having captured 57 wickets for 593 runs The record stands : Won, ten ; lost, one : drawn, four. Appended are the batting and bowling averages :—

BATTING.

	No. of Ings.	Tms not out.	Most in an Ings.	Total Runs.	Aver.
W S A Brown	16	4	154*	1,032	86
H D Brown	13	9	37*	178	44·50
H D Wyatt	15	5	101*	383	33·30
T E Walker	13	1	123*	377	31·42
L Walker	16	0	141	391	24·44
A B Horsley	12	1	115*	239	21·72
J T Tulloch	12	0	47	164	13 66
F C Trapnell	3	1	19*	26	13 00
H A Morgan	6	1	53	58	11·60
N Spicer	12	0	39	87	7 25
W B Beckett	6	1	10	35	7 00
L J Willis	4	1	4	8	2 66

* Signifies not out.

WILLINGHAM v. TRINITY COLLEGE SERVANTS.

Played on Tuesday at Willingham, and resulted in a victory for the visitors by two runs.

WILLINGHAM.
A Ingle, b Marshall .. 2
E Ellwood, b Bryan .. 3
E Jones, b Bryan 2
P Poulter, b Bryan... 0
S Ingle, not out 34
W Ingle, b Marshall .. 3
J Few, c Anable, b Bryan 8
O Smith, b Bryan 9
C Hayden, b Bryan... 0
H Childs, c Auable, b Bryan 1
A Kidd, b Bryan 0
Extras 10
Total 62

TRINITY COLLEGE SERVANTS.
H Clarke, b Poulter .. 31
Crohill, b Jones 3
W Bryan, b Poulter.... 15
D Marshall, c W Ingle, b Poulter 8
A Hopkin, b Hayden .. 2
A Hunt, run out...... 0
Lander, run out 0
Nobbs, c Few, b Hayden 2
Brown, c Jones, b Hayden 0
Anable, c Poulter, b Hayden............ 0
Gadsby, not out 0
Extras 8
Total........ 64

CAMBS. v. M.C.C.—This match will take place on Bank Holiday and Tuesday. The Cambs. team will be as follows:—E M Butler, F Roberson, P H Smith, H Gray, G E Winter, P W Cornell, Hayward, O'Connor, Coulson, Watts, and Brown.

On Friday and Saturday Cambs. will meet Oxfordshire. The team will be chosen from the following, in addition to those given above :— H S French, Rev E R Douglas, A Hayward, and H Edwards.

POLICE INTELLIGENCE.

CAMBRIDGE DIVISION PETTY SESSIONS.

SATURDAY.—Before Messrs. W. W. Clear, J. Bester, and Dr. Kenny and Dr. Donald MacAlister.

DRUNK AND DISORDERLY.

Charles Gibbs, a labourer, of Stapleford, was summoned for being drunk and disorderly at Stapleford on July 11th.—Defendant pleaded guilty.—Mr. Alfred Miller Barker, the parish constable, proved seeing the defendant drunk and disorderly. He gave information to the police.—Defendant was fined 10s., including costs.

WITHDRAWN.

Edward Webb, of Shelford, was charged with threatening to kill his father, John Webb, on July 22nd.—The complainant asked that the case might be withdrawn, the defendant having promised to be better than before.—This was allowed by the Bench.

CAMBRIDGE BOROUGH POLICE COURT.

TUESDAY.—Before Messrs. A. S. Campkin and J. Burford.

POTATO THROWING.

Sidney Burgess (17), labourer, of 4, Dover-street, was summoned for throwing pieces of potatoes in Brandon-lane, on July 22nd.—Defendant pleaded guilty.—Warrant Officer Evans saw the defendant throwing pieces of potatoes at pigeons.—Defendant was dismissed with a caution.

An Article Compiled During September 1905

PART TWO

Australian Summer Reprise: The Keynes Family And Cricket

My father took his bride to live in a newly built semi-detached house on the outskirts of the town. At the end of Harvey Road to the East was Fenner's cricket ground.

(Geoffrey Keynes, 'The Early Years')

GOLDEN AGES AT THE FENNER'S MARGIN

In July 1897 J.M.K. won a scholarship to Eton, tenth out of twenty scholars, and at seventeen was elected to 'Pop' (the exclusive debating society). He played well at the Wall Game and took a casual interest in rowing; cricket was left in the margins. In that era of 'Prizes' he piled up the awards; the Chamberlayne Prize for coming top in the Higher Certificate Examinations in 1901 brought him £60 a year for four years.

In October 1902 he went up to King's College, Cambridge, on an open scholarship in Mathematics and Classics, becoming a member of the Apostles and President of the Union at the turn of 1905. He completed his mathematical studies that summer and was about to embark on a fourth year at Cambridge studying Economics when he wrote this essay.

AN ARTICLE COMPILED DURING SEPTEMBER 1905

It is now barely a month since 'breakfast' meant the spartan dining room of the Montenvers Hotel, followed by a combination of busy Chamonix social froth and the wild Alpine slopes. The experience of these at first hand, as opposed to the glamorous myths surrounding such figures as Leslie Stephen, led me to ponder; could any environs could be finer than tea and toast in bed at Harvey Road with the knowledge that a cricket match was soon to start on the somewhat flatter acres just across the road? Now, returned safe to haven, I breakfast with Pigou who, although devoted to Kent cricket, is equally keen to discuss the plans for a railway to the Sea of Ice[1] and the likelihood of avalanches at Argentières this winter. It is no wonder that I try to hurry him off sports and onto my new passion, Political Economy.

The dwindling evenings and the noisy press plaudits oblige me to acknowledge that another Australian summer of cricket has come to an end. This is the fifth of which I have been conscious, but it only serves to remind one of the sweetest and most pregnantly significant; the tour of 1896, which affected me deeply even though the Australians didn't have a fixture at Fenner's. The changes of season and of study also prompt me to wonder quite how much cultural baggage a child of Harvey Road carries around in his head years after it might seem reasonable for a polite jettisoning to take place, and how both the individual and social memories contained therein are taken for granted? For I believe it is fairly straightforward to shew that 6, Harvey Road was (and is) at the margin of two of the mightiest cricketing nurseries in the Empire, which could not fail to leave their mark upon an inquisitive child being brought up there during the final ascent to the summit of the Victorian Age.

I have been quoted as saying that if the theory and history, but not the practice, of cricket were to be examined I would do well in the subject;[2] this is still my contention, although I do not follow county or Test cricket closely in the press and rarely go to the cricket at Fenner's, Eton, or Lord's any more. However, given my upbringing I will always be able to claim an intimate understanding of what happens on the field of the cloth of cream, although it is clear, to be fair, that I am no performer. This is hardly an insurmountable problem, however; nobody deprecates the opinion of the music critic of *The Times* because he is terrible at playing the cor anglais or, for that matter, at bowling lobs.

These musings were fed by my father turning through his diaries for that 1896 summer and also by the unearthing of an old exercise book in which I collected cricketana for about two years. Stimulated by these treasures, I have tried to encapsulate some flavour of that watershed year when W.G. with his hundred centuries was eclipsed by the exciting new record-breaker, Parker's Piece's very own Prince, Kumar Shri Ranjitsinhji. What sort of cricket did I grow up with, and what sort of effects may this time-consuming passion have had on me? The answer to the first question, to judge from the Wisden Almanack of 1897, is very good, if not quite the best, cricket of the both old school and the new Golden Age. My memory is that players like Thornton still eschewed pads and gloves, even against Jessop, while Ranji was both technically and artistically a precursor of the new century. The Australian visit to our shores in 1896 was during a hot, high-scoring summer, and the University had good wins over Yorkshire and Somerset which were inspiring

GOLDEN AGES AT THE FENNER'S MARGIN

For J.M.K. Montenvers and Chamonix were more like a prison than a romantic nirvana. In 2002 the former could still take on an austere appearance.

to watch. M.C.C.'s visit induced awe rather than interest, W.G.Grace and Ranjitsinhji sharing the same field. The key freshman was Jessop, and the captain was Frank Mitchell, later to play for both England and South Africa. The Varsity match was highly controversial and entertaining, producing a correspondence in *The Times* that set brother (Hon. E.H. Lyttelton) against brother (Lord Cobham). The local Cambridge hero, Tom Hayward, was on song for both Surrey and England. As to the question of the season's effect on my life, this essay can be but a preliminary answer given in a somewhat perambulatory manner, for one can argue that it is still too soon to tell.

A thirteen-year-old keeping records of the 1894–6 seasons produces a misleading image of an ardent swain swooning at the feet of flannelled Corinthians, vowing to follow in the train of the deity (that is, W. G.)[3], and sucking at a pencil and noting down individual runs while seeking to understand nothing of the context within which they happen.[4] Nothing could be further from the truth, however. Perusing again that child's exercise book[5] I find it contains hand-written humorous epitaphs, a stock of riddles, a timeline of what I then considered to be the most significant historical events (only Mahomet, Charlemagne, William the Conqueror, the Reformation, and the French Revolution merit a mention after the life of Christ), plus some rather more carefully collected and significant cricket items.

148

AN ARTICLE COMPILED DURING SEPTEMBER 1905

The cuttings are from an unidentified daily national newspaper and date from the day after the end of the first-class season in September 1894, September 1895, and September 1896. This is not some passing fad. To do this I must have been organised enough to get the same newspaper on the correct day each year and keep track of this particular exercise book. The choices also show a remarkable lack of partisan feeling; I was looking at the game at an overall level,[6] one might say. Thirdly, it was preserved; it was important enough to me and to my father for it to be kept.

The first set of clippings go into the 1894 Surrey-Lancashire tie in detail, and lists Stoddart's team for Australia (including Cambridge University blue F. G. J. Ford). The complete county and first class averages show Hayward (playing for Surrey, but very much of Cambridge) to be 5th in both the batting and the bowling. The section is simply headed in hand-written ink 'Cricket 1894'. The same set of cuttings is pasted in a year later under a similar ink inscription, but there is an additional large hand-written message; 'Cambridge beat Oxford'.

The 1896 section is the largest, with a special report on the Australian tour, plus a review of the season which says that the weather for May – July was superb, and that W.G. was 'simply miraculous'. Spofforth was top of the bowling averages with 23 wickets at 9.4 runs apiece. The most striking table is of a format now rarely used. A list of the 18 first-class teams (14 counties plus the universities, Australia, and M.C.C.) shows the pecking order in terms of batting (runs per wicket) and bowling (ditto). Cambridge comes 2nd only to Yorkshire in the batting list, but is one below Oxford at 11th in the bowling. The totals are a statistician's delight, showing of course the total runs scored to be the same in each list.

Here, then, are nearly thirty pages of exercise book devoted to a detailed but wide-ranging and medium-term overview of the game in England, containing details relating to the greatest players of the age. I was aware that the batting averages had an 'exceptionally heavy character' in the words of the newspaper's commentator. I knew that despite W.G.'s hundredth hundred in 1895 a new age was dawning with Ranji, C. B. Fry, and Jessop. I knew that I had seen cricket in which the bowlers had struggled. I knew that controversy and changes of the law were continuously not only under consideration, but also carried out. The weight of this knowledge and understanding resonated far beyond considerations of just cricket.[7]

The amusing series of jottings made by my father between April and August 1896 is clearly a farewell to my youth and were written out of necessity, it seems, rather than whimsy, almost as a purge. He realised how crucial the coming campaign to acquire my scholarship would be, and also how severely taxing it would prove to be. I cannot really recollect any of the attributions made to me and my father seemed to layer huge folds of meaning over trivia which now seem manic in places. Why, crucially, should I break with Marshall when all he has done is to describe and partially explain that which truly exists in the world of political economy? These wobbles seem to reflect my father's character rather than mine. This *opus* has very little of interest.

GOLDEN AGES AT THE FENNER'S MARGIN

My father's official diary, although leaner, is much more instructive and of far greater value; for here was a man who was so busy, so precisely conscientious, almost unnaturally engaged in the detail and quantity of his workload, whose working year was culminating in a tidal wave of examinations, and yet we can find references to Fenner's as if it was the back garden. Indeed, our back garden is not mentioned once, but there is a sound geographical explanation for this.

To walk home from the Fenner's Pavilion we would at once cross Gresham Road to the corner of Harvey Road, immediately cross that road itself, and then walk down it to the third house. The distance from the Pavilion front door to 6, Harvey Road's front door was exactly sixty six yards as the batsmen sprint three runs. There were no intervening buildings, so from front window to front window you could communicate by semaphore, were it not for three inconvenient Fenner's trees. Indeed the Fenner's Pavilion is on such a tilt as to be directly pointing at 6, 7, and 8 Harvey Road.

After several examinations of the classic 1902 photograph of Fawcett's[8] 1874–7 Fenner's Pavilion in Ford's History of Cambridge University Cricket Club I came to apprehend that the building in the background of the top right hand corner was none other than the home of my schoolboy friend F. H. Smith at 8, Harvey Road. This shows the extraordinary cheek-by-jowl existence of Walter Watts, groundsman, and John Neville Keynes, University administrator; how deliveries of post, coal, and newspapers were shared; how clearing the street rubbish in the summer and the leaves in the autumn were of common concern. So, most certainly in good weather, Fenner's would hold out more promise as a theatre of relaxation and entertainment than our back garden, and through its proximity this would be in return for very little extra expenditure in energy.

My father's diary for April 1896 was dominated by the organisation of a large conference at the end of the third week. After that work picked up so much that at the beginning of May he complained that he had 'hardly any time for stamping', an indoor pursuit of which the theory and practice went hand in hand with the wallet. Bridge and walking are activities mentioned in May, as is the heat. A year earlier he had noted that he hadn't used coal fires for some time, only to bemoan a change in the weather soon afterwards.[9] 1896, by contrast saw such a consistent spring and early summer that coal is only mentioned in connection with a different matter. My school sports day took place at Fenner's towards the end of May.

June 4th saw the triumph of steering the new Syndicate for women's degrees unopposed through Congregation.[10] After nearly five hours of meetings about this, previous exam exemptions, and a Business Details Subsyndicate, what did he do? Go for a stroll along the Backs? Search out a colleague with whom to go for a drink? No:

> Afterwards half an hour at the cricket match with Yorkshire
> ... I have a kind of holiday feeling.

On the 12th he had to invigilate examinees from 9 a. m. to 11.30 a. m., return home for lunch and later in the afternoon go with a large party of family and friends to the boat races, finishing with a supper where the preacher from Emmanuel Chapel joined

AN ARTICLE COMPILED DURING SEPTEMBER 1905

THURSDAY, JUNE 4, 1896.

(156-210) Corpus Christi.

12.15 Council
12.30 Congregation
The new Syndicate for women's Degrees gets through unopposed.
Discussion on Locals Report on Exemption from the Previous Examⁿ: No remarks made.
4 Business details sub-Syndicate
Afterwards half an hour at the cricket match with Yorkshire
It is extremely hot, & the pressure of work being over (though there is still a good deal to be done) I have a kind of holiday feeling

Florence has been speaking at Bury St. Edmund's to-day on the principles of the Charity Organisation Society.

23rd Week.   FRIDAY, JUNE 5, 1896.   157

(157-209)

Maynard's 13th birthday.
His principal birthday present is to be a visit to London next week.
He is growing in height at a great pace just now. In very little more than two months he has put on nearly an inch & a quarter.

2.30 Press Syndicate. The Master of Peterhouse rather annoys me.

Mr & Mrs Dale to dinner to talk over their projected trip to Switzerland.

After two lessons of half an hour apiece Margaret can bicycle quite nicely. She & Florence are getting up quite a bicycle mania.

AN ARTICLE COMPILED DURING SEPTEMBER 1905

164   FRIDAY, JUNE 12, 1896.   24th Week.

(164-202)

9–11½ Invigilate

Mrs Spokes & Helen West arrive to lunch

Cricket

To the Boat races in the *Alice*
     J N K   F A K
     Mrs Spokes   Helen West
     Miss Rotmann & the three children
        Upward
        Atlee
        Spicer
        Jessie Forsyth
Dr Forsyth joins us at supper and Spokes arrives a little later

GOLDEN AGES AT THE FENNER'S MARGIN

TUESDAY, JUNE 16, 1896.

(168-198)

Invigilate 9–11
11½–1½
4–7

2¾–3¾ at Fenner's — M.C.C. (incl. W.G. Grace and Ranjitsinhji) v. the University

There are 7 M.A. candidates. I am at once beginning to look over the papers.

Macmillans write that a new edit^n of my Scope and Method will be wanted before long. I am not at present inclined to make many alterations, but I shall have to think the matter out in the Long Vacation.

AN ARTICLE COMPILED DURING SEPTEMBER 1905

SATURDAY, JULY 18, 1896.

I shall be busy at the office for the next fortnight; but there are no serious arrears –

Lunch again with Mother.

Match at Fenner's between Goodchild's boys and the Paters – the latter won by one wicket.

Goodchild speaks very highly of Maynard's mathematics and says that he is equally good at classics.

GOLDEN AGES AT THE FENNER'S MARGIN

30th Week.   TUESDAY, JULY 21, 1896.   203

(203-163)

Lunch with Mother

Florence to Bedford for the night to help at a bazaar to-morrow

Sugar at Fenner's without success

us. Yet amongst this hectic schedule in the mid afternoon we find a single word printed given equal weight of spacing and lettering to the other items;

Cricket.

A possible variable factor has been removed by the revelation that my mother was in Bury St. Edmunds on June 4th but at home on the 12th. Father was not a secret cricket watcher.

The 16th is even more remarkable. He invigilated from 9 to 11, 11.30 to 1.30, and 4 until 7. He had seven M.A. candidates whose papers he started to look over at once, plus Macmillans, his publisher, had written asking for a new edition of his book, which must have filled him with gratitude and dread in equal proportions. But what did he choose to do with his few precious free moments that day?

2.45–3.45 at Fenner's – M.C.C. (incl. W.G. Grace and Ranjitsinhji) v. the University.

The temptation to see the greatest player to date batting with the wunderkind of 1896 was far too great to resist. I had been disappointed the only time I had sought out the 'Prince' on Parker's Piece, for he had been dismissed by Camden for a low score.[11]

Later, at Eton, I faced the full truth of the adage that our heroes will be found to have feet of clay. The impression of languid, intelligent movement in 'Great Cricketers' at distance was demolished in a particularly brutal way by close range scrutiny and interrogation of one particular master about the whys and the wherefores of his art. This specimen of batsman generally gave the impression that the questions were coming far too fast off the pitch for him. By the time I entered King's I was of the opinion that one could not expect cricketers to show more than bottomless ignorance.[12] This merely reinforced the knowledge that Ranji was peculiar.

I have never got round to telling my father about my slice of fortune during the University's match with M.C.C., even though he would have been delighted; it seemed to be such an intensely personal moment that I'm not sure I could have described it adequately to him, and there is no indication that he heard it from Goodchild. For as luck would have it my headmaster was in the melée around the pavilion when Ranji emerged at the end of play one day, and by sheer force of personality he managed to engage the great man in conversation. Spying his pupil at the periphery of the crowd he steered a passage towards the ground exit by way of me. I grew nervous as they approached, although the familiarity of Goodchild's prattle was reassuring.

'Here, sir, is a most unusual boy, an exceptional boy, who is devoted to following the game of cricket ...'

'Very unusual, eh? So you know what the Champion and I were up to today, don't you?'

The mouth and facial features looked serious, and the tone of voice was earnest, but there was a playfulness in Ranji's eyes that was quite startling and gave me the confidence to try a clever answer.

'Yes, sir, to get as many runs as possible – but without losing your wickets.'

'Oho! Capital thinking, "to get as many runs as possible – but without losing our wickets" indeed!' He looked so pleased with this retort that I thought he was going to congratulate me on my utilitarianism. He proceeded, however, in a most unexpected direction.

'That would be effective, but an exceptional boy should never overlook *style*. The Champion taught me that, and today our aim was also to narrow custom, and enlarge individual judgement and expression. Can you remember that?'

'Yes, sir,' I said with more confidence than I felt, and then he was gone. But I did remember it, and the memory seems to get stronger and more real as I get older. It was the only thing a cricketer has ever said, I suspect, that was of lasting importance.

In retrospect I cannot think of any other creative person or technician (be it painter, author, politician, dancer, or academic) who has given a better goal for life's endeavour than that curious Victorian; 'narrowing custom and enlarging individual judgement and expression'. Kumar Shri Ranjitsinhji was the link between the Victorian and the Edwardian, the scientific and the artistic, the popular Parker's Piece and the sectarian Fenner's, the accumulative hedonist and the abstract aesthete. It is hard to think of anyone else in Cambridge in 1896 who could have been considered more important than the batter who had eclipsed W. G.

One of the great joys of the Reverend F. M. Butler, the Master of Trinity, was that he had an entry in the Births and Deaths section of each year's *Wisden Almanack* as a member of the winning 1851 Harrow XI.[13] He was delighted, therefore, to arrange the September celebration dinner in given in honour of Ranji's magnificent feat in surpassing W. G.'s record aggregate of runs for a season.[14] My father hoped to go but failed to get an invitation. He fretted as if the Empress herself had passed away, and wondered if the Master of Peterhouse had engineered an embargo on his attendance by some fell method. He could imagine the motives.

The official diary entry for July 18th contains the thought that he would be busy at the office for the next fortnight yet on that same day he went to Fenner's to see the Fathers XI take on my fellow school pupils at Fenner's. The 18th is of interest in four ways. First, cricket was a sufficiently important part of the fabric of life for the head to be present and available for parents:

> Goodchild speaks very highly of Maynard's Mathematics

Indeed, Goodchild himself had turned out for the Trumpington side in its first season against Grantchester about three weeks earlier, and had been tickled pink at scoring 12 not out in the innings victory. Second, my lack of playing ability in no way inhibited my father from attending or deflected him from the occasion. Third, the match was played at Fenner's, not adjacent to the school at The Leys.[15] Fourth, and most important, a hardworking, dedicated university administrator at a busy time of the year did not hesitate to participate in a seemingly minor event at Fenner's.

AN ARTICLE COMPILED DURING SEPTEMBER 1905

Reeve's book on Cambridge notes for plate 105; 'Liberal Club Athletic Sport at Fenner's in the late '90s. The famous cricketer Ranjitsinhji is the sixth from left in the middle row, behind the Reverend and Mrs. Austin [sic] Leigh in the centre.' There is interesting work to be done here as the suspicion is that several other cricketers are in this group, possibly members of the Hobbs, Hayward, and Carpenter families.

The Eton XI in 1858 with R.A.H. Mitchell elongated on the ground on the left: A. Austen Leigh, the eleventh member, is notable for his absence.

GOLDEN AGES AT THE FENNER'S MARGIN

The 21st takes us to the heart of Fenner's myth and encapsulates the way Cambridge society interlocked in a continuous weave despite commentators' current habit of dividing stories about Cambridge into discrete portions.[16] Tuesday July 21st contains the cryptic note

> Sugar at Fenner's without success

Here, in just one word, 'Sugar', I am transported home listening to father fretting about dogs, and a particular person's dogs, and that particular person's dogs at Fenner's. This marplot has already been mentioned (detrimentally) in the diary, but this later entry was, it seems, a cryptic message of smug satisfaction, heavily linked to the earlier complaint. Within the humdrum business of a bureaucratic life, Fenner's can be seen to be providing the colour of controversy, gossip, and revenge; hardly what we associate with J.N. Keynes, I hope you will agree.

What am I getting so nostalgic about? There is agreement that dogs were not welcome in Fenner's Pavilion, but astonishing contradictions emerge in the telling of the story. Rev. Ward had banned them and left a regulation to that effect as part of his legacy. Mr Ford, in his history, gives an imaginary account of Ward confronting a dog-owner, but it is so Dickensian in its portrayal that it actually beggars belief. The dog-owner pays a life subscription in his dog's name and is supposedly welcomed to the pavilion as a capital japester who will be forgiven and allowed in with his pet to enlarge the already corpulent legend concerning the generosity of the C.U.C.C. President; 'Haw! Haw! Haw! Come and have a glass of sherry, James!', the story ends. The date of the death of Ward invalidates this cosy drama, however, if the dog-owner is correctly identified as Dr James Porter.

For it was not until several years *after* Ward had died that Porter, the Honorary Treasurer of C.U.C.C., with reckless regard for the written rules, paid five guineas for his Dandie Dinmont dog Hugo to become a life member. This dog was a small terrier along the lines of a Yorkshire, but altogether more Scotch in looks and temperament. Sadly the dog was killed in an accident; so a new one, Rollo, was acquired. This one was also elevated to a life-membership, and went on to outlive Dr James Porter, who died in 1900.

On my 13th birthday, says father's diary, he crossed swords with the Master of Peterhouse after one *séance*;[17] the Master of Peterhouse was none other than Dr James Porter, Treasurer of the C.U.C.C., and owner of that canine life-member. The club President, Augustus Austen Leigh (also Provost of King's), had assumed his C.U.C.C. office shortly following the death of Reverend Ward in 1884, as did Porter.[18] Both were opposed to Henry Sidgwick and my father on the subject of degrees for women, a matter that was boiling up to the crisis during the spring that followed that Australian summer. If my memory serves me right the Master was inordinately proud of being the first person to ascend Mont Blanc with only one official guide, which perhaps serves to show what sort of man he was.[19] As a student in the late 1840s he claimed to have bathed in the Cam every morning one year. This puritanical streak stretched to his Vice-Chancellorship which was the last to be accompanied by hand-written accounts. But such dogmatism did not mark all his decisions; his capacity for blowing with the wind was shown when he supported the establishment of the New Theatre after it was clear how popular it would be. He courted popularity in the town as an Improvement Commissioner, Councillor, and Alderman, taking a leading role in sanitation,[20] the library, and Cambridgeshire cricket, even in its crisis of support in 1896.[21] At Fenner's he was quick to take Reverend Ward's well-known spot on the top of the pavilion after he died and claimed to have trumped Ward's efforts twenty years earlier by writing 3,000 letters in his own hand during the drive to buy the Fenner's freehold in the 1890s.

Returning to 1896, it seems that Dr Porter was going walking (although I am certain that he would have said 'climbing') in the Alps during the Long Vacation of 1896, and was convinced that his dog would feel happiest during his absence near Fenner's where he could be walked daily in familiar surroundings. Would my father look after him at Harvey Road for the month? Clearly it never entered the imagination that our family might also seek recreation in August, and father asked how familiar the hound was with Yorkshire.

In July, well after the university season had finished, Porter was still trying to board his new dog near Fenner's pavilion. In fact he visited Walter Watts himself and asked if he would provide a month's lodgings for 'a member', but this was received with coolness amounting to a diplomatic incident. The terse comments in my father's diary seem to confirm that he observed it with pleasure from a close distance, while his neighbour dealt with the pompous foe.

To an outsider (particularly if American) researching the meagre clues in the diary this might all remain a mystery. To those of us who feel at home at Fenner's it is crystal clear, for both Hugo and Rollo were known to all and sundry by the nickname 'Sugar', the very word used by my father in his official diary entry for the 21st.

This all suggests that Fenner's went beyond pleasure and interest; it was an intimate and intrinsic part of my household, as accessible as the garden and of more interest than the plethora of tennis courts that can be seen on the map surrounding 6, Harvey Road. It was partly a social outlet, partly a place of relaxation, but it was chiefly a theatre where a whole system was on display, where great technicians, practitioners, and actors struggled to control their fates and the environment using defined skills of a mental as well as a physical kind. It was where you could see the most famous Victorian of all, W. G., on the same bench as the most famous Edwardian, Ranji. It was the cricketing home of the greatest Victorian's son (W. G. Junior). It was where most of the authors of the Badminton Book of 1888 had served their apprenticeships (chiefly Steel and Lyttelton). It was next to Parker's Piece, where just a generation before 1896 the professional Cambridgeshire side (including Carpenter, Hayward, Buttress, Diver, Smith, and Tarrant) was to be measured on a scale with Surrey or Yorkshire. It is worth far more attention than it has so far been given, but seems so slight and incidental on the surface that it may not be treated with due care by those who were not directly affected

A Second Article Compiled During September 1905

Some Thoughts On Cambridge Cricket From The Fenner's Margin

'I do not know which makes a man more conservative - to know nothing but the present or nothing but the past.'

(John Maynard Keynes, 'The End Of Laissez-Faire')

Cambridge cricket was established primarily in the first half of the nineteenth century, although clubs like Wisbech (in the north) and Royston (part of Cambridgeshire until nearly the turn of the twentieth century) were late eighteenth century in origin. William Glover[22] bored all my father's generation with his stories of how he saw Pilch, Wenman, Mynn, Felix, and Redgate play in Cambridge during his youth before the days of Parr, Hayward, Carpenter, Tarrant, Diver, Arnold, Buttress, and Cornwall. He even saw Pilch and Fenner play together in a triangular match on Parker's Piece. Fuller Pilch played for Cambridge Town in 1832 and was a regular coach of 'quiet ease and frankness'. Glover was vehement that the example from the finest players in the land on Parker's Piece provided national (*sic*) lessons for Cambridge people which were engraven on the tablets of memory. As young boys we found his ramblings risible, but my father was able to forage a little deeper for the reasoning behind these grandiose claims and pass it on to me after the old man's death.

For Glover the key was Parker's Piece, 'the sacrifice of a few acres, which became a treasured possession for all time'. Fenner's ground was private, and therefore had interest for only a sector of the Town. As mixing between Town and Gown dwindled, so did the Town's standards, and in the end so did the universal enthusiasm. Gone were the days when every Cambridge youth would look forward to the visit of the 'Marabuns', as M.C.C. were usually described by Town enthusiasts. For Glover cricket was a safety valve for youthful excitement and a possible escape from drudgery and penury. Parker's Piece, as a gift to the people, was a miracle, albeit diminished by Fenner's. John Stuart Mill, he claimed, tapping my father on his waistcoat to emphasise the point, would have resisted the state intervening to provide play areas in all the nation's large modern towns. However, he would have been perfectly content to buy the land, if possible in a better world, for £400 million with the acquiescence of an 'obedient' upper chamber, and organise a paternal distribution of much needed grounds by the ruling classes. But Parker's Piece was the dream turned into reality, and at no cost at all, located between the area of greatest need and the area of greatest affluence, freely allowing the hungry to imitate those who were overflowing with riches, creating heroes from such diverse personalities as Tarrant and Hayward. Hence the miracle.[23]

What did the Town slowly lose as Fenner's became established after 1846? Glover reminded us of the 1856 return to Parker's Piece of the Town/Gown fixture after nine years at Fenner's Ground, which raised enormous public interest even though the Town lost. No such crowds have been seen in recent years, and the fixture disappeared some time ago.

Top cricket according to Glover (and I am more in sympathy with this view now than I was a decade ago) depends on displays of patience, honour, justice, courage, endurance, and self-control; these make up what Ranji later called 'the spirit of cricket – of the game itself'. Cricket could not co-exist with meanness, evasion of laws, sharp practice, violent changes, riotous violence, or abused private interest. Townsmen like Carpenter and Hobbs were bound up with men like Balfour and Goschen[24] eagerly

Fenners' Old Pavilion, removed about 1877.

reading the cricket reports. When Arthur Milner had to nurse his leg intensively during 1895 he chose to do it at Reigate while watching W. G. and Ranji play at cricket. You may have cricket conducted without these virtues, but will it attract such a wide range of spectators? Essentially it is a contemplative game; Professor Marshall has said in another context that if excitement deafens our ears to the more delicate tones then it is wrong, whereas relaxation gives us a greater power to appreciate delicate harmony.

Currently Cambridge is generally taken to be synonymous not with Town but with University cricket.[25] The reverse was true fifty years ago, and when the first team from England set off for North America some of the best players available were indeed professionals of Cambridge Town. In the 1848 publication *Sketches of the Players* by William Denison one can deduce that eighteen were from the south-east, eight from Nottinghamshire and Leicestershire, while fully eight were from Cambridge itself. Two were college servants, two had no occupation outside the game, and the others were a cook, a tobacconist, a licensed victualler, and a brazier.

The variety of cricket on Parker's Piece alone would have been dazzling, involving many Gown and Town teams on equal terms. There is a very rare Felix print of Cambridge Town posing with the University team, possibly at the new Fenner's ground, but more likely Parker's Piece.[26] The Cambridgeshire side of the mid-nineteenth century was not only a top county side, but contained the two greatest English batsmen in Thomas Hayward and Robert Carpenter, and also the best fast bowler in George F. Tarrant. William Buttress, the father of leg-spin bowling, had a prodigious record against All England Elevens, and his tricks as a ventriloquist made him popular with the public. He took 11 wickets in the 1857 innings victory for the Town versus the University. The names Carpenter and Hayward were as familiar in the early 1860s as

SCORES, 1846.

THE UNIVERSITY v. THE TOWN.

Played on Parker's Piece, May 25 and 26. Though assisted by Boudier, an ex-"blue," who scored liberally, Cambridge suffered a bad beating by 10 wickets, Arnold and Fenner doing a lot of damage with both bat and ball.

R. T. King, b Arnold	4	b Fenner	13
G. P. Ottey, b Arnold	0	c and b Fenner	1
R. Seddon, b Fenner	17	b Arnold	1
A. M. Hoare, b Arnold	20	b Arnold	3
John Walker, b Arnold	7	b Arnold	3
G. J. Boudier, c Fenner, b Arnold	26	b Arnold	31
E. Macniven, run out	6	c and b Arnold	22
O. C. Pell, c Arnold, b Fenner	1	run out	4
S. T. Clissold, c Boning, b Fenner	3	b Fenner	3
H. T. Wroth, not out	2	not out	20
J. M. Lee, b Arnold	0	b Arnold	3
B 8, w 2	10	B	15
	96		119

The TOWN scored 209, and 9 for no wicket.

SCORES, 1861.

THE UNIVERSITY v. THE TOWN.

Played on Parker's Piece, May 9 and 10. The Town, though not at full strength, made the University follow on, and eventually won by 6 wickets, Carpenter, Hayward, Buttress, and Tarrant all being successful at least in one department of the game.

The TOWN scored 168 (Carpenter 54), and 38 for 4 wickets.

T. E. Bagge, b Buttress	1	not out	20
E. B. Fawcett, b Buttress	6	b Buttress	6
H. M. Marshall, b Buttress	10	run out	25
D. R. Onslow, c Tarrant, b T. Hayward	2	b T. Hayward	18
A. E. Bateman, lbw, b T. Hayward	2	c Tarrant, b Buttress	0
H. M. Plowden, b T. Hayward	8	b Tarrant	16
W. J. Lyon, not out	19	b Tarrant	7
R. Lang, b T. Hayward	0	b T. Hayward	27
F. C. Hope-Grant, c Pryor, b Buttress	2	st Winterton, b T. Hayward	3
H. W. Salter, b T. Hayward	4	b Tarrant	2
F. Lee, b T. Hayward	17	b T. Hayward	2
B	3	L-b 3, w 1	4
	74		130

UNIVERSITY BOWLING.

	Overs.	Runs.	Wickets.	Overs.	Runs.	Wickets.
Salter	44.3	62	5	12	12	2
Fawcett	14	22	0	...	...	...
Plowden	15	40	1	...	...	...
Onslow	15	27	3	...	...	...
Hope-Grant	...	...	...	13	20	2

A SECOND ARTICLE COMPILED DURING SEPTEMBER 1905

Grace and Spofforth in the late 1880s. In 1861, 1862, and 1863 only four batsmen made 1,000 runs in each season, making twelve occasions. The famous names who achieved this are Daft, Griffith, Anderson, E. M. Grace, and Mortlock (twice); the other six are Carpenter (three times) and Hayward (three times). As late as 1870 Hayward and Carpenter put on 305 at Radcliffe out of All England's 504 made over seven sessions of play.

Robert Carpenter made so good he could later afford to live in a solid town house in Cambridge at 45, Mill Road between the Durham Ox pub and Sturton Town Hall, just the other side of Fenner's ground from Harvey Road. He was also a great skater and cribbage player, and organised a cricket match between 22 of Swavesey and District and the full Cambridgeshire XI, with Hayward, Tarrant, and Smith, during the coldest period of January 1867. This precedent inspired the Town/Gown three-day match in December 1878 when Dan Hayward and Carpenter put on 132 for the 10th wicket. The University replied with 274 for 4 to the Town's 326, and in view of the C.U.C.C. triumph over the Australians earlier that year the Mill Road pubs were full of Christmas talk of Cambridgeshire once more being the champions of the world.

Curiously, given the precedents of Hayward and Carpenter, the stereotypical view of professionals as bowlers had been promulgated, and it persisted despite additional late-century evidence from Spofforth, who contended that E. M. Grace (the amateur) was rated as a much less stylish batsman than Carpenter (the professional) by the Sydney crowds of 1863.[27] This gets us into the territory of Say's Law, for who was to do the teaching of the gentleman if not the professional?[28]

This was shown on pages 364–6 in the 'Gentleman and Players' chapter of the *Badminton Book* of 1888, where a string of great professional deeds is recorded if not fleshed out. For example, Lyttelton describes the 1864 Lord's game briefly:

> Tarrant and Willsher bowled unchanged throughout the match

but without developing the drama of the M.C.C. intervention in the laws that followed it. This involved the legalisation of overarm bowling and also the beating-off by M.C.C. of the last great challenge to its authority, by Surrey. Lyttelton emphasises that Hayward, Carpenter, Parr, and Daft as batters carried all before them.

James Pycroft wrote in 1868 about the decade of dominance by Cambridgeshire and Surrey in uncomprehending and derogatory tones, not deigning to mention any of the offending characters by name, although he was clearly thinking of the rough Tarrant and the lamplighter Buttress. For all the charm of his other writings the myopia of the following paragraph suggests that what he saw in cricket was not what the masses perceived:[29]

> Professionals of late years have become very numerous. The demand of schools and clubs has stimulated a forced and unnatural supply. Lads remembered at Cambridge as the common cads of the town, from constantly serving about

Parker's Piece, have attained to proficiency, and got places as practice-bowlers, and played much before the public. One or two of the same grade have played great matches, and have travelled with all the luxury of gentlemen, and been received and feted as cricketers in a way truly ludicrous to those who remembered the very dunghill from which they rose. No wonder, therefore, that, petted and spoilt, they lost their balance, and, like beggars on horseback, rode rather fast.

Yet if one examines *Reminiscences of the Old Players* one finds that Pycroft has chosen only one line drawing which he puts at the front of the volume, and it is not of the 'Gentlemen', or of Thomas Lord, but of Hayward and Carpenter!

Richard Daft is far more illuminating when reminiscing about this era mentioning 'Ducky' Diver and his fine singing voice; Tarrant and his vainglorious boast to Parr that he would not be seasick on the way to Australia; Hayward and Carpenter duelling for top score when All England played the United Eleven. Daft was emphatic that only Surrey could rival Cambridgeshire:

Cambridgeshire was for some years as good a county as any, as well it might be, having two such batsmen as Hayward and Carpenter, and such a bowler as Tarrant. It possessed an excellent little player, too, in Jack Smith, who was a fine batsman, and as good an outfield as anyone I ever saw. Diver was another of its best men, and D. Hayward, a brother of Tom, was a useful player. Fred Reynolds, an old All England Eleven man, who has been at Manchester for many years was a first-rate bowler. C. Warren was a good man with the bat for some years.

The glories of the Cambridgeshire sides of 1850–70 were not matched by later physical or financial fortune in life. C. Arnold, M. Arnold, F. Bell, W. Buttress, A. Diver, T. Hayward, C. Newman, G. Smith, J. Smith, and G. Tarrant had a pitiful average lifespan of just 40 years. Those with other skills and means of income did much better, especially if they escaped the harsh, damp housing conditions of Cambridge in winter.[30] C. Warren (clergyman), W. Watts (Fenner's groundsman), R. Carpenter (umpire), F. Reynolds (Old Trafford manager), H. Perkins (MCC Secretary 1878–99), and F. P. Fenner (absentee landlord) had an average lifespan of 80 years, fully double the others'.[31] How the Cambridgeshire committee of 1896 would have wished for a brigade of fifteen similarly talented cricketers.

'Tear'em' Tarrant presents one with a particularly poignant story. Five foot seven and a little over nine stone there is no doubt in Daft's mind that the amount of work he had to do on the field shortened his life. The circus of All England matches versus eighteens and twenty-twos required all-round proficiency, and more than once Tarrant opened the batting with Daft. But Tarrant is at the centre of an inter-hemispheric bowling event of major consequence; when the ten year old F. R. Spofforth of Sydney saw the tearaway George Tarrant, of Cambridge, carrying all before him during the visit of Parr's team, his determination to bowl as fast as possible became strengthened. Spofforth described the adoration in his heart as follows in *The New Review*, April 1894:

A SECOND ARTICLE COMPILED DURING SEPTEMBER 1905

Above; Parr's XII for North America. 'Ducky Diver' sits in the centre, Thomas Hayward is standing right back, and Robert Carpenter is standing back left.

Right; The great pair of Cambridgeshire batsmen about to depart with Parr for North America (or have they just returned?); Tom Hayward and Bob Carpenter. The next Cambridge generation included T. Hayward of Surrey, H. Carpenter of Essex, and the self made John Berry Hobbs.

> I remember that what made most impression upon me personally ... was the bowling of Tarrant. It was a perfect treat to me to see him. His tremendous pace on the hard wickets positively scared the batsmen. When he hit the wicket, time after time the stumps were knocked completely out of the ground, and it was no uncommon thing for them to be split into pieces ... I myself, I remember, never failed in my allegiance to Tarrant, and continued to bowl as fast as I knew how. People expostulated, and prophesied that I should overbowl myself; but, with the admiration of Tarrant before my eyes, I could not change my plan of campaign. Indeed, as I grew older and stronger I found that my constancy was rewarded.

Spofforth was still able to top the English first-class bowling averages in 1896 at the age of forty-two, not through speed but by 'constancy' to his second and third models, Lillywhite and Southerton.

Adorned in his pink-spotted All England shirt[32] as a twenty-two year old round-arm whirlwind in 1860 it is easy to believe that Tarrant was the man who later inspired the young spectator to become the 'Demon'; he also acted as Parr's bodyguard on the 1863–4 tour. Alfred Diver, the Cambridgeshire all-rounder who went to North America with Parr four years earlier, got his nickname 'Ducky' from his antics at longstop to Tarrant; sometimes a pair of longstops were required on the hard bouncy grounds in the days before industrial groundsmanship. But Tarrant would be dead from pleurisy in 1870 at the age of thirty one years and seven months. In the July 1870 copy of *Sportsman* a piece about Tarrant appeared entitled 'In Memoriam' by 'Batsman':

> At school the boy was never taught to care,
> nor dream in summer of a rainy day.

An M.C.C. photograph of Parr's XII on the ship deck travelling to North America in 1859 marked the dawn of a short age of glory for Cambridgeshire who could claim the two top batsman (as well as Diver) in Carpenter (far left) and Hayward (standing at the back on the right). Hayward and Carpenter also went to Australia, four years later and Spofforth saw them bat nearly all day against twenty-two of Sydney.

Ford, in Ranji's 1898 *Jubilee Book*, describes Cambridge cricket as someone familiar over many years with both the town club cricket on Parker's Piece and the University cricket:

> It is no small debt that Cambridge cricketers and their visitors owe to F. P. Fenner and to Walter Watts, who for thirty-six years has had the management of the ground and running-track ... Five-and-twenty years ago [*i.e.* around 1872] "Association" [*i.e.* soccer] was hardly known[33] ... There also haunted "The Piece" a class which has perhaps died out, of rather seedy-looking professionals, provided with bat and ball and stumps – no net – ready and anxious to bowl to any passer-by for a casual shilling; and often was he who journeyed up to Fenner's for athletics invited to stop and "'Ave a few balls", if a specially bright and warm day accidentally appeared during the rigours of a Cambridge March.

A SECOND ARTICLE COMPILED DURING SEPTEMBER 1905

This may seem scarcely credible to the modern reader who knows Cambridge, but it was the real world of my parents. Did my father ever try out the sport that had become all the rage on Parker's Piece in a pre-echo of his wife's later 'bicycle mania'? He will not say.

At the same time University cricket in Cambridge was by no means the mighty organisation it appeared to be in 1882 when my parents moved into 6, Harvey Road and Jack Hobbs was born in poverty in Brewhouse Lane on the other side of the Mill Road workhouse (Pycroft's 'dunghill').[34]

The transition from chaotic to top-quality is bound up not only with W. G. but also Reverend Ward, A. G. Steel, the Lyttelton family, and a host of Town professionals. It happened largely in the twenty years that followed Parr's tour of Australia, and unfolded thereafter close to the homes of Hayward and Hobbs and on the very doorstep of the Keynes family. There was a symbiosis in Cambridge with Town and Gown interdependent at many levels of the game. Jack Hobbs's father was in charge of the grounds at Jesus College, while T. W. Hayward's revered father, Dan junior, was the groundsman for Parker's Piece, and another of his sons (Dan again) seems likely to succeed Walter Watts at Fenner's.[35]

The young Dan is groundsman at Corpus Christi and additionally took on the university football ground in 1896. He was a considerable bowler having taken 13 M.C.C. wickets for 69 for Bury St. Edmunds in a two innings match, and all ten Norfolk wickets in an innings when playing for Cambridgeshire.[36] Back in Cambridge, Ford described the college grounds in 1897 as each having one or more professionals. He affirmed that Trinity and St. John's were good enough for 'any' county match, and that Jesus (the Hobbs ground) was a 'pretty little ground'.[37] Ford made it clear, however, that overall Fenner's was the 'prince' of grounds.

The townsman Fenner created a source of continuing glory for the University, but it was Ward who developed it. He not only boasted a pair of formidable godfathers (Peel and Wellington) but was also named after them. Between 1856 and 1860 he was Curate of All Soul's, and then became vicar of Saint Clement's. Well known as the hearty President of C.U.C.C. from 1873 until his death in 1884, Reverend Ward found it a hard struggle to make both ends meet. A bucket of water from the tap was the lavatory at the old pavilion which was approached by a mud road. Only in 1861 was £300 of debt repaid and mains water and a metal surface installed. The athletics circuit which surrounded the boundary (which was a third of a mile long) was not aesthetically pleasing, but the income from its use subsidised the hiring of the bowling professionals each May. These were not just townsmen, but later great names such as Richardson and Mold. Ward did achieve some reward for his hard work in living to see the replacement of the wooden pavilion adjoining the gaol yard on the north side of the ground by the 1877 pavilion designed by W.M. Fawcett on the west side, and the demolition of the hated gaol in 1879, fifty years after it was opened. Building plans have always created problems for financiers; the 1874 estimate for the new Fawcett pavilion on Gresham Road was £2,400, while the actual bill in 1877 turned

GOLDEN AGES AT THE FENNER'S MARGIN

There were many changes to the skyline as seen from the Fenner's pavilion between 1882 and 1899, the first seventeen years of Jack Hobbs's life. Chief among them Hughes Hall, another Fawcett construction. The wall beyond the far boundary built out of remains from the gaol is extant today, and its buttresses serve as reference points for comparison of these views.

out to be £3,780. Each college except Caius, Jesus, St. John's and Trinity (who had their own grounds) paid a poll tax of three shillings in 1880 to rally round with regard to the bills.

Ward's foibles were many (such as the blanket banning of dogs, the term 'Fenner's', and walking sticks from the Pavilion). He was much-loved for the prodigious breakfasts of salmon cutlets and champagne he served to all the cricketers who came into contact with him, but is most famously the Cambridge captain who didn't play at Lord's, in 1854, either because he was ill or because the crowd gave him such a rough ride on account of his enormous girth. His proudest boast was that he wrote 1,500 letters in raising the money for the lease and pavilion of 1876–7, one of which elicited investment expenditure by the Prince of Wales, who remembered his own period of Cantabrigian cricket-mania four miles west of the city at Madingley Hall where in 1861 he installed his own cricket ground.[38]

Ford tells us that at Fenner's in 1897 were

> engaged some dozen professionals, many of them the pick of the bowling talent of England; and on a fine day the long row of nets is fully occupied, while the "fags" in the out-field have their hands full indeed ... for the contestants [of college cricket] there is plenty of fun ... [and when] to this the various club matches [Quidnuncs, Perambulators, Etceteras, Magpies, Kettles, Hawks, Pilgrims, Jackdaws, Chaffinches] are added, and it is remembered that the nets are going all day and every day, it will be seen that there is at least no dearth of opportunity for the Cambridge undergraduate.

One of those undergraduates in 1896 was Horace Gray, who was also a townsman, a member of an eminent local cricketing family, and an alumnus of the Perse School. He didn't get his Blue that year on account of a troubled shoulder, but did play for Cambridgeshire as well as the Old Perseans.[39]

The next Cambridgeshire generation was reared to make money from cricket. In 1896 Robert Carpenter's son Herbert was able to open each innings for M.C.C. at Lord's against the University side as Essex did not have a match. Despite a capital innings of 161 the *Wisden Almanack* didn't mention his name in their report because of a sensational fourth innings charge by the University to win the game. Perhaps the pressure of expectation was felt by the Carpenter and Hayward offspring; or was it over-competitiveness? When the famous son (Herbert Carpenter) and nephew (Tom Hayward) met on the field in 1896 there was no magic. In the Surrey versus Essex match at the Oval each got a duck, although Hayward picked up 6 wickets. In the return at Leyton, Carpenter failed with the bat, Hayward didn't bowl, and he only scored 44 and 8 as Essex easily won by an innings. Most poignantly, in the Gentlemen versus Players match at The Oval (just after the Varsity match) they batted at three and four in the order, the scorecard evoking memories of that ravaged Cambridgeshire side of the early 1860s. But in total they could only muster 45 runs in their four innings.

As Herbert's star waned so his contemporary Tom Hayward's waxed. Hayward followed up his South Africa tour of the winter with appearances for England versus

Australia in only his fourth proper season. Wisden says Carpenter showed a 'falling off', as Surrey pipped Essex for fourth place in the table.

Hayward, of course, is one of the country's most prolific batsmen[40] and is as important a figure to us in Cambridge as Alfred Marshall.[41] This pride and enthusiasm in Cambridge cricket encouraged the production of further raw material for professional cricket, and perhaps surprisingly (given the stereotypical view of the sweaty net bowler and the languid undergraduate batsman) professional batters were the result. E. J. Diver, the nephew of 'Ducky', was one example, scoring a thousand runs for Warwickshire in 1899 ten years after being both Secretary and Treasurer for Cambridgeshire. George Watts, son of Walter, the Fenner's groundsman, was born in 1867 and played for Surrey in the early '90s. John O'Connor was also 29 in 1896, and a Cambridgeshire teammate, but his foray into the first class game would be in 1900.[42]

Some of the Cambridge gods are rarely seen playing at Fenner's. T. W. Hayward started playing for Surrey in 1893, a year after playing for the likes of The Anchor public house at Fenner's.[43] John Berry Hobbs followed him to The Oval, but much later on, being only six months older than me. As a thirteen year old following the Australians' progress through England I would have loved to do likewise, but I hadn't the talent to match the will, and anyway my path was already pointed in a very different direction, as I then thought.

An Article Compiled During May 1909

Concerning The Various Strings That May Loosely Tie Cricket To Economics

'[J.M.K.] had no special athletic gift, but he suggested both in movement and talk, a keen dark-metal rapier, with light and shadow playing quickly over it. 'A dark ray', I once described him.'

(G. M. Young)

J.M.K.'s formation of friendships with like-minded followers of the philosopher G. E. Moore, such as Lytton Strachey, Clive Bell, and Duncan Grant, was an important part of the organic growth of 'Bloomsbury' during the Edwardian years. More prosaically, Keynes came second in the Civil Service examinations in August 1906 with very little preparation, having resisted Marshall's pressure to become a professional economist. Work in the Military Department of the Indian Office soon made him reconsider the Victorians' idealism of public service and also bored him. There was a lot of time for his treatise on probability between 1906 and 1908 when he resigned, despite moving to the more interesting Revenue, Statistics, and Commerce Department.

Elected a Fellow of King's in March 1909, he took up a post at Cambridge lecturing on the Principles of Economics, the Theory of Money, Currency and Banking, Company Finance, and the Stock Exchange. This post was offered by the new professor, Arthur Cecil Pigou, and the decision to return was helped by J.M.K.'s parents who gave him an additional allowance, the size of which was in excess of the salary level. In May 1909 he continued his winning ways with an essay on Index Numbers that took the Adam Smith Prize (£60 down).

AN ARTICLE COMPILED DURING MAY 1909

§ 1. Economics and Cricket.

Cricket was undoubtedly the first ball sport to become hugely successful in terms of mass spectatorship and organisation. This was in the late 1860s, ironically after the peak of Cambridgeshire's progression. G. E. Moore told us that while at Dulwich College he had to debate in favour of the motion that cricket was an inferior game to football (the devil's advocacy indeed). In spring 1896 he too was to be found near Fenner's, trying in hs fourth year at university to find at least one true friend, and succeeding (in the shape of Desmond MacCarthy). Nobody, it seems, in our society, was able to evade the rise of cricket in some form or other, whether it was welcome or not. It is insufficient, therefore, to say that cricket's (literally) spectacular success was solely due to the phenomenon of W. G. Grace (although it was clearly bound up with him), or to say that it was because MCC had revitalised itself and reunified the national scene.

It is more arguable, in my father's view, that cricket was unique among the sports on offer in appealing to both the working and managing classes as a metaphor for the new liberal economy, and specifically the competitive world of manufacturing. At the same time its conduct and surroundings suggested a better, more pastoral, and relaxed world, that had disappeared as the factory system arrived. Although these various arguments have been forwarded piecemeal I have never seen them put together, and there is a danger that cricket's historic part in the emergence of mass spectator entertainment is being written out of the history books by new reference works from America. It would be cruel if baseball and football, rather than cricket, were to be credited with creating modern sport.

Why should this matter? In particular, why to me, a mathematician, an economist, and a golfer? Perhaps after more than a decade's reflection I can begin to make some sort of sensible explanation for the instinctive feelings I have on this matter. In essence it comes down to a simple distinction, which, since it derives from the relations between quantifiable properties involved in the process of the game, is mathematical[44] rather than artistic or sociological:

Cricket is like Economics, Business is like Golf.

In golf you compete against someone else by a total immersion in your own activities. If you compete better, you win a moral as well as a technical victory, since the competition takes place on a level playing field, in modern business parlance. It is always in your power to get better, therefore you can account for your wins and strive to reverse losses. The golfer is an optimist, at least on the first tee. Even I am an optimist, although I also know that I am an appalling golfer. If asked why I play such a simple game (in terms of ideas if not co-ordination) I reinforce this analysis of the individualistic golfer *versus* the communitarian cricketer by saying that at least in playing golf I am not wasting anybody *else's* time. The decrying of 'Good Business Men' is often thought to be of no more significance than a fit of envy by one golfer at another's prowess, but the comparison with cricket reveals this to be an insufficient judgement. Within itself there is less to be lauded in good business practice than in the sound running of a whole economic system. The destruction of technical and social potential for production and the loss of welfare to society in general is far greater in a small crisis of the business cycle than that resulting from the closure from incompetence of even a large joint-stock company, and the consequences are distributed indiscriminately to both the deserving and the undeserving. The 'Young Man In a Hurry' to get from the golf course to the boardroom is, thankfully, far less of a lynchpin than he imagines himself to be, while the steadiest, most immovable Chancellor may be guaranteeing society's future supply of manna to a far greater degree.[45]

Arguably, however, cricket is uniquely suited to be an inspiration to Economists because it takes place in a marketplace, at the wicket; instead of producers and consumers we have bowlers and batters, but the key point is that they have totally different aims and are performing totally different activities. with totally different methods and utensils. One side is not even allowed to touch the ball with their hands, while the other has to, and has no bats. Everyone must keep off the wicket because it is the capital that the process depends on. The authority of the umpire as arbiter and custodian overarches both teams. But most importantly, the teams cannot achieve their ends without the co-operation of their rivals, and yet in the enjoyment of these endeavours they are trying to beat them. This is also the complex relationship of the firm to the household; the employers know they must try to entice consumers to buy the product, while simultaneously they try to keep wages as low as possible. Draws are so important because their avoidance pushes captains into imaginative action, trying to keep the spark of belief in possible victory alive in the opposition's hearts.

Cricket is a system of individuals *en masse*, and involves a far more complex relationship between the competing teams in many more ways than any other sport. As G. E. Moore said about life in what he labelled 'the real world', in cricket

> not everything can be secured

and so there is scarcity in our game, bringing with it choice and opportunity cost. There is specialisation, perfect (and less than perfect) competition in changing market conditions, and so a moral dimension lacking in golf (and business) which makes even foursomes a much more limited activity then a Test Match.

But cricket supports Moore's vision in terms of its action as well. Consider pages 160–1 of *Principia Ethica*, where a number of problems are listed concerning desirable conduct in society. The third of these is where

> the usefulness of a rule depends upon conditions likely to change

or where a

> change would be as easy or more desirable than the observance of the proposed rule.

On first reading this brought into my mind the Varsity Match fracases of 1893 and 1896 about the follow-on law which made such an impression on my youth. My father claimed I was staggered to find M.C.C. intervening so often to change basic law, but this rather reflects his own reaction, I feel. At a tender age I merely absorbed the reality and assumed this was a normal way to deal with problems in a changing world, much as Goschen a few years previously had considered the innovation of the pound note as a rejoinder to economic crisis.

As far as batting goes Moore's thesis that

> Egoism is undoubtedly superior to Altruism as a doctrine of means.

is clear; acquisitiveness is appreciated by all the team as the batsman at the crease is the representative of the side as a whole. The same goes for our interests in society as consumers, or insurers, or shopkeepers, or producers. In the next section Moore paraphrases Ranji when talking about discounting:

> Goods which can be secured in a future so near as to be called the present are ... in general to be preferred to those which, being in a further future, are ... far less certain of attainment.

Ranji trumps Moore in perfection of image and language in his Jubilee book, however:

> the disproportionate value of a run in hand and a run to be made is greater in the fourth innings than in any other.

But the area where Moore pinpoints why cricket may have become such a success with the working-class spectator as a model of life is on page 221, where he claims that the cognition of things evil or ugly, which are purely imaginary, is essential to the Ideal. In the same way that an evil fairy could inhabit a ballet to our benefit, Jones could bounce Grace[46] and England could collapse to Spofforth. The suffering does not matter in such tragedy, but it makes possible the appreciation of compassion, courage, and self-control in the same way as war does but without the damage.

One of my strongest beliefs is that good feelings are too often stimulated by evil happenings, and that one should search for ways of living that can by-pass this problem. Clearly a reaction against the Boer War of my childhood, with its uncountable futile gestures and heroic tragedies, made this a pressing concern.[47] I had a clue to the solution of this problem at Fenner's in the mid-1890s where I discovered living dramatic art and later found a home for my belief in the ballet and the theatre; they shared an identity as places where noble feelings were possible without appalling consequences.[48]

It is not just that cricket is a team game. All the codes of football ordain a team game, but the aims of each team and the general method by which they will pursue those aims are the same as each other. The nature of the competition is still manifest, only tactics will differ. Cricket has far more subtlety. I am talking here of cricket proper with four innings, not the single-innings base version limited to one day's play, which I would label (because of its frivolous nature) 'Fricket'. At any one moment in the game it is worth emphasising the two teams have totally different motives, employ totally different concepts and skills, and are looking for totally different outcomes. They are not directly comparable at any point until the match is over. This is because at any given time one team is batting and the other is in the field. That progress occurs at all is due to a series of transactions; the cricketer even calls them 'deliveries', the jargon of the economist. It is arguable that this feature makes the game specially bound up with the science of Marshall; it positively reeks of Marshall's 'two blades of a scissor' model with which thousands of students have struggled in the economics textbooks.

§ *2. Time and Cricket.*

One of Marshall's greatest contributions to Economics was the rigour with which he tried to distinguish between different time-periods when looking at the process of recovering equilibrium after a shock. It was clear that quantities and prices as the key signals in the market would have constraints of varying types through time and he tried to systematise these through a memorable analysis of fish.[49] Marshall developed those two phrases of our ancestors and gave them a rationale: 'many hands make light work', and 'too many cooks spoil the broth'. W. E. Johnson gave us the technical terms that he said represented *tendencies* acting in opposite directions in physical markets as output increases; increasing and diminishing returns.

The problem can be seen at once; this rationalisation involved complex terms. The principle of diminishing returns in the short run shows us that when the optimum point of output (*i.e.* lowest average cost) is reached by increasing the factor of production that is easiest to expand, we should then increase the next factor as well. This usually is labour followed by capital, but in times of changing technology it may be capital followed by structural unemployment. If all three factors are increased Marshall talks of the long-term, and calls the reduced average cost 'economies of scale'. These may occur inside the firm, as suppliers give discounts or bigger capacity machines can be employed, or may occur for all firms regardless of size, as the consumers or workers are attracted to a particular geographical concentration, or a new bridge is built to accommodate extra traffic, for example.

Beyond the short run and the long run there is the trade cycle, which was explained in terms of buildings-up and runnings-down of stocks or inventories every two years by Kitchin, and a mysterious business pattern of seven years (Juglar). Jevons, mercilessly mocked by socialists such as Hyndman, had a hypothesis that the cycle must be related to the sunspot cycle of eleven years, through the size of harvests and subsequent changes in the price of grain.[50] Would that Hyndman had had any such clear and logical hypothesis.

Silvio Gesell's *The Natural Economic Order* has a chapter on Free Money in which even he struggles (when refuting the law of diminishing marginal utility for money) to operate without resorting to the language of cricket:

The mighty fortunes of our epoch could never have been formed if after reaching the first million their possessors had said: "We have acquired enough, let others now have an innings."[51]

Cricket operates in a series of discrete time-periods that mirrors the economy. Each delivery is a transaction in the market between bowler (supplier or firm) and batsman (consumer or household). The batsman can try to get satisfaction or can forego it in the hope of greater return later. Then there is the over (now of six balls) akin to a batch of output which requires planning by the firm and effective production. The captain will be thinking about bowling spells (shifts of work), the most efficient allocation of the fielders, and trying to tailor the deliveries to the consumer in order to maximise returns. The batsman will be thinking in terms of survival each ball, each over, and each session (usually two hours or a certain number of overs) as well as over the whole innings; there is a sort of life-cycle of income analysis that observers apply to an innings; 'getting the eye in', 'opening out a bit', 'filling your boots', 'a final flourish'. The sessions have a rhythm or cycle within the day. A careful morning with the damp surface and new ball, the golden carefree afternoon as the outfield speeds up and the pitch becomes truer, then the playing for stumps as the new ball is due. The pattern may be made more or less complex as the composition of the team, the fitness of the individuals, the luck of the bounce, and the mental processes unwind, but there is still a general *post hoc* pattern to be discerned. It is clear that this interplay between long and short run, multivariate processes, and individual and aggregate components makes cricket a far more apt metaphor for an economic system than soccer or fishing, although clearly these also have changes of behaviour through time according to the conditions in a more simple format.

The soccer commentator in a crowd may say to his fellow, 'I really think they'll have to push further forward now, and this may leave the team exposed at the back.' But three cricket enthusiasts can mount a real discussion. Says one: 'If he gets the new ball now he may get a third spell from the quick men, who could rest overnight before the follow-on.'

The second breaks in: 'I disagree, he wants to put the left-armer on with the old ball and get the lower order reaching out. Besides the hard ball may go for more runs if they hit out, and also there's a doubtful forecast of weather for tomorrow afternoon so the pace bowlers won't get overworked.'

The third gives a shake of the head: 'But you are both forgetting that the fielding side is one up in the series with only two Tests to play and they haven't managed even to draw a series against the batting side for a decade, so why should they risk injury or defeat by doing anything other than slowing the game down, and placing over-defensive fields for the next day and a half?'

These time-periods in cricket also have rhythms that approximate to cycles. We have a rate of interest (wickets falling) that regularly goes down on sunny afternoons and up on cloudy mornings; we have an approximation of the working week, the product life-cycle,

GOLDEN AGES AT THE FENNER'S MARGIN

and interlocking factors that can produce complexity and unexpected, even chaotic, shocks. This is the very stuff of Economics, as is the long-run pattern made up of a series of short-run solutions (reflected *post hoc* in cricket's averages and tables).

I am not claiming exclusivity for this linkage of Economics with a common pastime. It is equally clear that a host of United States Economics brethren ought to be examining Baseball very closely, while the Austrian School should perhaps take up the cudgels on behalf of Gardening, which in most aspects would seem to be an even more fruitful avenue than Cricket, although equally liable to be subject to a range of ghastly mixed metaphors.

§ 3. Money and Cricket.

Gesell made an attempt in his 1906 *Die Verwirklichung des Rechtes auf den vollen Arbeitsertag* to link football to monetary economics, but the success of the paragraph quoted below hasn't the punch it should, following a section on elasticity that would make sense in terms of a bowler, but not a soccer player.

> The players do not concern themselves with the material of the ball or with its ownership. Whether it is battered or dirty, new or old, matters little; so long as it can be seen, kicked, or handled the game can proceed. It is the same with money. Our aim in life is an unceasing, restless struggle to possess it, not because we need the ball itself, the money-material, but because we know that others will strive to regain possession of it, and to do so must make sacrifices. In football the sacrifices are hard knocks, in economic life they are wares, that is the only difference. Lovers of epigram may find pleasure in the following: Money is the football of economic life.

To this, of course, I say 'nonsense!' *Strokes* are the money and cricket is the metaphor as it seems to be transactionary in a dynamic and complex way like no other game; perhaps like no other activity. It is emulated to a lesser extent by the aforementioned baseball as well as softball, real tennis, and rounders.[52] Perhaps more precisely, for 'Money' in Cricket we can investigate the *range* of strokes available, with the fundamental problem, as ever, being what *is* money and what is not? Wickets are definitely interest; I think my father's informal diary of 1896 gave some interesting insights on that, although he put them into my mouth.

When it comes to analysing price inflation in cricket terms I would argue that no matter how feeble the bowling and pathetic the fielding, unless the batter is willing to attempt the use of attacking shots there will not be any runs scored. It is not sufficient that W.G. and Ranji had increased the range of strokes available (*i.e.* money). There may be byes, wides, and no-balls, but there is no guarantee that the batter will take advantage of the situation; ask anyone who has watched a side bat out the final innings for a draw. It is clear that the idea of an increased supply of loanable funds (*i.e.* appalling bowling) is not going to lead to an increased level of demand (*i.e.* fours and sixes) through a change in the rate of interest (*i.e.* the chances of losing a wicket). It is a long run lack of previous investment that is constraining the scoring, not the bowling (*i.e.* the tail-end batsman is painfully inept because of lack of practice or lack of skill).

§ 4. *Uncertainty and Cricket.*

Cricket also has strong representation of my other current obsession; expectations, and in particular expectations in conditions of uncertainty.[53] A crucial strength of the model of Cricket as Economics is the role of uncertainty inherent in the drama of the game. In given conditions any pundit can estimate what *should* happen (the rate of scoring that could be expected, the likelihood of a bowler getting on top, the eventual result, etc.) Listening to Test Match crowds at the start of play what is fascinating is the degree to which patriotism and ignorance in equal measures add to the certainty of the predictions cast, and how at the end of play the incorrect prognoses are generally explained away with a player scapegoated, while the successful ones are paraded as signs of the prophet's great sagacity.

Uncertain knowledge does not mean events like the toss where the probability is clear, although in practice a captain could call incorrectly a hundred consecutive times. Nobody won all five tosses until 1905, and Noble has won consecutive tosses since the Test at Melbourne on January 1st 1908. It is quite possible that he will never lose another toss, and P. G. Wodehouse's hero Psmith would be the pundit of the hour.[54]

But we are rather talking about a matter where there is no scientific basis on which to form any calculable probability whatsoever. We simply do not know and *cannot* know whether our fast bowler will break down physically, or how much time might be required to bowl out the opposition in the fourth innings, although we are required to take action despite our uncertain knowledge.

If the spectators were placed out in the middle they would apprehend the relentless psychological warfare that marks Cricket. In some moods a batsman can hit any ball for a boundary, and a bowler can come to believe that is inevitable. Other bowlers[55] seem to take wickets with balls that should be routinely despatched to the boundary. Statistics are *post hoc*, not predictive in both Cricket and Economics; anyone brought up just three cricket pitch lengths away from Fenner's would be deeply aware of this.

The state of confidence, based on the degree of certainty a captain can impart to his players, is subject to sudden and violent changes. The practice of implacable calmness breaks down. New plans and hopes will suddenly form the basis of conduct amid the collapse of the well-regulated facade. The team tries to deal with the present by making polite references to the past and submerging the fear that it can know very little about the future.[56]

Ranji, in the 1898 *Jubilee Book* innocently suggests that this mirroring of uncertainty in cricket with the uncertainty of economic life as an income earner is a source of cricket's popularity in the late-Victorian age:

> A run is more difficult to make than to save, because batting is in its nature a far less certain and reliable thing than bowling and fielding ... batting is, besides being

GOLDEN AGES AT THE FENNER'S MARGIN

Tom Hayward's charity cricket match on Parker's Piece, September 1910. Hayward, 'the famous Surrey and All-England cricketer', organised a number of matches to benefit Cambridge institutions – this year the District Nurses' Home. Several Surrey players were included, and a large crowd watched Hayward, Hobbs, Hitch, Smith and Jephson perform. Jack Hobbs would become Cambridge's most famous cricketer. Back row, left to right: G. Smith, H. Coulson, H. Tebbutt, E. Moule, A.S. Scales, A. Titchmarsh, E.B. Darby, Reg Hayward. Third row: Dan Hayward, G. Watts, A. Hobbs, S. Speller, Tom Brown, W.C. Hunt, F.E. Collier, E. Bryan, H. Scales, W. Rumbelow, F. Addison. Second Row: E. Swann, F.A. Dalton, E.E. Stubbings, F. Hayward, Tom Hayward, W.C. Smith, D.L.A. Jephson, H. Faulkner, Jack Hobbs, R. Phillips. Front Row: F. Stubbings, W. Hitch, O.J. Stibbon. Tom Hayward's team of twelve players beat Frank Hayward's fourteen players. Frank stumped Tom on 79, the highest score; Jack Hobbs hit three 6s and nine 4s, and Jephson, the underarm bowler, took four wickets.

more difficult in itself ... far more subject to chance. A batter may bowl a bad ball or a fielder drop a catch without losing all chance of retrieving himself ... A bowler can without doubt be much surer of bowling a good ball, a fielder of catching a catch, than can a batsman of keeping a ball out of his wicket or scoring a run off it.

This reminds me of watching Ranji bat at Fenner's in 1896 (against W. G. Grace junior, I think it was). Ball number one swerved in from a high arc and beat the inside edge, only to hit the pad. Ball number two was of a similar line and trajectory and Ranji adjusted for the experience of the ball before only to find the seam grip the turf and send the ball leaping past his outside edge. Ball number three was of a sharper pace, delivered from a lower arm and seemed to be of yorker length. Ranji played back to dig it off its toes, only to find himself beaten in the flight, but again the seam gripped and the leather merely whispered past the edge of the bat and the off stump. Grace now seemed more full of purpose than ever. The next delivery seemed to be an orthodox, slow half volley, of the sort I had seen Ranji despatch routinely during other bowlers' spells for an inevitable four. However, this time the ball stopped as it kicked against the seam that had been cunningly held crosswise in a flat grip. The ball left Ranji's fully driving bat in a gentle, looping arc towards mid off, who dropped it. The rest of the team showed remarkable self restraint, especially when the fifth and last ball of the over was swept to deep square leg, the site of the old gaol (fortunately for mid off, now demolished). This four brought up Ranji's fifty, and fully exemplified the truism that cricket's real glory is its uncertainty.

§ 5. *Summary*

Morgan Forster has argued that life cannot be compared to a game of football because the rest of the side is too influential with regard to an individual's destiny. In our discussions he has also dismissed bridge for the opposite reason, that too much control can be exercised by the individual; in bridge fate is insufficiently unfair. When I have argued, however, for cricket as a middle way he has reacted with horror, and retaliated with the devil's final compromise: piquet! Herein fate is indeed dealt, but disaster can be accelerated or retarded by the effort of individuals. He says one day he will prove his point in print, and at least in the meantime we are agreed that, to a realist, life is *nothing* like golf. But in ignoring cricket he is succumbing to both ignorance (I doubt if he ever considered Fenner's seriously) and prejudice (convinced of the barbarous frailty of Muscular Christianity, as expounded by Leslie Stephen nearly half a century ago). For consider batting as an exercise in psychology.

The solitary batsman takes on the opposing eleven, in the way an individual labourer without the benefit of combined union confronts a firm that seems to have a monopoly of power. In the same act the batting side resembles the demand side of the economy, able to attempt to hoard and withhold spending power (*i.e.* stonewall) or loosen the purse-strings and enjoy the fruits of luxurious consumption (*i.e.* go for his shots). The explosion in spectator interest in cricket must have rested on the sympathy of the worker for the solitary batsman as the representative of the heroic worker/consumer in the middle. They don't just want an innings (liquidity); they want to see the satisfying spectacle of an innings with strokes (money being used on consumption). Hence the concepts of time, money, and an individual's place in the system all meld together into the pastoral appearance of the cricket field in a very *industrial* manner.

Another contemplative source of wonder confronts the spectator in cricket. The players take decisions, but how exactly? What is the evidence on which a proposition is based, and is it, in addition to being correct, *relevant*?[57] A crucial consequence of both the rational and empiricist approaches to cricket is that evidence may be unreliable and the future *unknowable*, requiring the intuitive action of the cerebellum. To any batsman this makes sense in a way that may not be clear to non-performers; the turning ball may have spin imparted on it by design, and previous experience may have shown that the pitch is receptive to spin, but it is unknowable if the seam is going to grip and rip during any *particular* delivery.

I recognised a decade or more ago that batting can appear to be magical, defying the empirical possibilities (how could the body process so much information in less then half a second?) It also suggested to me two types of uncertainty; the randomness in nature, and ignorance. Watching captains deciding to change the bowling showed me the process of ranking probabilities without the ability to measure them (you can't even tell after a terrible spell if anyone else would have done any better).[58] This belief about probability gives us in turn the accompaniment of a lot more freedom of choice, and no one put it better than Ranji did when we had a short conversation at Fenner's in 1896; cricket is about

> narrowing custom and enlarging individual judgement.

If one is to try to intrigue a total novice and explain the attitude of the players and the principles of the game (as opposed to the laws) this approach would seem to be as likely as any other to succeed. We could start with the 'Unathletic Swot',[59] who despite his other strengths, professes a blind spot for sport that raises a cheer every time he mentions it in public. He should rather be moved and humbled that thousands would turn up to a Victorian cricket ground to empathise with the solitary batsman in his unequal struggle, a true metaphor for labour in its struggle in the factor market.

An Article Compiled During October 1915

Some Thoughts On The Passing Of 'The Champion', W. G. Grace.

'[A master] must possess a rare combination of gifts ... must combine talents not often found together ... He must be purposeful and disinterested in a simultaneous mood; as aloof and incorruptible as an artist, yet sometimes as near the earth as a politician ... a dealer in the particular and the general, the temporal and the eternal at the same time.'

(J.M.K. on Professor Alfred Marshall)

J.M.K.'s career ambitions were set high, but along very academic lines before the Great War. In 1911 he was asked to take over as editor of the Economic Journal *and two years later became Secretary of the Royal Economic Society. His expertise on India led to membership of the Royal Commission on Indian Currency and Finance (with ex-Chancellor Austen Chamberlain as Chairman) as well as the publishing of his first book* Indian Currency and Finance *later in the same year, 1913. As the war started a memorandum drafted for a friend in the Treasury about averting a banking crisis sealed his reputation as a 'high flyer', and he was invited to join that body between January 1915 and June 1919. Although the world of the British Establishment was a tight one, it moved quickly when required to accommodate outstanding talents, even those as idiosyncratic as J.M.K. and Lloyd-George, 'the Goat'. The field in 1915 was also very small; there were few universities in Britain and even fewer courses in Economics. The literature was growing but still limited, and J.M.K. had already made an indelible impression which was soon to grow to international proportions.*

AN ARTICLE COMPILED DURING OCTOBER 1915

§1.

We were playing bridge at The Wharf, with the 'Umpire'[60] as usual an epicentre of calm control while Margot and her titans whirled about him. Like Robert Carpenter at Fenner's surrounded by Ranji, Jessop, and Grace in 1896, H.H.A. appeared to be the dullest present, although he had in his time done and achieved it all. Margot was extolling the virtues of tennis and chiding me for not playing. I tried to explain away my snobbish attitude as a reaction against the myriad courts surrounding my house as a child, which seemed to bubble with social froth while the really substantial sport was unfolding down the road at Fenner's Cricket Ground, the hub of our local suburban oasis in Cambridge. She dismissed my explanation with characteristic airiness.

'I must teach you, you're an ass not to play. Think of your bridge – if you didn't play you wouldn't know a cat!'[61]

The butler brought in a telegram and after a protracted perusal of it the 'Umpire' informed us that W.G.Grace had died earlier that day. There was a mixed reaction, with loud cries of astonishment and disbelief from some mixed with quiet rumination and downcast expressions from others. As the evening progressed talk was dominated by consideration of what this news meant to us and the country, and more interestingly why we felt so affected by the passing of one who, when compared to the likes of Newton and Darwin, was so trivial. My contribution took the conversation in a very philosophical direction and was rather badly thought out and even worse received by most of the company. It nevertheless set me considering the matter for the rest of the weekend, and this paper succeeds, I feel, in illustrating the gargantuan vacuum W.G. has left not through statistics alone, but by showing that he was the embodiment to Victorians of what their society had grown from and into. He was, historians will come to note, the most famous of Victorians, beyond the Queen Empress herself.

The trail starts with a curious popular song Lytton Strachey pointed out to me some months ago, from a collection called *D'Urfey's Pills To Purge Melancholy* which was published in the reign of Queen Anne. In it a lady (Aminta) and her maid (Molly) stay at an inn in the room next door to a young (male) admirer. Through the thin wall he can hear them sharing the same bed and debating who should have first go with the chamberpot. It is trivial but also striking, because it is so different from the Victorian society in which I and my circle were supposed to have been raised. If a lady had a personal maid two hundred years after Queen Anne, every means available of asserting one's superiority was used, to the point of denying any similarity between one's own physical functions and those of the servant. Is the war changing this? We will have to see. But in such ways did the Earnest Evangelical succeed in changing the English stereotype from bluff to opaque so that we are now capable of misleading the whole of the rest of the world and each other; masks are expected to be used to give passion and forces some social control. How did the Earnest Evangelical manage to unseat the Rural Roisterer so completely?[62]

GOLDEN AGES AT THE FENNER'S MARGIN

In addition to the effects of the French Revolution in undermining the natural assent to authority and creating the need for artificial dividers (or masks) in England, there were the effects of Adam Smith's division of labour, following the 1776 publication of The *Wealth of Nations* and the ferocious success of the factory system. This meant specialisation at a type of trade, so that instead of nineteen individual cottage pinmakers one entrepreneur would organise nineteen people doing different stages of the manufacture in one place, boosting daily output from a few hundred to many tens of thousands with the same inputs. But it led on to a lot more than pin money.

There grew up another division between labour & production (activity in the firm) and leisure & consumption (activity in the household). There grew up a third division of labour from capital on geographical grounds, in terms of spatial segregation. There arose a fourth division (or more properly a diminution) of labour's memory from not only its origins but of its immediate past. The resolution of these fractures will come to absorb a great deal of time and energy in a post-industrial society. The method for reconciling these problems in the summer if you were an Edwardian in Yorkshire, or a late-Victorian in Cambridge, was to become absorbed in cricket.

As far as the middle and upper classes of society were concerned, cricket was clearly not merely a Rural Roisterer's pursuit, as there is plenty of evidence that Bespectacled Scholars and Earnest Evangelicals were equally fascinated, and of course the game had, as the Roisterers knew, rural origins. All three types of gentleman could be (and were) encouraged or even enforced to take an interest. But why did they absorb it into the culture so swiftly and so seamlessly? Are there particular features of the game that raise a mirror to society exciting its pleasure and its curiosity in itself?[63] The giant figure of W.G. gives us clues to the answers to both questions.

§2.

W.G.'s pre-eminence was based on both his technical revolution and his being a typical representative of the pre-Victorian age, the legendary stories about him being out of place and out of time even as they were being created.[64] Unlike a museum, however, he was not lifeless, but an active and progressive propagandist for cricket as a plastic art, and so a rare and valuable national possession. The technical discussion must lean heavily on Ranji's *Jubilee Book*, the first part of which is merely a coaching manual divided into traditional areas (batting, bowling, fielding, captaincy). Other sections have named authors.[65] There are claims that C.B.Fry was responsible for most of the rest that one might attribute to Ranji if one didn't know better. Since the named author was presumably in a position to reject what he didn't agree with I will continue to refer to it as Ranji's book. Ranji memorably claims that Grace turned

> the old one-stringed instrument into a many-chorded lyre ... and, in addition, he made his execution equal his invention.

In other words, through *science* a game became a national institution, and, later on, an international industry. As W.G. blew pastoral breezes through bleak Sheffield, dusty Kennington, and grim Manchester, passions and forces were aroused which led to imitation and organisation; new championships, increasing overseas touring, and a true frenzy of public curiosity in 1895. This was near the peak of my interest in the game, and saw W.G. become the first player ever not only to score a hundred centuries, but also to score a thousand runs in May. The astonishment of the public was all the greater given his age and the appalling winter weather that continued until April and must have had all England's bowlers licking their lips. Even H. D. G. Leveson Gower,[66] the 1896 captain of Oxford University and my favourite childhood pantomime arch-villain said:

> Nothing W. G. Grace ever did, nothing any other champion at any other game ever did, achieved such widespread and well deserved enthusiasm as his batting in May when he was in his forty-eighth year.

He was a great bowler and fielder but clearly this was overshadowed for the public by his batting. It is possible, however, that his fame has led to a lack of public apprehension of other, equally great, changes in the game. It is not denied that he greatly expanded the range of strokes on both back and front foot (and I have equated this to expanding the quantity of money in other writings). But Ranji, Hayward, and Hobbs continued to pile up the huge scores and aggregates which W.G. had introduced on a scale such as to dwarf even the 1860s scoring of Carpenter and the earlier Hayward. Other factors to do with the ground, the weather, the laws, and players' expectations need to be investigated and given the prominence they deserve. Having imparted due weight to the rest, W.G.'s true stature will be even clearer; and I am confident that, through comparison with these changes in general conditions, his individual contribution will seem even more astonishing than before. To investigate such a grandiose hypothesis I will revisit my father's writings on the deductive method of economics, in particular with regard to inflation, and try to illustrate the argument with both cricketing and economic examples. There are several passages from his Scope (pages 351, 220, 212, 234, 231, 217, 237, and 239) worth seaming together through the next few paragraphs.[67] There is first the usual caveat that we must be sure of our ground when appealing to figures; are we comparing like with like and can we trust the evidence?

> If arguments based on statistics[68] are to be of any value, particular attention must be paid to the following points; (a) the sources from which the statistics are obtained, with special reference to their reliability; (b) their true meaning and significance; (c) their completeness or incompleteness as covering the whole range of the phenomena to which they relate; (d) the manner of their grouping, with special reference to the taking of their averages.

Surely *Wisden* and the thousands of eye-witnesses cannot be denied as authoritative sources of statistics? Then again, even if W.G. did revolutionise the range of strokes available, are we sure that the rise in team scores (and his) are due solely to this fact?

GOLDEN AGES AT THE FENNER'S MARGIN

My father's cricket diary of 1896 is clear that many features led to the bowler's struggle becoming greater in the 1890s.

> Take again the theory that an increase (or diminution) in [the range of strokes available] the quantity of money in circulation tends (*ceteris paribus*) to be followed by a general rise (or fall) in [the level of scoring] prices. This is, in a sense a hypothetical law; it does not enable us to say that whenever there is an actual increase in the quantity of money in circulation [range of strokes available] there will actually be a rise in prices [the level of scoring]; nor does it even enable us to say that if we find an increase in the quantity of money in circulation [range of strokes available] taking place concurrently with a general rise in prices [the level of scoring], the latter phenomenon must of necessity be wholly due to the former. For the cause in question is not the only one capable of affecting prices [the level of scoring]. Its effects may, therefore, be counteracted by the concurrent operation of more powerful causes operating in the opposite direction. But while this is true, it is also true that wherever the cause in question is present, it does exert its influence in accordance with the law laid down, and plays its part in helping to determine (positively or negatively) the actual effect produced.
>
> The problem of the effect exerted on [the level of scoring] general prices by the [the range of strokes available] the quantity of money in circulation is first worked out deductively, and then illustrated and tested by the examination of instances in which changes in [the range of strokes available] the amount in circulation have occurred on a considerable scale. In some cases the confirmation may be very clear and decisive; but sometimes there may be the greatest difficulty in allowing properly for the effects of [the weather] an increase or the diminution of the general volume of trade, for the effects of [the factors affecting the speed of the ball travelling towards the boundary] an expansion or contraction of credit, and so forth, the tendency of which is to counteract or exaggerate the effects proper to the cause specially under investigation.

Perhaps it was just less attractive to be a bowler in an age of faster, smoother outfields and better prepared amateur batsmen to whom the umpire would defer? Perhaps a job in the mine or the tannery seemed a better bet than an uncertain career as a professional bowler during a period of crises such as the Barings debacle of 1890? Perhaps W.G. even as he aged was faced by a less penetrative set of opponents because the counties would not pay high enough wages?[69]

> Suppose that it is desired to to determine the relation, if any, between the general [level of scoring] commodity purchasing power of money and the [wages and bonuses earned by professional bowlers] price of securities yielding a fixed rate of interest. Can the method of concomitant variations suffice for a solution? Statistics are available in abundance. The average [wages of bowlers] price of

Consols is known for every year, but however perfect our knowledge may be, we could never, by simply comparing the general [level of scoring] commodity purchasing power of money and the [wages and bonuses earned by professional bowlers] price of securities yielding a fixed rate of interest, obtain even approximately a solution of the given problem. For whatever may be the effect of the general [level of scoring] purchasing power of money on the [wages and bonuses earned by professional bowlers] price of securities, it is at any rate likely to be insignificant by the side of other influences, such as the [attendance figures and takings at the turnstile] condition of the money market or the [condition of the pitch] political outlook. It is true that the investigation, if it is to be complete, requires knowledge of the general characteristics of periods of rising and falling [scores] prices, such as can be gained only by experience. But it also of necessity involves deductive reasoning of some degree of activity.

Furthermore is it not significant that the very year after W.G.'s 1,000 runs in May Ranji passed his record aggregate for the season, and within a few seasons such a comparatively lesser figure as Tom Hayward passed 3,000 runs in a season? Hadn't the pattern of cricket changed for everyone, in which case can we be sure of the significance of the 1895 events? Inflation and high run-scoring are not as easily explained as they once were. Gesell, still assenting to Say's Law, claims inflation is a problem of money's velocity of circulation, *i.e.* that good bowling constrains the scoring of runs and that bad bowling allows runs to be scored.[70] This is not what the classical view predicts in which there is an assumption that a strong batting side will score runs even against a good bowling side (i.e. that [runs] prices are determined by [strokes] the quantity of money).[71] I suspect both views are insufficient.

This is where one must bring in realism in the form of other factors. A good score may indeed be predicted (if not guaranteed) if the pitch, weather, and match conditions permit it.[72] But one might believe that the past level of investment, the position in the business cycle, and the level of international competitiveness affect the extent to which an increase in demand (particularly from the consuming public) will be matched by improvements in supply by firms.

The *Badminton Book*, in particular the riveting final chapter on Cricket Reform, should be mandatory reading for any economist. It is a tract about the problems with, causes of, and solutions for inflation, and is written by someone who knew the system inside out (Hon. R. H. Lyttelton). The absence of W.G.'s revolution in batting[73] as a cause of the rise in scoring, and the multifaceted approach to the problem he takes instead, make it clear that Lyttelton was not a believer in the cricketing version of the quantity theory.[74] Interestingly, it shows that high cricket theory was more open to complex analysis and policy prescriptions than Economics at this time (1888), but the writer was still clear about the problem facing him:

> The gigantic scoring is an evil.

Lyttelton has no doubts, and uses the history of round-arm bowling, over-arm bowling, chucking, and in particular the developments in groundsmanship to explain it. This is not some anaemic fusty relic; some of the reforms were tried and put aside while others were, and are still, successful. The reform on page 403 to reduce the time between innings while the wicket is repaired and to keep the crowds off the playing area while it happens dates from this tract's recommendation. The idea was to tire the batters more, both mentally and physically.[75] My father said:

> The [cricket] economic world is subject to continuous changes. Certain assumptions may be realised at one stage of [cricket history] economic progress, and nevertheless be in violent opposition to facts at another stage. Hence without the aid of an extensive knowledge of facts, there is danger of ascribing to [cricket dogmas] economic doctrines a much wider range of application than really belongs to them.

It seems clear that although we can ascribe the rise in scoring to a number of factors, we shall never be able to settle with absolute certainty on the extent to which W.G.'s example of strokemaking has caused the result. That is, in spite of all the statistical figures that will be used in the obituaries to be published in the days ahead, we cannot be categorical *rationally*; we cannot prove, in any sense, that W.G.'s revolution in batting caused the mammoth scores of the Golden Age rather than the introduction of the boundary rope, the Ransomes grass-cutter, the introduction of the six-ball over, the increased revenue available for groundsmanship, the improved knowledge of loams and fertilisers, or the hot weather speeding up the passage to the boundary. We could debate the proportions to the end of time.

> All laws of causation may be said to be hypothetical, in so far as they merely assert that given causes will *in the absence of counteracting causes* produce certain effects. As a matter of fact, in the instances that actually occur of the operation of a given cause, counteracting causes sometimes will and sometimes will not be present; and, therefore, laws of causation are to be regarded as statements of tendencies only. It follows that all sciences of causation, and pre-eminently sciences employing the deductive method, – including political economy and astronomy – contain a hypothetical element.

Nor can we insist that W.G. was free from all faults with regard to Ranji's 'spirit of the cricket'; there are umpteen tales of intimidation of umpires, expenses beyond the norm, and rows in the committee room. Even (perhaps especially) the titans will have their detractors, and we need to keep a clear head to distinguish between genuine, concerned criticism and sheer spite or envy. With regard to the opposite problem, deference, it is also often said, for example, that Cambridge economists are too closely associated with the doctrines of Ricardo, but I cannot agree; there is too much independent spirit (like my father's) around for that to occur.

Ricardo's writings are not free from grave faults; many unjustified assumptions, many ambiguous terms, and even many wavering utterances.

As a fourteen year old in 1897, however, when one read the new *Wisden* one did not rush to 'wavering utterances' (the note disclaiming the expenses paid to W.G. at The Oval, or the editorial about the associated strike by some of the professionals). Rather one pored through it in vain for some reference to the already legendary encounter the previous year between W.G. and the Australian express bowler Jones. Had the former growled 'Now then, Jonah!'? Had the latter replied 'Sorry doc, she slipped'? Did the ball bounce only once before it reached the boundary behind the wicketkeeper? Had it really bounced so steeply that it flew through the Champion's beard? Already the other players' recollections conflicted and were unclear; the legend was enhanced yet again, and that surely is what made W.G. the keystone holding together our national game. Most mortal players would have been so traumatised by the experience that they would never have played at the top grade again. The same elements that allowed W.G. to come through it while adding to cricket mythology ensured the ongoing rumbles about such matters as his appealing for leg before wicket from the line of mid-off on his wide follow-through when bowling.

So in spite of the statistical doubt, the faults, and the fading memories, the enormous feeling of loss expressed on the occasion of his passing is evidence that we still remain certain in our belief in the Champion. We assume, rather than reason, that it was his example that enabled Ranji, Hayward, and Hobbs to set their sights so high rather than the other factors favourable to high scoring mentioned. In fact one only had to witness him striding onto the field, as I did at Fenner's in 1896, to realise that here was the embodiment of how the Victorian age saw itself. He was tall, with long arms that fell in rhythmically with a determined tread which spoke of the final afternoon of harvest. The sun-worn face had been tricked into a permanent expression of smiling optimism through years of squinting into the bright light of summer. The rest of the fielding side passing from the pavilion over the boundary, *sans* the jizz of the Champion, seemed to gravitate around him and shelter under him like ducklings entering a previously unvisited pond. Once the team had reached the centre of the ground and the crowd had settled one was surprised to find that that breathing was coming rather fast. In the effort of trying to miss nothing, blinking had been avoided, eyelids had been kept as wide open as possible, and a curious physical sensation emerged, rather as if one had *peeled* one's eyes. This was someone who could never be taken for granted, and whose physical presence was more powerful than any other I can recall.

When such a reversal of reason by sentiment can be so readily comprehended and forgiven there must be a truly outstanding and extraordinary force involved. For cricket is an easy game to play, but very few come to excel. The paradox finds its explanation perhaps, in that any new Champion must possess a rare *combination* of gifts, must combine talents not often found together. He must be purposeful and disinterested in a simultaneous mood; as aloof and incorruptible as an artist, yet sometimes as near the earth as a politician; a dealer in the particular and the general, the temporal and the eternal at the same time. Without doubt such was Dr W. G. Grace.[76] Will it be possible for such a reputation to be made at the present day? That is the way I carefully phrase my query, for I have great enough faith in cricket as a plastic art to believe that even such a talent as was W.G.'s may be repeated in years to come in terms of quantity (i.e. statistical magnitude) but never will he be transcended in terms of the quality of his revolutionary science.[77]

W.G. junior and senior; the son was 16 in 1891 when this was taken, and died just fourteen years later.

§3.

On this basis it is unfeasible that an adolescent cricket fan like myself, living just across the road from one of the most organised and prestigious centres of the game in the world, could not have been partly moulded by the events not only at Fenner's, but the prodigious deeds of England's greatest Victorian as he travelled around the country. W.G. was such a fundamental figure in late-Victorian society that one should really be able to link together any members of that society through reference to his theatre of action, so wide was his sphere of influence.[78]

In 1896 I was coming to realise that Henry Sidgwick's wife was not only Principal of Newnham but also the sister of Arthur Balfour (Edwardian Prime Minister and Philosopher.[79]) After Eton, Balfour had studied at Trinity College under Sidgwick, following a parallel career to the Hon. C. G. Lyttelton (Blue 1861–4) who became 8th Viscount Cobham in 1888.[80] Balfour (the most extraordinary *objet d'art* our society has produced) was a broken man (or perhaps, from a different perspective, a determined bachelor with new excesses of energy for politics) when two years into his courtship of May Lyttelton she died of typhoid in 1875. Who knows whether that red-headed lady might have changed history more than any of her more exalted brothers?[81] It should not be forgotten that Balfour's mother, Lady Blanche Cecil, was, like Rev. Ward of the Cambridge University Cricket Club, a godchild of the 'Iron Duke' and that Balfour was given the name Arthur for that reason. Spencer Lyttelton (officially G.W.S., but recorded by contemporaries as S.G.) was Balfour's closest friend; it was Edward Lyttelton (Ranji's 'Ed') who broke the news of May's death to him.

The first, as opposed to 8th, Lord Cobham was somewhat earlier hanged a heretic and provided an anti-hero for Shakespeare to exploit in the character of Falstaff. The Sidgwick/Balfour/Lyttelton axis was real enough not to require this extra dose of mythology, however.[82] Cricketers refer to the 4th Lord Lyttelton, father of C.G. and seven other cricketing sons, as if he were more a bestial curiosity of stud history than a player of flesh and blood with a name. In point of fact he was George William, under-secretary for the Colonies in 1846, and the grateful settlers in Canterbury named Christchurch's port after him. He committed suicide in 1876, the year after May's death. There featured, in addition to the immediate Lyttelton progeny, J.C. (who was 12th man for Eton in 1900), my contemporary G.W. who did play at Lord's (1900–01), and the Reverend C. F. Lyttelton of Eton and Cambridge (who got Blues in 1908 and 1909): all Cobham offspring to keep the waters running deep. Quite how deep were these?

Hon. G.W.S. (Spencer, Blues 1866–7) not only played county cricket for Worcestershire, Shropshire, and Northamptonshire, but was also chief private secretary to Gladstone between 1892 and 1894. The irony here is that Balfour had been the previous Prime Minister's secretary at one time (he was also Salisbury's nephew), so even a change of governing party implied limited change from one Trinity College student to another. Hon. Edward was a Middlesex player, excellent at other sports, an ex-head of Haileybury, and the current headmaster of Eton.[83] Having been winning Cambridge captain in 1878 he handed over to his equally adept brother Hon. Alfred in 1879 who played in Test Matches as well as county cricket for Middlesex and married a sister of Margot Asquith. He became M.C.C. President (1898), played soccer for England, played in a winning F.A. Cup side, and was M.P. for Warwick from 1895 to 1906. Not only was he Balfour's Colonial Secretary from 1903 to 1905, but through May he was also nearly Balfour's brother in law, and therefore also nearly a brother in law (of sorts) to Henry Sidgwick, who would also have been familiar with Hon. Arthur Temple Lyttelton (M.C.C.),[84] and Hon. Robert Henry (a tennis Blue, M.C.C. and the most accessible of the lot through his writing six of the sixteen chapters in the 1888 *Badminton Book*). Alfred Marshall, our Professor of Economics at Cambridge University, was not to be left out. Balfour wrote to him in 1891 asking that he serve on the Royal Commission on Labour. This he did, interviewing expert witnesses such as Sir Robert Giffen the statistician and economist; the report was completed in 1894, ready for Salisbury to read on his return to power following the governments of Gladstone and Rosebery.

As one of the most prestigious of the great Lyttelton brothers in terms of both cricket and rank, it is of interest that Cobham's followers came off so badly in the argument conducted through *The Times* over the 1896 Varsity Match that their position on the follow-on has never been revisited by M.C.C. His coterie lived on to fight more winnable wars for conservatism, becoming the progenitors of the Wisden myth on the eve of the Great War that such a great game as cricket did not *need* to tinker with its laws or regulations, and should certainly not indulge in change for the sake of change. Like Balfour they said they believed in progress, but as slowly as possible, and that the only thing to be said in favour of H. G. Wells (hence Socialism) is that his father was a damn fine bowler for Kent. The events of 1896 (indeed the whole Golden Age) showed, of course, just the opposite, and I was as aware of changes in the number of balls per over, the size of stumps and balls, and the follow-on law as Jack Hobbs was.

One major question remains now that W.G. has gone. Will cricket not become an anachronism in general?[85] Once the current war is over it will continue, of course, to be Ranji's 'heroic' pursuit in substitution for war. Agamemnon, Achilles, and their peers will still go to the wicket, one against thirteen (for the umpires also wear white). The foremost of these heroes was the Champion, and his example redirected the ambitions and energies of the present-day young; perhaps Jack Hobbs will take up the mantle in future?

The twentieth century Rural Roisterer in England will not generally box bare-knuckle, but he will try to cut a fast short ball for four. More pertinently, he will not generally be encouraged by his mother to box. The twentieth century Rural Roisterer will be decreasingly apt to hunt, either from conviction or from social pressure or from a combination of both. As to the Earnest Evangelical, religion in England will become a private activity of the adolescent and the old. The two groups are linked in decline; hunting abolitionists are much more aware than the bourgeois middle ground of the almost theological basis of hunting, going back to Assheton Smith in Napoleonic times.

Interestingly the Ranji thesis that cricket helps heal the class divide is also a key tenet of the hunt's defence. The English (and fox-hunting has been almost entirely English) have usually been able to persuade themselves that there is a serious moral force behind whatever they enjoy.

I am agnostic on the hunting, though a true believer in the riding,[86] but the hunters have still to be convinced that their activity will not only define an attitude to animals that is no longer acceptable, but will also define to outsiders their own mentality in a way that makes them less trustworthy and less worthy of respect. This is eventually what happened to the Rural Roisterer, or 'blood'; cricket saw the wind change during the Lambert betting controversy early in the nineteenth century and, in self-preservation, purged itself of the betting tendency for the next hundred years. Perhaps that is what out the true greatness of W.G. into sharpest relief; we know his performances came from superior skill, performance, showmanship, and achievement because we never felt suspicion that the unfolding of his long career was determined by any significant perversion of the context in which he was acting.

An Article Compiled During April 1935

In Reaction To The Announcement Of The Retirement Of J. B. Hobbs, Professional Cricketer.

'I should no more regard Maynard Keynes as a typical Bloomsbury than I should regard J. B. Hobbs as a typical member of the Surrey County Cricket Club.'

(G. H. Hardy, as reported in Robbins, 1983, and Moggridge)

J.M.K. had his own division at the Treasury within two years, became Companion of the Bath in 1917, and third in the Treasury pecking order by the time of the Versailles negotiations. Despite such success he had limited power to intervene decisively, and despised all the governments he came into contact with; his conclusions were that they were necessary but that like British industrial management, they should be doing much better. Written at Charleston, Sussex, during the summer of 1919 The Economic Consequences of the Peace *was published in December and made J.M.K. world famous (his book on probability was less populist); and rich. It was noted as much for its Strachey-like anti-establishment tone as its anti-treaty message, and the opportunity cost was the end (as it seemed at the time) of his Treasury career.*

'Noises off' predominated in the 1920s; marriage in 1925 to Russian ballerina Lydia Lopokova, speculation reverses to his personal fortune in 1920 and 1929, the Bursarship of King's College, and further iconoclastic publications (notably A Tract On Monetary Reform, The Economic Consequences Of Mr Churchill, *and* The End Of Laissez-Faire*). His influence was also of some direct practical import, helping the government of Germany considerably in various ways during the difficult period of 1922–3.*

The 'big' book was to be A Treatise On Money *(1930), which received a muted welcome during the 'Great Depression', as did the policies he advocated (investment in public works and a low long-term rate of interest). The majority in Britain held the opposite 'Treasury View' (although Swedish, German, and the U.S.A. experiences seemed to support his heresies). In Cambridge his mother, as Mayor, rebuilt the Guildhall and he himself gave life to the Arts Theatre ('Footlights', like J.M.K., was born in 1883). But despite battering away on both the Macmillan Committee and the Economic Advisory Council he was unable to persuade national bodies to act.* Essays In Persuasion, Essays In Biography, *and* The Means To Prosperity *came out in the early 1930s, but the real work on the* General Theory *was happening behind the scenes with the* Cambridge Circus *(a group of young, radical, non-Soviet thinkers) and at Tilton (the Keyneses' summer residence from 1925 adjacent to Charleston). In 1935 the British might have concluded from the media exposure about J.M.K. that a promising career had reached its zenith through shameless self-publicity and was now fizzling out. How wrong they would have been.*

Some have more pleasant duties than others to perform. Our Foreign Secretary continues scuttling hither and thither in the manner of the previous Sir Samuel Hoare M.P. trying to field the thunderbolts at long-stop from 'Bob' Lang on Harrow's playing fields.[87] I, on the other hand, sit back with satisfaction far from the scuttle diplomacy, a finished draft of my new book in front of me ready for retouching. However, I feel I must mark a rather different termination with a few thoughts and memories. For at last, at a time of life when it is all I can do to climb the stairs for a balcony view of Gordon Square, my fellow Cantabrigian Jack Hobbs is retiring from playing first class cricket for Surrey on the enormous sward of The Oval that he made his own. To those of my age this a greater passing than that of the old Empress in 1901.

Hobbs is the highest run-scorer of all time, the biggest century-maker of all time, and the model professional who other professionals acquiesce with the public in calling 'The Master', a term reserved in the *Badminton Book* of 1888 for W. G. Grace.[88] It is hard to imagine that any man will ever again score around a hundred first-class centuries after the age of forty. In addition, one should really estimate Hobbs as something of a rebel. This may sound curious, but since the days of Hambledon there have been professionals, yet they have always been viewed as a separate and rather disparate group kept apart from the amateurs. This has altered greatly in this century, and is due in no small part to Jack Hobbs.

From the almost feudal rules governing his qualification for Surrey until 1934 Hobbs's career marked an epoch of social, political, and economic revolution. Could the changing status of professionals have been achieved without him? One is tempted to think not.[89] This went beyond cricket, for cricket was (it is hard to imagine it now) *the* English summer game, just as soccer was the winter game. Hobbs therefore changed the situation for professionals in *all* leisure activities. It will take some sports (such as rugby union football) longer than others (rowing) to adapt to his rebellion. Hobbs not only overcame a far less promising background than mine in Harvey Road but at the peak of his success and beyond he refused to bow to either hubris (compare and contrast the Cambridgeshire gods of the 1860s) or triumphalism.[90]

The clues to an explanation for Hobbs's successful rebellion lie way back in the 1898 *Jubilee Book of Cricket* by Kumar Shri Ranjitsinhji. Chapter XI concerns the world that Hobbs would bring about; the opportunity for the professional to inherit the world of cricket.[91] Ranji was playing Isaiah, if not John the Baptist, to the adolescent unknown, Hobbs of Rivar Place. It is this chapter that many seem to have completely misinterpreted, telling us that Ranji wanted the professional to revert to the pre-1846 (Clarke's exhibition match) role and was warning us that a professional could not be trusted to captain in the interests of the side. This is exactly what Ranji denies in explicit terms, saying that cricket in future would require full professional participation and would be the *better* for it:

> The two interests [local and spectacular] join and make the system a very strong one. Its value I have tried to prove.

GOLDEN AGES AT THE FENNER'S MARGIN

The Holford Report in the 1950s recommended Cambridge's wholesale redevelopment, and highlighted two areas with photographs; Sleaford Street (with Rivar Place a few metres off to the right) and Burleigh Place (just over East Road from Brewhouse Lane). Even when he was 70 Jack Hobbs could have revisited the disadvantaged poverty of his boyhood.

The conservative thesis is the reactionary stereotype invoked to this day against which Hobbs led his successful rebellion. What did Ranji really say?

His first task is to convince us that the division of household leisure from labouring at the firm produced in the second half of Victoria's sixty years an important explosion in the market for cricket as a product, and that this meant that it was now a completely different game from that of the early period; it was now a visual art that could attract paying spectators in very large numbers.

> a professional cricketer's life does somewhat resemble that of an artist ... I would rather be a professional cricketer than a man who toils to make a large income out of some business that he hates, in order to be able to spend it on something he likes.

Yet the professional becomes the rentier of trapped labour who throng to spectator sports in the post-1846 era. Taken by an Oxford graduate to see Nottinghamshire play at The Oval, a German friend of Ranji was astonished that three hundred or more policemen were not required to control the crowds. Was this the 1892 match which broke all previous record with 60,000 spectators paying to see the first two days? Others have suggested rather that it was England versus Australia in 1888, but the point of substance was not the fixture, but the *crowd*. People were not only trying to watch the spectacle, but trying also not to obstruct other spectators' views. Ranji summed it up as memorably as Hippolyte Taine might have done:

> Something that keeps 25,000 people in order without external direction or suppression must be very real.

He then attacks the criticism (which he tactfully imputes to foreigners) that these people should be trained militarily, not in games; that cricket is in itself a waste of time and energy. This is daring stuff, for despite the traditional lack of a standing army the Empire was on a growth path towards its twentieth century Georgian apogee that required policing, yet Ranji says that cricket is superior to military training because of its better 'atmosphere' and because there is 'zest' for it. This coded message is pointing out that venereal disease had become a threat to the whole country because of barrack life rather than rubber bat handles, and that the authorities would try and stem the supply of spectator sport to Demos at its peril. He makes it as explicit as he can that this is a revolution to be welcomed:

> Cricketers and footballers are far more likely to realise their possibilities for good than are hastily-trained soldiers.

He then struggles to put into words why the game holds this fascination for late-Victorian men, women, and children. Why did Colman's, mustard-makers of Norwich, base their advertising campaign on W.G., and feel able to show an equal number of women and men on the poster spectating at a cricket match? Which segment of the market was thought to be susceptible to changing brand, or increasing the proportion

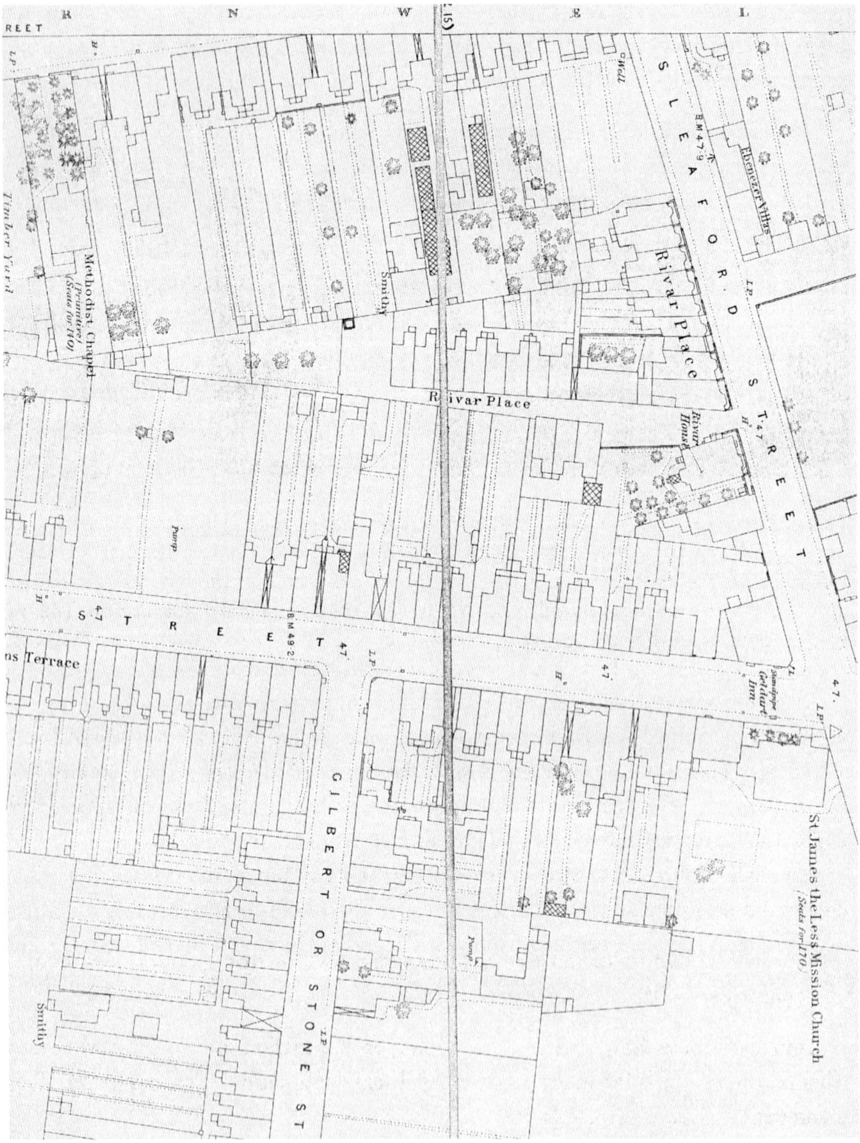
REET
Timber Yard
Methodist Chapel
Smithy
Well
SLEAFORD STREET
Ebenezer Villas
Rivar Place
Rivar Place
Rivar House
Pump
STREET
ns Terrace
Geldart Inn
GILBERT OR STONE ST
Pump
Smithy
St James the Less Mission Church

AN ARTICLE COMPILED DURING APRIL 1935

The numbers seem to have changed ends in Rivar Place, where Jack Hobbs learnt to bat using brussel sprouts and cabbage stalks. Number 4 seems to have become number 5 judging from the old photograph kept in the window of the current number 4. How upwards of a dozen people lived in the house requires considerable imagination. The map (left) reveals that the houses facing Sleaford Street were also called Rivar Place; the poorer alley behind backed onto a forge and some glasshouses.

of their hard-earned income on an edible comfort good on the basis of the promotional appeal of a mere *game*? The answer is that cricket was an heroic spectacle familiar to *all* Victorians, a fundamental assumption we must not discard in dealing with the 1890s. Cricket left room for individual gallantry that could affect the end-result.[92]

Ranji falls back on a phrase that suggests he is at a loss; but all those who know cricket understand him precisely:

> ... it is the spirit of cricket – of the game itself – that glorifies everything connected with it.

Ranji then traces how cricket, in becoming an occupation rather than a recreation, relies on professionals 'naturally', in the Gesell sense of a natural economic order. There is competition and a marketplace:

> ... A demand for exhibitions of first-rate football has arisen, and been met by the inevitable supply ... if this is true of football it is doubly true of cricket.

and

... without professionals ... it would be impossible to fill up the county teams with players possessing the requisite amount of skill.

and

... The chances are that a strong popular desire, if not bad, is very good, and consequently ought to be satisfied.

so

Now the increase of the number of professional players is a natural result of the evolution of cricket into its present state and dimensions.

For Ranji cricket professionals are not the doomed rentier class of the mid-1930s County Championship being made even more marginal by Hitler and Mussolini;[93] they are the future, to be led by Hobbs then others to an inheritance of the organisations and tradition guarded for so long by the gentleman amateur against the animals of Pycroft's 'dunghill'. Let us examine this 'dunghill' more closely.

The East Road area of Cambridge was regarded as a 'nether world' from the 1850s onwards, where anecdotes of hopeless poverty and despair match any to be found elsewhere in the Empire.[94] This is where Jack, the oldest of the twelve Hobbs children, was born in 1882. He eventually moved with his siblings to a small terraced house in Rivar Place off Sleaford Street, Sturton Town. Cambridge's 'East End' by the railway lines was as near to us in Harvey Road as The Leys School in terms of minutes spent walking, but very far removed in material circumstances and activities. One was punctuated with the sounds of tileworks and wagons on the sidings, the other by the sounds of cows on Sheep's Green and the splashes of bathers and boaters on the river.

Hobbs was not bound for Eton and a Blue. He left York Street Boys School (fees fourpence a week) aware of the riches in professional cricket:

> they were getting five pounds a match. It seemed big money ... Cricket had become with me an all-absorbing passion. It was my supreme ambition ... Love of the game must have been bred in my blood.

We can still stand on the same ground outside the Rivar Place terraced house where he used to play with a brussels sprout for ball and a stalk for a bat as a young man, and ponder the contrast with the world of the Darwins, Lyttletons, and Balfours, indeed even the Keyneses.

The culture of purposeful non-conformity, duty, and service was shared between our families, however, and the most striking feature of Barnwell/Sturton Town at that time was the number and range of evangelical and missionary initiatives aimed at easing the grinding material and spiritual poverty, free from the palliative of alcohol.

It is more than doubtful that we met at Emmanuel Chapel or in the Ainsworth Street bible class, but it would be fitting to think that The Master cricketer and I mingled occasionally on Parker's Piece in the early 1890s without realising it. Hobbs said in his

AN ARTICLE COMPILED DURING APRIL 1935

This faded moment of glory for The Anchor cricket team shows Fenner's in 1892, and is in Reeve's book on Cambridgeshire as well as Hobb's first autobiography. It is clear that this is a very unusual pub side as there are several top players present. Reeve says 'Included in this group are H. Carpenter, later the well-known Essex professional; Tom Hayward of All-England [sic] and Surrey fame; J. C. Hobbs, father of Sir Jack Hobbs; G. Watts who kept wicket for Surrey; and of course, as did J. O'Connor, father of Jack O'Connor, the Essex batsman.' Tom played for England, not the All England club, of course, as did Jack O'Connor in the 1920s. Jack Hobb's book *My Cricket Memories* gives us more information; Second from left, front row, J.C. Hobbs, father of J.B.; seated first in the second row, Tom Hayward; seated in the background Dan Hayward, Tom's brother; standing wearing a straw hat is Mr F. C. Hutt, to whom J. B. Hobbs owed his introduction to Surrey. Hutt was the scorer at Jesus, and a sort of father figure for Jack after the death of J. C. Hobbs.

autobiography that he attended the Australia match in 1893 at Fenner's. I do not recall exactly, but it is doubtful my father or I could have resisted a visit across the road to such a prestigious event.

Kelly's Directory surveys the Cambridge populace annually. Here we can see George Burbage, of 29, King Street, replying in 1874 that he was a 'professional cricketer', although he never played in a first-class match in his life, and Cambridgeshire is not thought of as a professional's county. This is also what Jack Hobbs's father said later in Brewhouse Lane, that most notorious of Cambridge slum streets, and then again in 1896 after the move to Rivar Place. The cricket professionals littering the Kelly Directory didn't get a winter 'dole', and their earning lives were short. This is the true curse of the label 'first-class' cricketer; it diminishes the memory of all those net bowlers and assistant groundsmen (and there were many) without whom the Fenner's showcasing would have been impossible.

It must be remembered that the background to Hobbs's success was a home and family in Cambridge that would have implicitly and explicitly placed constraints around his life and forbidden contemplation of such ambition as playing for England. A slum birth in Brewhouse Lane hemmed in not by one but two breweries at least. A servile relationship to Jesus College and the University, such that Parker's Piece rather than Fenner's was to be his training ground. A surrounding culture of long working and drinking hours for little reward, and tragic deaths and heavy responsibilities within the family. The expectations, the probability, of success must have been low, and the height of rebellion could only be, surely, taking the temperance pledge, and associating with a Mission rather than mammon? Indeed, his first century was for the Ainsworth Bible Class, a coterie of fellow rebels mustering in the mission rooms on the next terraced street along from Rivar Place where the family had escaped to from the East Road nexus. Halfway along the walk to Fenner's on Mill Road lay the workhouse.[95]

The ambition to turn one's back any further than this on one's heritage would be seen as lunacy rather than bravery. It is clear that what other advantages he had he was loathe to use; it was left to family friends to make chance suggestions to Hayward about a Surrey future, as he never countenanced doing this himself. He found the secret of making artefacts, divorcing himself as a person from what has been created, almost by streaming it out from the cerebellum untainted by personal memory, consciousness, or effort. The irony of this world is that we label such creations 'work' or 'craft'; to Hobbs, rather, it 'came naturally'. I can hardly say that exactly of my own output. The curious nature of Hobbs's rebellion is compounded by his circumventing the Cambridge establishment. It was very much carried out from the Fenner's margin, with deferential good manners that signalled integrity rather than cant. This makes the scale of it now seem prodigiously large, and places him ahead of me as a rebel, however much the next generation of young economists may come to talk about 'Keynes's revolution'.[96] The crucial condition was a lack of inhibitions, even an inherent degree of uninhibitiveness.

Hobbs was conditioned by a never-ending series of environmental and conceptual constraints at the Fenner's margin, the most pervasive of which were the ubiquitous working-class parochialism and insouciance which so frustrated Evangelical and Anglo-Catholic missionaries alike in the established Church. Eglantyne Jebb, after whom one of my niece's was named, was encouraged by my mother[97] to write a study of Cambridge's social questions a generation ago. She put this in an apt way:

> The majority will, indeed, drift into the common resources of idleness, but there will always be a few adventurous spirits who, finding their lot cast in grey, dull surroundings, will defy society and find an outlet in breaking its laws.

AN ARTICLE COMPILED DURING APRIL 1935

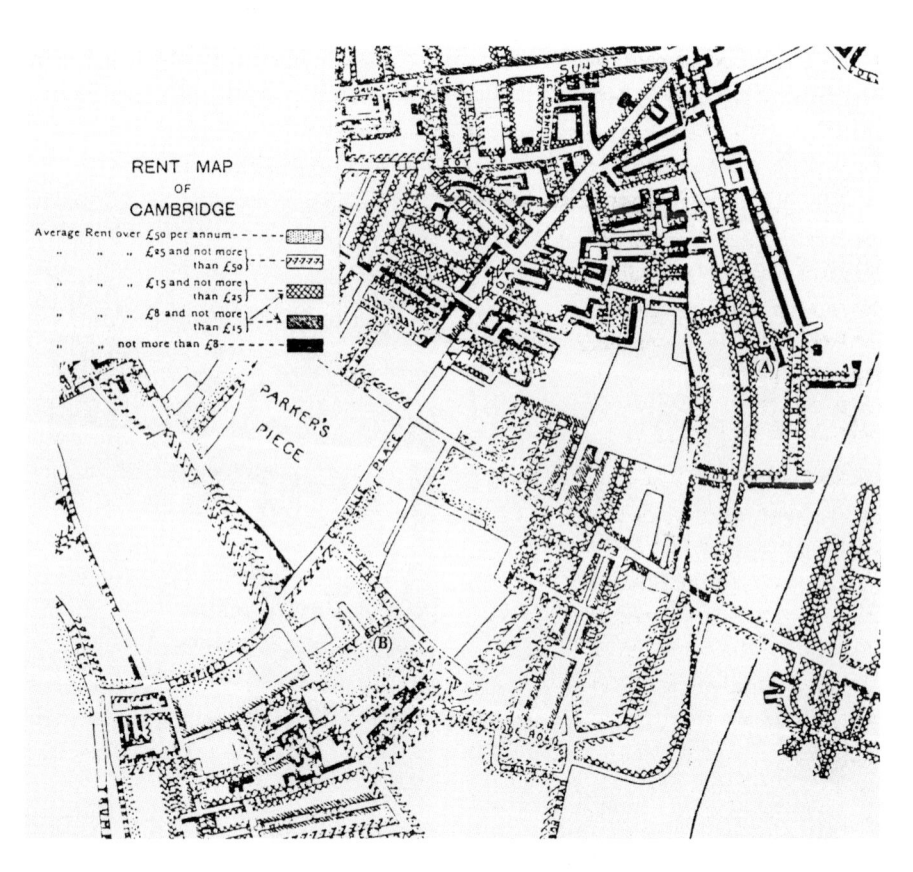

Despite Gwen Raverat's error in the key, the map in Eglantyne Jebb's book squarely contrasts the poverty of the Hobbs family (A) with the comfort of the Keyneses (B)

Or, alternatively, in breaking its *bounds*, for part of his rebellion was in trying to be *good* ('even if I failed miserably', Hobbs says). That a Hobbs would break out rather than break laws was not really considered as a possibility by Charles Darwin's genteel grand daughter, and because he clearly had an exceptional ability his example may have resonated only dimly through the rest of the slums of Barnwell and Romsey Town. By his modest public manner he may not seem to be one to defy social norms, but his mother gave him an early example in life by keeping a pet duck in the household called Cyril which followed

The two Ambrose prints used by Fry

her wherever she went. Hobbs is on record as detesting Brewhouse Lane and later Rivar Place, not because of Cyril, or the pet rabbits, or the local bullies, but because of the contrast with other areas of Cambridge that he explored in the summer holidays:

> I envied those who had big houses and who could hold up their head in any company

How must it have felt to see his parents managing a family of six boys and six girls in that small cottage in Rivar Place while Margaret, Geoffrey, and I seemed to luxuriate in Harvey Road just sixty yards from Fenner's? Gwen Raverat's iconographic map for the 1906 Brief Study is pathetically eloquent on this point, showing Brewhouse Lane and Rivar Place darkly shaded ('not more than £8 per annum' in rent) while Harvey Road is in the top order ('over £50 per annum').

Hobbs's escape may have been unexpected but the contributions made by his father, and then Mr Hutt and Tom Hayward, were clearly more in line with Eglantyne Jebb's prescription:

> ... to foster interests which will stifle vicious or merely frivolous tendencies is not simply to assist the cause of temperance, morality, and thrift, but to raise the whole level of existence.

That conditioning makes the picture of him by Charles Ambrose in an Edwardian charge a genuine portrait of a revolutionary, indeed the great Cambridge rebel of the century. Ambrose seems to have given us a disturbing insight into the power of the rebel in that portrait showing Hobbs leaping out at the ball like Constantine senior. It was widely seen in C. B. Fry's magazine which ran from 1904 to 1911. The pose is so uncharacteristic of Hobbs (where is the long nose, bony look, and legside shot?) and so different from the other Ambrose portraits in the magazine series that the question has to be asked: is this a mistake? Isn't the languid leg deflection the true portrait of The Master's economy? Although the Fleurs de Lys is there on the cap this must be an accretion on a Caribbean sketch, or perhaps a borrowed item of Surrey headwear on someone else's head. As the librarian at Lord's pointed out, even if it is labelled 'Hobbs' in the original publication that could have been done in error, as even the best publishing manager might not oversee the project to perfection. Another puzzled expert thought it was Learie Constantine, but recognised it was too early and could not be so. It seemed to be an intractable problem and a delightful reminder that in a capitalist, as in a communist, society the winners write the history; if Fry published this as Hobbs, then it will be Hobbs to all future generations of researchers.

The discovery that 'Tear'em' Tarrant was also likely to undergo accidental censorship further entrenched such a gloomy line of thought. Pupils of modern history are always shown the famous photograph of Lenin in full, passionate flow on the podium with Trotsky at his left hand; teachers then show them how under Stalin the podium was extended and Trotsky has been removed. Now poor Tarrant is to share that fate; page 6 of *The Graphic* dated July 20th 1901 shows a photograph of 'Three Famous Cambs.

GOLDEN AGES AT THE FENNER'S MARGIN

THREE FAMOUS CAMBS. CRICKETERS.
Carpenter, Tarrant and Hayward, senr.

PICTURES OF THE PAST:
No. 467.

"Tearem" Tarrant, one of the greatest of all Cambridge cricketers, who gained world-wide fame as a bowler. He was contemporary with those other renowned players, T. Hayward (uncle of the great Surrey batsman) and Bob Carpenter, whose photograph was recently hung in the Hobbs Pavilion on Parker's Piece (reproduced at the time in the *Cambridge Chronicle*). George Tarrant (his real name we are told in Wisden's was George Tarrant Wood) was born at Cambridge on December 7, 1838, and died on July 2, 1870.

Above: But the press got it wrong: the third player is DIver not Tarrant, and this is the trio who went out to North America with Parr in 1859–60. Tarrant went with Hayward and Carpenter on the Australian tour of 1863–4.

Right: This is the genuine article.

Cricketers, Carpenter, Tarrant, and Hayward senr.'. But the man in the middle is also to be seen in the photograph of Parr's North America party of 1859 – and Tarrant didn't go to North America on that tour. The great (and, one hopes, authentic) picture of Tarrant in his All England gear was reprinted in *The Chronicle* on page 9 of the 7th June 1933 copy and shows a totally different man, clean-shaven not with the 'Newgate' whiskers, and with level rather than angular eyes.[98] Is it too late to save Tarrant, and does anyone care enough to do it? In fact it was simple to find multiple references to the player in Parr's party and likenesses to back up the correction; the third famous Cambridgeshire cricketer in *The Graphic* of 1901 was Diver, not Tarrant.

Encouraged, I went back to Cardus to read about the pre-war Hobbs. Then there was no doubt; the rebel was a dancer down the pitch. I looked at the cigarette cards that have been used as promotions, and the photograph of Hobbs on the boat to Australia for the Edwardian tour; there was the curve at the cheekbone and the unexpectedly full face. Then to a photograph from the Surrey C.C.C. collection showing the shot which

AN ARTICLE COMPILED DURING APRIL 1935

Ambrose had worked on. The mystery was solved; he had taken a view not from wide mid-on like the photograph, but from an imagined position at wide mid-off which makes the shot look much more dramatic, violent even. The sun is the same, giving that deep shadow over the face and yet the clear view of his fore-arm; the sweater is off (characteristic of Ambrose) to give dramatic impact. Purposefulness is amplified to produce the final effect of theatrical captivation.

This is the Cantabrigian who had to live idly in Surrey for two years to qualify, and also missed four of his best years (and a huge tranche of benefit income) during the Great War, during which he worked at a munitions factory before joining the R.A.F. Despite losing these six summers he revolutionised batting techniques between 1905 and 1913 when swerve, seam, and googly threatened to swamp all other batsman. He then, between 1919 and 1934 became not only a legend for his play, but, more significantly, a legend for being a professional

The photograph of an effervescent Hobbs.

batsman. Looking at the two Ambrose prints I can finally and confidently express a preference for the offside shot, the genuine and disturbing portrait of a rebel, quick on his feet, alert in mind, and joyfully aware of the possibilities that youth is offering him.

There is so much in this man's spirit that breathes warmth into us and reminds me of a conversation held with Virginia Woolf over a decade ago about her male literary characters which she raised again at Tilton last August. She knew, she said, that Peter Walsh believed, wrongly, that cricket was important, was no mere game, but why did he believe it? 'I mean,' she finished on one occasion, 'look at how much fuss is made over that funny little boring man Hobbs!' Cricket certainly entered her books in ways that no other Bloomsbury author entertained. In *Jacob's Room* Mrs. Flanders surprises herself by mentioning cricket to Captain Barfoot; she subconsciously realised it was a subject he would consider to be important. Lord Gayton would spend all day at Lord's; Dr. Holmes advised that Septimus Warren Smith should notice real things and play cricket.[99] In *To The Lighthouse* there are constant references to the children (including Prue) playing cricket before bathtime, with the tap of balls upon bats and the sharp sudden bark of 'How's that? How's that?' Near the beginning of *On Not Knowing Greek* Virginia opined that the main elements of village life include the farm (for working), the church (for worship), the club (for meeting), and the cricket field which is for *play*. I was delighted that she put it that way; it is where we play *with* others, for we can only

215

compete against them by co-operating with them to create the marketplace at the wicket. Virginia has often said that one of her deepest contentments at Rodmell was looking out of the window to watch the village boys playing cricket.

Her comment about Hobbs, or more particularly her recognition of his fame, reminded me of *A Room of One's Own* in which she concluded from a perusal of the newspapers that 'England is under the rule of a patriarchy'. One of the key bits of evidence was the splash in the serious dailies that 'somebody' had made a big score in South Africa. Note the 'somebody'; maybe it was Mead in 1923, or Tyldesley in 1927, but it wasn't Hobbs, or Woolley, or Chapman. These were names that she would have remembered, but it was just a 'somebody'[100] – yet they still took up more space in the headlines than the Foreign Secretary or the Judge (who only get second and third mentions). Virginia knew indeed that cricket was thought to be important, even though that view was wrong, through its association with the patriarchy.

The temptation for me was to retaliate in defence of cricket by giving Lydia's opinion of *Mrs. Dalloway*, that there were no characters but only puppets, while in cricket (or ballet) the drama is in seeing the dynamic of character. Who will grasp the chance to express their true personality and *not* behave like a puppet in the given situation? (In defiance of the growing academic interest in modern literature, this has always seemed to me to be the problem with fiction. Why read Forster or Woolf when you can read *Principia Ethica* or Marshall[101] and taste Cambridge *first* hand?)

So instead I pointed out some obvious points, like the appeal to our pre-industrial memory of toiling in the sun on a field, and the precarious uncertainty of the vulnerable batter (a labourer) surrounded by the opposition (commerce!) waiting to make profit from his error. I then tried to approach cricket from the point of view of inflation, deflation, and the return to gold. Cricket was a simplified model that provides parables, even ideals, for how we would wish economic success to be earnt by skill and persistence rather than rights, monopoly, and inheritance. That this does not reflect the harsh reality of a world where primogeniture and sex matter merely gives cricket an added contemplative, even tragic, air that is absent in other, less leisurely, games.

I cited the situation of the French franc of early 1926 as being equivalent to a sticky wicket. In my articles of the time I was offering four explanations for the low French price level; time-lags, hoarding, capital flight, and price ceilings. 'My analysis' (I exaggerated to her for effect) 'came to me from Cricket as much as from Economics.' The four options could be translated respectively from Economic language to Cricket language in the following ways: confidence to play shots would emerge through time spent at the wicket during which one would become accustomed to the nature of the pitch (time-lags); some would always be fearful and stonewall (hoarding); some will try to draw this match, hoping that other results will work for one and that one will try to win the next match (capital flight); the last explanation is that it is following skipper's orders (price ceilings). The cricket-viewing public would hardly equate the drama of the sticky wicket exchanges on the cricket field with those in the foreign exchanges of the City, but there would be meaning drawn even from such apparently tedious play as play-

Virginia and Vanessa Bell playing cricket in St. Ives, 1894.

ing out a draw that could be similarly found as a topic of discussion in the chophouses off Lombard Street.

Virginia was patient but looked at me in a manner that suggested cricket was more akin to Greek than Economics. I persisted with my presentation this time citing gold, and in particular the position of early 1927. A possible policy at that moment was to return to the aim of earning more in exports to finance investments overseas, requiring either wage-cuts or a rise in the world price of gold (or leaving the gold standard). This, in cricket, was the equivalent of waiting for a change in the championship points system while hiring more professional bowlers. A second policy was to continue with depressed trade and unemployment; this is clearly the attempt to grind out defensive draws. The final option was to redirect the unemployed resources from previously-exporting firms and the idle hoardings into domestic production and investment (particularly in housing and light industry in the south). This would correspond to a batsman going onto the attack in a knife-edge situation, prepared to lose gloriously (and enjoy it) in the attempt to win. Surely Virginia could see that the reaction to England's Ashes win at The Oval in 1926, when Hobbs and Sutcliffe counter-attacked on a sticky wicket, was public exultation that could only be explained by this sort of close relationship with the reality of their political and economic situations? I paused for breath to see if I had convinced myself.

Virginia said, 'But Maynard, won't they see through these delusions and get awfully depressed? I mean, Churchill likes to see himself as a hero in a crisis but generally he fumbles the catches so badly we pack him off to the boundary.' Sensing victory, I seemed to bend to agree, but concluded that I was therefore glad that she had conceded my main point; since he had rarely failed us when we looked to him for heroics, Hobbs must be more heroic than Churchill!

And now he's gone, let nobody forget it.

An Article Compiled During July 1937

Can The Field Of The Cloth Of Cream Withstand Scrutiny From Marshall's Twin Blades Of The Scissor?

'[J.M.K.] had a keen eye for the mutual relevance of apparently widely separated problems.'

(Sir Roy Harrod, 'The Life of John Maynard Keynes')

The General Theory Of Employment, Interest, And Money *(or should it be Enjoyment, Wickets, And Strokes?) went on sale in February 1936 and was acclaimed as widely as the* Treatise *had been ignored. There were many factors behind its success; the sheer impotence of traditional remedies (whose advocates reviewed the book savagely), the coherence of J.M.K.'s attack on the apparent Soviet successes through Planning, the deep frustration of younger economists, the growing influence of quantitative analysis, the beguiling degree of difficulty of the guru's message, as well as his reluctance (although presented with myriad opportunities) to say 'I told you so' all contributed to the Keynesian Revolution.*

J.M.K. invented the need for, as well as the subject of, macroeconomics as we now understand it. Denying that supply creates its own demand ('Say's Law'), that thrift is needed to fund investment, and that public budgets must balance to avoid the 'crowding out' of private enterprise, he allowed governments to alter their priorities with regard to the economic system, and encouraged intervention for the achievement of those aims. A 'magic rectangle' with the aims of growth, low inflation, low unemployment, and balanced trade should replace the balanced budget mantra, even though these aims were tethered in pairs that pulled in opposite directions (e.g. high growth and low unemployment generally bring rising inflation and trade deficits). Economics could now be an interesting holistic art, not just the removed and mechanical engineering of public finances. Dangerous gluts of output might persist (bringing increasing unemployment), and the lowering of interest rates and of taxes might be needed to raise overall demand, which would then restore levels of savings and tax revenues as the unemployed were soaked up into jobs.

J.M.K.'s articles in The Times *in January 1937 (How To Avoid A Slump) helped popularise the main elements of his ideas, and signalled that he might soon become genuinely the most influential figure in British economic policy. The swift subsequent appearance of an explanation of the business cycle, through the interaction of the multiplier effect and the accelerator (which can now be achieved in minutes by an adolescent on a p.c. spreadsheet), confirmed the universal belief that Economics had changed forever. But in May 1937 at the age of 53 J.M.K. suffered a massive coronary thrombosis from which he only recovered slowly. He was told to take it easy and convalesce far away from pressure in North Wales.*

AN ARTICLE COMPILED DURING JULY 1937

So here I am at death's door confined in a room where even rice pudding and calves' foot jelly are forbidden luxuries, yet my imagination continues to run riot. They cannot quell the questing spirit by just telling one not to work and after a vivid dream last night I feel another cricket article coming on. I have an inkling that this may partly be stimulated by my medication. I had a most curious and feverish nightmare during which I must have been half-awake; I was the manager of a textile factory manufacturing cricket flannels, and was keenly aware that the level of profits was judged to be in direct proportion to the amount of disarray I could create amongst my bedclothes. Judging by the tangle of counterpane and blankets strewn around me by the morning it must have been a satisfactory trading period. The connection between cricket and business stimulated me to ponder on the renewed current world downturn and also the experiences of 1929–33. These events culminated in Britain's desperate (but separate) attempts both to create an economic *modus operandi* in a fracturing world, and to regain the Ashes in a world dominated by Bradman (even to the extent that in the Covent Garden season in 1934 no fewer than *three* newspaper writers compared a ballerina to 'The Don', who was piling on the runs and in renewed favour following the 'Bodyline' controversy).

It would have been difficult for the Australian authorities four and a half years ago to have chosen a more provocative word than 'unsportsmanlike' for their famous telegram to M.C.C.. The implication that the Jardine approach was legal but not in the spirit of the game could hardly be expected to wring concessions out of Lords. Perhaps the Australian estimation of what was meant by the phrase 'it isn't cricket' had got out of step with the English? Certainly Learie Constantine, one of the most notable of thinking sportsmen, realised in 1933 that it was up to the legislators to sort out the possibility of a direct attack on the batsman; an appeal to one side to abandon an advantage it had created within the existing laws of the game was an irrational expectation, for reality can hardly be *uninvented*.

Besides, there were plenty of possible avenues for retaliatory challenges to be made; what about the incessant noise of the barrackers which was, to say the least, a contrast to the atmosphere at a British snooker, golf, or cricket event? Was it in the spirit of the game that Australian players should broadcast or report domestically on the same day that they were playing in a Test Match? Was it in the spirit of the game that such a fuss was made about Larwood and Voce that their careers should be imperilled? Should champagne be allowed on the field (or off) as a restorative for bowlers since it could be argued it is a stimulant? Did Barton King breach the spirit of the game in developing swing by shining one side of the leather ball more than another? Certainly it was widely felt that the 'Bosie' 'wasn't cricket' when it was introduced, for the action was deceitful with regard to the result. There hadn't been any obvious, major betting scandals in English cricket for over a century, and there could surely be no greater devotion to the spirit of the game than the elimination of that particular canker.

Archie Jackson, A. A. Milne and B. J. T. Bosanquet were among the more celebrated critics of the Australian response, emphasising how cricket had always been a batsman's game punctuated by exogenous bowling shocks like Bart King's swing, the googly, and the Gregory-McDonald partnership of 1921. Then of course there was always the possibility of direct retaliation, which might have hastened a change in the laws of the game, but might also have required the Australian authorities to pick an aborigine, Eddie Gilbert, for the national side. They clearly thought that this was a less acceptable option than the aforementioned telegram. By such curious currents are the fates governed.

The 1935 change to the L.B.W. law as championed by my boyhood hero Frank Mitchell, the 1896 Cambridge University captain, to entice bowlers back outside the offstump was a fairly prompt and reasoned response to the crisis. However, the revision of Law 42 on unfair play relies on the necessarily normative judgements of umpires. A more active response, even to the extent of short-term over-reaction was possible, with a maximum number of balls per over at a particular height, a limit on the number of legside fielders, deadening of the pitch composition short of a length, even restricting the bowler from delivering the ball from above the top of the cranium, and, of course, penalty runs for infringements. It seems the prompt response to Mitchell's own crisis at the Varsity Match was not to be repeated now as it would be an admission that M.C.C.'s own captain had exposed gaping holes in their own legal architecture.

The 'timeless Test' concept was introduced as a rather soporific method of dealing with the bat's predominance (what Lyttelton called an 'evil' and against which Ranji also declared his opposition back in 1901). But as the fates would have it Jardine almost immediately made the change in regulations redundant. What was clear was that with 'bodyline' we entered a cricketing as well as an economic period of deflation; the range of shots that could be attempted was drastically reduced, and although the velocity of circulation was interestingly raised (*i.e.* Australia scored at an above average rate), the actual totals plummeted compared to 1928 and 1930. The classical function of such recession (or indeed the second new ball) is to ensure that we get 'idle forms to perish and error to decay'.

The standard economist's position in a slump was to repeat a belief in Say's Law; that if output has been created the payments made for its production to the factors of land, labour, and capital must be sufficient for that output to be consumed. If there is any unemployment it must result from a maldistribtution of income created by some groups of workers having excessive wages compared to others. Unions, for example, may be raising some sectors' pay too high above the subsistence mark set by the informal agricultural labour market. Since the financial institutions guarantee that all loanable funds saved will be lent for investment or consumption, and mechanisms such as the Gold Standard ensure the balancing of trade, the only possible source of destabilisation might be a budget deficit. This will (through the government having to borrow from the pool of savings) lead to a crowding out of private investment and lower future growth. The obvious policies in a slump are therefore threefold; first, curb union powers and seek wage reductions to price labour back into jobs; second, raise taxes and lower spending to restore the government's balanced budget; third, raise interest rates to encourage saving which will supply increased finance to firms for higher investment. This was what my father rather grandly called (with all the authority of scholars like Whewell) 'the explication of conceptions', not to be followed, one hopes and presumes, by '*ignoratio elenchi*'. The logical relations established in the above arguments seem so perfect it seems almost unfair that they should be wrong.

Part of the error comes from a misunderstanding of equilibrating as a concept; people are brought up to think of a parallel with a central heating thermostat. They picture a fixed temperature which can be chosen at which inputs will be switched on or off to balance with the outputs, or losses. This 'hydraulic' approach isn't helpful. I prescribe a day at Fenner's as a cure. The rate at which wickets fall is neutral, necessarily happening at the same rate for the bowling and batting sides, but the outcome of a myriad of different decisions, possibly favouring one side's ambitions, possibly the other. It is *income* that equilibrates savings to the stimulus of investment, and only cheap money will embolden firms tripped up by falling expected returns and low sales and high stock levels. The public budget should, like the trade balance, be left to itself, as any deficit in a downturn can only act as a helpful stimulus, just as any surplus in a boom can only restrain growth from creating inflation.

It is very suggestive that at a time when in certain quarters it is fashionable to talk of how many people Lenin or Stalin has killed no one is whispering the question how many did the depression of 1929–33 kill? It is a taboo concept, for the capitalist-classical system is a neutral, automatic mechanism that cannot be admitted to kill actively. In fifty years time there will still be no one asking the question, let alone answering it, although all will be taught how many Stalin, or Mussolini, or Hitler killed. Yet we know that carts were going around the streets of Santiago in Chile in 1931 picking the dead off the street. We know there was malnutrition in Chicago and Berlin. How many did Mr Hoover kill? We are not allowed to ask.

In Australia the looking glass world of the classical response to deflation was completed by my old friend Otto Niemeyer prescribing the full Treasury remedy when visiting from the U.K. as an 'expert'.[102] Justification for such a role was not hard to find at a time when the U.S. banking sector was in such evident disarray (with almost more runs than Bradman in evidence) compared to the British reactions to crises in 1847, 1857, and 1866; despite the provisions of the 1844 Act the Bank of England directors were permitted to issue notes such as to prevent further crisis against securities. Generally the mere threat of an 'illegal' note issue was enough to encourage confidence. It was overlooked that the German operation of legal issues above the limit in return for a 5 per cent tax was even more efficacious as it obviated the mental strain of bankers awaiting the suspension of the Bank Act.

However, since the Australians were net debtors to the U.K. Otto's detractors in 1930 could portray his suggestions for tax rises as attempts to ensure that they would not default on the interest payments during the depression. Otto was merely a greedy garnerer of *gelt*. This was typical of the paranoia engendered on all sides by the destabilising weight and longevity of the recent slump; in a fast-changing world where the deflationary spiral seemed to be unstoppable it was difficult to tell where the economic power really lay between nations. Just as the creditor could only see the debtor gaining from the use of the loan and suffered the constant threat of default on a huge asset, the debtor could only see an endless drain on its current account and the possible growth in size of the liability if negative inflation took hold; each assumed she was being exploited by the other. The Ottawa smokescreen and Balfour committee merely added to the illusions that both the mother-country and the dominions held about each other, the stability gained developing into potentially ruinous inertia.[103]

Inertia is one quality most individuals in the workforce still require, as work for the majority is claustrophobic, repetitive, and, if not requiring definite concentration, generally forbidding liberty for the imagination and any expression of verve. Spectacular cricket still provides an antidote. At The Oval a man can relax the eye and sinew, and contemplate a range of possible outcomes at each stage of proceedings. Routine is provided but is ever-varying. There is space for conjecture and cause for wonder. It is not surprising that they pay and require professional heroes.

It is quite daunting to think, however, what it will mean for cricket if this state of affairs should change. My fear is that with the rise of services and the decline of secondary industry, cricket will increasingly become another outlet of nationalistic fervour, which will make the 1932–3 series seem by contrast to have been in tenor more like the sort of unfortunate punting expedition on the Cam, ruined by someone leaving Aunt Bessie's parasol loitering at home under the front door porch so that the poor dear develops a sunstroke which means she has to miss the archdeacon's tea party.

One of the strongest forces the colonial powers will exert in the second half of the twentieth century is in restructuring the world's economy to their advantage along the following lines. Rising domestic productivity which threatens job security will naturally be resisted by unions in manufacturing and, more strongly, by white collar managers with large home loans to repay. Fortunately for capitalists this may not matter too much, for these categories of productive factors enter into the process of production at a relatively late stage, and so the top level manager earning a fabulous salary working every hour God sends in the week, and more, will comfort himself that he is not inhibiting profit unduly.

The cost of capital represented by work in progress will be greatly reduced, however, by increased productivity at an *earlier* stage of production. In a way this is similar to the use of the off drive after a rain break in cricket; the longer you wait to use it the more likely it will be to go to the boundary for the outfield will have dried. Your expenditure of energy yields greater results.

There will be, therefore, relentless pressure on imports, on commodity production and prices by the colonial power, a desperation in the attempts to gain economies of scale in their distribution, and a constant anxiety about costs in the energy sector. If it proves to be an era of flexible exchange rates this will encourage sheltering from competition in a concentration on non-traded output (*i.e.* services) in the more economically developed nations. The result is likely to be both growing world inequality and more adverse terms of trade for the poor and indebted nations. The Christian Utopians (what Marx called the soft-hearted capitalists) will try to resist this trend in vain, and if successful will only succeed in impoverishing their own communities and creating a deflationary vortex of investment inactivity and muddled uncertainty.

Is this bleak prospect completely unwelcome? Not entirely, for accumulation must occur somewhere in the poorer nations as the manufacturing process is shifted away from the most advanced, and therefore care should be concentrated on guiding the path and destination of that divestment by the colonial masters. In addition, methods will be sought (successfully by some) both to resist the downward terms of trade and to hurdle over a complete level of development to focus on a later stage of production with its higher reward for the rentier and the labourer. True entrepreneurship in these undertakings will be shown but rarely. Its standard will usually be championed by the very rentiers who have succeeded not through their own enterprise, but by an inexorable global tide that has carried them up rather than down river. They view the helpless stranded on the shingle of the curving river's inner edge and become the bores of tomorrow, moralising about *laisser faire*, unions, and, of course, enterprise. To switch metaphors in midstream, a rentier is one who occupies the crease, while the entrepreneur changes the match.

For the English knowledge and understanding of cricket such economic changes may prove devastating without compensatory measures.[104] The move to services means that nostalgia will emerge for industrial rather than pre-industrial relics. This will remove the yearning for wide grass spaces, for slow but purposeful ritual, and lead to a demand for more noisy and immediate excitement, with a corresponding shortening of the concentration span. With the rise of electronic calculating and the decline of the manufacturing calculus (services being a more quality-driven sector) people will lose the ability and desire for the complex of quantification that cricket provides; the concept of the nil-nil draw, or the knife-edge win, or the unlucky defeat over ninety minutes will be at the limits of desire. Above all, the assessment of input (usually dignified as 'effort') will be of more interest than the data output, because this is what employees will be increasingly judged by. This could also undermine the idea of teamwork and rewards being egalitarian (whither the Test match fee?)

It has also to be admitted that the familiarity of the public with the game through the newsreels means that the the *conjuring* element has all but disappeared from the lower reaches of the game. Fifty years ago a Parker's Piece spiv could offer 'a few balls' to a passer-by and feed him a series of full tosses and long hops that would be easy to hit with a scything motion; when venturing to suggest a few pence on the punter's ability to keep the remaining balls out of the stumps he would then alter his length subtly to defeat the customary scythe with ease, and complete his fairground swindle by magically bowling the bamboozled batsman. Nowadays the importance of the straight bat is demonstrated regularly to all cinema visitors and has become temporarily part of the nation's psychology. The time will soon come when the British have no idea why a straight bat is an important metaphor.

The counter side to the drug of excitement, however, is the increasing awareness of and dissatisfaction with boredom, and a constant fear that life is getting greyer. There will be charges of hypocrisy every time the activities held to be superior show any signs of flagging (*e.g.* the tedious play up and down the touchline in the first half of a soccer match between two keen rivals). People will become so bored for large stretches of their life that there won't even be rebellion, for that takes the sort of long, careful planning and execution that will be beyond the future worker. My mother related how her rebellious safety valve as a young teenager consisted of secretly putting up her mother's sacred umbrella (kept ceremonially in the parlour) and walking round and round with the umbrella aloft and her tongue out.

On reflection perhaps I was too optimistic in my *Economic Possibilities For Our Grandchildren*. Even if there is a continued and, by the standards of previous generations, sizeable rise in future incomes it will be of little consequence if it is accompanied by a loss of ability to pursue pleasure meaningfully. A distinction can be made between 'money' and accumulation; as I've said before the 'love of money' (*i.e.* drive to accumulate) is a somewhat disgusting morbidity, one of those semi-criminal, semi-pathological propensities which one hands over with a shudder to specialists in a mental disease.[105]

The class antagonisms which were so mischievously stirred up by the marxian and classical tendencies may also reappear. Since in the accounting identity liabilities plus proprietorship equal assets plus profit, any increase in profit raises proprietorship (*ceteris paribus*). But a capitalist cannot make *any* output without labour, and with no revenue there can not only be no profit, but there will ensue as a matter of course losses, due to fixed costs, *plus* the loss of income for the alternative uses of the capital that were foregone. It seems clear to labour, therefore, that the capitalist owes it more than the sum the capitalists deduce from marginal productivity theory. Without the labourer, they hold, the capitalist is like a groundsman with a ball, stumps, rolled pitch, umpires, and batsmen waiting but with no bowler or fielders available; there is no prospect of any enjoyment without them. The capitalist sees this through the looking glass; the former argument represents a treacherous holding to ransom of the capitalist after he has taken the risk with his capital on the understanding that labour will cooperate. If no profit is made, no output can be produced that will ensure employment in the future. There will be no enjoyment from the game in such an atmosphere, which would be further blighted by a wave of inverted snobbery in which the English cricket tradition will be seen to be a relic of Eton and Cambridge rather than Old Trafford and Kennington.

The irony is that those who champion soccer as the working man's game and decry cricket as an upper-class remnant will be more bourgeois than ever before. They would do well to remember that such a view bestows a genteel patina on cricket's halo that doesn't square up to the reality of history. For example, before the *Enigma Variations* of 1899, it was Hubert Parry, not Edward Elgar, who was the doyen of English music, and one could hardly name a more austere or revered figure within the imperial Establishment. Parry was also, of course, one of Eton's long line of cricketers. He achieved cricketing fame not for his play during the 2nd XI match against Winchester, but for a spectacular display of hooliganism at Windsor station on his return. This was so keenly felt by the stationmaster that the composer of the 1882–3 Cambridge Symphony had to skulk around in crowds (for he could not disguise himself given the distinctive garb expected of all pupils) every time he required railway transport for some time after.

An Article Compiled During February 1946

A One-Way Bet To Global Divergence; Why Cricket And Economics Are Likely To Fail Us In The Real World

... how we all bear relation to each other in this small wide world ...

(Lydia Lopokova to J.M.K. in 1924).

GOLDEN AGES AT THE FENNER'S MARGIN

By 1939 J.M.K.'s health had recovered sufficiently to allow him to consider how best to marshall the nation's resources for the impending conflict and combat the danger of both demand-pull and cost-push inflation. His approach was again set out in The Times *(in November 1939) and turned into a booklet three months later (*How To Pay For The War*). In July he was given a roving government commission (with a desk in Whitehall, but no salary) and the next May saw him begin the series of six journeys to the United States which spanned the last few years of his life.*

The first involved finalising the details of Lend-Lease but the even more serious negotiating later on was about the post-war global settlement. The Keynes and White Plans were distilled to produce the Bretton Woods settlement, witnessed by 44 nations in July 1944. There was more White than Keynes, but J.M.K.'s influence was so pervasive that any U.S. economist a decade earlier would have excoriated White's ideas as louche recklessness.

The final version was vital in committing the U.S.A. and Europe to seeking a renewal of liberal, open economies as soon as practicable, while setting up international (almost supranational) bodies, like the I.M.F. and the World Bank, to prevent the return of the destabilising autarchy of the inter-war years.

Now Baron Keynes of Tilton, he defended the settlement in the House of Lords in May 1944; two months later he made the closing speech at Bretton Woods, was given a standing ovation, and serenaded with 'For He's A Jolly Good Fellow' by the delegates.

AN ARTICLE COMPILED DURING FEBRUARY 1946

§ 1. Divergence In The National Economy

The tenth anniversary of the Arts Theatre's inauguration has passed off with a most interesting and enjoyable event, thanks to the persistence and selflessness of Norman Higgins. But the evening was staged in surroundings far removed from the uncomfortable Cosmopolitan Cinema he opened in 1933. Lydia and I rearranged our weekend schedule and arrived for a supper in Norman's flat with Rylands and Kennedy.[106] Our host then surprised both Lydia and me by showing a series of excerpts from commercial motion pictures that he had identified as being fully in tune with my economic theories. This was by way of recognising that the next day was also the tenth anniversary of the appearance of my *General Theory* in the bookshops.

Accordingly the Frank Capra[107] works he chose to screen for us are, fundamentally, films with a powerfully modern economic message, conveyed in a populist way that by-passes the dry sterility of the textbook, and, therefore, are to be applauded (or in the case of Lydia and Kolenkhov, Mischa Auer's Omsk wrestler, in *You Can't Take It With You*, roared at with hysteria). One can sense the director's mistrust of *laisser faire*, hoarding, inflexible financial regulation, and the power of new money. *You Can't Take It With You* should be stopped where Anthony P. Kirby receives the news of his rival Ramsey's death and the triumph of his deal. *American Madness* should be stopped where Dickson is slumped at his desk having failed to raise any short-term liquid reserves to stop the run on his bank. In both however the last dramatic scenes involve the 'little things', the birdfeed woman, the John Doe of U.S. folk history.[108]

Higgins's coup, however, was to find out about a new R.K.O. idea entitled *The Greatest Gift* and he managed to obtain the three preliminary scripts for us to see. The core speeches have been completed although there are many parts of the film where planning remains weak, and, unfortunately, since it is with Charles Koerner it is lost to Mr Capra.[109]

Capra puts some powerful speeches into the mouths of Dickson, Grandpa Vanderhof (and one day, I would wish, George Bailey) which can scarcely be bettered for showing how the old world of *laisser faire* had to be tossed away as bankrupt not only on moral grounds, but also on the grounds of efficiency. In the Kaufman and Hart script for *You Can't Take It With You* A. P. Kirby rants, and is rebuked by Vanderhof, who reminds him that he can't take his money with him:

> 'I've got the longest and the sharpest claws too. That's how I got where I am – on top – and scum like this is still in the gutter!' ... 'When your time comes I doubt if a single tear will be shed over you, the world will probably cry good riddance!'

In *The Greatest Gift*, the hero's fluent streams of conviction tumble out in anger when the local monopolist tries to use his power to shut down his only competitor, the small independent building society the hero manages. The monopolist complains that the generous policy of lending gets us:

> a discontented, lazy rabble instead of thrifty working class

Our hero is well aware that he is implying that, as friends, these workers were being favoured in an unbusinesslike way. The response is that they did

> help a few people to get out of your slums, and what's wrong with that? Why, you're all businessmen here – doesn't it make them better citizens, doesn't it make them better customers? You said they had to wait and save their money before they even thought of a decent home. Wait? Wait for what? Until their children grow up and leave them? ... Do you know how long it takes a working man to save $5,000? ... this rabble that you're talking about, they do most of the working and paying and living and dying in this community. Well, is it too much to have them work and pay and live and die in a couple of decent rooms and a bath? ... to [my father] people were human beings, but to you, a warped frustrated old man they're cattle.[110]

Dickson, the bank manager in *American Madness*, is more specific when confronting his board of governors who want him to be less liberal. When the rebels say that in such times 'a bank should keep liquid' Dickson is clear:

> The trouble with this country today [1932] is there's too much hoarded cash; idle money is no good to industry. Where is all the money today? In the banks, vaults, socks, old tin cans buried in the ground. I tell you we've got to get the money back in circulation before you get the country back to prosperity ... It's a vicious circle, my friends, and the only place to cure it is right here at the source ... Let's get the right sort of security, not stocks and bonds that zigzag up and down but character – Alexander Hamilton's idea ... You want me to hang onto our cash; well, I don't believe in it. The law demands that I carry a certain legal reserve and I'm doing it. The rest of my money is out working, working to help industry, to help build up business.

Capra made a much more important series of seven films with Anatole Litvak when he was attached to the army unit under General George Marshall[112] responsible for explaining by film to eight million U.S. servicemen *Why We Fight*. These pictures have been widely-viewed in Britain, thanks to Mr Churchill's insistence,[113] and are part of the canon of every U.S. servicemen; but how rarely will *Prelude To War* be shown to the next generation, or the one after that? The narrator of the films was Walter Huston, who played Dickson in *American Madness*. According to Higgins and Lydia this is the most Keynesian of Capra's creations in both spirit and looks, for which I must be suitably grateful.[114] The method Capra used to convince the public that the free nations would be taken over unless they resisted by all means possible was to show them the enemy's view of themselves in propaganda films like the Nazi Party's *Triumph of the Will*, directed by young Leni Riefenstahl who also put together the film about the 1936 Olympic Games. Thus Capra's efforts were closer to documentary than propaganda in style and content; the editing was the main method of imparting the message. It clearly worked.

The ultimate test is to imagine what the world would have been like without one's own life touching so many others, in the fashion of *The Greatest Gift*; it would in my case, perhaps, be a world where Robbins and Hicks remained indefatigably on the right, where Hayek was unchallenged except by the likes of Henderson and the planners, where there existed no young generation of American 'Keynesians', and where there was no belief that, if necessary, governments can intervene to maintain demand or avoid inflation.[115]

§ 2. Divergence In The International Economy

At the end of the evening's viewing Norman remarked to me that he was sorry to say he had been unable to locate a single motion picture that made imaginative use of cricket. He had eschewed archive material as generally being tedious and wooden, and opined a fear that the peculiar Englishness of the game and its decline in Philadelphia prejudiced the odds heavily against the Hollywood system committing resources to any cricketing ventures in the future. This left me thinking once again that night about my boyhood dreams regarding the game and the nagging words that closed my father's informal and fancy-filled diary for the spring of 1896. By morning I had formalised the thoughts into a number of notes on trade, gambling, and the inadequacy of cricket as a model of how the real international arena works, and was forced to admit that my father's writings had been more prophetic than I had imagined.

Cricket is indeed a very strong metaphor for trade and the balance of payments, but in a rather unexpected way. It highlights how the belief in the importance of 'fair play' still exists in the popular imagination, even though all the evidence of social, economic, and political development over the last few centuries is that fair play can only be afforded by a victor. Crucially the failure lies in the connection between betting and the players; or, rather, the *lack* of it.

What exactly happened when the champion cricketer in the world was involved in a betting scandal and was banned? William Lambert was a partner with Osbaldeston in the double-wicket challenge against Lord Frederick Beauclerk and T. C. Howard in 1810 at Thomas Lord's first ground for a stake of fifty guineas. Illness meant that Osbaldeston couldn't play and in the final innings Lambert hit on a desperate plan to try to snatch an unlikely victory. Lord Frederick had a fearful temper, and Lambert bowled wides deliberately to arouse it. It worked and when he eventually bowled a straight one he got through the defences. As a result in 1811 wides were included in the extras. Despite being thirty-eight years old in 1817 Lambert made two hundreds in the same match at Lord's; no one else performed this feat in England until W.G. in 1868. He became implicated in the match between England and Twenty-Two of Nottingham (who won by 30 runs) at the Forest ground just before his pair of centuries. He failed badly all round, bringing suspicion upon himself, although it was rumoured that both sides had sold the game. The fact that such activity had extended from betting on single-wicket matches to wholesale bribery in a game involving thirty-three players revealed that the scale of money involved was massive, and the effects were manifestly chaotic; the Committee at Lord's was galvanised by fisticuffs just outside the pavilion between two players of the same team who had been bribed to take opposite courses of action. This farcical situation required action, and the 'legs' were cleared from 'The Green Man and Still', and public betting over the next century became associated with horseracing. Beauclerk was in a particularly ticklish situation as someone who admitted to making six hundred guineas a year out of cricket matches but was in the hierarchy expected to deal with the situation. In 1826 as M.C.C. President he delivered an unconsciously humorous speech, extolling cricket as a game

> unalloyed by love of lucre and mean jealousies.

Is it a triumph that will ultimately elude what Joan Robinson calls the 'Cambridge Circus'? Despite fleeting visions of victory, such as the 1944 White Paper on employment and the Federal Reserve's notional commitment to the level of employment, defeat looms in the form of a potential dictatorship by the short term financial transactions section of the capital account of the balance of payments. The feeling within the British establishment that nothing can be done is growing, and this will make Economics, and then Business too as nonsensical a game as the cricket I countenanced in those last diary extracts of August 1896; even more so than the sort of cricket being worried over by the President of M.C.C. in 1826.[116] But it is the earnest *cleaning-up*, not the corruption, of cricket which followed that finally convinced me of its inadequacy as a realistic model of the economy.[117] I turned my back long ago on the practical world of cricket, but began what may prove to be a forlorn attempt to clean up the world of political economy, following the guidelines of Ranji's *spirit of cricket*.

The 'American Dream' can be readily imagined by picturing the hopeful golfer at the first tee. Its deepest revelations and proudest appeal to the working man are that anyone with skill, perseverance, and luck can make an impression from there. The Fenner's system and my own golf indicate that this is patent nonsense. I have been rebellious enough, however, to wonder if it could not be so impossible as to construct a viable alternative model for the common aspirations. It is this confrontation with dogmatic free marketeers that marks the true spirit of my attempted revolution in theory.

The text book method of explaining the balance of payments is to assume fixed exchange rates, and to make trade in visible goods and in services appear paramount. If the other flows (interest, profits, dividends, transfers, and transactions in foreign assets/liabilities) still leave one with a deficit, then one must draw on one's reserves or borrow. The reality is that trade is *not* paramount, that rates need *not* be fixed, that reserves are miniscule compared to the resources of speculation, and that capital flows are a tail that can not only wag the current account dog, but are effectively the new lead. Without any capital controls the concept of a meaningful divide between long and short term financial transactions on the capital account becomes a matter of mere sophistry, for a 'committed' company may dispose of its 10 per cent or so shares in another company one day and move the spoils into another currency the next. This is not exactly the sort of timespan I had in mnd when I pointed out that in the long run we are all dead.

The reality was acknowledged in 1932 for example, by an innovative Austrian economist Robert Eisler, who put it thus:

> Purely speculative exports of liquid capital, *e.g.* from London to New York because of a boom in Wall Street and the ensuing high rate of call-money in New York, can force the Bank of England to raise its discount rate and thereby to restrict not only English industrial activity and employment but also the financing of world-trade by means of sterling bills.

This is the equivalent of match-fixing in cricket on the basis of the weight of bets laid and odds given in particular match situations. Even an economy performing satisfactorily in its trade of goods and services can face a depreciating currency and the necessity of deflation if capital is being withdrawn. This startling dilemma may arise not due to a lack of confidence in that economy's firms, but because of difficulties abroad in the investors' domestic economies. A big spender's own firms' and households' problems can very easily ruin a third party's development programme for years. Avoiding the acquisition of unsustainable debt in leafy Hampstead is more likely to help world economic development than buying imports from poverty-stricken overseas territories.[118]

We know that the world economy is not like a multilateral cricket match, that the game breaks down as a metaphor for trade, but we can be charmed that so long after that golden Fenner's summer of 1896 we still cling to the idea that the outcome should be determined by performance rather than the market. Cricket, indeed all sport, is ultimately inherently childish in its aim, although it may have admirable side effects. So admirable, perhaps, that it is worth fighting to reverse the assumption in the world's economic system that it is those who place the bets (rather than those who play the game) who should determine the result. Why do we not say the same about the economic system as we do about cricket, that it is rendered as meaningless by arbitrary large-scale capital movements as cricket was at Lord's by the betters, those calling the odds, and their 'legs'?

A Second Article Compiled During February 1946

An Uncomfortable Posture; Britain Caught Between the Nuts and a Hard Place.
Will Mr Keynes's Iconoclasm Finally Desiccate Cricket of all Utility?

'... *there was a tension, even a fissure, between Keynes's nationalism and internationalism, which required a fabulous formula to overcome*'.

(Lord Skidelsky, 'Fighting for Britain')

GOLDEN AGES AT THE FENNER'S MARGIN

The end of the war in August 1945 saw the abrupt cancellation of Lend-Lease by the USA, who were not going to allow the peace to be dominated by newly-restored European empires underwritten by Washington. J.M.K. was Britain's chief negotiator with the Truman administration, but his hopes for grants as a reward for Britain's heroism were soon dashed, and U.S. terms for a loan seemed harsh to a bemused Attlee government. J.M.K. himself realised that the dreams of an autonomus Sterling Area were no longer viable, and that the loan was the only way of avoiding Nazi or Communist methods. It would buy time until something else turned up.

Thanks to the legacy of Keynes's own optimistic economic templates things did turn up, despite his death in April 1946. The European Recovery Programme of 1948–52 was overtly Keynesian, and the 1950 Schuman Plan was fully Keynesian in the clever generosity of its practice as well as in its spirit (although Britain was painfully slow to grasp the significance of the latter event). It should not be thought, however, that J.M.K.'s last years were single-tracked. He was appointed a Governor of Eton College, to the Court of the Bank of England, and a Trustee of the National Gallery. He was the driving force behind the creation of the (yet-to-be-chartered) Arts Council (previously the Committee for the Encouragement for Music and the Arts) and was Chairman of that as well as the Trust which revived Covent Garden's Royal Opera House. The gala reopening of Sleeping Beauty *took place on 20th February, 1946, but was marred by J.M.K. suffering another heart attack. Almost immediately, however, he was on a ship again bound for New York with time to spare.*

A SECOND ARTICLE COMPILED DURING FEBRUARY 1946

The Europe that Hobbs and I grew up in was a Europe of empires and Britain was indisputably the greatest of those, reaching its maximum in terms of geographical and population size during the reign of George V. Arthur Ransome could drink Imperial Stout during 1917 and reflect that the skills learnt in Deptford and applied in honour of Peter the Great two centuries before were only recently relevant to Britain with her first and only Empress Queen. Neither of us could have predicted in 1896 (or perhaps even 1919) how quickly the Empire would become not a source of strength and riches to Britain but a painful economic burden, a political liability, and a psychological block that would paralyse active political economy half a century later. Like the man at the billiard table who screws in cleverly off the coloured ball but curses, for he only seems able to do it when he's playing snooker, we now seem to have been over-confident to the point of being buffoons.

Yet we were the *liberals*, who shared Baldwin's view of the mass intake of Conservatives (voted in dutifully by newly-enfranchised matronhood during the 'khaki' general election of 1918) as

> hard-faced men who look as if they had done well out of the war.

As early as my book *Indian Currency and Finance* I was impelled to write on page 71:

> The time may not be far distant when Europe, having perfected her mechanism of exchange on the basis of the gold standard, will find it possible to regulate her standard of value on a more rational and stable basis.

Perhaps a customs union leading on to a single currency? By the time of my plan (watered down by the Americans for the Bretton Woods conference) I felt confident enough to propose an International Clearing Union and Bancor as a world currency. By 1919 I had digested the remedy for withered empires and set it out very clearly and boldly and without much theoretical dissent in *The Economic Consequences of the Peace*. Chapter VI, 'Europe After The Treaty', was one of 'pessimism'. The next, 'Remedies', held out the vain hope that the Treaty of Versailles might be rewritten. What should it include?

> Economic frontiers were tolerable so long as an immense territory was included in a few great Empires; but they will not be tolerable when [the Empires] have been partitioned between some twenty independent authorities.
>
> A Free Trade Union should be established under the auspices of the League of Nations of countries undertaking to impose no protectionist tariffs whatever against the produce of other members.

I foresaw that some would object to this. In a striking reversal of the famous quote about 'the long run', I asked critics indeed to look at the long run, because peace involved making assumptions about what was desirable and attainable in the long run.

It would be objected, I suppose, by some critics that such an arrangement might go some way in effect towards realising the former German dream of *Mittel-Europa*. If other countries were so foolish to remain outside the Union and to leave to Germany all its advantages, there might be some truth in this. But an economic system to which everyone had the opportunity of belonging and which gave special privilege to none, is surely absolutely free from the objections of a privileged and avowedly imperialistic scheme of exclusion and discrimination.

This was so important I put it before sections on 'The Settlement of Inter-Ally Debt' and, that fore-runner of 1945, 'An International Loan'. It was the only chance I had to paint a large picture of a new system for Europe; I was too engaged in the minutiae of the British struggle against the U.S. to do a similar job recently. But I have not changed my opinions, and have hopes that there are agents who may be able and willing to put them into action.[119]

Churchill was not alone in assuming in 1919 that India would still be part of the Empire in 2000, although perhaps by then it would be ready for the sort of Federal devolution of government that had so successfully been implanted in the white-dominated Dominions of Canada and Australia. For him the British were not to be part of any European Union, because of the Empire, although this was not the impression given in his 1930 article in the American *Saturday Evening Post* ('The United States Of Europe'). In 1919 I also thought the imperial model was a viable an economic system for growth, but hoped we would become part of a free trade area, or, even better, a customs union.

Where I parted company from Churchill was in the aims of Empire (and any European Union). I was always an inveterate peacemonger who detested war in all its forms, was committed to international co-operation, and saw no sense of failure if conditions could be merely described as an absence of war. In 1929 I concluded my review of Churchill's book *The World Crisis: The Aftermath* with a careful statement outlining a position which I still hold:

> With what feelings does one lay down Mr Churchill's two-thousandth page? ... A little envy, perhaps, for his undoubting conviction that frontiers, races, patriotisms, even wars if need be, are ultimate verities for mankind, which lends for him a kind of dignity and even nobility to events, which for others are only a nightmare interlude, something to be permanently avoided.

Perhaps I was too careful. I should have added that we should be very wary of politicians who are apt to become too heady about the splutter of musketry. At this point an unlikely villain, Winston Churchill, has been many things to many people. Along with the times he was breathtakingly right there are some fundamental points on which he was hopelessly wrong. He was also less original than is now presumed; we have left behind the references upon which he built famous phrases, such as Baldwin's;

> When you think about the defence of England, you no longer think of the chalk cliffs of Dover. You think of the Rhine. That is where our frontier lies today.

A SECOND ARTICLE COMPILED DURING FEBRUARY 1946

That was July 1934. When in 1944 Mr Butler set out in private to the premier his proposals for all pupils to stay on longer at school, Churchill reacted not by stopping him, for which future generations may be thankful, but by saying of the more highly-trained adolescent workforce of the future:

... they will be my powder monkeys!

Presumably to save the Empire? Myriad such examples make trying to sort out where Mr Churchill's strengths actually lie a highly contentious business, because they are so often disingenuous.[120]

Why is the Empire still felt to be so vital in 1946? It is not just civilisation abroad that is held to be at stake; easing the pressures within Britain on the ruling class's way of life is still a vital consideration amongst Her Majesty's Opposition; Churchill would accept as a given Robert Eisler's point, made as recently as 1932, that:

> The vast empty regions of the Empire cannot be populated by the surplus of the over-crowded mother-country unless a temptingly high standard of living can be maintained in the overseas country; this would involve the export of British capital.

However, thanks to the redoubtable year at the helm when Britain was alone facing Hitler (plus six months of uncertainty after he turned east in June 1941) Churchill has developed a legendary image of indomitability that cannot be tarnished by his current delusions, and can only grow in the future as more removed generations are fed nationalistic myths. It will also become a common tenet of future generations (just as it did after the Napoleonic wars when the multilateral and multinational nature of Nelson's navy was whitewashed out of history) that the key difference between the Britain and the rest of western Europe is that the Britain wasn't invaded, and that British citizens have a unique view of what victory in World War Two really meant. Germany has lost and can be put back in her place, while Britain picks up the threads with the Empire and creates a welfare state to keep the Thirties at bay.

I don't hold with this view at all. From the Spanish Civil War onwards British civilians knew they would be targeted and involved in the the new style of conflict in an intimate way. Democracy brought with it a conundrum, for if the government in a representative democracy claims legitimacy through the votes of the people, then those voters themselves become real targets for any enemy of the nation rather than innocent bystanders as in previous centuries. 'Innocence' becomes a scarce commodity when even mothers suckling their young have cast votes for a leader who is perceived by others to be an enemy. Furthermore it was direct experience of death and destruction and close association with the enemy, and the leadership of both sides through the radio and newspapers, that made a sustained popular response possible after the Blitz. Just listen to any genteel lady among the flattened empty ruins of Plymouth, a nurse perhaps, explaining how people had come to say in 1941 'yes, *bomb* Germany' knowing that this meant burning mothers, children, and old people in their homes on a scale far outweighing the damage done in Britain The view of a distinctively imperial experience of war, aloof from the grubby complications of invasion, underestimates the British resolve to defeat the Nazi ideology by whatever means possible, in order to be free from the continual subjection by such methods in the future.

Where Britain *is* different and usually fails is in the peace, as does the U.S.A. in a rather different way (oblivious to echoes of Kipling's 'white man's burden', with its dire warnings about the thankless nature of the liberated mass). Britain is not a direct neighbour of Germany and will come to feel that it does not have to continue the business of reconciliation and peace-making beyond the first generation unless a new politico-economic arrangement is brought about.[121] It takes a lot of hard work in each new generation to create an ongoing peace, and the U.K. has the additional handicap of the generation of politicians who are either imperialists or imperators by means of Planning. It runs peculiarly in parallel with cricket, in particular *vis à vis* the popular attitude to the Ashes. The complacency of the selectors before the 5th test of 1930 seems to have been made of the same ostrichlike stuff. At least Jack Hobbs, one of the advisory team, was honest enough to say that although the decision to drop Chapman was unanimous it was a mistake. The chairman of the selection committee was the 1896 captain of Oxford, my childhood bogeyman Leveson Gower.

One must finger the politicians rather than the populace. Purely because of the party political situation it has not been clearly explained to the British people just how impoverished (and dependent on the United States) the economy is. It is inconceivable, even if *per capita* annual income was ever again to reach parity with the U.S.A., that we could even hope to begin to catch up with her in terms of assets and net value. It is even more inconceivable that the U.S.A. would countenance allowing us as a single sovereign state to do so, even if we were able to. In a weak confederation with others we may hope for an existence of sorts; independence from Washington, however, is out of the question without economies of scale of the economies of states closer to home; Briand's dream of federation may yet be the only way to prevent an American hegemony smothering the fissiparous cluckings of the European governments. When Harold Nicolson asked me to rebut Funk's plan for a New Europe I queried whether he wanted me to

> ... outbid Funk by offering good old 1920–21 or 1930–33 i.e. *laissez faire* aggravation by heavy tariffs, unemployment, etc., etc.

From the moment it was clear that the war was won in the Soviet Union, probably as early as Tehran in 1943, the U.S. behaved towards Britain like an alien power operating against Britain's interests; but this could hardly provide the basis for a new Beaverbrook crusade in the press. Roosevelt and Stalin were purring at Morgenthau's plan to pastoralise Germany, and F.D.R. was indifferent to Europe's future other than the undressing of the empires.[122] I certainly felt a foreboding about Morgenthau:

> ... these issues are extremely likely to be settled by those ... who have not given continuous or concentrated thought to it.

In a 1944 letter to Lord Simon I was very clear that

A SECOND ARTICLE COMPILED DURING FEBRUARY 1946

> ... the Americans are strong enough to offer inducements to many or most of our friends to walk out on us

while the proposed Commercial Policy the U.S. pushed heavily towards the end of the war ruled out Preference and doomed the idea of an imperial economic bloc. More recently, Churchill's speeches in the Commons with regard to the American loan read, just as they sounded, as a cowardly evasion.

How can we make the people understand that we are not what we once were? There are no such problems with Wittgenstein who masks the realisation by teasing me that following the end of Lend-Lease he is my most powerful bargaining tool; or rather, his pain at the scarcity of detective magazines in Britain is a weapon. Apparently I should tell Washington that if they don't 'cough up' some Street and Smiths we won't give them the philosophy, and

> America will be the loser in the end. See?

I think that the language has permeated through our whole generation on this side of the Atlantic as well, for I am told that I too have been addicted to the exaggerated use of words like 'crazy' and 'nuts', even when it comes to figures such as Cunliffe and Winston. Perhaps I overuse them to avoid my habitual confusion between the words 'barmy' and 'balmy'.

I may have been scathing about the Churchillian model for the post-1945 model of Europe and Britain as summed up by Beaverbrook, but none of us can afford to be under any illusions that the U.S. will allow Britain to salvage a coherent worldwide system.[123] One also has to be blunt about the ineptness of the intent of politicians wanting to:

> build up a separate economic bloc which excludes Canada and consists of countries to which we already owe more than we can pay, on the basis of their agreeing to lend us money they have not got and buy only from us and one another goods we are unable to supply.

Exports may hold up over the next few years. But to keep up with imports of food, materials, and capital they will have to triple to an area that is more self-sufficient than before. Without a workable imperial system, defeated in the peace by *Pax Americana*, and with a psychological delusion of greatness bolstered by being in the van against a potential Soviet threat, the strategic dilemma for the U.K. economy will not be inflation, even if there is a long boom, but the constraint of the balance of payments.

Thinking of the U.S.A. takes me back, perhaps perversely, to Canada. It was interesting to meet Wynne Plumptre there again in 1944. He recalled his days at Cambridge, and how he found Pigou to be easier company for a pupil than I was. Reading between the lines he felt that Pigou never used his reputation to intimidate. If you were not female and expressed an interest in climbing you could be a friend of Pigou's for life. Cricket, he emphasised, and particularly the cricket of Kent, was a standard topic of conversation at their supervisions in the spring of 1930.

There are several points that make this noteworthy. Firstly, although supervisions were meant to be academic, the Professor of Economics at Cambridge University thought it more useful to discuss Percy Chapman's captaincy and the forthcoming Ashes series with his pupil than Economics; will this be tolerated in the Cambridge of the future? Secondly, that pupil was Canadian not English, but cricket was still a major item on the agenda. Thirdly, the pupil's father was Kentish (or, possibly, of Kent) and so the pupil was expected to take note of what was said regardless of his own predilections. Fourthly, although conversation between myself and Pigou about cricket was only ever superficial, we shared nevertheless a very particular understanding of and approach to the world. W.G., looming large, was as much part of our shared cultural inheritance and understanding, as firmly lodged, as Ricardo on rent or Marshall on time-periods. Fifthly, fourteen years later the pupil was expected to create a favourable, cultured impression of Canada for me when, exhausted, I was hosted by Ramsay MacDonald's son while seeking further Canadian aid following the Bretton Woods conference. Plumptre and the others succeeded in the task to the extent that I said that

> if one ever had to emigrate, this should be the destination, not the U.S.A.

What I dread is that *my* United States, the U.S. that likes to think of itself as a 'Puritan Republic', will be under increasing threat from another U.S., a 'Gaudy Empire', in the decades ahead. It is clear that the best defence from this for the U.K. will not be the Commonwealth as predicted by Winston Churchill, but full participation in some European cooperation, for which we really need to start again and go back to a perhaps surprising authority: Lionel Robbins. As early as 1939, to his credit, he was emphatic when he wrote (in a section of *The Economic Causes of War* entitled 'The United States of Europe') that Hamilton and Madison were correct to say that there is no safety in confederations, and

> unless we destroy the sovereign state the sovereign state will destroy us

Neither *Staatenbund,* nor *Einheitsstaat,* but *Bundesstaat. Genossenschaft,* not *Herrschaftsverband.* The politicians largely need to destroy their sovereignty by pooling it, to create what Spinelli has called in his *Ventotene Manifesto* of 1944

> the indispensable condition for the elimination of imperialist militarism

His sources of authority for the division of powers, or federalism, included Acton, Seeley, Sidgwick, Beveridge, Lothian, and Robbins. He might also have included both the current Prime Minister and his predecessor.

Clement Attlee is likely to have a far greater significance for the long-term future of this country than Winston, now that he has the majority in the Commons; for while some with such popular backing tremble in case the support drops, he has never been in any doubt about what he is in power for. Perhaps surprisingly, this does not overconcern me, partly because his government is so constrained that they cannot do very much more damage than the Nazis have, but also because of the precepts of the man himself. For Attlee is, unlike Churchill, not only a cricket lover, but educated to understand cricket. We were able to discuss these matters when MacDonald convened his Economic Advisory Committee and we sat rather inconsequentially together trying to be constructive on stony ground. The small preparatory school he attended was religious, but the orthodoxy was Cricket not Anglicanism. Every afternoon outside and all moments of the day indoors were suffused with cricket and the thought of emulating W.G. Grace, then at the height of his renown. Other worthies like Lord Kennet (MacDonald's Minister of Health) and the current Lord Chancellor, William Jowitt, were similarly grubby, short-trousered boys at the same tiny school, trying to learn the mystery of the breakback and the leg-draw.

Then on to Haileybury, to study at the feet of, and in the ambience created by, the Headmaster, the Hon. 'Ed.' (as Ranji called him) Lyttelton, the most interesting of the eight great cricketing brothers. This was also the school that helped another contemporary, Dulwich's P. G. Wodehouse, create the best of the schoolboy cricket stories, *Mike*, although in a somewhat negative way; Haileybury's Antiquarian Society (or, for Wodehouse, the archaeological group of Mr Outwood at Sedleigh) and the Haileybury protest after the relief of Ladysmith (or Wrykyn's Great Rebellion in the Wodehouse world) were both part of public school folklore. Lyttelton caned seventy-two 'patriots' who took a day off to celebrate during the latter, and was thereby suspected of having Boer sympathies by those capable of only superficial analysis.

Attlee survived this upbringing and also his role as a lecturer at the London School of Economics to break free from Jingo and the Invisible Hand when the experience of London's East End converted him to a very pragmatic form of socialism, not so far from the experience of my sister Margaret that I couldn't appreciate the mechanism. When he entered politics he had the additional advantage of the first-class Colin Clarke as his Private Secretary, and imbibed a sound approach to the place of statistics in the modern world from him. He was never destined to be bamboozled by a Henderson or a Bevan with such experiences behind him. However, in Foreign Affairs he may well be stymied, not by Bevin, but rather by the people's uncritical support for Bevin, of which he is unfortunately acutely aware.

This will be a pity, for Attlee has a realistic view of western Europe as currently being a collection of disunited elements lying between two great continental powers, and is on record as saying that

> Europe must federate or perish.

His problem is that most citizens don't realise this, and still see western Europe as the dominant theatre of action in the world, with Britain in semi-detached superiority, as if aircraft and the telephone had still to be invented. Attlee's current opinion is that Churchill will use his new role as elder international statesman (and his spare time as a rather miniscule opposition leader) to tour demolished economies and tout rebuilding by federation. He can pursue this apparently radical course safe in the knowledge that if he ever regains power he can use the Empire (for to him it will always be that rather than a Commonwealth) as a means of escape from following his own advice. It wasn't always thus.

In 1940, just as Attlee was moving into Downing Street to act as Winston's deputy there was a lot of work going on in the Anglo-French Organising Committee. Churchill as P.M. was, after Dunkirk, bent on Monnet's plan for a full union between the two countries as a final statement to Hitler and the world that Europe meant something more than Aryan autocracy. He nearly got it, if the rumours of a 13–10 vote in the French Cabinet are to be believed.[124] Although union was a project with rapidly diminishing prospects it involved my meeting Jean Monnet, who was the most interesting Frenchman I ever met (and the only one who was a British civil servant during two world wars)[125] mainly because he seemed to believe in the future. My proposals on 24th May 1940 showed that I was never afraid of pooling sovereignty (in this case foreign currency reserves) and Benelux has celebrated its second birthday doing just that. In 1919 there was some unitary sovereignty for the large European nations to guard. In the current ruins of Europe there is none that is not illusory, and for most citizens on the continent it seems clear that the past should not be reconstituted. The party leaders and I are equally convinced that union is a model worth following, but in Churchill's hands currently it is only useful as a stick with which to beat Attlee, and the latter is entrapped by his party. The helplessness of politicians is sometimes too pitiful to be believed.

Arnold Toynbee dressed this all up in very metaphysical terms as befitted a mandarin up in a garret of the F.O. who was working on the mysteries of Planning.[126] But although intellectually assenting to the premises and logic of our dilemma he is still unable to commit us to specific *action*. Churchill is likely to commit lots of action that will be a waste of energy going off in the wrong direction (by the law of averages he is due another Antwerp, Norway, or Gallipoli).[127] The neo-realists (they approve of maximum pretension in a label, which is why they dub me a Reforming Whig) say that once again that with regard to European cooperation I am being far too optimistic. This is very gratifying, because when they have said this in the past my ideas have born fruit later on after theirs have withered in the frost. Am I not mindful, they ask, that there will be great transitional difficulties after the late conflict on the road to union? Surely union should be delayed until a plan for transition can be worked out to everyone's mutual satisfaction?

On this matter the anti-federalists forget that the founders of union in the U.S.A. lived at a time when New York had imposed tariffs on Connecticut fuel and New Jersey butter, competitive depreciation meant the currencies of Rhode Island and Georgia (over 15 per cent of the states) were worthless, and Pennsylvania was committing atrocities in the Wyoming valley against Connecticut settlers. Is it not possible that, on the contrary, the current lull after the third major Franco-German conflict in seventy years forms the very circumstance in which larger nations may assent to being squeezed with Benelux into the federal model? Furthermore if we try to join forces to stand up as a unit against the U.S. and the Soviets, we will create the possibility of staying in the first division; if we wait and see what happens we will surely be kicked down to a lower league.

A SECOND ARTICLE COMPILED DURING FEBRUARY 1946

Churchill drives from Luxembourg to Metz on July 14th 1946, past cheering crowds in villages like Évrange on the road now marked by bollards commemorating the U.S. army's liberation in the area. During the speech Foreign Minister Robert Schuman looks on approvingly; he is less comfortable inspecting the troops, while Churchill is in his element.

The grimness of it all merits a footballing analogy. Everything depends on a happy coincidence of leaders being dealt out to us. There is no plan that can provide us with that essentially human pre-requisite.

It is inconceivable that we could wait to go into some arrangement later and expect to get anything out of it. The shock will be all the greater when we find that, instead of Churchill's memory dominating Europe, Britain counts for little in the ideas of the community, or in its hopes for the future. Given that most politician try to cure the ills of their youth rather than those of the present time, however, 'wait and see' is probably what will happen.[128]

After the Great War I argued for a European free trade area and was ignored. I argued for a European clearing system and was ignored. I argued for a world currency in 1943 and was ignored. Along with many other of my croakings I suspect that second time around these ideas may take wing, but with whom and how it is too soon to tell. Perhaps I underestimate the dead weight of opinion within the Foreign Office (and particularly their actual and potential political 'masters', Messrs. Bevin and Eden). Perhaps I am too sanguine of Attlee, Churchill, Spinelli, and Robbins, and too ignorant of other champions waiting in the wings; but that they are there somewhere, I am certain. There is in British circles a profound misapprehension about, or even ignorance of, the close bonds between Jean Monnet and the Democrats in the U.S.A., for example, that might confound Foreign Office orthodoxies in the not too distant future.[129] I hope that the impulse towards reconsideration of my prophesies will not involve further starvation or ruin or humiliation, and that Washington will be swift to support what must happen first; reconciliation between France and Germany. On that at least Winston is correct.

But it is crucial also that Britain as a whole must also be reconciled with the continent, and I am far from certain that either Winston or the Americans see that as being in their own narrow interests. When my father mentioned Metz in *The Scope And Method Of Political Economy* it was as a great 'modern military fortress'. After what Europe has been through since the 1890s that has to change. In the future will we not rather be able to think of Metz as a cultural centre, or as a border focus of reconciliation? I fervently hope so. But is the will for peace there, not only throughout the vanquished nations, but among the victors?

An Article Compiled During April 1946

Prospects For My Little Protégés In The Latter Half Of The Twentieth Century

'A will to civilization may exist among the Veddahs of Ceylon or the Meg, of the Gold Coast, but no sign of it appears on the Stock Exchange or in the Trade Union Congress'

(Clive Bell, 'Civilization', 1927)

J.M.K. was frustrated by the compromises made for the Bretton Woods agreement; the Fund was really a bank, and the Bank was really a fund, and neither should have been sited in Washington, disagreements over trade liberalisation held up G.A.T.T.'s formation for years, and his world currency (Bancor) was only partially implemented much later through the Special Drawing Right.

Harnessing and guiding the global driving-force of the U.S.A. was essential for European liberalism's survival, but what hope was there for the future given the cultural gulf between the governing classes of Washington and London et al? One infamous story seemed to sum it up; J.M.K.'s speech at the Savannah inauguration of the I.M.F. and I.B.R.D. alluded to Sleeping Beauty when he hoped that no Carabosse would blight the future of the newly-christened twins. The foremost U.S. official, 'Judge' Vinson (a tough but straight Democrat), was heard to make a remark along the lines of 'I don't mind being called malicious, but I do mind being called a fairy'.

However, with the newly-flexible national approaches to economic organisation, the new global architecture did lead to the demytholigisation of gold; there was now an onus on countries to balance rather than maximise basic balances on the current account; and the world growth of G.D.P. between the European Recovery Programme of 1948 and 1973's oil crisis outstripped that of any other equivalent period. This was not merely a bungee 'bounce-back' following the destruction of Europe's capital stock during the depression and World War Two; decline during the first two years of the peace was disturbingly persistent, and it took managed changes of policy with promised injections of demand to initiate the 'Golden Age'.

Such progress in development was made in the Mediterranean and the near east during the 1950s that the UN was confident enough to make the 1960s its first global Development Decade, the expectation being that Europe's success could be imitated from Ghana in Africa to Fiji in the Pacific and to the Caribbean Federation in the backyard of the United States. In the event the conservative counter-revolution and the lack of constructive political institution-building resulted in stagnation and disillusion that still poisons meetings between North and South. At the end of his life J.M.K. seemed to be well aware that progress could be as easily blocked by self-interest and caution as it could be by cowardice and ignorance.

AN ARTICLE COMPILED DURING APRIL 1946

The binding on my 1881 copy of *Every Boy's Book* has let me down as badly as my heart, it seems. At least, the vital portion of it that kept the front cover attached to the imposing maroon and gold ribbed leather spine is thoroughly ravaged, and the ensemble has a sadly spavined aspect. I took the volume down after our walk down from Firle Beacon today to remind myself about Sliding. There it was, on page 360 between Skating and Swimming, reminding us of the joys of taking off along the pavement on hob-nailed shoes in winter. It is not something I have performed for fifty years, nor do I expect to do it ever again, but as I read the passage the memory of the experience was as real as the dose of medicine I was putting off taking.

> What can be jollier or more enjoyable than sliding for an hour upon a crisp wintry morning when the snow is lying three inches deep on the ground?

Indeed. Or perhaps the Microscope, or Electricity, or Fireworks, or Tinselling, or Foot-ball (two codes), or Gardening, or The American Game Of Baseball further on in the book? Here is Postage Stamp Collecting, Or Philately, on page 840, worn thin through my fingerings in the 1890s. How did we read such small print on those dark gaslit evenings in the pre-electricity days of Harvey Road? Then there is Cricket on page 150:

> The game of cricket is the noblest of the English pastimes. It combines athletic power, grace, quickness of eye and of hand, nimbleness of leg, and scientific skill. It is played by high and low, rich and poor, man and boy; and there is no game, either native or foreign, can compete with it for manliness, fairness, and healthfulness. Every one should learn to play it, and all should begin early. How it originated or who evolved its beautiful laws and regulations, it is now difficult to discover. We have nothing like it among the sports of the Greeks and Romans...

Indeed, I would still rather see one stroke by W.G. Grace than read all the words of Homer again.[130] Somehow this funny little island (capable of latching onto, falling in love with, and developing the activities of others, like the ballet of the Russians) has created a plastic art that is travelling worldwide in ways unimaginable in previous eras. My mind drifted off to Susan Salaman, one of the most ingenious theatricals of our time, and her creation of the humorous dance sketch *Cricket*.

All those who will live on after me yet create nothing! I have thought of one in particular considerably over recent days. The ultimately baffling stalemate that developed between Hubert Henderson and myself can perhaps only be illustrated without the use of hindsight by sensing the gulf in temper between our writings. Where I like to be bold, Henderson is cautious, where I suggest optimising Lenin's advice (two steps forward, then perhaps one back) Henderson prevaricates for for fear of slipping up before he's begun. It is only decades later that this tendency can be seen to be not only annoying and self-fulfilling (if nothing changes you can justify not setting out to change things) but on important occasions plain wrong. He denies that fiscal policy was the chief factor in the major recession of 1921 ('essentially a slump in international trade') whereas this was perhaps the most characteristically 'Keynesian' recession experienced anywhere so far in the twentieth century.[131]

At the time we hadn't the tools to analyse it, and with the succession of Chancellors (Lloyd George, Mackenna, Bonar Law, Chamberlain, and Horne in under ten budgets) there wasn't a chance of understanding how to implement policies to avoid the craziness of 1920–1. Sir Robert Horne gave the orthodox view:

> The only hope of ultimate full employment in this country is … a reduction of prices and correspondingly in wages

while inflation would be cured by balancing the government budget. Austen Chamberlain's anxious letter to me asking for advice at the time was a classic of its sort, and even four years ago I concluded retrospectively that the dose of dearer money, if not cuts in government spending, were necessary. The Geddes Axe was much-heralded, but the timing was a bit too late, or that's what I assumed until just recently.

It is now clearer that there were boom conditions in the 'peace' economy of 1919–20, with supply bottlenecks notable from 1915 onwards that kept prices rising at a rate of 20 per cent p. a. The inflation that mattered, however, was the early stuff; we can now see that of 1920 as merely a storm blowing itself out. Despite this partial 'boom' there were falls in overall output and rising unemployment between 1919 and 1921, which I now attribute to the running down of the 'war' economy and time-lags between demobilisation and the effects of such capital investment as was necessary to absorb the returning workers. Unfortunately, by the time the adjustment could be made, concurrent massive fiscal tightening damaged confidence, deterred the necessary private investement, and reduced consumer demand; the 'homes fit for heroes' were full of unemployed, where they were built at all. Dear money (7 per cent by 1921) meant that over half of government expenditure had to go on debt servicing, yet £300 million out of £2,000 million raised in revenue was used to repay debt in 1920 and 1921 while 2 million were unemployed and another million were on strike.

Despite all this the 1921 budget was carefully planned to do almost nothing. Excess Profit Duty and Corporation Tax were raised when losses were being made, the wobbles in the exchange rate meant the size of debt was a moving target, duties on death were put up just as the nation went into a mammoth crisis of mourning, and one couldn't even drown one's sorrows since spirit and beer duties were both put up as well. Still the hard-faced men thundered for Chamberlain to reduce the national debt, which was 900 per cent higher in 1919 than when he had given his last budget in 1905. Given the experience of 1939–46, the period 1915–21 holds a horrifying fascination, like the sight of a drunken snake approaching the edge of a volcano's mouth. How little we knew then! Inflation has to be caught early, and recessions have serious long-term consequences. Economists have to be a lot more artful than just balancing the budget and trusting to competition among the business and working classes.

Henderson was quite clever enough to grasp his errors later on and change his mind.

He didn't. We start to see a writer who ultimately wants the conservative, sensible-sounding, majority view to be corroborated, whatever it is.[132] He also actively steers us towards it, and away from progress and even liberation, until the new becomes the familiar and can be safely embraced. In the 20s I could never have believed that he would prove to be so ordinary. Despite all the thinking we shared in *The Nation* and *Can Lloyd George Do It?* Hubert was really of no help whatsoever on the budget of 1941. He had thrown up his hands in horror at *How To Pay For The War*, and yet five years later is quite happy to continue working into the future on the very basis of assumptions and analysis laid down by that budget.

So the Hendersons of this world act as brakes not only when change is first sniffed in the wind but when those very new conditions ultimately change again. My father, it seems, was right when he prophesied

> Methods are attacked for not doing what those who advocate their use never imagined they could do;

How long will it be before the 'young' members of the 'Circus' or the seemingly more aged Hicksians will boil down the word 'Keynes' to mean all that is risible in the world of Economics? Worse, will Economics survive? Already the methodology is being skewed beyond recognition by American mathematicians who claim to be positive scientists establishing uniformities; will there be room in the face of these managers for normative firebrands determining ideals, or for artists formulating precepts? Will, rather, the new electronic calculating machines head off the automata and allow us to move from our static, physics-like models towards dynamic, biology-like models, as my father recommended all those years ago?[133]

I fear that the language of my father's book and the Cambridge revolution of the thirties seem to be doomed. As businessmen regain control of consumer demand from social institutions who will recall that Victorian teachers of *laisser faire* would emphasise equally with my father that

> nothing can be more deplorable than that the economist should be understood to imply that, in his industrial dealings, a man is freed from the ordinary obligations of justice and humanity.

How curious that I, with such an ancestry, should be accused of setting up a travesty of capitalism, while the Aunt Sally in Kingsley's *Alton Locke* remains more widely read than Mill and Marshall combined! What a wise father who could see that the errors of Social Darwinism would be continually replicated among the supporters of *laisser faire*, arguing that because such and such has happened like this *it ought to go on* happening like this.[134]

* * * * *

I would like to leave on a more sanguine note, akin to my *Economic Prospects For Our Grandchildren*. Assuming there is some *rapprochement* that makes life in Europe worth living, assuming Stalin's system slowly withers until the Mahometan majorities disintegrate the Soviet Empire, assuming the Americans provide a cocoon of world security compassionately 'liberating' the oppressed while despising their allies, assuming some return is made from autarchy and nationalism to the global world economy of the Edwardian era, what would I hope life will be like for My Little Protégés?

A greater chance of a balanced diet and physical vitality than Jack Hobbs's family had in Rivar Place of Victorian Cambridge. A chance to decide how much education one wants and when. Information about what is happening around the world free from the dictates of news moguls. An example from one's elders that inspires one to reach further. An upbringing that includes an understanding of what life was like for one's forebears, not just two but many generations back. An expectation that the wisest leaders should be chosen, not the ones who will do most for oneself in the short-term. A freedom to run against the tide, especially when the tide calls itself a democratic mandate. Companions with whom one can play cricket, not just opponents to play other games against. A systematic view of the world, where rational deduction is as respected as empirical induction, and both are understood to be as interdependent as the private and socialised sectors of the economy (since to some extent a firm's profits necessarily fall due to the government in return for the purchasing of public and merit goods).

On the negative side there will be increasing dissatisfaction amongst M.L.P.s with God (about which very little can be done) and also umpires (in the widest sense of the term), although all will be agreed on the theoretical value of an independent judiciary. When the demands come to pay 'umpires' by results (*i.e.* the correctness of their decisions), as technology improves and the educated public apprehends what is happening, then we will be in a bind. Should there be continual monitoring and adjustment, or should they be appointed periodically with relegation and promotion? Will we see betting return, not on the players but on the correctness of umpiring decisions?

An indifferent executive, separate from the legislature, is also critical to the running of the system for M.L.P.s. In which direction will the Europe of the future creep? Will an American spirit of litigation infect our own approach? With the French and German traditions being closer to Cricket than the U.S. Congress, perhaps the prospects are not so dire. Harrod has questioned me in the past about the pre-suppositions of Harvey Road; it is to be hoped that through the exemplar of continental co-operation the dutiful, professional executive may become a pre-supposition of M.L.P.s.

I've been rereading my cricket articles and hope that if anybody exhumes them in the distant future they will echo something I wrote last week about Bernard Shaw's portrayal of Isaac Newton's mode of conversation:

> The words are right, though it is inconceivable that they could have ever issued from the closed lips of that secret man.

> But, please providence, they won't say 'closed' and 'secret' about me, rather may the words 'public' and 'impish' will spring to mind.

> This suddenly all seems very inadequate in a world of frightening and frightful

change. Ludwig has an expression that he uses almost as a mantra, which has some value in this context; *Ein Ausdruck hat nur im Strome des Lebens Bedeutung*, or

> an expression only has meaning in the stream of life.

My hope is that both Economics and Cricket will continue to be taught as having relevance. My fear for M.L.P.s is that in the very heartland that gave birth to both of those beautiful traditions, they will not be passed on in such a manner.[135] If in fifty years time, when seeking to come safe to haven, cricketers and economists still feel they can descend with certainty on Cambridge, then it will all have been worthwhile, for the world that preserves such an organic trinity as Cambridge, Cricket, and Economics cannot be based on wholly ignoble foundations.

> *J.M.K. died in April 1946 in his bedroom at Tilton*
> *following yet another heart attack. He was 62.*

Appendix; May 2000 – May 2003

The Luxembourg Visitations

These problems cannot be solved by individual states. They must be solved by the Community as a whole. The single currency is vital to this now, because of the single market'.
                (Sir Edward Heath, see Steinherr, 1994)

Be in no doubt that this appendix is a genuine conceit. The editor has hazarded a guess at how J.M.K. would have regarded the long, western European peace since 1945 in view of his multifarious and oft-related opinions, and those famous pre-suppositions of 6, Harvey Road. The evidence is that J.M.K. was committed to globalism, liberalism, and intervention rather than nationalistic laisser faire. *He was averse to war as a solution for nearly anything, and saw material progress as merely a precursor for artistic and personal progress. He saw no merit in either restricting liberties to make financial gains or in restricting financial gains to preserve spurious liberties. He did see merit in winning a debate.*

When it comes to the great dividing line of postwar British politics, i.e. Britain's place in Europe, there can be no doubt that J.M.K. would have stood with, if not ahead of, Heath and Jenkins, and firmly against Gaitskell and Thatcher. Funk's July 1940 plan outlined in Paris for a New Order in Europe was praised by J.M.K. for its content, but equally damned by him for its origins. The gestation, by contrast, of the E.U. (whose history is still all but neglected in the U.K.) would arguably have delighted him. Among the range of the EU's opponents (including 'enemies within', such as de Gaulle and Thatcher) he would have recognised his own opponents (with odd, sad exceptions such as Dennis Healey, Bill Morris, and Clement Attlee).

J.M.K. was skilled at sifting rhetoric from reality, and would have discerned that the success of the long, western European peace rested on the EU's economics as much as N.A.T.O.'s politics. From 6 nations and 4 languages in 1957 the E.U. had grown to 15 nations and 11 official languages by 2000, with 12 more countries waiting close in the wings to pool resources and sovereignty. E.F.T.A. had failed. The simple generosity of U.S. missiles in Europe bought time, but the simple generosity of the Schuman Plan in Europe brought inspiration. Even 'Sleeping Beauty' Russia draws nearer to the E.U. as this book is published.

In late 2001 the world was, we were told, 'changed forever' in a different way. To many in liberal England the first few years of the current millennium in fact held few surprises, and panned out according to a remorseless logic of inanity pre-ordained by the errors of previous generations (particularly in the U.S.). The media seemed to disagree. Would J.M.K. have fallen in line, or were the foundations of his vision for the good life rather more flexible than those of the skyscraper and the oilwell?

APPENDIX; MAY 2000 – MAY 2003

§1. Mid-2000
The long, western European peace;
advantages of a more perfect union.

It would not be surprising if people have felt my presence in recent summers on occasions at various cricket grounds. The Luxembourg pasture at Walferdange in particular is in delightful countryside, and I now recant my opinion of 1919 that Luxembourg is a boring place. It has seen the sort of stirring, country house style of cricket that I so enjoyed at Fenner's in the mid-1890s. I feel more at home there where the game is loved and understood than in most parts of Britain, which can seem pretty hostile to civilisation at times. I, like most listeners, was open-mouthed at the viciousness displayed by Lord Tebbit on the B.B.C. Radio 4 *Today* programme in discussion with Yasmin Alibhai-Brown, which made one feel like going on the air oneself and *patronising* him. Tebbit seems to eulogise the Edwardian era and imagines he would have got on well with Balfour, Cobham, *etc*. He wouldn't have. His notion of British traits may be good or it may not be, but it is increasingly mismatched against reality, and I suspect he would perform less well than he assumes against Edwardian criteria. Perhaps he can say his nine times table and thinks he knows the rules of grammar, but how is he on the tonic sol-fa, or on *troches*? More pertinently, how many twenty-first century white children whose families have clung for generations to Norfolk clunch or Surrey loam have committed to memory the Sermon on the Mount, or the names of the rivers of Yorkshire, or know how many chains are in a furlong, or could talk for five minutes on the subject of 'Duty'? Tebbit revealed a reductionist ignorance worthy of a Marxian and elevated the external symbols of colour and lineage to obscure both the internal similarities between people and the gulf between his perception (let alone his idealisation) and the real world. I bet that he keeps his fingernails over-neat. In doing all this he really did endanger the meaningful use of the word 'British' at a time when Yasmin and her fellow-commissioners were producing an excellent report called *The Future of Multi-Ethnic Britain* that I commend. He should have read his Gesell on Free-Land; in the E.U., nations are merely administrative boundaries or geographical descriptions, not a basis for rights.

Naturally I have much more time for my biographer, Skidelsky. He has, however, expressed anxiety that the last eighteen months of my life [October 1944 – April 1946] were wasted and I should have rested in contentment having earned the right to bit of personal peace once international Peace was established. This is very solicitous, but as he himself has pointed out, the new war for Britain had begun and was being lost; the Empire was not to be tolerated in the *Pax Americana*, and without the system of empire, Britain was economically lost. I ask everyone to think clearly about the conflicting pressures that required continuing action on my part.

All the domestic negotiators were under pressure not only from the extreme wings of imperial preference and dirigiste planning, but also from those in the middle who favoured tinkering in the short-term. People like 'Otto' Clarke wanted me to imitate Quintus Fabius Maximus, in the hope that external shocks would precipitately

> P. W.
> rond-Point Robert-Schuman
> L-2525 Luxembourg
>
> le May 9th, 1994
>
> Dear Mr. Rium,
>
> I am sending you under this cover for the archives of the Club the original of the Message of Prime Minister John Major delivered on July 4th 1992.
>
> Sincerely yours,
>
> Pierre Werner

> BRITISH EMBASSY,
> LUXEMBOURG.
>
> MESSAGE TO THE OPTIMISTS CRICKET CLUB
> LUXEMBOURG FROM THE RT HON JOHN MAJOR MP,
> PRIME MINISTER OF THE UNITED KINGDOM:
> SATURDAY 4 JULY 1992
>
> I warmly congratulate the Optimists Cricket Club on opening their second innings at Walferdange, thanks to the generosity of the Commune. It is a particular pleasure to see our Presidency of the Community marked by the celebration at the heart of Europe of our national game. We must all be Optimists about Europe. I wish the Luxembourg Optimists every success, in their match with the MCC and thereafter.

Pierre Werner, President of the Optimists Cricket Club, passes on a memento of the opening of the new ground in 1992 at Walferdange which now officially bears his name.

change the context. They favoured a minimal loan from the Americans with no promises in return on the commercial front about trade or sterling. This really was wishful thinking, which I knew to be a commodity which can be hoarded only to lose its value very quickly in an inflationary spiral of events; I wanted everything signed, sealed and delivered before I left the scene (perhaps to be followed swiftly by a departure from memory, although I was self-confident enough to think perhaps not). The loan we agreed ultimately guaranteed a satisfactory outcome whatever happened in the immediate future, which is why I was able not only to accept but recommend it; if there wasn't a dollar shortage (which I hope is what we all wished) the multilateral system would be what we had wanted all along. If there *was* a crisis, it would show the Americans just how wrong they had been at Bretton Woods and in Washington (I suppose Skidelsky would say 'meaning how right Keynes had been'), and they would *have* to take action, even if it meant suspending the rest of the machinery until the crisis was over.

As to the medicine for that crisis, a dead man couldn't say 'I told you so' to Congress, but the memory of my (sometimes tempestuous) warnings would return to haunt the guilty men. The whole of George Marshall's team could see me sadly shaking my head beside them as they made their tour of inspection of Europe in 1947. When they got back, infected by the spirit of second thoughts, they pressed for Keynesian solutions.

Truman became so infected that he said his government should frighten the (Republican) Congress with *anything* to get the European Recovery Programme package through. That stream of sorry but necessary anti-communist rhetoric has, of course, blinded historians ever since to the battleground of economic theory; most of them just don't know enough about political economy to look for any other explanation than fear of Stalin for such generous intervention. 'Otto' was completely taken in, justifying his position using *post hoc* observation and reasoning typical of a plump and balding weights and measures inspector spectating at a Test Match. His illusions about the Marshall Plan and the dollar shortage led him to the conclusion that the liberal precepts of 1945 had been reversed two years later, as the U.S.A. was now granting Europe the right to discriminate against it! From the other end of the telescope, however, one could see Congress being told what it wanted to hear, a British refusal to realise that 'Starvation Corner' (*i.e.* no loan) would have put convertibility and free trade on the back-burner for a very considerable period of time, and that the main effect of Marshall Aid was in fact to cement most of Europe to a liberal, multilateral long-term future. The assumption that delay and austerity (the policy of recovery back in 1932–7) would have led to the the same conditions in 1947 as my grand plan, and that G.A.T.T., the I.M.F., and the I.B.R.D. would have developed in the same way is an uncricketlike phantasm. The rebuttal belongs to Mike Brearley (and his use of Botham and Willis); even an expensive spell by a bowler may lead to something else happening in the game, and no one can know if a different choice might not have been much more catastrophic, leading to a totally different situation later in the day.

There are two major questions begged by the policy of 'Otto' and his supporters. Would negotiations on a grand scale about commerce and finance have ever re-started if they had been stopped in 1945, and if so who was a grand enough personality in Britain to re-start them? Also, would as much Marshall Aid have been granted to a Socialist government that not only practised a more class-driven form of Monnetesque planning but also based its whole credibility on being anti-convertibility and anti-free trade? I never entertained the slightest doubts on this matter, and surveying the confused situation (even given my lead) in 1948 only convinces me how right I was to chase the rainbow. As coherent an economist as Austin Robinson could write in bewilderment on the 27th of October to the Cabinet Office from the Paris offices of the O.E.E.C. administering Marshall Aid:

> ... I do not know whether or not H.M.G. has any thought out policy ... we do not know what you others have been thinking and assuming in this field. I myself have always assumed that it was our idea to move rather slowly from the controlled economy in Europe to the liberal economy in Europe ...

so three cheers for my Cambridge colleague.

My own feelings about Marshall Aid reminded me of Harrod's reaction a few years earlier on the train back to Oxford when he read about the U.S.A. proposal of a scarce currency clause ('an exhilaration such as only comes once or twice in a lifetime'). It lifted thirty years of depression about Germany from my mind, and, with the prospect of new and viable export markets, opened up all sorts of alternatives to the sterling area for Britain. The pity is no one had the vision to see the possibilities of a match-changing innings at the wicket of the European Coal and Steel Community after the Schuman Declaration of 9th May, 1950; Heath, after a dashing cameo on debut, played a gritty back to the wall innings following Macmillan and Wilson's collapse, but I'm afraid people like Sir Ted and Trevor Bailey are seen as relics rather than role-models in the U.K. of today.

While on the subject of the 1950s/60s I am surprised that more hasn't been made of the finest Cold War satire to see the light of day, unintentional prophecy of the highest order though it may have been. I refer to Roger 'Syd' Barrett's charming ditty *Effervescing Elephant*, written before his Pink Floyd days. I knew exactly how that elephant felt by the time of my death; the American tiger had pretty much finished Britain off, but I suppose that sub-text wasn't in the forefront of the mind of a songwriter who was born around the corner from Harvey Road just when I was leaving the scene. Whether, consciously or not, 'Syd' was in touch with the *zeitgeist*. He intuitively felt what Truman *et al* were up to, and the real nature of the U.S.S.R. (theoretically well-meaning, but a drunken buffoon, as likely to squash those around it by accident as design). The U.S.A. was the tiger in his song, and western Europe was the hippo. Zebra and mongoose were the first line of eastern satellite states, and I have a fond feeling that the water bison were E.F.T.A. (including the U.K.). 'Syd' also predicted exactly how the matter would abruptly end leaving a disturbing vacuum. Let me remind you:

> An effervescing elephant with tiny eyes and great big trunk
> Once whispered to the tiny ear, the ear of one inferior,
> That by next June he'd die, oh yeah!
> Because the tiger would roam
> The little one said 'oh my goodness I must stay at home
> And every time I hear a growl I'll know the tiger's on the prowl
> And I'll be really safe you know, the elephant he told me so'
> And everyone was nervy, oh yeah! and the message was spread
> To zebra, mongoose and the dirty hippopotamus who
> Wallowed in the mud and chewed his spicy hippo plankton food
> And tended to ignore the word preferring to survey a herd
> Of stupid water bison, oh yeah!, and all the jungle took fright
> And ran around for all the day and the night, but all in vain
> Because you see because the tiger came and said 'Who me? You know
> I wouldn't hurt not one of you, I much prefer something to chew
> And you're all too scant, oh yeah!'
> He ate the elephant.

The official history of the Cambridgeshire High School for Boys (now Hill's Road Sixth Form College) dismisses Pink Floyd in under six lines, saying;

How far the experience of the school had any impact on the later careers of the two Rogers as immensely successful pop stars is debatable.

This is too modest. The school was directly responsible for the Christmas number one which began with the festive words 'we don't need no education'. But did 'Syd' really want us to be trapped by *The Wall* of Roger Waters? That may have been the Waters reaction to the negative tedium of Cambridgeshire High School, but for 'Syd' the greyness merely made playtime more precious. The oppression which later enclosed him was that of success, the tedium of its execution, and the expectations it aroused for the future; so he retreated within, and back to Cambridge. He was not as successful as Jack Hobbs in rebelling against the expectations and wishes of his own environment; his mother's home in Cambridge, like mine, was a refuge for life (in Barrett's case her life, in my case my own life). Jack Hobbs moved to the south coast.

Where does Barrett fit in, then? His was the third generation to live at the margin of Fenner's after the change of University regulations in the 1880s. My parents' generation contained the pioneers of the new mixed-sex university, self-confidently defining its role as agent of both town and gown midway between the colleges and the railway line. Barrett, two generations on, had lost the authority of purpose. He loved the woods, fields, animals, and bicycles of Cambridge, but hated the schools, regimentation, and constraints of the civic life there. He was flailing at the latter while trying to hold on to the former, and the inability to do that under the pressures of superstardom led to Barrett, like The Monkees, committing professional suicide for the sake of his sense of well-being. I wonder how often in later years the rebel would wander unrecognised into Fenner's and feel that this was closer to being at home than doing a sound check at The Marquee?

That Roger 'Syd' Barrett was a moderately successful revolutionary can be seen in that he not only did something unprecedented which changed the way everyone else thought of things, but in so doing destroyed his ability to carry on enjoying the life that had produced his revolution during the unfolding of its consequences. This was very different to the writer of the original *The Piper at the Gates of Dawn* (which was Chapter VII in *The Wind in the Willows*). This was written in 1908, the year in which its author, Kenneth Grahame, retired from his job as Secretary at the Bank of England for reasons of health. Grahame must have been invigorated by the reactions to his master work because he lived for another twenty four years. His second book (of 1895) had coincidentally gone out under the title often given to the period 1948–73, *The Golden Age*. The 1929 Introduction to A. A. Milne's play *Toad of Toad Hall* carried a justification for the theatrical representation of the real and comic aspects of the book. Milne also tried to reassure potential critics that

> we are not going to add any fresh thrill to the thrill which the loveliness of *The Piper at the Gates of Dawn* has already given its readers.

But this is precisely what Barrett claimed to be doing when he allowed the first Pink Floyd album to go by this name. It was the equivalent of my letter to Bernard Shaw in which I claimed to have written a book that would change Economics at its roots. Barrett thought that he too was being successfully revolutionary rather than merely rebellious.

Rick Wright's early songs for Pink Floyd (*Paint Box*, *It Would Be So Nice*, *Remember A Day*, and *See Saw*) were touching tributes to Barrett's influence, imitation arising from inspiration; others, from Messrs. Bolam and Bowie to Messrs. Albarn and Coxon, have indirectly followed suit ever since, usually unconscious of the stream's source, which retreated thirty years ago, eventually trying to lose himself in Cambridge. A passage from Quentin Bell, written about Vanessa, provides an appropriate analogy to explain the meteoric rise and demise of 'Syd' as *the* pop revolutionary of 1966–7:

> To belong to the 'forlorn hope' of any victorious company is perhaps honourable but not wholly enviable. Leaders get wounded, or perhaps merely breathless; they stumble as they cross the glacis and leap into the trench.

En passant, have you noticed the remarkable facial likeness between the young G. E. Moore and Johnny Rotten in 1977?

Back in 1945 I was much more worried about the government in the U.K. than in the United States; there was no one able to grapple with the strategic economic opportunities (which were then seen as threats) of a combination of Indian independence, the O.E.E.C., and the Schuman Declaration. Winston was perceived by anyone hopeful of living into the last quarter of the century to have gone nuts (to use Wittgenstein's favourite detective-comic parlance), and was mentally straitjacketed in the Commonwealth until his demise. Attlee correctly forecast that the Churchillian statesmanship as a man of Europe would swiftly evaporate if he actually got back into power. Every October when I visit the Vianden nut festival in the north of Luxembourg I am overcome by two complementary warming feelings (a third is prevented by my physical inability to imbibe the liqueurs); there is the satisfaction of seeing the good life return through socialised investment in such a short time to a castle and a town that had been ravaged by the Battle of the Bulge (and much before) – and also the pleasure of running through in my mind's eye all the gaga bankers, economists, and politicians it had been my pleasure to have described as 'nuts' during the first half of the twentieth century. All this while watching a mediaeval throng purchasing kernel comestibles. To return to 1950 on the theme of nutty slack, we had, of course, Mr Morrison who said the Durham miners wouldn't wear the E.C.S.C., to which I would have replied:

> in that case they'll soon be wearing an eleemosynary hairshirt instead.

Should I have tried cunctation in 1945, in the hope of a miracle cure for my medical condition, ready to rise from the sickbed to be a champion again once conditions had changed? Could I have put more gusto into G.A.T.T., once it eventually got going? Could I have shoehorned the U.K. onto the continent once the imperialists' dreams were punctured? I never fully realised until it was too late that I was an Archie Jackson, in Ranjitsinhji's heroic mould – only able to display my batsmanship if I simultaneously used up the dregs of my life force. Nevertheless, despite the tragedy of the process that unfolded, the answers must be no, no, and no.

This isn't just because I am unconvinced that the unholy alliance at home could have been reconciled to convertibility or multilateralism later without my grand design behind them, or that the U.S. would not have adopted a reciprocal habit of minimal gradualism towards Britain if we had approached on tiptoe. Would a Socialist, dirigiste, and yet still imperialist, Britain have been invited to take a meaningful part *at all* if it had resiled from any commitment to the liberal order in 1945? As it was, the Acheson, Marshall, and Truman approach (so welcome after the Soviet-inspired madness of White and Morgenthau's plans for Germany) of encouraging supranational European co-operation was rather stymied in 1947 by the choice of Oliver Franks as O.E.E.C. Executive Chairman, which was akin to spiking a double whisky with Bisto.

In truth, even had I relaxed and lived on to fight another day, I would again have been a voice on the margin, trying to avoid both the glutinous and isolationist tendencies, accused once more of pro-German sympathies. It was unlikely I could have staggered on to become an octogenarian during Ted Heath's first push into Europe in 1962, although Jack Hobbs just made it; Dr Barnard's heart operations in the late 60s would have come too late for me. Without the political backing to weave magical dreams into technical possibilities there was very little point in prolonging my life; there were others to carry the torch now, particularly in the U.S.A.

The plate shows the endpaper from 'Stable Money' by J. Eisler (1932) embodying the full weight of the mythology of gold. Gesell, on the other hand said it was time to substitute cellulose for gold; 'money only needs to be countable, the rest is mere ballast'. Even cowries, the single currency of North Africa and the sub-continent a millennium ago, were preferable to 'the archetype of death', gold.

There should be little doubt that I would have had the stomach, if not the heart, for the fight. I was never a great fan of the Ottawa agreement of 1932, imperial preference, the sterling area, or the restabilisation of 1936 and Roosevelt's barmy financial policies (which made Klotz seem like a big spender). Imperialism was dead in the water after the Atlantic Charter signalled U.S. intent to do to the U.K. what it had already succeeded in doing to Spain. A new system of prosperity (as opposed to survival) should hve been sought actively from that moment. The Schachtian system of bilateral barter when compared to my vision of growth through multilateral trade reminds me of one-day 'Fricket' compared to Test Matches, in particular before the invention of the fielders' circle. Germany blocking the Danubian balances to obtain forced loans was like putting all the fielders on the boundary during a run chase in the second innings when the opposition had not done so in the first. They simply dispensed with the whole business of wickets (*i.e.* interest, the signal for the allocation of finance). These transactions and all their subtleties of uncertainty and expectations were to become autonomous.

But for what would I have fought had I lived on? The substantive clues are there in the archives, along with a generally liberal and internationalist tenor. Perhaps, as an observer, I have become really engaged during only four periods of late twentieth century activity of political economy; time spent shadowing the High Authority President in Luxembourg between the vote against the European Defence Force in France and the elevation of De Gaulle, the era of the Solemn Declaration at The Hague and the production of the *Werner Report* 1969–70, both the administrations of Commission President Delors in Brussels, and back in Frankfurt since mid-1997 for the birth of the euro.

Despite the revival of interest in me that it led to, I would not have made the mistake of equating the 1992 E.R.M. exit with the 1931 Gold Standard collapse; the adverse British public reaction to both these and the 1949 and 1967 devaluations arose largely out of pagan belief in government being an upholder of the exchange rate as a virility symbol. I maintain also that a 1945 devaluation would have been entirely an inappropriate signal at the start of the post-war era. Well before that, the Treatise reply to the Cunliffe Report showed the way I would have supported the current benign neglect of the euro-dollar rate eighty years later; concentrating on price stability within each bloc has been adopted with the bonus that negative inflation is clearly seen as an equal danger.

The chaotic failure of floating rates in the 70s and 80s combined with fissiparous economic nationalism was a swing of the pendulum away from the Gold Standard that would have driven me equally to distraction. Once the U.S. became a deficit nation in the 1960s and 1970s it was clear that none of the new surplusive nations was big enough to be decisive, and all were reluctant to sacrifice domestic economic objectives for the purpose of external balance. Clearly a bloc would find it easier to stabilise the world system with the U.S. than even a confederation of states. So economic sovereignty as a concept had a lingering death in the E.E.C., euthanasia coming in handily through Cohn-Bendit's rioters in May '68, but, as Richard Gardner said, the need to sell half of France's gold stock on that occasion

> can hardly be considered part of the permanent adjustment mechanism!

APPENDIX; MAY 2000 – MAY 2003

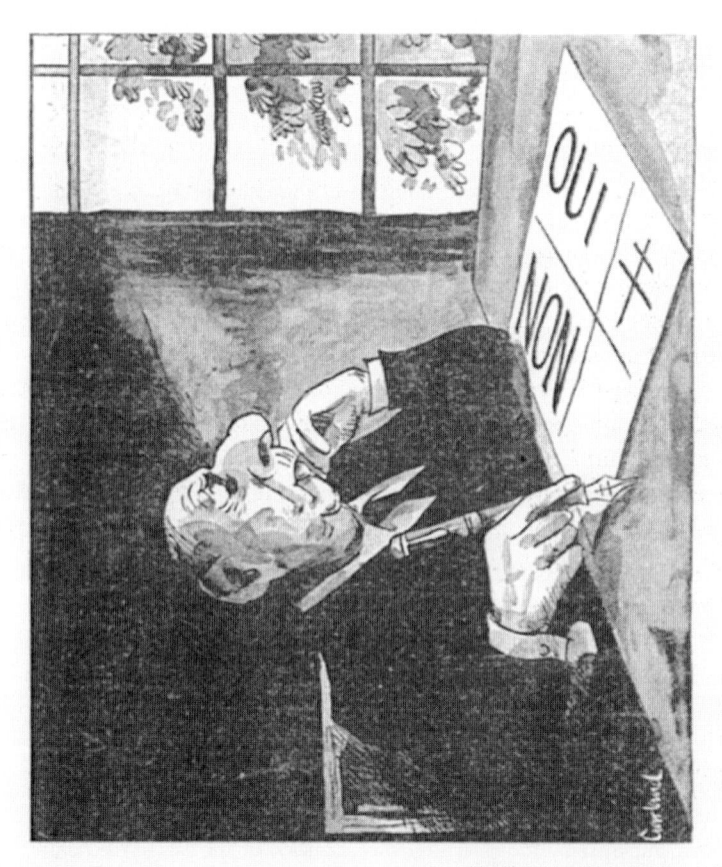

'FIVE' FEAR CIVIL WAR IN FRANCE

GRAVE EFFECT ON MARKET

By WALTER FARR
European Affairs Correspondent

BRUSSELS, Thursday.

THE danger that President de Gaulle's broadcast could lead to civil war in France was stressed by representatives of her five Common Market partners in Brussels tonight.

Even if he succeeds in maintaining order without the use of troops, his Market partners expect the French crisis to drag on for months in a way which could paralyse the Market and have grave economic repercussions in their own countries.

Ministers and officials of the Five were expressing this view in private meetings aside from a Common Market Ministerial Council session in Brussels which began shortly before Gen. de Gaulle was due to broadcast.

The council took the unprecedented step of adjourning so that Ministers could hear the General's declaration in a room near the council chamber.

The Daily Telegraph, Friday May 31st, 1968

GOLDEN AGES AT THE FENNER'S MARGIN

In the U.K. 'economic sovereignty' still seems to have some resonance although it is backed up by vehemence more than evidence.

But even De Gaulle had to bend politically for some external stability. Can anyone really doubt that I would not have been moved to hear that arch-nationalist and gold-hoarder in Germany clutching the whole nation to his heart by telling them, in German, 'you are a great people!' in January 1963? Kennedy had only managed to sound stridently desperate in Berlin as he affirmed he was a doughnut. Why are the television clippings of Kohl's tears both at Verdun and at Mitterand's funeral not considered to be stock clips of the most significant moments of the last century, if not millennium? Could the E.U. have endorsed any better anthem than Beethoven's setting of Schiller's celebratory *Ode to Joy*? Could I have resisted supporting any project that could choose such a credo? Could we believe our eyes as the other three Beatles tried to save Ringo from a tiger by singing it along in chorus with Patrick Cargill? From *Triumph of the Will* to *Help!* in only a quarter of a century.

What are we to say about the conveniently cosy view of the post-war development of Europe as a conspiracy of the élite? I describe it as cosy because it is expressed at its strongest in the U.K. as a static explanation of forces that have in fact been continuously pervasive through the last half-century, and because its *raison d'être* is to bring comfort to those who oppose the process of integration. There is no real drive either to investigate or correct the nature of the problems that would arise from halting the process. The alliance of green, anarchist, anti-capitalist, and Marxians would actually *prefer* the Bilderberg Group to maintain its policy (born in 1954) of not publishing minutes, but one can estimate the degree of muddled thinking here by their parallel attitude to Keynesian national income statistics.

At an initial glance they seem to have a point that Net National Product is a pretty strange beast if it increases as a result of a motorway pile-up; how can that, along with increased sales of burglar alarms, be an indicator of rising development? But try pointing that out to the many minions employed by the great insurance agancies, or the garage mechanics, or the sales reps., or the shops where they all buy their food and shoes, or the newspapers who sell them opinions, or the highly-indebted poor country that sells them a cheap holiday in the sun. Of the two hundred countries in the world, by any indicators of human progress, where are the erratics, the exceptions, if one looks at the top or bottom twenty? Perhaps Barbados with its liberties enshrined in a constitution and good schools, in spite of a low national income. Perhaps Saudi Arabia with high material inequality, and even higher gender inequality in such matters as literacy, despite a high G.N.P. But these are rare exceptions, not a basis for dismantling the whole macroeconomic edifice. Hospitals, schools, recycling, police, transport, theatres, *etc., etc.* cost money, and require income. Alternative development may mean alternative routes and methods, but it can't escape the monetary nexus to some utopian barterland imagined by the Seattle rioters now any more than it could to the Fabians' fairyland a century ago. We have to make the system more human rather than escape it.

The anti-globalisers must have been disappointed when the Trilateral Commission started publishing their minutes in 1973, and then put a brave face on things when the

European Round Table (E.R.T.) stated their views very clearly in newspapers which were accessible to all in the early and mid-1980s. At the same time there was hardly a furore of scuffling pickets at the Grace Gates each summer at Lord's, despite the strong evidence that British company board-members still prefer to discuss decisions in their clubs, such as M.C.C., rather than official (minuted) meetings. What is curious is that there has been little effort made to open up from the exterior the discussions held in the early days of the Bilderberg Group in the same way the 'secret' Apostles society of my era was opened up to scrutiny; nor has there been an acknowledgement that since the single market began on January 1st 1993, the influence of the Group and the E.R.T. has declined considerably. They have made their mark, and the debates should really have moved on.

This is why I can say that everyone has been very easy on the bleating band of self-styled modern historians and 'pro' E.U. journalists. They seem to me to have contracted a form of collegial fugality with regard to the long western European peace and the E.U. Like the *laisser faire* school of thought they can advocate no constructive course of action when put on the spot or given power, but continually criticise when any intervention is implemented, giving the impression they would do something else and do it better. Timothy Garton-Ash is particularly annoying because he should know better that the E.U. couldn't go meddling in the Balkans without an attainable aim, and that agreeing on that would imply the sort of deepening process in the E.U. that he has always said he mistrusts. It's the buildings syndrome all over again; too shabby and one can't be expected to take the institution seriously, too expensive and they must be wasting public money. There remains the question of motive; are writers currently being intimidated into pitching their work too far towards the old order of ideas (exemplified in what the Americans call 'new' Europe) to market it more easily with the publishers, or are the current writers of such low intellectual calibre that they do not see the contradictions and omissions that give them away? Or are they scared of the 'new right' rather than part of it?

We should never forget that crucial period between 1981 and 1986, in which nothing less than the viability of Europe as a distinct economic and social system was addressed, with far greater perspicacity and success than was the case in the inter-war years. One cannot find anything in the English-language textbooks on this; there is the odd nod to Lord Cockfield, but also widespread misunderstanding of his role, which essentially was to nail the politicians to what they said they agreed to in theory. It is Etienne Davignon who was the instigator and architect of the single market strategy, but he is almost completely ignored by most U.K. 'authorities' who fondly imagine ESPRIT to be some form of motor manufacture rather than a key part of late twentieth century British history.

The crisis was real and it was looming. One intimidating statistic said it all; Europe provided 30 per cent of demand in the world for information and communications technology, but only 10 per cent of the supply. Every future growth sector in the world economy would follow a similar pattern unless something was done. The U.S. would, far from meekly, inherit the earth. In addition to the problem of market size there was the problem of the relations between the existing European firms; these relations were almost non-existent and impossible to develop in the existing framework. The second state of affairs meant that the first would also further collapse, so the outlook was set for continued deterioration with the Japanese and U.S.A. becoming rampantly dominant as capable organic unities compared to the disjointed portions making up the E.U. Consequently, with diminishing prospects for industrial survival, any distinctive European social design would wither and die. Between 1961 and 1994 E.U. labour productivity nearly tripled; but without the equivalent U.S. stimuli of economies of scale and a socialisation of space/military investment, the E.U.'s capital productivity fell by a third and job creation was hampered by demand constraints. Delusions of national independence with regard to monetary policy were dwarfed by the dandified illusion that individual European nation states could hope to keep up with the U.S. in a world of mobile capital. These dreams are still pumped out daily to the British people by lunatic media who should rather be holding a stake in that very widening of performance.

I would have got a lot of publicity if I had published an assessment along these lines; the 1984 D.G.XII pamphlet by the Forecasting and Assessment in Science and Technology Group (FAST) was equally elegant and persuasive, but has never received enough attention from the public or even from scholars. If the 'National Curriculum' is to mean anything, it should include a requirement that all school-leavers should have visited the document on the website and read pages 70 and 165.

This prospect of economic extinction, as I.C.T. and later biotechnology by-passed the European economy, led to the simultaneous proposals of the Common Market programme of Cockfield and the Delors programme for social development. The latter has been traduced *ad absurdum* by the British academic and media circus, who fundamentally dismissed the President as a joint-venturer in the final failure of 'Keynesianism in one country' during his participation in the Mauroy government in France. What they never bothered to assess was the extent to which 'Keynesianism in one continent' (a system with far lower propensities to import and export, and a far greater potential for economies of scale) *was* a viable alternative response, when compared to the alternative policy of a counter-revolution along *laisser faire* lines.

There was some notion in the U.K. that the Thatcher Revolution of the second term was a sort of vanguard for a return of the Manchester School of free marketry, following the failure in its first term to act as a vanguard for the Chicago School of new monetarists. But when serious analysis of the early union reforms and later privatisations is undertaken it is clear that there was no interdependent strategy that led to fundamental changes in the course of events in successful parts of the E.U. economy such as Luxembourg. This heresy was denied by most business pundits even two years into the U.S. stock market crash (which started a year *before* the collapse of the Twin Towers, a fact currently subject to populist revisionism). In fact the state interventionism seen in Docklands was more typical of the prevailing philosophy of the mid-80s. Delors, despite being defeated in terms of the scope and depth of his social plans, had a far more pervasive and long-term influence over the economic structure of the E.U. (including, ultimately, the U.K.) than Thatcher. A pertinent phrase made by Michael Ramsey (brother of my late, lamented philosophical colleague Frank, and an ex-Archbishop of Canterbury) is as hard to dislodge from the memory as a cobweb was from his huge eyebrows; when asked what he thought of Mrs. Thatcher in 1979 he paused and then said as carefully as he could

I, I, I, feel v–v–v–very sorry [pause] for *Mr.* Thatcher.

The basis of the Delors approach was a personalist philosophy that led to a policy of concertation between government, employers, and unions (the social partners). The crucial change from previous presidencies, however, was his sense of how dynamics required more than the traditional 'log-rolling' between heads of state (*i.e.* bartering support for various courses of action to gain unanimity to defer the threat of any country vetoing your desired policy); the structure was now too complex for that. In technical terms Delors sought dynamics through integration projects rather than functional spillover. In everyday language this meant the use of two further strategies in addition to 'log-rolling'; these were 'flanking measures' and 'Russian dolls'. The former is where, in order to achieve the admission at a low authority level of the unpopular course of action that one is *primarily* seeking, you introduce a proposal at a higher level with an accompanying issue that is acceptable. The 'Russian doll' is when a proposal is put forward that is irresistible to the partners, but will necessitate consequences that were not wanted by them at all. These may be unforeseen (hence the epithet) but it may not matter if they are recognised.

There is an argument (peddled primarily by national leaders) that the Delors social package (his major 'flanking measure' to combat the negative effects of the Single Market) was successfully repulsed. But if it was in rhetorical terms, it was not in substance. The Danish insisted on health and safety being linked to the core project in 1985; there was a growing share of the budget for cohesion (regional policy) at the expense of agricultural support in both 1988 and 1992 (in the last fifteen years farming has lost over a third of its share of expenditure), and of course there was also the Social Chapter.

If victory is the hallmark of even a defeated 'flanking measure', then the success of a 'Russian doll' is inestimably spectacular; it entails cascade effects with an almost Marxian inevitability. For Delors the Commission's unstinting support for the Single Market was the best way to create a dynamic between such diverse leaders as Kohl, Thatcher, and Mitterand. He backed it to the hilt, a socialist betting on the vision of the supposedly free market Bilderberg Group. Why? He saw that the necessary corollaries of a genuine single market would be a single currency, greater regional transfers, and a social contract between the employers, unions, and governments over social affairs, all of which were suitably Monnet-esque achievements to leave to posterity in the Delors Report of 1989. Facing a more politically-diverse E.U. it could be less openly federal than the *Werner Report*, but Delors is quoted by Werner's daughter as saying his aim was to model his proposals as far as possible on the predecessor of 1970. That the 'doll' took shape in the Luxembourg package of December 1985 and is still unfurling its consequences over fifteen years later is a mark of the enduring qualities of federalism. The reaction against a strong Commission after 1992 has led to the predictable failure when the member states decided to set up the pillars of the E.U. for internal and foreign affairs themselves; that their impotence shows a return to supranational solutions is clearly needed is the most powerful tribute that could be paid to that difficult but indispensable intellectual fixer, Jacques Delors.

Of course the facility with which the E.U. can be traduced demands constant vigilance against both misrepresentation of the process and the process itself being diverted. I have had plenty of lively arguments in the celestial ether with Hundertwasser since his death, asking him why both the Green and the Development movements have got into destructive opposition to the EU, the W.T.O., the I.M.F., and the I.B.R.D. to the delight of nationalist and fascist leaders everywhere. Like the shrilly misdirected young communists of my Cambridge in the '30s, he cannot see that the break-up of the liberal order is worth avoiding and responds by attacking the technocracy that has built up the E.U. with only belated democratic representation. At this point Altiero Spinelli came up and laid into the record of national governments blocking a bigger role for the people's assembly (now European Parliament), and then Jean Monnet started giving examples of how quasi-democratic governments have used the Commission that they appointed to hide behind whenever any unpopular decision they had taken in the Council of Ministers had to be implemented. I then pointed out that the Court of Auditors has continually rejected the Commission's accounts in recent years chiefly because national authorities are not controlling the disbursements from the E.A.G.G.F. and R.D.F. properly and there are a number of incompatible accounting systems being used masking transparency. The B.B.C. has now given up making this a big annual story because not even the British members of the Court will give them the big corruption scandals they are looking for.

Spinelli came back in to back this up by pointing out that the Parliament's flexing of its muscles against Santer's Commission was made possible by the Treaty of Amsterdam rather than an evil conspiracy against the people, and Hundertwasser, if he was a democrat, should have welcomed the turmoil that led to the formation of Prodi's Commission rather than using it as an excuse to wash his hands of the tainted E.U. altogether. Altiero got so carried away that by the end of this I was feeling almost sorry for an architect I admired very much. But then I remembered him shouting at me that

> to adhere to the European Union is to betray Austria!

with Jimmy de Goldsmith nodding at his side, and I shuddered. I didn't go to Schengen to 'see in' 2002, but headed instead for the Costa Del Sol to delight in observing all those retired Conservative Blighty pensioners starting to use euro notes and coins and finding that they didn't after all turn into pumpkins. For the first time since I left Britain in 1946 I nearly died laughing.

Anyone who fails to believe in the reality of an afterlife is a fool, for even atheists such as myself and Gesell believed in the latter's precept that

James Watt in his grave does more work today than all the horses alive.[136]

So far I have managed to avoid John Buchan up here, which is just as well, for I might lose my privileges after saying all that deserves to be said about his traducing Lydia in *The Island of Sheep*. I don't mind his portrayal of me as Barralty, because it has all dated so badly that no one will be able to connect with that character any more; but to drag my wife in like that was (nearly) unforgivable. Things could be worse, however. Hell in heaven will be Margaret Thatcher rounding up Marie-France Giraud, Elizabeth Guigou, Denis de Rougemont, Alberto Miele, Henry Coston, E. F. Schumacher, and Leopold Kohr to harangue me about the E.U. while Isaac Newton, Charles Darwin, and I are trying to watch Jack Hobbs open the batting with Tom Hayward in the sun against Malcolm Marshall and Sylvester Clarke on a true wicket at the Kensington (*sic*) Oval.

§2. Late 2001
Widening and deepening both the E.U. and the Channel; weaknesses of the existing confederation

Great Bustards sound like a music hall joke, but my dream in 1896 was to be awarded one. This sounds like lunacy, given that Great Bustards are among the rarest birds in Europe, but the explanation is both simple and poignant. If you are awarded your Cambridgeshire colours you get an embroidered Great Bustard in the middle of your cricket sweater. I wanted to emulate the heroes of my youth; Tarrant, Hayward, and Carpenter.

In June 1991 European environment ministers were meeting at Dobříš Castle in Czechoslovakia. They requested that a report should be prepared about the pan-European environment. Pages 198–199 make disturbing reading for a Cambridgeshire supporter. The Great Bustard, plentiful in previous centuries on the lightly managed pastures of the county, is now close to extinction. There were only about 25,000 left in 1995, 60 per cent of which were in Iberia. Between 1945 and 1995 they disappeared from Germany, Poland, and Yugoslavia. More worryingly, the strong protection provided by the national government in Hungary had also proved insufficient, because, inconveniently for nationalist politicians, temperature variations (and so migration patterns) are not bound by national limitations. The report concluded that a multilateral agreement was needed on a continental basis (*e.g.* the Bonn Agreement on Migratory Species). Local initiatives are, of course, also welcome, such as the attempt by The Great Bustard Group to introduce forty chicks each summer for four years (2004-7) from Russia to Salisbury Plain. But the idea that a national government can have some unitary sovereignty over the largest species of bird that can fly is cuckoo.

Agreeing on a need for multilateral agreement such as the Rio Summit and the Kyoto Treaty, seems to be a modern orthodoxy, with myths peddled around schools during an

GOLDEN AGES AT THE FENNER'S MARGIN

APPENDIX; MAY 2000 – MAY 2003

1957, like 1948, was a year of great hope for a federalist. The first European School (top Left) was completed in Luxembourg to join the High Authority (above, soon to be moved to Brussels as the Commission) and the Court of Justice (below left).

adolescent's Geography classes, photocopies distributed just days after after the headlines are dry. The pupils emerge imagining that everything will be all right, because the politicians have agreed to 'talk'. But the real world outcomes of multilateral agreements are generally too small and too late. The United Nations, the Bretton Woods system, and the second and third pillars of the European Union are evidence that they do not generally work well at all, although they are an improvement on unilateral and bilateral methods.

The High Authority of the European Coal and Steel Community *did* work, however, and the Commission of the European Community *can* get things done occasionally. The lesson of the Great Bustard is that the federal system does indeed rely on decentralisation through subsidiarity, but that this means giving the Commission proper power in a number of areas that national bodies cannot even multilaterally manage.

But (to take on the stylistic mantle of Roy Harrod) why federalism? Why not good old British divide and rule pragmatism? Surely the E.U. should be about economic co-operation not high politics? The genesis of the project, however, suggests that we should be aware of double standards being applied when commentators decry political motives for change in the E.U. What was the urgency for aiming to widen the E.U. by 10 states in 2004 and a further 2 in 2006 if not political? It could not be economic in the short term – Poland, Hungary, and the Czech Republic had a huge income gap even with Portugal, and could arguably provoke wage depression, flows of capital away from the U.K., and economic uncertainty; a recipe for deflation, and further unemployment in the medium-term in Western Europe unless positive countervailing forces could be unleashed. The example of Germany's catch-up since unification in 1991 is there as a living example (although free marketeers insist rather that Germany has an immobile labour force, full stop). This doesn't mean that the political gains haven't been worth the economic sacrifice. However, it should seem clear that for a near-doubling of the number of states in the E.U. in perhaps a decade the veto, regional transfers, agriculture, and migration should all be sorted out at E.U. level. The British government can do nothing by itself about this and should have made that clear to the people, who also have a responsibility to assume in engaging with power at the E.U. level rather than calling for 'red lines' to be drawn at each successive summit. As an M.E.P., the East Enders star of the 80s Michael Cashman has a more important role in the U.K. of 2003 than whoever currently happens to be the leader of the Tory party, and is more worth lobbying and reporting.

The moves to E.M.U., however, have always had a sound theoretical economic basis. Following the 1969 Solemn Declaration at The Hague about currency union the *Werner Report* of 1970 foresaw a single currency by 1980, leading to lower costs, less uncertainty over import/export prices, a transparent single market in goods and services, and a stronger European voice in world trade negotiations. North Africa and Russia would move towards the eurozone rather than the dollar (over 100 million people in 13 African countries entered it *de facto* in 1999). Other regions like West Africa and the Caribbean approve so much that they are trying to fashion similar institutions. The floating of the dollar and the oil crises of 1974 and 1979 with their subsequent inflations held up the process, and yet reinforced the desirability of the end in view. Steps such as the introduction of the e.c.u. in 1979, the E.R.M. (particularly 1987–92), and the Maastricht criteria have been spectacularly successful in terms of inflation convergence (astonishingly so in the case of Greece), but the pain of adjustment to the Bretton Woods breakdown has become confused with the effects of the euro's introduction.

The irony of the hostile position of the current Tory party is that it echoes the old Cambridge Labour view of early 1971, expounded by Nicky Kaldor, and supported by Austin Robinson and Old Pauline Richard Kahn, in response to the Werner Committee's report. Kaldor is worth two extensive quotations.

> My main criticism of ... the post-war policies of economic management ... is that it treated the problem of full employment and (implicitly) of growth as one of internal demand management, and not one of exports and international competitiveness.

> If we enter the Common Market and the Community proceeds with its plans for currency integration and not just customs integration, our economic dilemmas are likely to become much greater. For not only shall we be precluded from employing the instrument of a managed exchange rate but our existing instrument of ensuring a continued growth of domestic demand through fiscal policy

will itself be far more difficult to operate. Unless we manage to become the fast-growing industrial centre of the Community – a difficult prospect, if we start off by being the slow-growing area – we may be faced with the same problem of declining total demand and employment as our development areas have had during the last twenty years, and with no more ability to counter it by local policies without external assistance.

The illusion is of a dichotomy between Economics and Politics, which to the old Cambridge school of Political Economy would have seemed illogical. The need to keep open the option of devaluation is neutralised by the knowledge that every administration that has used the instrument by accident or design since 1945 has been sent to electoral oblivion as a result. It is such a form of self-destruct that that seems to me to be the end of the argument, period, full stop, game set and match. Did the Conservative leadership want to change the peg against the German mark in August 1991 when the rate was under such pressure that meltdown seemed imminent, or did they have an eye for their seats in the general election that had to come next spring? Why is anyone trying to defend an instrument which will never work by design but only by accidental good fortune? The tax rises of the early 1990s to plug the P.S.B.R. was another complete reversal of the policy espoused at the time, but equally vital in making the late 1990s, fortuitously, a period of growth. Tax rises, devaluation? The Conservative Party? Please!

It is also entertaining looking at the literature from the mid-1990s predicting disaster across the water for the euro; only two countries would pass the tests, the speculators would tear it apart in the intermediate stage, there would be mass unrest. It was clear to federalists that nobody in the British media had the faintest idea of or interest in what was really going on. The euro debate was just a background to the continuing process of political warfare in the U.K., which provided the real news for parochial bodies like the B.B.C. and the *Guardian*. What was risible was that such organs were being accused by europhobics of being pro Europe. No one can fault the consistency of the conservative blocking element since 1950 when it comes to both putting the U.K. behind in the game, and ultimately being wrong, and now it happened again. The Lipsey and Chrystal tome, which has passed for an elementary Economics textbook instead of a doorstop for generations, could say of the single currency in its eighth edition of 1995, for instance:

> The debate in the next few years is going to be more about the principle; the detail will come later, if at all.

Thus were students prepared for the start of the euro in eleven countries less than four years later; that says it all, really.

Well before the 1997 election we were hearing through whispers at the European Investment Bank that the Bank of England's only real worries about the euro were differences in the U.K.'s stage of the economic cycle and U.K. mortgage traditions. Little did we think that a new Labour government with a huge majority would capitulate to these concerns in what the sadly-missed Hugo Young in the *Guardian* has rightly called 'cowardice'.

The arguments of the eurosceptics (I will call them 'Septics') who generally claim to be free-marketeers, with regard to the Stability and Growth Pact (particularly with regard to P.S.B.R.s over 3 per cent) and the euro in general are a mere publicity diversion to buy time. They would have made the 1970s monetarists laugh, since what is the use of retaining tools of control like devaluation and fiscal policy in a world of self-regulating markets? These people believe that in reality fiscal policy can only affect growth in so far as a P.S.B.R. crowds out private investment, and so a balanced budget is paramount even if it means raising taxes in a recession. Only supply side reform of the economy's structure can increase output and employment, they say, nurtured in a stable price environment that is maintained by targetting monetary growth.

But my followers are as astounded as true monetarists by the muddled thinking in evidence; are our opponents, in criticising the restrictiveness of the Pact, accepting that it isn't only the supply side that now works as a lever? Interestingly in these supposedly *laisser faire* times most commentators seemed to share that neo-Keynesian assumption when they criticised Japanese fiscal policy in 1997 or the handling of the Thai current account in 1996. Indeed, interest rate changes in the U.S. and the U.K. are now directly presented as mechanisms for fine-tuning demand-pull pressures on house prices and consumption (and thence cost-push pressures on wage bills for firms). The idea of an independent central bank creating a stable monetary environment to limit inflation is hardly mentioned by the media. Perhaps, after twenty years of being told that fiscal policy *can't* regulate real output and that a monetary framework is all that is required macroeconomically, it would be embarrassing to have to raise taxes to compensate for a lower interest rate. But I can't think of a single other disadvantage for the U.K. V.A.T. revenue is not high by E.U. standards, the G.N.P. is skewed towards consumption and away from investment, and the public services are cash-starved. To delay over the euro is once again to deify the Bank of England's monetary policy, while denying the efficacy of all other controls at the same time as saying that they mustn't be pooled with our neighbours'.

As far as mortgages go, the idea that a Briton would be confused by the (untraditional) prospect of a mortgage fixed at 5 per cent for twenty years is preposterous; dazed, perhaps, but not seething with rage at Brussels. Perhaps the Bank of England is more concerned about the work implied for uncompetitive and monolingual U.K. financial service companies than the borrowers? On economic grounds, then, there is no bar to joining in as soon as possible; the first day of 2000 would have been a welcome symbolic choice.

The much-vaunted idea that 'the rest' have to make their labour markets more flexible is also a dangerous red herring, not a viable new orthodoxy, and suggests that it is time to re-read Cairnes on the immobility of labour and capital after a century and a half. Andrea Lamorgese's study of U.S. cities (National Institute Economic and Social Review no. 170) shows that social security and transfer payments are the most important channel of income smoothing, followed by investment income and then, firmly in fourth place, intercity labour mobility. In terms of geographical and occupational (as opposed to perceived institutional) rigidities the 'rest' of the 15 are a long way ahead of the U.K.; the large Portuguese presence in Luxembourg shouldn't exist, according to British pundits, until unions have lost their power and the rights of employees are reduced. Presumably the free marketeers haven't heard about the successful experiment by Mather and Platt to introduce an eight-hour rather than a nine-hour day? That this happened as early as 1893–4 and can be read about in my father's textbook is quite arresting. When trilingual journalists start exercising their right to work rather more in the U.K. perhaps we'll hear less about labour mobility. It is hard to estimate how many young Belgians, French, German, Danish, Swedish have word-perfect English, have never visited the U.K., yet are eyeing the exchange-rate distortion of wage-rates and planning to try out the single labour market in Britain. What percentage of U.K. residents would pass the Cambridge Certificate of Proficiency in English? Perhaps the U.K. should look to the language-entitlement of its pupils instead of lecturing the rest of the E.U.?

Indeed, the contradictions took an even more curious turn with a host of scare stories like the Czech refugee saga and Italy's implementation of the Schengen agreement; these quite ignored the fact that the U.K. has always supported widening of the single market, and thus the free movement of Czech peoples. The U.K. opted out of the full Schengen accord which really requires unanimity to work properly in creating a credible external border control. It is a naive contradiction that implies the government has sieves for brains, unless (as with Thatcher/Major's 1990 DM2.95 E.R.M. level for the pound in the E.M.S.) the aim is to make the whole policy fail.

The 'Septic' press has also tried to tangle up their opponents by claiming the public is more sceptical than the papers, Charles Moore and Neil Kinnock clashing at a Press Institute seminar on the matter. This gave rise to a particularly depressing reaction by Peter Preston in the *Observer* which proved Kinnock's point. The 'Septics' finesse the current situation by claiming that the *Daily Mirror* (Tony Parsons?), *Financial Times*, the *Guardian*, the *Independent*, and the *Daily Express*, plus the B.B.C., are europhile. This would be enough to make a federalist (who has tried in vain during recent decades to see any mention of the 'f' word anywhere that isn't derogatory) weep.

Kinnock's major problem was that it has never been the Commission's function to be explanatory and it has no resources to do that; even when it has tried governments like John Major's blocked the circulation of documents saying it was an 'encroachment'. The extensive websites are a red rag to the tabloids who claim that they are mis-spending on propaganda while they simultaneously challenge europhiles to debate properly – the room for circular argument, hypocrisy, and evasion is enormous. Preston spots a flaw in the Moore thesis (that it downgrades the press to a reactive, not opinion-forming, rump) but doesn't follow it up by pointing out that this diminishes the need, in the Moore psyche, to have a balanced or an objective view, for, if the press is held to be unable to influence proactively society, who cares if every paper is like the *Sunday Sport*?

The series of referenda surrounding the enlergement of 2003–4 has been given an intensity of reporting within the B.B.C. according to an inverse relationship with the

GOLDEN AGES AT THE FENNER'S MARGIN

"Some day you may be President of Europe."

If you had said to average Punch readers in 1961 that more people would relate to the top than to the bottom cartoon forty years later they'd have thought you were off your head.

"I need two for my fifty!"

likelihood of a no vote. Hence a whole programme of *The Food Programme* on Radio 4 was devoted to looking at Polish peasant farmers who were, we were told, mobilising opposition to entry. The Polish vote was in fact 78 per cent 'yes', which was not given as much air time. The television news report of Esthonia's 'yes' vote (67 per cent) was gleefully tailed off by a warning that the next vote, in Latvia, would be much closer with a large degree of scepticism anticipated. The 'yes' vote was again 67 per cent, and was barely mentioned on television; there was so much to pack in about the Swedish euro vote which had provided a much better result for news managers.

The drip, drip of ignorance and mischief-making was crystalised in one particular feature. To hear the old Minister for Europe Keith Vaz go on Radio 4's *Today* programme and be asked why we should have a European Year of Language when everyone else is learning English was sufficient to destroy Moore's claim; if the B.B.C. were europhile they would have talked to the Commissioner responsible (Viviane Reding of Luxembourg) and then, when told the aim was to have every E.U. child learn two (not one) foreign languages, they would have interrogated OFSTED about why this was not happening nearly thirty years after E.C. entry, and then they would have reported why the national Parliament was failing to hold national bodies of the executive to account, before concluding that the U.K. was falling behind in economic competitiveness even more, and that the national Parliament had better quickly learn to do fewer things better or it would lose all relevance. It has already abrogated responsibility for national networks to private companies (*e.g.* the railways) and charities (*e.g.* the Sustrans cycle path system). The fire in the funicular railway tunnel at the ski slopes before Christmas 2000 was even worse; a European human tragedy was reduced to a sort of nationalist league table of death in the *F.T.*, the *Indie*, and the *Guardian* as well as on TV, to the point where it became unbearable. You just wanted someone to say something like the distraught TV commentator at Bradford City's football stadium during the 1985 fire; 'Oh, those poor, poor people!'

The most significant premier that the U.K. has had since World War Two, Ted Heath (none of the others could have summoned up the combination of pragmatic and rhetorical achievements displayed in getting the country into the E.U. and also winning the Charlemagne Prize) was very clear that the way to bind Britain in more closely was by monetary union. With one of those characteristically casual, majestic sweeps of imaginative certitude that could make listeners grin, gasp, or grimace depending on their prejudiced proclivites, he would assert that the finance ministers of Europe should just get together one night and announce the next morning that agreed exchange rates against a new currency were now in force and that national currencies no longer existed. Then a single market might start to become a reality.

At present, although the E.U. market currently accounts for over half of the U.K.'s trade, the consumer and small business person can get little intelligible price information about either the product or the factor market. So the most important benefit of the euro's arrival in Britain will be the end of exchange rate uncertainty and a large increase in the efficiency of the price mechanism as a resource allocator. That this is a dynamic and a substantive change rather than some static change of regulation indeed makes it hard for the media to convey to the public. The situation will be changed in ways that we cannot presently predict with accuracy. But that is not a reason to give up; why not pose an opposite case, and let the readers judge the likely consequences, e.g. the setting up of seven regional currencies in the U.K. with local futures and options markets? Imagine the chaos of West Yorkshire being forced to devalue against Middlesex because the latter put up its interest rate to defuse the housing market, and Lancashire refused to intervene by selling its reserves of southern currency.

The current unpredictability in the U.K. is a disincentive to capital-formation in anything but a nationally-based service unless the firm's market sector is uncompetitive and the firm has a strong brand in place. In the U.K. in particular non-traded services have increased as an employment sector because of the reluctance to invest with a background of poor quality information and volatile trading prices. The consequences of E.M.U. for the U.K. will include therefore a wider European capital market, more manufacturing investment, more research and development, and further (sensible) corporate rationalisation. There is no point in the current pursuit of a well-educated, mobile labour-force if the only long-term, knowledge-intensive investment and jobs are in the U.S.A. To resist U.S. monopolies in microbiological and pharmaceutical (as well as the computing and aeronautic sectors) the euro must be embraced with vigour and soon. This will lead to improved productivity and lower unemployment in a way that lower wages will not.

An effect that cascades on from these changes is that small and medium size enterprises will be stimulated into competitive trading, resulting in more intra-E.U. trade and a virtuous cycle of more investment and more employment. It is extraordinary that the benefits of E.M.U. are portrayed as being skewed towards large firms; the removal of regulations and exchange rates must necessarily favour S.M.E.'s proportionately as they start from such a hopelessly low base, flummoxed by current conditions in a supposedly single market.

There are other points. The government will no longer be able to influence rates of interest for electoral purposes. In addition, the political clout of the euro should enable the E.U., in the G3 arena and thence the markets, to stop the U.S.A.'s periodic exports of unemployment. It is curious how the analysis of the U.S. labour market dominates articles, as if it is the cause of some miracle of growth; product price in the market is assumed to be determined paradoxically by both the wage-rate and the extent to which firms have switched out of labour. So perhaps a reminder of a third factor is in order; the exchange rate. For example, from the French/German/Benelux perspective the U.K. inflation rate from summer 1996 to summer 1997 was more like 28 per cent than 3 per cent. The price of a video, or a burger, *or a worker* shot up, not because of tight labour markets or over-regulation but simply because sterling appreciated. It is extraordinary how perhaps only 1 per cent of the population comprehends that point, and it is simply weird that our broadsheets don't try to put it over.

Furthermore, and this may seem a small point, but it is one that has huge resonance with the Frederick Forsyth/Bill Cash school of thought, how should the windfall benefits be used? Usually the media assume the British are keen on coming into windfalls, so why aren't they being told about this one? This refers to that misunderstood national treasure, the pile of foreign exchange reserves. Not only is it irrelevant if our reserves are pooled in Frankfurt rather than squirrelled in London, but there will just be too many reserves for the needs of the euro. Our pundits should be calling for surplus foreign exchange and reduced reserve management costs to be used for regional support and employment creation when the E.C.B. and the euro are more democratically supervised. Or will they just play Jingo and say the British should pay less of the budget? That will help unemployment nicely.

One recent insidious trend is the castigation of the single interest rate as 'one size fits all' for the eurozone. Suddenly everyone on Sky TV is an economic expert, and insists that the regions must have the same inflation rate or long-term there will be civil war. At least this delays the prospect of falsification indefinitely, and reverses the tactic of making short-term predictions (which turn out to be hopelessly wrong) that has marked the humiliation of euro-scepticism in the U.K. for over half a century.

The heavyweight critics, however, are all familiar with the Balassa-Samuelson theory which invalidates this populist nonsense, but are cynically covering it up for their own benefit. Norman Lamont has been particularly devious in regard to the Irish miracle, declaring it to be a 'disaster', just as he says the Stability and Growth Pact is for German growth although he has always claimed that economic theory shows that fiscal policy can have no effect on real variables like output and employment. However, the free-marketeer (he only admits to being a Post-Keynesian) Samuelson back in 1964 showed that a country with rapidly-expanding productivity in the tradeable goods sector will necessarily experience higher inflation in non-tradeable goods than its competitors. It is to be expected and natural; a haircut costs more in Luxembourg than Newcastle. It will particularly affect land and housing. To say that higher inflation in Ireland or Portugal than France and Germany is a disaster is to smear totally and deliberately a success story; will the locals there be moaning about the increases in their property value?

At the same time they compare eurozone growth rates in 2002–3 with those of the U.S. and talk about 'disastrous' growth and the 'disastrous' appreciation of the currency to nearly $1.20; in 2000 they were talking about the 'disastrous' depreciation below $0.90! They then deliberately fail to point out that the U.S. cycle (bottoming out two years earlier than the eurozone's) was marked by a massive recession whereas the eurozone's trough of 2003 was at a far greater level of growth and employment than that of 1993, and that this was due in no small degree to the low interest rates brought about by greater economic integration leading up to and following the euro's introduction. They are both trading on and reinforcing the economic and political ignorance that governments have woefully failed to address for the last thirty years or more. In October 2003 the standard quote about Concorde's last flight was that it made people 'proud to be British'; this of a project born of the highest ideals of co-operation with the French,

Beleaguered euro may have to bank on international rescue

HAMISH McRAE

Experts advised their customers to put money in the euro; as a result, their credibility is shot

IF THE collapse of the euro prompts a co-ordinated rescue of the currency in the next few months, what will be the long-term consequences?

The overwhelming balance of probability is that there will have to be some sort of internationally co-ordinated rescue. It will have to be co-ordinated because action by the European Central Bank on its own would not be credible.

At a minimum there will have to be a statement of support from the eurozone governments, coupled with assurances of continuing structural reform. But that might not be enough. Ideally, there would be a Group of Seven statement of support coupled with specific new structural reforms. And of course both such actions would have to be supported by co-ordinated central bank intervention on the foreign exchanges and an exemplary rise in eurozone interest rates.

We don't know the timing of this rescue, nor the precise form, but let's assume that it happens. Of course it is always possible that there will be a spontaneous recovery of the euro, but it is hard to imagine a sustained one. A rescue is therefore much more likely.

So what then?

The first point is that the markets will not trust the experts for a long time. None of the large investment or commercial banks forecast this weakness and I don't recall any even suggesting it as a possibility. As the currency weakened last year most of them urged their customers to put money into the euro in anticipation of a recovery. As a result, their credibility is shot.

This is serious. It is more serious than the lack of credibility in the ECB, because the poor old ECB never had any credibility to start with. It takes a while to build up a track record and there simply hadn't been time before the slide got going in earnest.

So for the next few years the euro is likely to be in much the same situation as the pound was in the late 1970s and early 1980s following the IMF rescue in 1976. Sure, people will buy it, but they will buy it for trading purposes rather than as a long-term hold. The result will be that the euro will be volatile, maybe for years to come, rather as sterling was. There will be a euro recovery and maybe quite a sharp one. But do not expect it to last.

Further bouts of weakness will compound the problem of an underlying lack of confidence. It took a full 15 years for the French franc to become regarded as a sound currency after the failed expansionary policies of the early 1980s, and the euro could find itself similarly disadvantaged. The ECB might have to run a tighter monetary policy than it would ideally like – as the French did – just to support the currency.

As far as the UK is concerned there will be profound long-term consequences. The pound is now quite seriously overvalued against the German mark, but it is fairly valued against the dollar. So if you are running an exporting company you will be having a

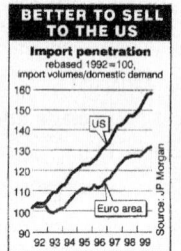

BETTER TO SELL TO THE US
Import penetration
rebased 1992=100,
import volumes/domestic demand

dreadful time exporting to Europe, but a great one exporting to the United States. The US markets have been expanding much quicker anyway. Indeed if you look not just as the faster growth in the US, but also its rising propensity to import over a long period (see graph), any sensible firm would direct its efforts to the US rather than the Continent. You put the effort into selling to the markets where you can make the best profit.

One further effect of the long-term weakness of the euro, then, is likely to be a re-direction of British trade away from the Continent and towards the US. The fact that, physically, Europe is nearer matters much less now than even five years ago. The communications revolution has changed all that. It is, after all, cheaper to fly to New York than it is to Rome and cheaper to make a phone call to the US than it is to Belgium. True, bulk transport will remain much cheaper to the Continent, so some industries will remain handicapped by the need for physical proximity to markets; but for most high-value-added industries a new freedom looms.

Also, from a British point of view, expect profound resistance by UK financial institutions to any plans to have British company shares quoted in euros, whatever the plans of the newly-merged London and Frankfurt exchanges. The experience of the past 16 months will have shaken pension-fund managers. The danger of having liabilities in one currency and assets in another has been brought home in the most direct of ways: would you like to have the size of your pension determined by the level of the euro?

As to British attitudes towards the euro – well, a new paper by Goldman Sachs concludes that Britain has achieved greater stability in GDP growth and inflation than any other industrialised country, including the US. One could add that the Bank of England has gained considerable credibility for its handling of monetary policy, certainly by comparison with the European Central Bank. It is quite hard to argue against success: if it ain't broke, why fix it?

Finally, it would be naive to think that there will not be political fall-out across the eurozone from the mismanagement of its currency. There is at the moment no focal point for the genuine concerns that ordinary people will have at seeing their savings devalued in this way. Remember how the phrase about "the pound in your pocket" not being devalued dogged Harold Wilson all his days. Ordinary people like the feeling that their currency is a valuable one: that they are being paid in real money rather than rubbish and that the long-term value of their savings will be preserved. This concern will be particularly strong in Germany.

I don't think it is possible at this stage to predict how this political concern will play out. But German voters in particular must feel misled. They were promised the euro would be as good as the mark. I don't think even the most enthusiastic supporter of the euro would claim that now.

LETTERS

multinational companies; the death and misery caused by Third World debt. I should have thought that these were issues of great concern.

But the crowds in London on May Day were made up almost entirely of under-30s. Where were the "respectable," middle-aged, even elderly, and middle-class people who made the protests against the WTO in Seattle such a publicity success? The fewer ordinary people there are at such events, the larger the minority of dedicated violent anarchists will be, and the less good will be done.

STEPHEN PRATT
Wincanton, Somerset

Euro fall foreseen

Sir: Hamish McRae's mischievous barbs against the euro seem to be becoming poison-tipped ("Beleaguered euro may have to bank on international rescue", 5 May).

He says the markets will not trust the experts. Nobody, he claims, even mentioned the possibility of such weakness in the euro. This is utter nonsense.

Robert Mundell, the Nobel prize-winner in economics, and other North American academics met in December 1998 in Luxembourg with over fifty others (such as Lord Skidelsky), plus bankers (such as Hans Tietymeyer), plus politicians (such as Vaclav Klaus) to discuss "The Euro as a Stabiliser in the International Economic System".

Professor Mundell's message was unequivocal and well reported. There was no dissent about his analysis, only about the timetable. He laid out five factors that will push the euro exchange rate down, and two that will push it up. The former will be in play at the start of the euro's life, the latter will become more evident after some time.

The E U, he says, should welcome the first phase as an aid towards recovery after the restrictive lead-up to 1999, but should beware the overvaluation that will eventually come, possibly threatening a trade-led recession. Mundell said this might be by 2010.

Both the Bank of England and the European Central bank have an inflation target, and both have largely hit it over the last 16 months. One has done it with interest rates a third lower than the other, so one currency has seen a rise, one a fall due to expectations of future interest rate changes. But McRae claims the Bank of England has "gained considerable credibility", while the ECB has conducted "mismanagement of its currency". This is misleading nonsense, because neither has been given a remit to target exchange rates.

No one living in the eurozone has seen any fall in the "long-term value of their savings" compared to anyone else in the eurozone. That is the whole point of it. Unless they are considering moving to Florida from Florence or to Sapporo from Strasbourg, why should there be a fuss?

ADRIAN WYKES
Luxembourg

The riposte from the sub-editor distilled it from the full froth outpoured from an irate reader. The full version was two pages long

Date: Friday, May 5, 2000 11:41 pm
Subject: LETTERS TO THE EDITOR; Euro dope or deceiver?

Dear Editor,

Hamish McRae's mischievous barbs against the euro and the E.U. now seem to be becoming poison-tipped (May 5th, p.19). He says 'the markets will not trust the experts for a long time'. Nobody, he claims, even mentioned the possibility of such weakness in the euro.

This is utter nonsense and should be denounced as such very clearly; the question is whether it is through lazy unawareness of his subject or wilful deception.

Robert Mundell, the Nobel prize winner in Economics, Prof. Cooper, Prof. Frankel, Prof. Henning, Prof. Andrews (all North American academics) met in December 1998 in Luxembourg with over fifty others (such as Lord Skidelsky), plus bankers (such as Hans Tietymeyer), plus politicians (such as Vaclav Klaus). They were there to honour Prof. Kindleberger and Pierre Werner (the 'father of the euro') and discuss 'The Euro as a Stabilizer in the International Economic System'. This was widely reported, and in March 2000, to celebrate the publishing of the 440-page book of the conference (Kluwer Academic Publishers, e-mail services@wkap.nl) and Prof. Mundell's Nobel Prize, over four hundred people gathered to hear him speak here again.

On both occasions his message was unequivocal and well-reported. It is in the introduction to the book, the papers he gave, and underpins the whole of the rest of the discussion. There was no dissent about his analysis, only about the timetable of events. He laid out five factors that will push the euro exchange rate down, and two that will push it up. The five bearish factors will be in play at the start of the euro's life, the other two will become more evident after some time. These can be found in full on pages xxvii, 65-72, and 293-294 of the book.

The E.U., he says, should welcome the first phase as an aid towards recovery after the restrictive lead-up to 1999, but should beware the overvalueation that will eventually come, possibly threatening a trade-led recession. Mundell said this might be by 2010, Cooper thought it might take thity years. The eventual build-up of capital flow surpluses will require a current account deficit, implying a period of faster growth and/or price rises and/or currency appreciation; it is vital, in Mundell's view, that the E.C.B. therefore continues to control inflation, and ignores the currency level *unless* there is a ridiculous *over*-valuation.

For years many people have struggled to get the pro-euro message printed and broadcasted in the U.K. while rhetoric and untruths from the anti camp have become commonplace, but when a column like today's is printed in The Independent it is time to protest strongly again and try to inject some pragmatism.

Both the Bank of England and the E.C.B. have an inflation target, and both have largely hit it over the last sixteen months. One has done it with interest rates a third lower than the other, so one currency has seen a rise, one a fall due to expectations of future interest rate changes. But McRae claims the B. of E. has 'gained considerable credibility', while the E.C.B. has conducted 'mismanagement of its currency'. It is very hard to believe that someone of his experience is unaware that this is misleading nonsense, because <u>neither</u> has been given a remit to target exchange rates.

In 1998 eurozone firms and households had to take account of over 20,000 internal exchange rate changes. Then the euro (the 'rubbish', says McRae) was born, and in 1999 there were none, zero, not one. No one living in the eurozone has seen <u>any</u> fall in the 'long-term value of their savings' compared to anyone else in the eurozone. That is the whole point of it. Unless they are considering moving to Florida from Florence or to Sapporo from Strasbourg, as some loud, conservative voices seem to be considering, why should there be a fuss?

Most citizens who are aware that their market (now the eurozone not a national one) has undergone at least a halving of the propensity to import, know this is a *good* feature not a bad one, as McRae's ridiculous diagram tries to show. They will continue to take out mortgages fixed for twenty years at 5%, continue to export with vigour, welcome the tourists and the jobs that go with them, and watch anxiously for signs of a rally in the exchange rate as Mundell suggested in March. They will be profoundly thankful that they do not live in the U.K.'s strategic straitjacket, and hope that after the sacrifices of the Maastricht criteria era they have now entered a Golden Age similar to the period between 1948 and 1973.

The euro has been a crucial precondition for such a reprise. It is particularly galling to have to read such stuff on the weekend of the 50th anniversary of the

Schumann Declaration, when Luxembourg is celebrating over half a century of western European peace. Tomorrow the Court of Justice's Thomas More Building is having an open day, and the Place d'Armes will be full of marquees, music, and celebration; Tuesday 9th is a holiday when the new European School will be inaugurated and the rest of the eurozone will be thanking the shades of Churchill, Monnet, Schumann, Spinelli, de Gasperi, Adenauer, et al for their efforts at reconciliation and integration. 2019 will see the 50th anniversary of the solemn declaration at The Hague about the single currency; does The Independent want these matters to be discussed properly before then or not?

With many thanks for your kind consideration,

Yours Sincerely,

that gave rise to the Airbus project, and provided a beacon for those who later sought to introduce the single market in order to enhance the possibility of further integrative projects. Yet for all the laughable and facile bone-headed prestidigitation involved in this propaganda the euro's champions in the U.K. have been left hanging by a supposedly pro-euro government of unprecedented strength.

So we are left with pundits who appear to think that the Texan dollar should have been devalued in 1986, and that the Californian dollar should have been appreciating since 1913 – oh no, *that* was the year, wasn't it, that the U.S.A. finally established a single currency (rather, twelve different dollars that have kept parity ever since)? The U.S. dollar, I believe, is the single currency that embraces such economically disparate places as Seattle, Honolulu, Fairbanks, Santa Fe, New Orleans, and subsequently (voluntarily) that inspirational well-developed dependency of harmony, Puerto Rico. Is the suggestion serious that Newcastle, Nancy, and Naples are *less* convergent overall and through the cycle?

Back in the Caribbean, the people of both Guadeloupe and Montserrat (those near-neighbours of Puerto Rico) are E.U. citizens, whereas those of Barbados and Grenada (ex-British dependencies) are not. But all of them would recognise among every age-group in large parts of the U.K. worryingly large quantities of a slave mentality which is articulated as a 'special relationship' with the U.S.A. This feeling, for it cannot be dignified with the term 'analysis', originated with the events of 1917–9 and 1944–7, and developed rapidly in the youth culture of the seventies and eighties. There is an unspoken assumption that if it all falls apart in Europe, 'over there', there will still be a rescue by our fellow English speakers, and an economic niche with them. This deference has been exacerbated in the media class by the U.S.A. boom in the 90s, the inability of journalists to keep track of the real German/French/Italian economies, and the total blindness until it was too late of what was happening in Asia. There are triumphal articles from people who should be more objective that are reminiscent of mid-1987, and they will return to haunt many who currently proclaim victory for the now offensively-titled 'Anglo-Saxon Model'. It is time to realise that times have changed. Splits over Iraq are a temporary red herring.

Until the government and the media acknowledge these dangerous fallacies, and educate a largely economically-unaware public how closely peace and prosperity in Europe depend on the E.U. it will always be forced to look down false trails towards E.U. 'leadership' and to enter new E.U. initiatives late. The time has come to state loudly and without regret that outside the central core of the E.U. the U.K. would be too exposed, vulnerable, and weak to cope with the ferocious economic competitive forces that will be generated in a euro/dollar/yen-dominated world. This message is as vital as my own warning in 1919 and Churchill's in 1946 about changing the mind-set and creating new organisations to deal with new world circumstances. Every action of this administration should be trying to lock it more tightly into that E.U. central core, and only then will the U.K. be able to give it some momentum of its own.

CONCERN OVER TREATIES

EUROPEAN INTEGRATION
From Our Own Correspondent
BONN, JUNE 1

Dr. Adenauer, the Chancellor, has decided to attend the conference in Rome of the Foreign Ministers of the six members of the Coal and Steel Community which opens on June 12. The original intention was that the deputies should meet to consider the draft of a constitution for the proposed political community, but in view of the coming Bermuda meeting, which is assuming ever greater importance in German eyes, the Chancellor hopes that Rome may show, especially to American public opinion, that the movement towards European integration is not stagnating.

The Chancellor has been influenced in his decision by the concern he feels over the delay in bringing the treaties with the west into force. The effects of Senator Taft's recent speech have, notwithstanding President Eisenhower's dissociation from it, not been erased. To the delay has now been added the uncertainty caused by Mr. Semionov's appointment as Soviet High Commissioner, and the danger of a rift in western unity. The Chancellor's view is clearly that the process of integration is in need of a new driving force.

POLITICAL COMMUNITY

The Chancellor's initiative follows the sudden visit of Professor Hallstein, the State Secretary for Foreign Affairs, to Paris at the week-end, when he saw Mr. David Bruce, the United States representative with the Coal and Steel Community, and assured him of the Federal Government's full support of the proposed political community. It is stated here that Professor Hallstein also raised the question of German association with the Bermuda meeting. The allied view seems to be that if Germany was represented, however loosely, it would not be possible to exclude other west European countries, and that such an extension would defeat the purpose of the meeting.

Herr Ollenhauer, the leader of the Opposition, has urged that the Federal Government should draw up a constructive plan for submission to the " big three," and at the same time prepare proposals, to be forwarded to Mr. Seminov by the Allied High Commission, which might test the sincerity of Soviet policy with regard to the future of Germany. The proposals, Herr Ollenhauer suggested, should deal with the scarcity of food supplies in the Soviet zone, the expansion of trade between east and west, and the removal of restrictions on inter-zonal traffic.

Herr Ollenhauer coupled with his suggestion the demand that " every possible step should be taken to prevent the ratification of the treaties "—a demand which a semi-official commentary describes as asking " the German people to get to work digging graves." Whether the Federal Government has direct contact or not with the Bermuda meeting, it will certainly have a comprehensive memorandum to submit to the three western statesmen.

STATE DEPARTMENT REORGANIZATION
From Our Own Correspondent
WASHINGTON, JUNE 1

President Eisenhower to-day proposed to Congress a reorganization of the State Department which will bring under the department's authority all foreign economic assistance programmes, including the Mutual Security Agency.

For administrative purposes a new agency will be set up to control the activities of the various foreign aid programmes, but the Secretary of State will be directly responsible for all decisions on policy. The new agency will be called the Foreign Operations Administration and will presumably be presided over by Mr. Harold Stassen, the present mutual security administrator.

Another part of the plan will establish a new governmental body, the United States Informational Agency, to conduct all foreign information programmes, now divided between the State Department, the M.S.A., the technical cooperation programme, and the Voice of America.

MEETING A CHALLENGE
WASHINGTON, June 1.—In a message to Congress accompanying these proposals, the President said they were necessary to meet the challenge imposed by the nation's role of leadership in the non-Communist world.

" Our nation to-day is dedicated to international action in concert with other nations — through the United Nations and in regional arrangements with other nations—for collective security, for economic and social cooperation, designed to foster a community of world law," he said.

" We have come to know that national security entails mutual security with other free nations. And we have come to know that their freedom, in turn, depends heavily upon our strength and the wisdom with which we use it."

President Eisenhower said the reorganization would fix clearly the central responsibility for foreign policy below the President and group together other programmes, at present scattered, which implemented foreign policy. " Slackness, confusion, blurred authority, and clouded responsibility—any of these can defeat the noblest purposes of any foreign policy," he said.

A key point in the plan would be the creation of a separate agency " setting forth official United States positions for use abroad "—that is, presenting the official American view on a variety of questions.—Reuter.

CRICKETERS KILLED BY LIGHTNING

PAVILION STRUCK

Three cricketers were killed and two seriously injured yesterday evening when, during a thunderstorm, lightning struck the home team's dressing room in the pavilion of the Co-operative Wholesale Society's soap works ground at Irlam, near Manchester. The team was playing against an Irlam district side as part of the Coronation celebrations. Players in the visitors' dressing room were unhurt.

PLANS DELAYED

As reported in a message published yesterday, the timing of the assault was delayed, largely through obstacles, caused

E. P. Hillary

by bad weather, in the crossing of the difficult ice-covered Lhotse face, which leads to the South Col. This delay led to rumours in Katmandu—whence they were spread abroad—that the pre-monsoon assault had failed. Although there was some sickness among members of the expedition, as well as the obstacle of bad weather, there is no reason to think a withdrawal was contemplated at any stage.
Copyright

LONG RECORD OF ATTEMPTS

MOUNTAINEERS' ROLL OF HONOUR
FROM OUR SPECIAL CORRESPONDENT
BASE CAMP, KHUMBU GLACIER

With the conquest of Mount Everest, one of the great prizes of adventure has been won. Everything about Mount Everest is big, and its long record of victory over successive expeditions is of course due principally to its stupendous size. Here at the expedition's base camp at the head of the Khumbu Glacier the array of mighty peaks that surrounds the Everest massif is spread in panorama. To the south are the two fine summits of Taweche, and just across the valley to the west is Pumori, the noble mountain that George Leigh Mallory first saw and named. The twin peaks of Lingtren stand to the north, with the romantic pass of the Lho La which leads dramatically, between towering heights, into Tibet. Behind the pass is the summit known as North Peak, and to the east is the enormous mass of Nuptse, from the south a menacing mountain wall, from here a gracious rock pile dressed in snow.

Very little seems to have changed in *The Times* over the last fifty years; concern over European integration and the treaties, quirky events at cricket matches, and nationalistic celebrations (although New Zealanders regard Hillary as exclusive to *their* history).

The level of debate in the U.K. is such that one is more likely to get in print by being Mr. Bean's brother (the other Mr. Atkinson is a noted 'Septic') than by posing positive thoughts. There are, in addition, plenty of current pundits like Norman Lamont with vested interests to protect, who are furiously diverting attention from the main points with trivial froth and deliberate falsehoods. They have their dupes even in the *Guardian* and the *Independent*. Hamish McRae on May 5th 2000 had a particularly extraordinary piece for a pro-EU paper (shown on p.282). On May 9th, the 50th anniversary of the Schuman Declaration, to its credit the *Independent* printed an edited version of a letter written in reply. The full reply is reproduced herein along with McRae's original article. But there wasn't a single item in the whole newspaper to do with that very special day apart from a few edited highlights from a humble reader's letter.

The situation can be summed up in a parable for our times. A cricket enthusiast born in 1940 who was run over by a number 72 bus on Hammersmith Broadway in 1962 at the age of 22 would have lived through two tours of England by West Indies cricket teams. A second enthusiast born in 1964 and run over by the very same bus on the same spot in 1986 (also aged 22) would have lived through six tours rather than two. A conservative is someone who appreciates the facts that the same machine administered both the blows in question and that no bogus reforms had disrupted the tried and tested routes and equipment of London Transport during this period. A Conservative, however, is someone who not only deplores the rise in West Indian influence during these years (with a concomitant fall in England's power) but also wants the London bus routes to be opened up completely to the chill winds of *laisser faire* forces. The distinction is not a subtle one, but then neither is the eurosceptics' claim that the *Independent* is rampantly europhile merely subtly different from the reality. The revolutionary American writers of 1787 (who published under the name of Publius Valerius Publicola) would struggle these days to get a federalist letter printed by the *Sun*; the tragedy for Britain is that the same letter would also struggle, sadly, to find a receptive editor *anywhere* in Britain.

§3. Early 2003
From the Euro to a Constitution;
proposals conforming to the principles of good government.

In October 1999 Pierre Werner (who died in 2002, having been Prime Minister of Luxembourg for most of the period between 1959 and 1984) gave a two-hour video interview in English, recalling the life of Robert Schuman, the genesis of the eurozone, and his own part in the history of cricket. He made it clear how dangerous the empty (French) chair of the mid-60s was for the E.U. and that the Luxembourg Compromise of 1966 was in fact not a compromise, but a unilateral full stop drawn up by France (or, rather, De Gaulle and the nationalists). It went without saying how the 1953–4 failure of the European Defence Community (an integrative initiative that was encouraged by the USA) and its allied political programme had also been close to catastrophic.

In fact Secretary of State John Foster Dulles went so far as to say, in Paris at the North Atlantic Council meeting of December 1953,

> If E.D.C. should fail, the United States might be compelled to make an 'agonising reappraisal' of its basic policy …

But Pierre Werner always returned to the positive. The 1955 Messina meeting had been given extra impetus by the collapse of the Pleven Plan for E.D.C., and the downfall of De Gaulle nearly fifteen years later, following his obstructiveness, was made equally spectacular by his isolation at the end. Above all, though, Werner emphasised the 'happy coincidence' that allowed the partnership of Jean Monnet and Robert Schuman to incubate the European Coal and Steel Community from its public announcement on May 9th, 1950. There was a symmetry with the 1960–1 Test series between Australia and West Indies, when, after three decades of rather dour, utilitarian strategy and tactics, zest and style were brought back into the game by the captains, Benaud and Worrell. That 'happy coincidence' has become a permanent yardstick, raised by cricket-lovers ever since whenever the spirit of the game or the attitude of the captains has become over-aberrant.

Werner said that without Monnet's political shrewdness and Schuman's honest humility the offer of the E.C.S.C. would never have been made to Adenauer, who (happy coincidence again) jumped at the chance of accepting the new challenge with a fresh slate, saying

> this is our breakthrough.

Listening to the clamour still made about Dunkirk and the Battle of Britain nearly three generations after the events, it is a cause of wonder how our British establishment (from R. A. B. Butler through to Gordon Brown) still resists celebrating other true turning points, of recent history, like Hitler's turning east in June 1941, or the Nazi defeat at Stalingrad two years later. But this is particularly true of May 9th 1950, Schuman Day, when the 'Golden Age' growth of post-Marshall Aid Europe was given a framework of cooperation within which Britain was welcome, holding the promise of further development in a way Commonwealth never did.

Pierre Werner was (contrary to Gregory Palast's extraordinary claims) the 'father of the euro', but in close attendance at the birth has been Robert Mundell, winner of the 1999 Bank of Sweden Prize in Economic Sciences in memory of Alfred Nobel. The media press one to take Mundell on board wholesale as a free marketeer who supports the euro, or reject him and be labelled an old-fashioned interventionist. The problem, not so much muddying the waters as turning them into opaque adobe bricks, is that most U.K. E.U. supporters are Keynesian and most antis are free marketeers. What is to be done about this cacophony?

The answer is to be critical of Mundell's assumptions and be pragmatically European in the application of the undoubted insights that have emerged since the breakdown of the Bretton Woods system in 1971. One can be sceptical about Mundell's regard for

GOLDEN AGES AT THE FENNER'S MARGIN

May 9th, 2000, the 50th anniversary of the Schuman Declaration, and the opening of the new buildings for the European School in Luxembourg; Jacques Delors is greeted by the Luxembourg Cricket Federation Patron (and government minister) Madame Hennicot-Schoepges. The Grand Duke and Grand Duchess are welcomed by the initiator of the original school, nonagenarian Albert Van Houtte.

gold and labour market mobility. The appearance of a speaker far in advance of his real age is partly accounted for by repeated references to these neo-classical props (as well as terms like currency boards and seignorage which are not in any Economics dictionaries that students will ever use).

One can be sceptical of Mundell's classical explanation of the U.S. success in the 1990s for a number of reasons. Firstly, it is not clear that wage reductions and low employee protection can explain the growth of jobs compared to the E.U. (rather than the imitation of Japanese investment strategies in high-growth sectors, spin-offs from the massive public investment in the military, and comparatively expansionary state and federal fiscal policy). Secondly, there is clear evidence that labour mobility *per se* is a neutral condition, which in the case of Luxembourg for example (as a high growth pole in a low growth region) has resulted in a higher rate of unemployment, as the Schengen agreement and the single European market have had their effects daily on trans-border migration (the 'frontaliers', or borderers). This seems to be particularly misunderstood in the U.K., where it seems to be assumed that 'mobility' does not include international geographical movements (in or out) of labour and that more labour mobility must lead to lower unemployment. Thirdly, there are his repeated harpings-on about the desirability of restoring some form of 'barbarous relic' like gold, and the barking argument that because Italian local authorities won't let him alter his new villa (even if he wants it to end up looking like a Star Trek set) the whole of Europe is over-governed.

The more attractive, positive, and constructive parts of the Mundell *oeuvre* centre on his initiation of a desirable rapprochement between short-run Keynesian analysis and long-run free market analysis. The outcome is that, according to the Nobel Press Release of December 1999:

> in a world of free capital mobility monetary policy can be oriented towards either an external objective – such as the exchange rate – or an internal (domestic) objective – such as the price level – but not both at the same time.

His monetary approach to the balance of payments dovetailed with Kaldor's analysis of the U.K. to suggest that the continual arising of external imbalance leading to internal deterioration as a means to restoring that balance would go on until international competitiveness was restored. For him that would imply a supply side revolution, for Kaldor an investment revolution. For me, it's whatever will work. Whichever way, it is the external deficit providing the brake. The ghost of Henderson again rebukes me for being too casual and flippant, but the brake is there, with or without the euro. It is bigger the longer the U.K. stays out, and at least I would take the decision to release it; I doubt if Henderson and his ilk would ever find that 'the time is right'.

But it is not just currency fluctuations. The businessman's attitude of Fortress Britain remains; the Softback Preview, the Laithwaites wine club, and numerous other potential export businesses all have one very significant sentence at the bottom of their advertising; 'Offer only applicable in the U.K.' But why such sheltering, when Luxembourg is closer physically and in spirit to Cambridge or London than Glasgow,

Truro, or Belfast are? There is no such problem with Rothschilds, who distribute wine in a remarkably similar operation to Tony Laithwaite; they simply don't think it is a problem to order from another country.

Within the eurozone the external constraint on growth has been transformed since it has a neutral current account balance, and the internal competitive dynamic has become more transparent and urgent. The independent central bank uses monetary policy to target price changes, and hence the external balance through competitive forces. Fiscal policy, more effective because under E.M.U. it is less subject to spillover effects from a single state to its neighbours, is, along with increased regional transfers, still available (and still controlled by government) to achieve internal balance between states. Over the whole eurozone fiscal policy could also reinforce sustainable growth and be more effective on a Keynesian basis if properly co-ordinated, because it would be carried out in a more closed system (*i.e.* the propensity to import is lower). If a sensible Stability and Growth Pact can be negotiated (and new rules for the E.C.B. allow it to have real effect) the growth potential within the eurozone will receive a step-change. To put it baldly, for one nation the share of the cake compared to another nation will become of less significance because the cake will grow faster through everyone pooling all the ingredients and equipment.

The Swiss have found out the truth of this to their great cost in their isolation of the last two decades, and the recent recession of that export-dependent island has been very poorly reported in the northern European 'Septic' press. The 'Septics' continuously commit the fallacy of composition, divining from the narrow evidence that oil-rich Norway is doing well outside the E.U. that a country like the U.K. (dozens of times that big and now without equivalent supplies of oil) will also be fine. A more dishonest folly is the complete disregard for the much higher levels of agricultural subsidies granted in Iceland, and Norway than the E.U., or the way subsidies have diminished in Finland and Sweden, for example, since they joined the E.U. The failure of national governments to set realistic production quotas in 1984, the success of the 1992 MacSharry reform of the C.A.P., and the significance of the 2003 'single payment' scheme are also invisible in media coverage by the 'Septics'.

The success of the Economics is going to be tied indissolubly to the integration of the Politics; notice the phrase 'still controlled by government'. That government, which has not yet fully arrived, is a collective noun implying sudsidiarity in a pluralist system of local, regional, national, and supranational government, and it is that government that the 2003 Fischer is quite rightly asking us to think about now, rather than the currency union of the 1971 Kaldor, Robinson, and Kahn. Thank goodness Nicky Kaldor had the chance to repent his euroscepticism in public with his 1984 Mattioli Lectures (citing me, along the way, as providing an example of one who would change his mind when proved wrong). He even promoted the formation of a European Central Bank and a single currency that might be involved in the reform of the Common Agricultural Policy, whereby the cost of accumulating buffer stocks would form the 'backing' for the currency rather than a charge on the taxpayer. He also saw political pooling in Europe as a possible method for by-passing U.S.A. hegemony, filling Mario Monti with joy over the sinner that repenteth ...

There remains of course the balance between the various policy instruments and agents which needs fine-tuning. What currently seems 'stupid' (to use Romano Prodi's term) to the outside world is constraining and fining the main motor of eurozone growth, Germany, for fiscal laxity when the eurozone is at the bottom of its cycle with a Public Sector Borrowing Requirement under 3 per cent, inflation only just above 2 per cent, the current account of the balance of payments at 1 per cent of G.D.P., and unemployment creeping nearer 10 per cent than 5 per cent (without incarcerating 4 per cent of the adult male population as the United States does it is hardly realistic to aim at a lower figure). Effectively, however, the 3 per cent P.S.B.R. ceiling is irrelevant at present, since the European Central Bank has the duty to adjust its monetary policy to whatever else occurs; if the Stability and Growth Pact was changed tomorrow to allow 10 per cent P.S.B.R.s, any use of the extra leeway might simply encourage the E.C.B. to tighten monetary policy in compensation.

For Hans Tietmeyer and other orthodox thinkers this would mean penalising the virtuous who have kept to the rules (which are, we are all agreed, probably flexible enough interpreted for the eurozone as a whole) and this becomes the argument to maintain the *status quo* although it creates unsustainable tensions between different national governments. But even altering (rather than just complaining about) the Stability and Growth Pact 'hard co-ordination' rules (Begg, Hodson, Maher, N.I.E.S.R. 2003) make up a sideshow when the equally 'hard co-ordination' rules of the E.C.B.'s inflation target of 0–2 per cent leads to a soft (and very unclear) adaptation of monetary policy with regard to fiscal policy. What is needed is not to loosen the constraints on the national fiscal authorities but an agreed means of modifying the cycle supranationally.

National politicians in all parties currently feel they have a lot to lose in terms of prestige and power and huff and puff furiously about the importance of Parliament at present whenever fiscal harmonisation is mentioned. What is vital is to discern the rhetoric of Blair and the Scandinavian nay-sayers from the reality of sovereignty-pooling that is being welcomed by the rest of the inaptly-named 'new' Europe.

All E.U. schoolchildren should make a comparative study of the United Provinces in the late seventeenth century and the E.U. of today, concentrating on the differences between the view from the outside, from where the organism resembles a messy confederation, and that from the inside, from where the organism resembles a federation. The tensions stem basically from there, and the crucial variable in terms of progress is the level of imagination present among the key decisionmakers.

That low-growth regions within the federation will have to rely on 'external' (*i.e.* federal) help from the supranational bodies is anathema to those opposed to further integration. Yet this is oxymoronic. Regional assistance from the federal power is not external assistance. It is the citizens of the E.U. that provide the federal powers with the ability to garner their 'own resources', which are deployed on behalf of the welfare of

GOLDEN AGES AT THE FENNER'S MARGIN

> **10 DOWNING STREET**
> LONDON SW1A 2AA
> 020 7930 4433
>
> THE PRIME MINISTER
>
> 29 May 2003
>
> Dear Neil,
>
> Congratulations on securing your Commission reform package.
>
> I doubt if anyone who had not had extensive experience of cajoling, haranguing and outmanoeuvring in a previous life could have pulled it off. You really did lead from the front. You must occasionally have felt more like St Sebastian than St George. But it is a real success. And all down to you.
>
> Well done!
>
> Yours ever
>
> Tony
>
> The Rt Hon Neil Kinnock

Hidden history; on the noticeboards in the staff areas of all E.U. institutions, but how many U.K. citizens got to see this message?

294

the citizens in the forms of agricultural stabilisation and regional aid; this is internal assistance, it is *our* community, and in the new federation, *our* federal powers acting for *our* benefit. If they are temporarily hampered by a Stability and Growth Pact that was accepted for tactical reasons to keep Germany on board, it need not necessarily affect the logic of the longer run. Invoking examples from Canada, Australia, the U.S., India, and probably the Roman empire as well should soon quell these fanciful notions.

The single currency requires greater regional transfer resources, more harmonised consideration of the automatic stabilisers, and harmonised attitudes to transnational companies. The latter are, as Mica Panic says,

> the one form of micro-economic organisation whose actions can turn to failure even the most imaginative scheme for intergovernmental fiscal co-operation and adjustment policies.

The aloof centralisation of the E.C.B. doesn't make such changes of rule and practice that will give it a change of direction unwelcome; the clear shift to a coordinated fiscal, monetary, liquidity, and incomes policy for the whole eurozone is what is needed to provide a dynamic single market for both output and labour. The fact that this will be seen to be at the expense of democratic legitimacy will in turn galvanise the search for real political reform, a subject to which one must next turn. Hans Tietmeyer concluded in October 2003 that the Commission is regarded as too political to be charged with intervening in fiscal policy. Which supranational institution should be given such a role, then?

Something is sure to happen; even the heads of state in the European Council aren't always going to be totally inept, although the current suggested changes seem nuts. Maintaining national discretion for fiscal policy in an uncoordinated policy environment, while giving more leeway than 3 per cent over the P.S.B.R. to those with lower public debt ratios rather than those most in need of the stimulus is a typical banker's solution. Imagine the public's response if a doctor refused medicine to one patient, but not to another who needed it less, and said the refusal was because the former was always being ill?

With regard to the much-needed increase in 'democracy', apparently the people and their media feel that this is a crusade the U.K. can lead the 'rest' in, with *the Independent* newspaper trumpeting particularly loudly to show that to be pro-E.U. is to be pro-democracy. This is going to be ill-received in the nations where proportional representation has always been used to vote members to Strasbourg, coming from a system that has until recently lost any meaningful semblance of local government, and from politicians who have lost sight of the true meaning and achievements of liberal pluralism since the 1930s, when the U.K. was in the vanguard of theoretical democracy. You have to be vituperatively and mendaciously against federalism to get into print about it these days. Seeley, Acton, Milner, Curtis, Churchill, Laski, Beveridge, Jennings, Robbins, Stead, Attlee, Bevin, Wootton, McKay, Toynbee, Wilson – even Hayek – wouldn't be able to get a positive word in.

The E.U. élite are said to be separate, out of touch; look at the Royal Institute of International Affairs conference on the euro in December 2000. Although sponsored by British Airways the fee was still £1404.13 for two days; and the euro had been in existence for two years already. This is true of all business conferences, however; they are a homogenous industry and there is nothing significant about that particular Thursday and Friday. Less was heard about the E.U.'s free digital satellite station 'EbS' that anyone could access on Eutelsat Hot Bird (13 °E), 12,47550 GHz, horizontal polarisation, widebeam footprint, 27,500 Mbauds, 3/4 FEC, and NO decoder card. In December 2000 this could be seen in Iceland, Riyadh, Kabul, Spitzbergen, and Gran Canaria, but was never relayed on B.B.C. Parliament, even during recesses when they put on a blank screen.

Tony Blair turned to the Centre for European Reform as a think tank on the 'big question' which has manufactured a pragmatic view of the EU's future designed to placate the voter. The 'f' word is rubbished as yesterday's thinking. The trailing of a new big idea for Britain in Europe such as 'EU2010' was meant to cause excitement and hope amongst pro-Europeans. The problem was the ideas proposed by the Centre for European Reform. More power for the European Council, the elected national leaders. Coreper to become a super-executive, diminishing the role of the Commission. Widening, not deepening.

But the wresting of control to 'democratically-elected' politicians is hardly a surefire recipe for the E.U. to regain popularity with its citizens; the foreign ministers' decision to impose sanctions on Austria when it lurched to the right was still generally portrayed and perceived as 'Brussels' being heavy-handed. Despite the reforms of the Finnish presidency Coreper remains the most suspect, democratically, of the E.U. institutions, yet Blair suggests making it a super-executive, and with Chirac and Berlusconi around he might just succeed whatever the fate of the Convention on the constitution.

Typically then, the politicians pin their hopes on a strengthening of national leaders through the European Council as a way to reduce the Commission. But woe betide us if Coreper, or the European Council, or the Council of Ministers are ever given even more power than now. Small states will resist this, and France and Germany should also resist the temptation. A centralised state like the U.K. will get more liberal democracy out of Fischer's federal proposals than either the French or British traditions. I would fight the latter as strenuously as the 'Septic' lunacies, because they stand a chance being taken up while ignoring not only Monnet and Schuman but also Lionel Robbins. Perhaps we could paraphrase the latter; 'if we don't coop up the nation state, the nation state will coop us up'.

By contrast, at Nice a series of nationalist vetoes, remnants of that dangerous Luxembourg Compromise of 1966 was put behind a 'red line' as if this was something to be proud of. The ability to protect the U.K.'s high rates of fuel and alcohol tax had been saved! The people and the *Daily Mail* were meant to cheer Jingo. Then, when it was realised that this had retarded progress to E.U. widening, the solution was to blame the French presidency. The latter had also heartened the national governments by snubbing the Commission President.

The main problem with this Blair Warsaw position is that it is historically wrong; it will not stop a two-speed Europe with greater federal accountability as the basis of deciding who goes in the fast lane. It just reinforces the view that Britain hasn't yet foresworn foot-dragging, centralisation by national government, and the grand gesture of futility.

There isn't a British monopoly on the politics of the barmy, of course. A lunatic misunderstanding of the fallacy of composition seems for good or ill to accompany most plebiscite voters by definition, upon which seeming law of nature Herr Hitler based all his faith in and practice of democracy. The tragic events of September 11th (Sweden, 2003) confirmed this, as the sizeable minority (dependent on multinational employment and exports) that voted for the euro were outnumbered by a majority who voted against entry despite being dependent on the employment of that aforementioned minority. The Swedes who live in the Malmo-Copenhagen and Stockholm conurbations are such good fellows and so all-but aware of this that one should not despair of persuading them to certify the rest of their countrymen. Foreign Minister Anna Lindh's murderer could hardly have been trying to save the sovereignty of the car industry, Saab being part of General Motors and Volvo of Ford. Edward Lyttelton would have likened the voters in euro referenda not only to the conservative Eton staff under his command but also the monks of some mediaeval monastery. The latter, when summoned by the abbot to consider new proposals, would as one fall soundly asleep, only to wake up when he paused in order to chorus 'Namus, namus' (short for damnamus, or 'we're against!'). They would then fall asleep again.

The Delors period showed, by contrast, how *experimenta fructifera* can only be achieved by a strong Commission when national governments are at loggerheads. Blair, Jospin, and Schroder seemed like a dream team compared to Thatcher, Mitterand, and Kohl, yet it was in the mid-1980s that the single-market breakthrough was made, thanks to the vigour and imagination of the Commission. How dangerous to imbalance the constitution on the basis of the coincidence of any particular set of personalities. The pitiful progress made on the 2nd and 3rd pillars of the E.U. since 1992 (the single Domestic and Foreign Affairs policies, left to the custodianship of the national leaders) show how it's crucial that when a logjam of national opinions forms (as they did over Iraq) there is an authority outside the European Council that will kickstart E.U. proceedings. Compare the tortuous ambulation towards a 'single' foreign policy to the *élan* with which Jenkins and Delors managed to get E.M.U. off the ground again at times when the governments were barely aware of each other's aims.

The British Government and the Centre for European Reform should replace their revisionist nationalist aspirations with grander designs that will reap more benefit for their citizens. They should develop matters where they have the understanding of the people. Every thinking person knows that the E.U. can do a better job than the national Parliament when it comes to cybercrime, to ferry safety standards, to harmonisation of taxes (people want that with reference to cars, drink, and petrol), and the big questions surrounding food, and the environment. The U.K. government could also lead changes of attitudes, for example by persevering with the resurrected common defence initiatives of the early 1950s (although the U.S. is now concerned rather than supportive) which briefly gave Blair some credibility as an integrationist in his first term. Without Tony Blair who else will pursue even a semblance of a sensible policy in the E.U.? Gordon Brown is committed to a life of picking a living at its periphery, the Tories have abandoned any accommodation with European reality, and the Liberal Democrats are hampered as ever by the voting system.

The events since the U.S. downturn really hit in the autumn of 2000 have demonstrated even more than those of autumn 1992 that the long-term future of the E.U. is only viable if it is avowedly, unashamedly federal as Fischer envisages. Charles Handy has convincingly demonstrated that federalism (with its subsidiarity, multiple citizenship, interdependence, common law, and separation of powers) has actually triumphed as the predominant model in the private sector of the re-globalised economy, although the public are somewhat tardy in recognising recent history. Let the benefits now be unleashed properly in the public sector in Europe as they have been in North America. It is time for politicians to lead the people in a pluralist direction rather than drift, to urge people to take their civic responsibilities more seriously rather than shrink them, to resist with equal fortitude both nationalist frameworks and nationalist ideologies wherever they are proposed, and to expose the self-serving vapidity and contradictions that lie at the heart of the New Right core of euroscepticism.

The Convention on the E.U. constitution seems to have headed partly in the right direction, even if the media barely reported it, trumpeting all the insignificant points, and drawing all the wrong conclusions. The Parliament at last will get the right to enact legislation (jointly with the Council of Ministers to begin with). The rotating Presidency will slow down from its giddying rapidity. The Commission's right to propose legislation is more or less unviolated. Everyone is complaining, and Giscard has been *insupportable*. About as harmonious a genesis as could be expected, with plenty of room for future reform. In particular there is still no real distinction made between the powers exercisable at national and supranational levels. But it will all look a lot tidier, and more easy to diffuse throughout schools (or are the democratic voters of the future still unready for that?) before the next movement to integration begins.

* * * * *

With the fifth E.U. enlargement complete, and the next wave of states soon to enter the eurozone it is clear that a two-speed Europe has all but re-emerged and that the important advantages will fall to those in the fast lane towards federation. It will become equally clear that Denmark, Sweden, and the U.K. have doubly hobbled themselves by staying out for the foreseeable future, and being seen to harm their fellow E.U. citizens currently in the eurozone by limiting the size of the single market, confusing E.U. price signals, and inflating transaction costs. But the U.K.'s disastrous three decades of policy mismanagement over Europe will chiefly rebound on its own citizens; how long will the markets hold back from launching punishing speculative sallies of selling private assets, government bonds, and currency to test the limited weapons at the disposal of the authorities? By the end of 2003 interest rate differentials were widening once again between London and Frankfurt; can anyone construct a case to explain that this was to the comparative benefit of U.K. citizens?

As the eurozone becomes more widely understood elsewhere the real effects of lower interest rates, greater mobility of factors and prices, increased competition, and higher investor confidence could lead to a golden age of investment, similar to the post-war consensus if a properly European fiscal framework is put in place. The U.K. would have been greatly advantaged if it could have joined through the removal of the balance of payments constraint on growth. The competitive services she can offer in high growth markets like retailing, finance, I. T., and leisure would have benefitted in particular. The sentiment of the country on economic grounds should be that those who are against the euro are also against the U.K. If there are other, possibly associated factors that are more likely to inhibit rather then promote growth they should be confronted from the inside rather than used as an excuse for yet more inaction.

High eurozone economic growth in the next quarter century can be generated by increasing volumes of more competitive intra-E.U. trade, staffed by immigration, and funded by internal E.U. savings against a background of balanced external trade. The prospect of growth, lower interest rates, and higher returns in the E.U. should encourage domestic investment. This means there will be less need for foreign direct investment, foreign credits, short-term foreign capital inflows, and the instability and uncertainty that go with them. However, this will be occurring just as capital flows towards the new euro reserve currency are increasing, with associated upward pressure on the exchange rate. Unless a catastrophic appreciation and import-led recession are to be endured, it will be Europe's painful duty to go through what the U.S. experienced during the 1990s: lower interest rates, borrowing more, earning more, consuming more, and putting up with lower unemployment.

What is needed is to refocus the E.C.B.'s monetary policy towards all four corners of the magic rectangle for the eurozone in its entirety, and admit some element of demand management, as envisaged in the *Werner Report*, that will target real as well as monetary indicators; 3 per cent annual growth, 5 per cent unemployment, and a 0 per cent basic balance on the balance of payments should be aimed at when permitted by the inflation performance with regard to a raised and widened target of 1–4 per cent. In a re-globalised world where foreign direct investment and portfolio investment are growing rapidly the basic balance (*i.e.* current account plus the long-term financial transactions on the current account) has become the most pertinent indicator of international trade. The ceiling on the P.S.B.R. should mature from the monetarist phobia of perceived Mediterranean irresponsibility to become a eurozone-wide guideline for normal recession. The E.C.B. will also have to be on its guard in the future to ensure that the velocity of money (that is, the EU's financial structure) is predictable (if not stable) and well-behaved, to target prices effectively. But how is this to develop when

GOLDEN AGES AT THE FENNER'S MARGIN

Europe's central bankers among others would still deny outright (this would probably surprise most of the casually-interested intelligentsia) that interest rates are set to manage consumer demand rather than achieve monetary and hence price stability?

The problem of *realpolitik* is in handing an even larger brief over to monetary policy decided by an independent, democratically unaccountable central bank. Additionally, in order for fiscal policy in the E.U. to have more effect on growth, coordination is required to stop one nation's push for expansion being cancelled out by another's 'prudence', and that means some political mechanism from the centre that may be generally indicative, but may become interventionist in extreme circumstances. V.A.T., for example, could each year be varied inversely with unemployment on a regional basis to neutralise the effects of national governments' attempts to meet the 3 per cent ceiling on P.S.B.R.s. The policy should be carried out by a new body and be redistributive only (*i.e.* fiscally neutral across the whole eurozone) with surplusive national governments able to offset the supranational burden with tax cuts (that would not be counted towards the 'golden rule' about borrowing across the cycle) if they wish. Other possibilities surround the European Investment Bank in Luxembourg; Mr. Antonio Guterres has already shown the way here.

National governments would then be left a more allocative role, with incomes policy (largely public sector) to control nominal wages, further rationing measures to share out the given jobs (more childcare provision and a 30 hour week perhaps), or tax incentives to guide the available credit to growth sectors. The irony is that currently they are even more impotent since their limited control over fiscal policy and the E.C.B.'s 0–2 per cent inflation target serve to inhibit some of the benefits of growth arising from the single market which governments could otherwise channel to their citizens.

It's ironic that Tony Blair praised a nationalist like De Gaulle in his Warsaw speech of October 6th 2000. Pierre Werner said that in 1966 De Gaulle was the man who came closest to bringing the E.U. project to a terminal halt while nearly plunging France into civil war. Werner was equally insistent that the Commission's function of proposing legislation must continue to be kept separate from the institutions which derive their legitimacy from the national state governments (*i.e.* the Council, Coreper, and the Council of Ministers).

My accommodation for his political recommendation is a revisiting of those forgotten Dutch initiatives of the early 1950s which so galvanised leaders like Spaak, and led to the sidelining of the Council of Europe (as well as the U.K.'s Eden Plan). The Beyen Plan and the draft European Constitution put forward in the Luxembourg Resolution of September 1952 foresaw a two-chamber Parliament, an idea that could be usefully revived with modification. The People's Chamber could carry on functioning, as at present, and solely in Brussels. In addition a small Senate, based in the Strasbourg parliamentary buildings, could be created as an an upper, independent house for the purposes of proposing pan-European legislation and regionally 'de-sterilising' over-tight fiscal policy (pertaining to those national governments too constricted by the Stability and Growth Pact for the good of output and employment levels). The Senate should determine the best method for achieving co-ordination between fiscal and monetary policy rather than the E.C.B. So the Senate should also be elected by the people rather than consist of a collection of national parliamentary representatives or appointees made by the European Council leaders as envisaged by Adenauer, de Gasperi, van Zeeland, *et al.* This would work in creative tension with, and not in the pocket of, the Commission and the Council of Ministers.

The advantage is that the Commission (whose leading representatives should also become members of the Senate, so that the Commission might be said to retain the right of co-proposal) would be able to concentrate on policing the nations which are failing to follow the laws they themselves have passed without the caricature of 'busybody Brussels' being raised at every opportunity. They would be insisting on laws proposed and passed by the people's representatives, not monolithically, but in two different directly-elected bodies, with the checks of the Council of Ministers and the Commission on hand to temper the furious fluctuations of the democratic will. The lower parliamentary house would continue to scrutinise and polish away at the budgets, the proposals, and the commissioners, as well as enacting legislation.

The first Russian Doll that a more unified and purposeful Europe should attempt seems to be very clear, and is not surprisingly extremely close to my heart; through vigour and foresight the E.U. should become, over the next few years, the biggest subscriber to the I.M.F. which should then be forced to relocate from Washington to a London that is in the eurozone. To many this may appear to be a token gesture of reforming liberal intent, but in reality it would be a small but decisive step (one that is well beyond the imagination of the current European Council) that would presage countless unfolding possibilities for rule changes which could have beneficial consequences

Mike Atherton settles in at the Fenner's wicket in the spring of 2000.

for a tri-polar global system over several decades. The anti-capitalist young and the conservative nationalist may protest and unite against this in a ghastly, unholy absonance but without further pooling, I'm afraid, the power of Britain to act as generously as the U.S.A. and the Franco-German alliance have during the current long, western European peace will never arrive.

The E.U. also needs a motto, or what these days would be called a mission statement, to which all its other activities should be traceable. When the *Luxembourger Wort* with nearly forty other Wstern European newspapers set this as a challenge to school pupils in the months running up to the 50th anniversary of the Schuman Declaration a maximum length of twelve words was stipulated. Thus it became a somewhat taxing exercise, since any motto needs to fulfil at least *eight* functions to be of use. The origins of a Europe divided must be made clear, with autarchy the expected order of the day. This was associated not just with austerity but real poverty, as any visitor from the U.S.A. between 1930 and 1950 (perhaps later) could testify. The need for recognition and forgiveness between the states and the peoples should be conveyed as a precursor for the sort of avoidance of war that should (*should*) prevent even such shrill issues as Gibraltar and the Elgin marbles becoming triggers for military action. The result of this should be a dynamic and gathering (rather than steady) movement towards potential economic progress, particularly through the pooling of resources, enterprise, and markets. This gathering of momentum as the future unfolds should make a return towards the old adherence to state supremacy increasingly unfeasible. After several moments consideration I came upon the following formula, which I still hope will suffice into the medium-term;

The E.U.
reconciling divided nations through a shared
vision of growing peace and prosperity.

It was ruled inadmissable by the judges as it wasn't in French.

The fact that we can be speculating (I hesitate to say making plans) like this shows how you have come such an unimaginably long way in the last half-century, farther than I could possibly have hoped my little protégés could travel. During my sixty two years plus on planet Earth I lived through two of the three European Civil Wars that centred on Franco-German rivalry and arose from the deification of the nation state. What sort of odds would I have laid in 1946 that the next sixty two would bring a long, western European peace of unprecedented prosperity and amicability amongst both people and politicians? However, without setting your eyes towards the next, more lofty peak you will not progress any farther. I'm afraid the flat tranquil turf of Fenner's may not be of any further help to you all, but I hope it will not be forgotten quite yet. Perhaps in years to come a corner of the Strasbourg Senate wallspace might be found for a pair of dusty black and white photographs recalling the era of 6, Harvey Road and the Fenner's Pavilion?

LITERARY REFERENCES

Altham H. S., Swanton E. W., *A History of Cricket*, (George Allen, 1926)
Annan N., *The Dons*, (Harper Collins, 2000)
Arlott J., *Jack Hobbs*, (Readers Union, 1981)
Ashley-Cooper F. S., *Eton V. Harrow at the Wicket*, (London, 1922)
Atkinson R., McWhirter N., *Treason At Maastricht*, (Compuprint, 1995)
Atkinson R., *Europe's Full Circle*, (Compuprint, 1996)
Avery G., *The Best Type of Girl*, (Andre Deutsch, 1991)
Backhouse R., *A History of Modern Economic Analysis*, (Blackwell, 1985)
Bacon R., Eltis W., *Britain's Economic Problem; Too Few Producers*, (Macmillan, 1976)
Bailey P., Thorn P., *Cambridge University Cricketers 1820–1992*, (A.C.S.H., 1992)
Bailey P., Thorn P., Wynne-Thomas P. *Who's Who of Cricketers*, (Guild, 1984)
Bainvill J., *Les Conséquences Politiques De La Paix*, (La Novelle Librarie, Nationale, 1920)
Barker D. A., *Cash and Credit*, (Cambridge, 1912)
Beckles H. and Stoddart B. (ed.), *Liberation Cricket*, (Manchester, 1995)
Begg I., *How to Pay for Europe?*, (Federal Trust, 2000)
Beldam C. (ed.), *Great Cricketers*, (Boundary, 2000)
Bell Q., *Elders and Betters*, (Pimlico, 1995)
Bell V., *Sketches in Pen and Ink*, (Pimlico, 1998)
Blaug M., *Great Economists Before Keynes*, (Wheatsheaf, 1986)
Blaug M., *John Maynard Keynes*, (Macmillan, 1990)
Bond M., Smith J., Wallace W. (ed.), *Eminent Europeans*, (Greycoat, 1996)
Borchardt K-D, *The ABC of Community Law*, (European Communities, 2000)
Bornschier V. (ed.), *State-Building in Europe*, (Cambridge, 2000)
Bosanquet H., *Bridge Street*, (Cambridge History Agency, 1976)
Boyle, D., *The Tyranny of Numbers*, (Harper Collins, 2001)
Brendon P., *Eminent Edwardian*, (Pimlico, 2003)
Bruce-Kerr J., Abrahams H. (eds), *Oxford Versus Cambridge*, (Faber, 1931)
Bryan P., Walker J. (eds), *Cambs. High School; the Second Half Century*, (internal, 2000)
Brodribb G., *The Lost Art*, (Boundary, 1997)
Brodribb G., *The Croucher*, (Constable, 1974)
Brookes C., *English Cricket*, (Readers Union, 1978)
Brown N., *Dissenting Forbears*. (Pillimore, 1988)
Burton J. (ed.), *Keynes's General Theory: Fifty Years On*, (I.E.A., 1986)
Camaiti R. (ed.), *Experiences and Problems of the International Monetary System*, (Monte Dei Pascha Di Siena, 1982)
Capra F., *The Name Above the Title*, (Macmillan, 1971)
Caravan B., *Economists for Beginners*, (Pantheon, 1983)
Cardus N., Arlott J., (eds), *The Noblest Game*, (Harrap, 1969)
Carey G. W., McClellan J. (eds), *The Federalist (Gideon Edition)*, (Liberty Fund, 2001)
Charlton M., *The Price Of Victory*, (BBC, 1983)
Chesterton G., Doggart H., *Oxford and Cambridge Cricket*, (Willow, 1989)

Chirac J., *Our Europe*, (Federal Trust, 2000)
Churchill W. S., *The Sinews of Peace*, (Cassell, 1948)
Clark J. W., *Cambridge*, (Bowes and Bowes, 1910)
Cornford F., *Microcosmographia Academia*, (Bowes and Bowes, 1908)
Coulton G. G., *Fourscore Years*, (Cambridge, 1943)
Cowie H., Pinder J. (eds), *A Recovery Strategy For Europe*, (Federal Trust, 1993)
Craddock P., *Recollections of the Cambridge Union 1815–1939*, (Bowes and, Bowes, 1953)
Daft R., *Kings of Cricket*, (Bristol, 1893)
Denman R., *Missed Chances*, (Indigo, 1996)
Denton G., *A New Transatlantic Partnership*, (Federal Trust, 1999)
Dewey D., *James Stewart*, (Warner, 1996)
Dow C, *Major Recessions*, (Oxford, 1998)
Dunn J., *A Very Close Conspiracy*, (Jonathan Cape, 1990)
Eddowes J., *The Language of Cricket*, (Carcanet, 1997)
Eisler R., *Stable Money*, (Search, 1932)
Engel M. (ed.), *Wisden Almanack 2000*, (John Wisden, 2000)
Eurostat, *European Union Direct Investment*, (EC, 1999)
Eurostat, *The Capital Stock In The European Union*, (EC, 1997)
Eurostat, *New Techniques And Technologies For Statistics II*, (EC, 1997)
Feinstein C. (ed.), *The Managed Economy*, (Oxford, 1983)
Figgis, J.N., *Civilisation at the Crossroads*, (Longman, 1912)
Finet P. (ed.), *Visit of American Financiers and Industrialists to the ECSC*, (European Communities, 1958)
Fischer J., *From Confederation to Federation*, (Federal Trust, 2000)
Ford W. J., *A History of the CUCC, 1820–1901*, (Blackwood, 1902)
Forster E. M., *Goldsworthy Lowes Dickinson*, (Arnold, 1934)
Forster E. M., *Abinger Harvest*, (Arnold, 1936)
Fowler L., Fowler T. (eds), *Cambridge Commemorated*, (Cambridge, 1984)
Friedman J., *The Keynesian Orthodoxy*, vol. III, nos. 3, 4, (Critical Review, 1989)
Frith D., *The Golden Age of Cricket 1890–1914*, (Lutterworth, 1978)
Frith D., *Silence of the Heart*, (Mainstream, 2001)
Frith D., *Bodyline Autopsy*, (Aurum, 2002)
Garnett A., *Deceived With Kindness*, (Pimlico, 1995)
George H., *Progress and Poverty*, (Kegan Paul, Trench, and Trubner, 1902)
Gesell S., *The Natural Economic Order*, (Berlin, 1916)
Golby J. M., Purdue A. W., *The Civilisation Of The Crowd*, (Batsford, 1984)
Grahame K., *The Wind in the Willows*, (Methuen, 1908)
Green J., *Days in the Life*, (Heinemann, 1988)
Griffiths R. T., *Europe's First Constitution (The EPC 1952–4)*, (Federal Trust, 2000)
Grubb N. P., *C. T. Studd*, (Religious Tract Society, 1933)
Hally N., *Sandeman: 200 Years of Port and Sherry*, (Sandeman, 1990)
Ham A., *Treasury Rules*, (Quartet, 1981)
Hamouda O., Rowley R., *Expectations, Equilibrium, and Dynamics*, (Harvester Wheatsheaf, 1988)
Hampden-Turner C., Trompenaars T., *The Seven Culture of Capitalism*, (Doubleday, 1993)
Hansen A., *A Guide to Keynes*, (McGraw-Hill, 1953)

LITERARY REFERENCES

Harcourt G., King J., *Review of Social Economy*, vol. LIII, no. 1, (Routledge, 1995)
Harrod R. F., *The Life of John Maynard Keynes*, (Macmillan, 1951)
Hart-Davis R. (ed.), *The Lyttelton Hart-Davis Letters*, (John Murray, 1981)
Haskell A. L., *Balletomania*, (Gollancz, 1934)
Henderson H. D., *The Inter-War Years*, (Oxford, 1955)
Hicks J., *Classics and Moderns*, (Blackwell, 1983)
Hill P., Keynes R., *Lydia and Maynard*, (Andre Deutsch, 1989)
Hobbs J., *My Cricket Memories*, (Heinemann, 1924)
Hobbs J., *My Life Story*, (London, 1935)
Holder J. et al, *Green and White, Fenner's Observed*, (CCAT, 1962)
Houghton G. and P., *Well Regulated Minds and Improper Moments*, (The Leys School, 2000)
House of Dickinson Staff Handbook, (John Dickinson and Co., 1928)
Howarth T. E. B., *Cambridge Between Two Wars*, (Collins, 1978)
Hundertwasser, *Architektur*, (Taschen, 1997)
Hunt F., Barker C., *Women at Cambridge*, (Cambridge, 1998)
Hutchinson G., *Edward Heath*, (Longman, 1970)
Hutton W., *The State We're In*, (Jonathan Cape, 1995)
Hutton W., *The World We're In*, (Little, Brown, 2002)
Hyndman H. M., *Commercial Crises of the Nineteenth Century*, (Swan, Sonnenschein, 1892)
James C. L. R., *Beyond a Boundary*, (Hutchinson, 1963)
Jebb, Eglantyne, *Cambridge; a Brief Study in Social Questions*, (Macmillan and Bowe, 1906)
Jenkins R., *The Chancellors*, (Macmillan, 1998)
Jenkins R., *A Life at the Centre*, ((Pan) Macmillan, 1991)
Johnson C., *In With the Euro, Out with the Pound*, (Penguin, 1996)
Kaldor N., *Causes Of Growth And Stagnation In The World Economy*, (Cambridge, 1996)
Keynes F. A., *By-Ways of Cambridge History*, (Cambridge, 1947)
Keynes G., *The Gates Of Memory*, (O.U.P., 1983)
Keynes J. M., *The Collected Writings*, vols. I-XXX, (Macmillan/Cambridge, 1971–89)
Keynes J. N., *The Scope and Method of Political Economy*, (Macmillan, 1890)
Keynes W. M. (ed), *Essays on John Maynard Keynes*, (Cambridge, 1975)
Kinross, A., *An Unconventional Cricketer*, (Harold Shaylor, 1930)
Lane C. (ed.), *A Century of Wisden*, (John Wisden, 2000)
Leijonhofvud A., *On Keynesian Economics and the Economics of Keynes*, (Oxford, 1968)
Lekachman R., *The Age of Keynes*, (Pelican, 1966)
Levy P., *Moore*, (Macmillan, 1979)
Lowes Dickinson G., *Autobiography*, (Duckworth, 1973)
Luff P., *A Brilliant Conspiracy?*, (Greycoat, 1996)
Lymington, Viscount, *Famine In England*, (Wetherby, 1938)
McWilliams-Tullberg R., *Women at Cambridge*, (Gollancz, 1975)
Macmillan H., *The Middle Way*, (Macmillan, 1938)
Marler, R., *Bloomsbury Pie*, (Virago, 1997)
Marshall, M. Paley, *What I Remember*, (Cambridge, 1947)
Martineau G. D., *They Made Cricket*, (Sportsman's Book Club, 1957)
Mason P., *The English Gentleman*, (Pimlico, 1982)
Mason R., *Jack Hobbs*, (Pavilion, 1960)

Mason R. (ed.), *Cambridge Minds*, (Cambridge, 1994)
Milne A. A., *Toad of Toad Hall*, (Methuen, 1929)
Milward A. S., *War, Economy,and Society*, (Allen Lane, 1977)
Moggridge D. E., *Keynes*, (Macmillan, 1976)
Moggridge D. E., *Maynard Keynes*, (Routledge, 1992)
Moorcroft Wilson J., *Virginia Woolf's London*, (Tauris Parke, 2000)
Moore G. E., *Principia Ethica*, (Cambridge, 1903)
Mundell R. and Clesse A. (eds), *The Euro as a Stabilizer in the International Economic System*, (Kluwer, 2000)
Myers A., Forsythe R., *W. H. Auden, Pennine Poet*, (North Pennines Heritage Trust, 1999)
Noble R. (ed.), *Recollections of Virginia Woolf*, (Peter Owen, 1972)
Notes from Nowhere (ed.), *We Are Everywhere: The Irresistible Rise of Global Anti-capitalism*, (Verso, 2003)
Oborne, P., *Basil D'Oliveira, Cricket and Conspiracy*, (Little, Brown, 2004)
Ormerod P., *The Death of Economics*, (Faber, 1994)
Ormrod S. J. (ed.), *Cambridge Contributions*, (Cambridge, 1998)
Page B., Leitch D., Knightley P., *Philby*, (Sphere, 1969)
Palacios J., *Lost in the Woods*, ((Boxtree) Macmillan, 1998)
Panic, M., *National Management of the International Economy*, (Macmillan, 1988)
Pardon S. H. (ed.), *Wisden Almanack 1897*, (John Wisden,1897)
Parker D., *Random Precision*, (Cherry Red, 2001)
Parry J., *Citizen of the European Union*, (European Movement,1995)
Partridge F., *Hanging On*, (Collins, 1990)
Payne S., *Down Your Street*, vols. I, II, (Pevensey, 1984)
Pevsner N., *Cambridgeshire*, Penguin, 1954
Phillips M., Phillips T., *Windrush*, (Harper Collins, 1998)
Pigott P., *Fenner's*, (F. and P. Pigott, 1948)
Pigou A. C., *Socialism Versus Capitalism*, (Macmillan, 1937)
Pinder J. (ed.), *Altiero Spinelli and the British Federalists*, (Kogan Page, 1998)
Poidevin R., *Robert Schuman*, (Imprimerie Nationale Paris, 1986)
Ranjitsinhji K. S., *The Jubilee Book of Cricket*, (Blackwood, 1897)
Raverat G., *Period Piece*, (Faber, 1952)
Rayvern-Allen D. (ed.), *Arlott On Cricket*, (Guild, 1987)
Rayvern-Allen D. (ed.), *Cricket Through the Pages*, (Andre Deutsch, 2000)
Reeve F. A., *Victorian and Edwardian Cambridge*, (Batsford, 1971)
Reeve F. A., *Victorian and Edwardian Cambridgeshire*, (Batsford, 1976)
Restany P., *Hundertwasser: The Painter King with the Five Skins*, (Taschen, 1998)
Reynolds P. J., *Political Economy*, (Wheatsheaf, 1987)
Roberts E. L., *Cricket in England, 1894–1939*, (Edward Arnold, 1946)
Robertson-Glasgow R. C., *Crusoe on Cricket*, (Pavilion, 1985)
Robinson J., *Economic Philosophy*, (Pelican, 1962)
Robinson J., *The Rate of Interest and Other Essays*, (Cambridge, 1951)
Ross A., *Ranji*, (Pavilion, 1983)
Ross A. (ed.), *The Cricketer's Companion*, (Eyre and Spottiswoode, 1960)
Rousseas S., *Post Keynesian Monetary Economics*, (Macmillan, 1998)
Sardoni C., *Marx and Keynes on Economic Recession*, (Wheatsheaf, 1987)

LITERARY REFERENCES

Sawyer J. A., *Macroeconomic Theory*, (Harvester Wheatsheaf, 1989)
Shaw G. K., *Keynesian Economics*, (Edward Elgar, 1988)
Sidgwick H., *Philosophy, its Scope and Relations*, (Macmillan, 1902)
Skidelsky R., *John Maynard Keynes*, vols. I-III, (Macmillan, 1983, 1992, 2000)
Soros G., *The Crisis of Global Capitalism*, (Little, Brown, 1998)
Spalding F., *Roger Fry: Art And Life*, (Granada, 1980)
Spalding F., *Gwen Raverat*, (Harvill Press, 2001)
Standing P. C., *Ranjitsinhji; Prince of Cricket*, (Arrowsmith, 1903)
Stanley L. T., *Life in Cambridge*, (Hutchinson, 1954)
Stanners D., Bourdeau P. (eds), *Europe's Environment*, (E.E.A., 1995)
Steinherr A. (ed.), *Thirty Years of European Monetary Integration*, (Longman, 1994)
Steel A. G. and Lyttelton Hon. R.H., *Cricket*, (Badminton Library, 1888)
Streit C. K., *Union Now*, (Federal Union, 1943)
Sugg W., *A Tradition Unshared*, (Real Work, 2002)
Swanton E. W. (ed.), *World of Cricket*, (London, 1966)
Swingle S. L., *Cambridge Street Tramways*, (Oakwood, 1972)
Trausch G. (ed.), *Robert Schuman, Jean Monnet, et les Debuts de l'Europe*, (Luxembourg Government, 2000)
Trevelyan G. M., *Trinity College*, (Cambridge, 1946)
Tugendhat C., *Making Sense Of Europe*, (Penguin, 1986)
Unwin F. T., *Pimbo and Jenny in Old Cambridge*, (F. T. Unwin, 1978)
Veritas Foundation, *Keynes at Harvard (Economic Deception as a Political Credo)*, (Veritas, 1960)
Ward A., *Cricket's Strangest Matches*, (Robson, 1988)
Ward R. and Doggett T., *Keeping Score,* (Central Statistical Office, 1991)
Webber R. (ed.), *Test Cricket*, Vol. I, (Playfair, 1939)
Werner P., *L'Euro: Un Defi*, (Luxembourg Government, 1999)
Werner P., *Union Economique Et Monetaire*, (Saint-Paul, 1992)
Wheen F., *Karl Marx*, (Fourth Estate, 1999)
Wild R., *Ranji*, (Griffon Press, 1934)
Williams C., *Adenauer*, (Little, Brown & Co., 2000)
Wilson, A.N., *The Victorians*, (Arrow, 2002)
Wilton I., *C. B. Fry An English Hero*, (Richard Cohen, 1999)
Woolf V., *Jacob's Room*, (Hogarth, 1922)
Woolf V., *Mrs. Dalloway*, (Hogarth, 1925)
Woolf V., *To The Lighthouse*, (Hogarth, 1927)
Woolf V., *A Room of One's Own and Other Essays*, (Folio, 2000)
Young, H., *This Blessed Plot*, (Macmillan, 1998)
Young W., *Harrod and his Trade Cycle Group*, (Macmillan, 1989)

VIDEO AND FILM REFERENCES

American Madness	1932	dir. Capra, 80 mins., Columbia
It's A Wonderful Life	1946	dir. Capra, 129 mins., RKO/Liberty
John Maynard Keynes; Life, Ideas, Legacy	1988	Mark Blaug, 60 mins., I.E.A.
Mary Poppins	1964	dir. Stevenson, 139 mins., Disney
Spend And Prosper; A Portrait of J. M. Keynes	1977	A B.B.C. TV production.
Whatever Happened To Britain?	1983	John Eatwell, series of 30 minute programmes, B.B.C.
Why We Fight (series of 7 films)	1942–5	dir. Capra, Litvak, 42–80 mins., US War Office
You Can't Take it With You	1938	dir. Capra, 127 mins., Columbia, Oscar best, picture.

MUSICAL REFERENCES

Syd Barrett	Crazy Diamond, EMI, SYD BOX 1, containing albums The Madcap Laughs, Barrett, and Opel, 1993.
Deep Freeze Mice	Hang on Constance, Let Me Hear the News, Cordelia Ericat 004
Deep Freeze Mice	Saw a Ranch House Burning Last Night, Cordelia MOLE 4, 1986
Pink Floyd	1967, The First 3 Singles, EMI 7243 8 59895 2 0, 1997
Pink Floyd	The Piper at the Gates of Dawn, EMI 7243 8 31261 2 5, 1994
Pink Floyd	A Saucerful of Secrets, EMI 7243 8 29751 2 0, 1994
Captain Sensible	Women and Captains First, A and M, AMLH 68548, 1982
Captain Sensible	The Power of Love, A and M, AMLX 68561, 1983
Percy Pavilion	The Cricket C.D., Talkcrest, TKCD001, 1995
Stereolab	Mars Audiac Quintet, D.U.H.F. Disks, D-UHF-CD05, 1994
Various	Bellissimo! (vols. 1, 2), Richmond Monde 11 & 12 CD, 1993

ENDNOTES

An Article Compiled During September 1905

1. Completed in 1908. J.M.K.'s younger brother Geoffrey would certainly not have agreed with this attitude to nature; he found climbing around Chamonix in 1913 with George Mallory, Geoffrey Young, and Jacques Raverat to be inspiring, if a little hair-raising. J.N.K. was no stranger to Chamonix either, having explored the area in September 1878.

2. Austin Robinson provided a similar quotation from J.M.K. himself in Lekachman's book celebrating three decades of the *General Theory*, which the latter reproduced in full in his Pelican summary aimed at the popular market.
   Harrod gets to cricket almost immediately on page 13 of his biography.

   > Fenner's cricket ground was at the end of the road, and he spent many hours watching the players and keeping records of their scores. For a considerable time he retained an intense interest in cricket, although he never became adept at the game in practice.

   'The end of the road' may suggest a long way away in the distance (conjuring up a metropolitan thoroughfare like Park Lane or Broadway), as if only youthful energy could prompt a Keynes to go and watch the cricket. Skidelsky is more confident, however (page 55, volume 1).

   > Like many children who have no aptitude for games, Maynard was entranced by them in their statistical aspect. He compiled lists of batting and bowling averages. In 1896 he spent every spare summer afternoon at Fenner's Cricket Ground, which adjoined Harvey Road, watching the University play.

   The university season was in fact a spring one (May and June) but in 1896 the weather was so good it could be fairly described as 'summer'.
   Moggridge's second and more substantial biography of J.M.K. has a very circumloquacious reference to cricket. The game is buried away apologetically:

   > In his second term, as well as beginning cricket, for which, as is perhaps inevitable for a small boy with the University Cricket Ground at the end of his street, he would develop a fascination, he went to the top of his class for the first time and, despite his comparative youth ,ended up second in the class for the term and third in the examinations.

3. Clement Attlee later claimed in his autobiography that W.G. stood for him 'next to the deity'; J.M.K.'s agnosticism could allow him to be less equivocal.

4. *i.e.* a trainspotter or a nerd.

5. *PP28*; part of the Keynes archive in King's College Library.

6. Macro, one might now say.

7. This is similar to C. L. R. James's thesis in chapters 13–15 of *Beyond a Boundary*, where he shows how solid a part of Victorian history cricket became, especially through the person of W. G. Grace.

8. Nicholas Pevsner described Fawcett as the most successful local Cambridge architect of this period but also damned him as being

   > not a man of much talent.

GOLDEN AGES AT THE FENNER'S MARGIN

Fenner's may have been his most successful and memorable building, both in terms of its functionality and its range of decoration. He had a curiously heavy effect on the Keynes's environment, because in addition to Fenner's he designed the 1893 Syndicate Building (enlarged from his own 1886 creation) in which J.N.K. worked, and the Hughes Hall building of 1894–5 that runs behind the current Fenner's pavilion and dominated the background view for any spectator viewing cricket from the Fenner's pavilion in 1896. In addition, the Cavendish Laboratory gateway and extensions of 1896 and 1908 were Fawcett designs, as was the Curator's House of the Botanical Gardens. With regard to Cambridge colleges, Fawcett added buildings to Emmanuel, King's, Queen's, and St. Catharine's (a hideous mediaeval reworking of the Hall, plus a new Master's Lodge). In rural Cambridgeshire he added Victorian Gothic to older churches at Haslingfield, Knapwell, and Longstowe, much to Pevsner's irritation. His main task at the time of J.N.K.'s cricket diary of 1896 was to prepare plans for additions to Wisbech's early nineteenth century Grammar School.

9. The frost of January-March 1895 inspired Arthur Ransome to write *Winter Holiday* and others born in 1882–3 like Clement Attlee also remembered the weeks of skating with nostalgia.

10. Having tried to interfere with the composition of the Syndicate (a deliberative not a judicial body), the blockers of degrees for women faced the possibility of defeat and so stopped trying to keep Sidgwick out of the frame. Instead they sought signatures of support for Memorials and published flysheets; Austen Leigh (Vice Chancellor 1894–5), Porter, and Marshall were in the van of the moderate wing of opposition. The period between June and October was thus a satisfactory lull for Sidgwick and Keynes in the trench warfare that was building up to the 'big push' of 1897 which resulted in serious defeat for Newnham and Girton.

11. This must have been 13 September 1894, when Ranji made just 3; a year earlier in the same fixture he had made 116.

12. The certainty of these remarks lead one to think he is not just talking about his contemporary 'flannelled fools', but senior figures, and R. A. H. Mitchell in particular. An assistant master at Eton from 1866 until 1901, 'Mike' died just five months before this article was written, and had had a breakdown shortly after teaching J.M.K. Classics just a few years earlier. The unwritten subtext of J.M.K.'s hostility seems to be that it was unreasonable that such a recognisably great batsman had got four Blues *against* Cambridge, had outshone everyone in bringing victory for Oxford in the 1862–5 matches, and, to cap it all, had no interest in or opinion of the mythical Cambridgeshire heroes of J.M.K.'s boyhood. W. J. Ford, very much partial to Cambridge, could still describe Mitchell in 1902 as

> the best batsman, especially for the 'Varsity match that either side has ever had.

He was Eton's principal cricket adviser and coach between 1866 and 1897, and cricket historian F. S. Ashley-Cooper assures us he would have been M.C.C. President had he lived longer. This was a powerful enemy and a seemingly unnecessary one. But Mitchell's orbit was through Oxford, the Gentlemen of the North, Buckinghamshire, Leicestershire, and Warwickshire, which left his experiences of the game totally detached from J.M.K.'s, despite the common Eton experience. Perhaps it was *because* of tales of that experience? For most of his coaching life Mitchell instructed his captains what to do on the field from the boundary edge, even more a comptroller than Diaghileff later on in the sphere of ballet.

Worse was to follow, for Mitchell's son Frank left Eton just before J.M.K. arrived and played cricket for Oxford and golf for England, no less, crowning his career with a knighthood for his services as George VI's assistant Private Secretary. Finding Mitchell's brain to be less sure than his bat must have been a great comfort to the Cantabrigian J.M.K., and would have assuaged any guilt or self-loathing he might have felt for having strong partisan urges that he would have derided in others.

13. Henry Montagu Butler made second top score and took two catches as Harrow won by 8 wickets in the two day match at Lord's at the beginning of August. He became Headmaster of Harrow before moving to Trinity College, Cambridge, in 1886. His sons and grandson also played for Harrow and a new pulpit and windows were inserted into the Harrow chapel by H.M.B.'s admirers in 1920, two years after his death.

ENDNOTES

14. 2,780 runs and 10 centuries. In 1871 W.G. had scored 2,739, but at an average of 78 compared to Ranji's 57.

15. 'Goody's' was not yet St. Faith's, as all the secondary sources imply it was, and indeed wasn't bought by The Leys until 1938. It owed its existence to the new university families, like the Keyneses, springing up in the recently liberalised inner suburbs. J. J. Thomson doubted whether there were more than sixty university families in Cambridge in 1881. Frances Spalding tells us that the Revised Statutes of 1882 led to a 'matrimonial rush' of 30 Fellows to the altar that summer. Even the sober historian G. G. Coulton called it a 'stampede'. Gwen Raverat enviously watched her brother, Charles Darwin, depart daily for lessons at 'Goody's'. Relations with The Leys public school arose by geographical accident. The name Faith was later added as a tribute to Goodchild's wife and daughter, both of whom were so named.

16. For example, E. M. Forster could write a book about Lowes-Dickinson and barely mention Keynes; Moggridge, in his first biography of Keynes, did not think it sufficiently significant to mention to fellow-economists that Keynes was possibly the worst golfer of the last, or any other, millennium.

17. See the 1896 unofficial J.N.K. diary entry.

18. J.M.K. was aware of Austen Leigh through seeing him at Fenner's from an early age. Later at Eton he researched the records of Pop (the elite Eton society) for 1854/5 and found mentions of the King's Provost-to-be plus his brother E.C., a Real Tennis Blue, later the assistant cricket master to 'Mike' Mitchell at Eton, and maker of a duck in his only appearance for Cambridge University at cricket. A team of 16 played at The Oval in 1861 against Surrey, and, despite E.C. Austen Leigh's failure and Caffyn's bowling, C.U.C.C. won by 14 wickets. Reverend Augustus Austen Leigh played in the two day game for Eton against Harrow in 1858 scoring 0 and 2 as an opener, taking one stumping off Mitchell, and suffering defeat by an innings despite excellent bowling by C. G. Lyttelton. He missed the team photograph into the bargain.

19. J.M.K.'s memory did *not* serve him right in this instance; this was the boast of Alfred Marshall, and the peak involved was Gross Glockner. In mitigation, Leslie Stephen regarded 'The Sunset on Mont Blanc', from *The Playground of Europe*, as the best thing he ever wrote, and the reporting of these claims in 6, Harvey Road may have melded together in J.M.K.'s infant memory. J.M.K.'s golden year of 1896 had coincidentally seen the opening of the first Alpine ski school at Lilienfeld in Austria.

20. On Sunday 26 April Dr Porter, as a longstanding member of the Town Council's Finance Committee, visited the site of the proposed sewage works with Professor Dewar (the Corporation's technical consultant) and Mr Hyde Hills (Chairman of the New Theatre Company). The latter was so impressed by the Town/Gown co-operation that he mentioned it in his speech at the Cambridgeshire C.C.C. annual dinner the next night. Residents were impressed more by the constant roadworks and disruption to traffic that accompanied the implementation of the scheme.

    Florence Keynes seems to have maintained a more balanced view of Porter, for she felt that University/Borough relations entered a new era in 1894 after six centuries of enmity, and that the sort of lead he and Horace Darwin provided blazed an integrationist trail for her own municipal career later on. Darwin, the founder of high-tech firm Cambridge Instruments, once described himself to the other councillors in the Chamber as 'a Cambridge tradesman' and was proposed for election as Mayor by Alderman Spalding in 1896. That summer saw further distinguished co-operation; a visitor from New Zealand named Rutherford (gown) was working successfully with one of the workshop men named Pye (town) on the magnetic detection of electrical waves.

21. The President of Cambridgeshire C.C.C. was the Newmarket M.P., H. McCalmont, from Cheveley Park over the border in Suffolk. He noted that never had such a small assembly (thirty diners) faced such a large deficit (£85), and if this could not be paid off that night they should quietly fold the club up. Such shock tactics worked, and for the first time ever the club was cleared of debt through the generosity of those present. Dr. Porter summed up the mood by declaring that despondency had given way to 'jubilant rejoicing'.

GOLDEN AGES AT THE FENNER'S MARGIN

A Second Article Compiled During September 1905

22. Author of *The Memoirs of a Cambridge Chorister* in two volumes, 1885, and *Reminiscences of Half a Century*, 1889.

23. The 'miracle' was rather an anachronism in legal terms. The Cambridge Corporation passed a by-law designating The Piece

    a common for purposes of recreation only

    but in failing to register it as a Town or Village Green before 1970 it was not protected under the 1965 Commons Registration Act.

24. A less-heralded Chancellor of the Exchequer who went on to the Admiralty and became the subject of a popular satirical rhyme:

    Goschen has no notion of the motion of the ocean.

25. Those who played with Johnny Wardle, Derek Parry, and Stuart Turner for the County would protest at such an assumption being made in the late twentieth century.

26. See *The Noblest Game*, by John Arlott and Neville Cardus, which also shows an 1854 etching of Parker's Piece showing four marquees, umpteen spectators, and several matches on the go. Plate 56 shows XII of Victoria playing Parr's All England XI in 1864; three of those XI were Cambridge professionals.

27. Even the modern writer Philip Mason reiterates this view with a caption under a picture of cricket at Eton in 1843 stating

    cricket was a bond between the classes and almost a religion. Only a gentleman had the leisure to be *taught* cricket. He was expected to be a more polished batsman than a countryman who had learned to take a swipe on the village green.

28. This was certainly the case at Eton as David Frith noted. Dr Christopher Brookes is clear that county cricket *required* professionals as:

    Only professionals had the time to acquire the skills and the consistency of application expected by first-class cricket's audiences, and only they were in position to play as often as required.

29. One can get the same feeling about E. W. Swanton when reading him on Graveney (the professional) and May (the amateur).

30. This was a commonly-held feeling at the time. Goldsworthy Lowes-Dickinson considered the Cambridge climate 'depressing', and felt all his life that it had a 'pernicious influence' on him (*Autobiography*). When Alfred Marshall returned to Cambridge and built Balliol Croft in 1886 he wanted his study to be as far away from the ground as possible; the architect persuaded him to have it on the first floor with a balcony to look out at the forest trees on Madingley Road.

31. J.M.K. carefully omits Henry's brother John Perkins, a batsman rather than bowler, who shot himself at the age of 63 when of unsound mind.

32. Coloured shirts were the norm until 1865.

33. Soccer was not considered for regulation on the Piece until 1883, in fact, and in 1896 the game was only permitted until the end of March. Cricket, however, had been central since the 1830s, with Daniel Hayward paid for groundsmanship duties, tents for hire at 10 shillings a week, and urinals, toolsheds, and a drinking fountain erected behind the University Arms.

ENDNOTES

34. C. L. R. James puts cricket pre-W.G. into perspective:

    The histories will say that the University match has been played since 1827. Yet up to 1862 ... the Oxford University Cricket Club was run by three treasurers, no one knew exactly who was to collect the eleven, and, *mirabile dictu*, there was never a definite captain, There were often two captains, both directing the field and changing the bowling; each of the treasurers had some sort of right, *ex officio*, to play in the eleven, even to the exclusion of better players. One conclusion is inescapable – such doings were responsible to no public interest or public opinion. Cricket at Cambridge was not quite so haphazard but only that.

35. Both Watts and Hayward died in 1910. The *Cambridge Express* printed an appreciation of Watts on 21 February 1908 and followed it up the next week with a photograph and biography of Daniel Martin Hayward. At the age of forty-two this brother of T.W. and son of Dan junior took over at Fenner's from 1908 until 1936, when Cyril Coote began his majestic tenure.

36. These were feats achieved at well-known club grounds like Kimbolton and Bury/West Suffolk; the photograph in the newspaper shows him standing outside Wolverstone Park, then a country house, later a boarding school for the Inner London Educational Authority, and now an élite Ipswich girls school.

37. It remains so, while other colleges, like St. Catharine's, are making proposals to replace their pavilions with structures that look as if they were built for battery hens.

38. It is hard not to watch Robert Morley in the film *The Final Test* and feel that the life of Ward played by the great actor would have made a much better story than Rattigan's turned out to be. In death the eccentricity of this character lived on. In the monumental 1984 *Who's Who of Cricketers* there are thirty one Wards listed, including A.R.'s father. Another was born in 1865 and apparently extant at 119 years of age. Perhaps this was, however, an error, as might be the total *absence* of Reverend A. R. Ward.

39. He was later ordained and left the county, playing cricket for Devon.

40. He was to hold the record for runs scored in a season from 1906 until Compton broke it forty one years later in 1947.

41. Robertson-Glasgow could put it more fully later on:

    To say that Tom Hayward batted at number one for Surrey and England is like announcing that Milton wrote poetry or that Disraeli often spoke in the House of Commons.

42. In November 1897 a further generation of Cambridge professionals commenced with the birth to John O'Connor of a son, named Jack, who played for Essex and England in the late 1920s. Jack's father had married Herbert Carpenter's sister and played for Cambridgeshire (also for Derbyshire, in 1900). Jack, became widely known much later as one of what Frith describes as 'a succession of top-class coaches' at Eton

43. The illustration is included in this book with notes by Reeve and Hobbs.

GOLDEN AGES AT THE FENNER'S MARGIN

An Article Compiled During May 1909

44. At this point there is a footnote with quotations from Edgeworth's *Mathematical Psychics*:

    Mathematical reasoning is not limited to subjects where numerical data are attainable. Where there are data which though not *numerical* are *quantitative* – for example, that a quantity is *greater* or *less* than another, *increases* or *decreases*, is *positive* or *negative*, a *maximum* or a *minimum* – there mathematical reasoning is possible and may be indispensable. To take a trivial instance; a is greater than b, and b is greater than c, therefore a is greater than c. Here is mathematical reasoning applicable to quantities which may not be susceptible of numerical evaluation.

    Mathematics is as it were the universal language of the physical sciences. It is for physicists what Latin used to be for scholars; but it is unfortunately Greek for many economists. Hence the writer who wishes to be widely read – who does not say, with French author, *J'imprime pour moi* – will do well not to multiply mathematical technicalities beyond the indispensable minimum, which we have seen reason to suppose is not very large. The parsimony of symbols, which is often an elegance in the physicist, is a necessity for the economist.

45. The quotations such as 'Unathletic Swot' and 'Young Man In A Hurry' are from Cornford's slim volume of advice to academic politicians, published in 1908. This had an effect similar to later humorous examples of 'advice', such as *The Peter Principle* and *1066 And All That*; the treacle of amusement was balanced by some astringent satire that hit the mark.

46. David Frith tells us that Ernie Jones's opinion of Larwood during the Bodyline tour was

    Him fast? Why, s'welp me, he wouldn't knock a dint in a pound of butter on a hot day.

47. And the Great War later on, of course, but more so. The desirability of the wish has recently been questioned quite severely by commentators seeking publishable material. Surely such feelings are bogus and not to be considered real in a world of Balkan unrest and Russian instability? A story of contentment from the Netherlands or Luxembourg is less likely to get printed than a tragedy in Romania or penury in Belarus. Perhaps the long, western European peace has dulled the imagination of such people, but they come close to suggesting that the first half of the twentieth century in western Europe was preferable to the second, or at least more 'real'.

48. Consequent to this analysis is the thought that J.M.K.'s love for ballet, and ultimately his successful marriage, may also have had its roots in the Fenner's margins. and on a more mundane level it may also account for the popularity of *Ready, Steady, Cook* on television.

49. In twenty-first century Europe let's try to illustrate this in terms of a small firm that earns revenue by digital processing and alteration of photographs. They may have a small office, three computers and three workers. If there is an upsurge in orders there might be a temptation to ration output through price rises. If there is confidence that demand will persist, a further shift of eight hours on the computers will involve the recruitment of three more workers, bringing down the average cost of each job because the capital and rent costs are divided amongst more output. If demand carries on rising a third shift of eight hours may be introduced rather than price rises. At this point the constraint of capital emerges; to increase output further a new computer must be ordered, which may take some time. The recruitment of the three extra workers will also take time, but the option of increasing quantity rather than price is still more likely to be taken by the confident entrepreneur. If there is no room in the office for a fifth machine an increase in the amount of 'land' employed will be required; time will be taken to get planning permission for an extension, or to find bigger premises. If the mistake was made of trying to cram too many workers and machines into the land available, productivity would go down, and average costs would rise.

50. Research and development clusters every half a century were all that Kondratieff could come up with to

ENDNOTES

explain the long wave observations which have given him lasting fame. Schumpeter later gave us creative destruction and the power of firms in imperfect competition to halt and accelerate developments in technology as profits demand, and by the World War Two Keynesians gave us the interaction between the investment accelerator (based on past changes in income and expectations about the future) and the multiplier effect. The Real Business Cycle of the New Right is beyond the power of this editor to put into intelligible format, but judging by Paul Krugman's crisp verdict on R.B.C. theory that is not a badge of shame.

51. This is mysterious, since the first published English translation was by Philip Pye in 1958, and Geoff Harcourt says Keynes could not read original works in German; he must have asked for, or been approached with, this translation. It is likely that the most handy translator would have been his mother, who gained a very good grasp of German from the age of 16 when she was sent to stay with the family of a pastor in Bonn before attending Newnham College, Cambridge. In 1888 she helped J.N.K. read Menger and Schmoller for *The Scope And Method Of Political Economy*. The choice of phrase made by the translator only further shows how fundamental cricketing terminology had become in Edwardian Cambridge.

This quotation links up with the only direct reference to cricket that I could find in J.M.K.'s major works, used precisely in this sense; of time-periods. A 1940 Macmillan copy of *How To Pay For The War* originally cost one shilling; a pristine copy in 2001 could fetch a price of £20. It is a short book, being an expanded series of articles originally run in *The Times* in November 1939. This is the Keynes of 1919 again inveighing against inflation; but now, as a man of power rather than just influence, he cajoles and directs worried readers in the direction of practical policy with little rhetorical flourish. Part of this task is communication by metaphor to reach and persuade the intelligent but untrained audience. What better image than cricket? When trying to explain the consequences of voluntary savings combined with price rises J.M.K. has the tricky task of showing how this is insufficient over time to prevent further inflation. He once uses a literary phrase:

> the second chapter of the story

and once betrays his gambling habits when describing policy options:

> we still have one more card to play.

But the main method for explaining the point is cricket, the Fenner's system, used on pages 63, 65, and 66;

> But in the next *innings*, so to speak, it will be added to the total of potentially spendable incomes ... only a small part of the £650 million ... will come on the consumption market in the second *innings* ... the profiteers continue to make a profit of £650 million in the second *innings*

The italics are added.

52. C. L. R. James claimed that it was art, and in response Mike Brearley agreed with the proviso that it is art on a par with cooking and ballet rather than architecture or sculpture.

53. This may sound strange to those educated under the 'New Right' who associate money and expectations with Friedman and Lucas, but even in 1975 Keynes's concerns are what good school teachers were busily emphasising to A Level pupils. All the rest stems from expectations and money, and if Cricket is to claim any affinity with Economics, let alone a special influence on Keynes, it must demonstrate equivalents for these two features. Skidelsky emphasises the point that the desire to play an innings *with strokeplay* is very hard to satisfy (Volume I, page 539):

> Keynes's vision, which was one can trace back to his youth, has to do with the logic of choice, not under scarcity, but under uncertainty.

54. Noble carried on winning the toss until August 1909 at The Oval, nine in all. He chose to bat first all

nine times, winning five matches, losing two and drawing two.

Psmith was famous for saying that one mustn't confuse the unlikely with the impossible, but had only appeared in one book by May 1909. Psmith called cricket 'The mimic warfare of our National Game' and was a slow left-arm bowler at Eton and Sedleigh. He followed socialism, as a 'great scheme'.

> You work for the equal distribution of property, and start by collecting all you can and sitting on it.

More importantly, however, he was the self-deprecating source of Keyne's famous concept of the animal instincts (or spirits) of the British Capitalist class. Over the last three generations many have quoted Keynes's 'animal instincts' but the full implications of the phrase's significance for the volatile nature of investment and capital flows have become both watered-down and obscured.

Wodehouse defined animal instincts as belonging to loud, boisterous, public school swashbucklers with a

> Whole-hearted and cheerful indifference to other people's feelings, treading on the toes of their neighbour, and shoving him off the pavement, and always with an eye wide open for adventure, they are not particular so long as it promises excitement.

This is the antithesis of Psmith's thoughtful approach to life so it is not suprising that Mr. Downing (in search of an incriminating shoe) was astonished at being covered in soot following a trail, laid by Psmith up a chimney.

> 'What did you mean by putting it there?' roared Mr. Downing.
> 'Animal spirits, sir,' said Psmith.
> 'What?'
> 'Animal spirits, sir!'

55. *e.g.* Botham?

56. This passage seems to have been re-written many years later in J.M.K. volume XIV pages 113–115. In *A Treatise On Probability* (1921) Skidelsky says J.M.K. was pessimistic about the possibility of using

> collections of facts for the prediction of future frequencies and associations.

The bludgeoning with mathematics that has taken place since the days of Keynes has arguably done more harm than good to the reputation of Economics; cricket also has a reputation as a refuge for statistical anoraks. In Economics the rational expectations theory seems particularly designed to be so mathematically complex that it defies non-experts to deny it. But the idea is simple (over time errors of forecasting overs and unders will cancel out), yet arguably tautologous; action taken on the basis of an over-estimate may lead to a feedback loop whereby the next expectation will be too low. This process of hysteresis is hardly new, and the fact that the errors of forecasting balance out by some simple application of a law of recursion doesn't stop the errant and possibly undesirable path that events are taking. Keynes would have seen this theory as a way to excuse the sheep-like captain who, for example, follows the shot with field-placement; Mike Brearley or Percy Chapman would dismiss it as elegant but irrelevant.

57. Skidelsky points out that Keynes was fascinated by the role of uncertainty as early as 1910, a contrast with most conventional theory at the time. Hyndman had talked about 'general uncertainty and doubt' as early as 1892, but did not define these terms precisely, and did not construct a model which suggested any specific, positive remedies. It is arguable that J.M.K.'s fascination with uncertainty was stimulated by the batsmen he saw at the Fenner's wicket in the middle of the previous decade. Between 1906 and 1911 he wrestled with the problem, determined to approach it from the logical rather than the mathematical side, and to focus on the relations between induction and probability.

58. As Mike Brearley was later at pains to point out in *The Art of Captaincy*.

59. *e.g.* Noam Chomsky?

An Article Compiled During October 1915

60. J.M.K. ended his biographical essay on Asquith by describing him as a

    wise and tolerant umpire.

    From this article it is clear that it was Robert Carpenter (one of the world's greatest batsmen in the 1860s and known to J.M.K. as an umpire in the 1890s) who Asquith most resembled in aspect and demeanour. W.G. died on Saturday 23 October 1915.

61. Lady Cynthia Asquith (wife to Margot's second son) reproduced this story in her diaries, but attributed the incident to October 12th.

62. Philip Mason's book mentions the Queen Anne ditty, possibly from another Bloomsbury source, and also tries to categorise the different types of gentlemen (*e.g.* the Corinthian). The Bespectacled Scholar as described by J.M.K. will survive, in the post-industrial age thanks to the revolution in information technology and the perceived necessity of continual study and the status that goes with it. This will aid Cricket in the future as it is a cerebral game (but will it help to revive Economics?) Another strand that is actively being reinforced by the new *2000 M.C.C. Code of Laws* is a fifth type of Gentlemanliness listed by Mason. *Gentillesse* was reviled by the Edwardians, he mysteriously claims, but cherished in Chaucerian England; however, it sounds as if it is very similar to Ranji's 'Spirit of the Game'. Robertson-Glasgow felt, by contrast with Mason, that *gentillesse was* a key feature of the Golden Age, epitomised by A. C. Maclaren, whose captaincy was a thing

    > of romance as well as of science. His plans might be subtle enough, but they were expressed in the action of chivalry and daring. He did things as they occurred to him, by intuition or analytical observation. They might be wrong, but they were his own.

63. There are real pre-echoes here of C. L. R. James, who was a huge admirer of Thackeray's *Vanity Fair* from a young age and later a telling commentator on the place of cricket in society. Born in 1901 in Tunapuna, Trinidad, the writer of *The Black Jacobins* produced his cricketing masterpiece *Beyond A Boundary* after the ascendancy of Sir Frank Worrell to the captaincy of West Indies and the exultant tour of Australia in 1961 which included the first tied Test Match. Pages 157–190, covering chapter 13 (Prolegomena to W.G.), 14 (W.G.), and 15 (Decline of the West) are also enough to keep one consistently revising one's view of what is and isn't evidence and what is and isn't history (particularly in these days of revisionist books about late twentieth century Europe). Chapter 15 passes Hobbs by with one phrase (after 1918 there was 'the long struggle of the amateur against extinction'), and is not of direct concern at this point. On W.G. and History James starts with a challenge:

    > A famous Liberal historian [Trevelyan] can write the social history of England in the nineteenth century, and two famous Socialists [Postgate and Cole] can write what they declared to be the history of the common people of England, and between them never once mention the man who was the best-known Englishman of his time. I can no longer accept the system of values which could not find in these books a place for W. G. Grace.

    Now A.N. Wilson joins Trevelyan. At least, Trevelyan said that the French revolution would have been avoided by cricket. There follow passages exploring the creativity of Hazlitt running concurrently with the creation of the modern form of cricket. Then Dickens, and the nostalgia of the industrial world for the pastoral. On to Arnold and the reinvention of manners and virtue needed to accompany the power of industrial imperialism and the freedom of the first Reform Act. The role of Dissent, flexing its muscles in freedom just as the renaissance of organised games took place in England, is affirmed as strongly as that renaissance, and both were to be copied worldwide because they contained considerable elements of universality. (The modern Olympic Games are now taken for granted, but they were only re-established in 1896). The communication of the creed to others through Thomas Hughes is addressed at length. Then, almost in a rush, we are taken through the changes in urbanisation, basic incomes, and working patterns; a people was waiting to be amused, and a new, unfamiliar stage was set for someone to become a star. So it came about that Clement Attlee could write:

> cricket was a religion and W.G. stood next to the deity.

James concludes the chapter thus:

> Prolegomena is a tough word, but my purpose being what it is, it is the only one I can honestly use. It means the social, political, literary and other antecedents of some outstanding figure in the arts and sciences. Grasp the fact that a whole nation had prepared the way for [W.G.] and you begin to see his stature as a national embodiment.

64. James puts it elegantly:

    > The characteristics of life as lived by many generations seemed to meet for the last, in a complete and perfectly blended whole ... What he lacked he would not need. All that he had he could use.

65. The book was put together with a variety of Oxbridge-educated writers. W. J. Ford wrote Chapter VII on the Public Schools and Chapter IX on Cambridge, Prof. T. Case wrote Chapter VII on Oxford, while journalist Mr Gaston helped in Brighton (along with Fry, of course), and Ranji's old mentor Dr. Butler, Master of Trinity College Cambridge, is also thanked. Chapter X on County Cricket was put together from individual county committee submissions. The major historical point of interest is Chapter XI, 'Cricket and the Victorian Era', first syndicated in July 1897 through publications like Blackwood's *Edinburgh Magazine*. The full book was published in 1898.

66. Pronounced 'looshen-gor', those under fifty please note.

67. These were references only in the original script but I have inserted them in J.M.K.'s text for the reader's convenience.

68. At this point there is a footnote of extraordinary length which seems to be a simple copy of parts of J.N.K.'s Chapter X on statistics. In the interests of verisimilitude I will include it here although it seems to be unrelated to the matter in hand.

    > The correct account of the derivation of the term *statistics* seems to be that it came through the Italian *stato*, which was in the fifteenth century first used in the signification of territory, or "state" in the political sense. Wappäus says "The Italians were the first to form a science of the state, and called it *Ragione di Stato*. There being in classical Latin no simple expression for 'state' in our sense the word *status* was used with this meaning. The Italians at the same time gave to anyone learned in the above science or art the name *statista*." Gottfried Achenwall, professor of law and politics at Göttingen about the middle of the eighteenth century, though not the originator of the Latin adjective *statisticus*, appears to have been the first to use the German substantive *Statistik*; and he is usually regarded as the founder of statistics. He meant by these a collection of noteworthy facts concerning States, not necessarily numerical or quantitative. Verbal descriptions took the first place, and figures were used merely as accessory thereto. Since the term has changed its meaning and the distinguishing mark is considered to be the employment of numerical data. In this sense statistics amy be traced back to the "Political Arithmetick" of Sir William Petty, and other English writers of the seventeenth and eighteenth centuries; and the influence of Quetelet and Knies was important about the middle of the nineteenth century

69. J.M.K. might have enjoyed the approach of Hoaglin and Velleman (1995), interpreted for a Eurostat seminar in 1997 by G. J. Wills. The American Statistical Association's data on baseball were investigated to see if pay was related to performance. Visual exploration by filtering and focussing linked computer windows studies of the small multivariate data set led to several clear conclusions:
    a) high salaries peaked among those players in the 7th and 13th years of their careers.
    b) it's impossible to earn high salaries in the first 3 years.
    c) income is loosely related to fielding position.

ENDNOTES

    d) hits *per annum* are a more highly-correlated with salary than home runs *p. a.*

    e) an erratic who was highly-paid despite a very low home run average and mediocre average hits turned out to be a player-coach.

70. Gesell, J.M.K. was saying, is so entertaining in contrast to Marx, for example, such fun to read, he makes you think, and he gives you a doorway to other more obscure economists like Brentano with his *Der Unternehmer*, perhaps even worth paraphrasing? Are there traces of J.M.K.'s 'academic scribblers' in the following, for example?

> In the teaching of economics a truth is recognised only as long as it coincides with the interests of a powerful party, and then only as long as this party remains powerful; if another party becomes more powerful, the most erroneous doctrines are rehabilitated if they appear to serve its interests.

71. It was still to be found until recently, *ad absurdum*, in Trueman on the radio, and one can get a whiff of it in Mike Selvey's comments (although he seems to make an exception for Selvey bowling against Richards in 1976).

72. The Trinidad dash by Boycott and Cowdrey in 1968, the Cronje declaration of 1999 against England in South Africa, and the Indians making 404 to win a Test Match all show the importance of the last factor. The 1938 pictures of 'Bosser' Martin and his Oval heavy roller exemplify the first. Everyone has their own personal triumphs and tragedies to illustrate the influence of weather.

73. C. L. R. James has gathered the evidence for the claim that Grace was the inventor of modern batting, combining back and front foot play into one system

74. Perhaps if Friedman were to read the chapter he would dismiss it.

75. In these days of 2-day tests perhaps Lyttelton would argue for change again? Someone ought to produce a collection of early 1990s Will Hutton, where the punches are much harder than in *The State We Are In*. In *the Guardian*, 7 May 1990, he put it pithily:

> If the price mechanism produces a stupid result – change the rules ... the heart of the Keynesian message is ... a structural fact of life about prices. They cannot account for an unknowable future, and so definitionally are incomplete purveyors of information.

76. So was Alfred Marshall, it seems, for J.M.K. expanded this elegiac paragraph in a biographical essay about his old professor years later.

77. A. L. Haskell, a close colleague of both Lydia Lopokova and J.M.K. in the Camargo Society, seems to have had access to this essay, since he used the same phrase about Anna Pavlova in his writings nearly twenty years later.

78. James concludes chapter 14 in decisive fashion, and it is worth recalling that he was no 'Little Englander', having lived for a considerable time in the United States;

> Never since the days of the Olympic champions of Greece has the sporting world known such enthusiasm and never since. That is accepted and it is true and it is important ... On what other occasions, sporting or unsporting, was there ever such an ... unforced sense of community, of the universal merged in an individual? At the end of a war? A victorious election? With its fears, its hatreds, its violent passions? ... If this is not social history what is? It finds no place in the history of the people because the historians do not begin from what people seem to want but from what they think the people ought to want ... Yet he continues warm in the hearts of those who never knew him. There he is safe until the whole crumbling edifice of obeisance before Mammon, contempt for Demos and categorizing intellectualism finally falls apart.

> The only figure in the editor's lifetime who has been so inventively and technically successful, respected by the masses, and ignored by the historians, is Jimi Hendrix who bestrode and defined the pre and post sixties.

79. Also Great War Foreign Secretary.

80. 8th Viscount Cobham (the 1886 M.C.C. President) was not unique, but, as J.M.K.'s essay points out, one of *six* brothers who played first-class cricket with aplomb; and there were two more brothers who nearly did, the family being completed by three sisters and three half-sisters. The 8th Viscount's grandson (C.J.) captained Worcestershire, toured Australia with M.C.C., became Governor-General of New Zealand between 1957 and 1962, was M.C.C. President in 1954, and then Treasurer in 1963. The 10th Viscount's part in the D'Oliveira affair was significant and of a reactionary nature. His father, J.C., was also busy, representing Droitwich for the Conservatives between 1910 and 1916, being M.C.C. President in 1935, a Parliamentary Secretary of State for War under Chamberlain (1939–40), and a distinguished President of Worcestershire C.C.C.

The best-known Lyttelton currently is the trumpet-playing Chairman of B.B.C. Radio 4's antidote to panel games *'I'm Sorry I Haven't A Clue'*, Humphrey, whose father, George (Keynes's contemporary G. W.), was a master at Eton, and (according to David Frith) wrote to the drama critic James Agate pointing out the startling fact that nobody ever saw Arthur Shrewsbury in the nude. Agate was a catalyst (with Clifford Bax) in getting C. B. Fry to reflect on the development of batting since W. G. Grace. A rare triumph in 1938 saw them avoid conversation about the theatre and Italy for once and concentrate on cricket, with Fry ranking Ranji, Grace, Trumper, Bradman, and Hobbs as the greatest batsmen he'd seen. The George Lyttelton/Rupert Hart-Davis correspondence revived the Fry list twenty years later, but G. L. got very irate about both Fry's inaccurate memory (confirmed by Iain Wilton's recent research) and the attempt to compare performers from different eras, calling the latter one of his 'bonnet's bees'. La Tchessinska, most famous of all the ballet dancers, was quite happy to compare performers from different eras conversing with A. L. Haskell, in an objective way that cricketers might do well to imitate:

> Many, who were greatly applauded, through their whole style would make one laugh today ... There are others, however, who could triumph, to-day just as yesterday ... There are some dancers whose performance excites you at the time, but who leave you with nothing ... The dancers of this time are technically very far advanced ... In the development of the artistic personality it is a different, more complicated matter.

In 1958 Rupert Hart-Davis was asked by Siegried Sassoon, along with the poet Edmund Blunden and J.M.K.'s brother, Geoffrey, to be one of his executors.

81. The sixth of the Ford cricketing brothers of Cambridge (Reverend L.G.B.J.) *did* succeed in marrying a Lyttelton, as well as becoming Headmaster of Harrow, although she wasn't named as such being the daughter of Lavinia Lyttelton (May's sister) and Dr. Talbot (later Warden of Keeble and then a distinguished Bishop). The Lyttelton girls were impartial when it came to public schools, however; the saintly Hester (youngest of the half-sisters, who only died in 1958) married Rev. Cyril A. Alington (Headmaster of Eton and Dean of Durham), the son of an Oxford Blue who got a duck in the match against Cambridge in 1859.

82. In 1940 a further twist was added as yet another Lyttelton (Oliver, later Lord Chandos) became President of the Board of Trade just as Keynes was undergoing full Treasury reintegration. They had little constructive contact; instead Lyttelton was supplied by Second Treasury Secretary Hopkins with the talents of Richard Kahn from Cambridge University's Economics Faculty. Lyttelton's grand title was later revived by Michael Heseltine when he reached the dizzy heights of Deputy Prime Minister.

The connections between the Darwins, Wedgwoods, Balfours, etc. have all been copiously noted with great detail by many authors (Noel Annan's *tour de force* essay *The Intellectual Aristocracy* being the prime example) but individual examples continue to resurface unexpectedly. It was over seven years after being captivated by *Job – a Masque for Dancing* at a Royal Festival Hall performance that I came to appreciate that the work only exists because J.M.K.'s brother Geoffrey commissioned it from his wife's cousin Ralph Vaughan-Williams, and that the set decor was by a Darwin sister-in-law, Gwen Raverat. Her nephew, Dr Milo Keynes, Geoffrey's son, has a photograph of 'Dadie' Rylands with Sir Ian McKellen on his desk to this very day, celebrating The Cambridge Arts Theatre's diamond jubilee in 1996. Ninette de Valois (who also worked at the Festival Theatre in Cambridge), Anton Dolin, and the Camargo Society spearheaded in *Job* what was not only the most important English ballet, but also one of the greatest English collaborations in the twentieth century arts; the music is even being revived for us by young producers in the twenty-first century as background music for B.B.C. Radio 4 documentary programmes. Maynard Keynes's Cambridge of 1936 is entirely tangible even now; that of 1896 is only half removed.

ENDNOTES

83. In fact from 1905 to 1916.

84. And later Bishop of Southampton.

85. To most English people in most specific situations it is apprehended as part of the stereotypical baggage to be escaped from, but as an international phenomenon it is still acknowledged to be thriving (in the future, one suspects, chiefly in Asia). Compared to fox-hunting, military service, and Christianity it has persisted in the mainstream bourgeois lifestyle remarkably intact, partly thanks to re-marketing but also due to inherent degrees of universal appeal and malleability as a product.

    Cricketers may be less aware that, along with Smith and Lonsdale, 'The Squire', George Osbaldeston (accent on the 'dest') was a leading example of both the Rural Roisterer; times have changed so much that he would now be reviled as a typical British hooligan. That attitude of self-disgust is one part of Arnold's revolution which survives, bolstered by the revival of *gentillesse* in the late 1960s . The cult of hunting and the high priest Assheton Smith really are under siege two centuries on.

86. J.M.K. often rode out with hunts over the next few years, but seemed to be rarely in at the kill. Reading his letters to his future wife, the ballerina Lydia Lopokova, a typical venture seemed to consist of several hours of trudging or cantering in the wet culminating in a broken shoe for the horse and sore buttocks (what Lydia called his 'poor halphes') for the rider.

An Article Compiled During April 1935

87. Lang was the great bowler who took 15 Oxford wickets at 6 runs apiece in the Varsity Matches of 1860–2; it is said he would never have made the Harrow XI in his wilder days without Hoare at long-stop saving the boundaries. No one except J.M.K.'s foe at Eton, R. A. H. Mitchell, could do anything against Lang at Lord's; their first battle was in the 1858 Eton/Harrow match, when only Mitchell scored over 20 in either innings for the losing Eton side.

88. Also, of course, later the first person to be knighted for services to cricket as a professional player. Robertson-Glasgow described him as

    > perfection in athletic balance and in judgement that flashes from brain to limb ... To crown all, he had the gift of smiling quietly at failure and triumph alike.

    Ronald Mason sums up the greatness of Hobbs best not in his biography, but in his *Sing All A Green Willow* of 1967 in which he wrote:

    > No king ever sat at a throne more easily or gracefully, scattered of his bounty to his subjects with such a friendly and liberal hand.

89. Concerning the title 'The Master', Arlott said:

    > There have been arguments as to who bestowed his extra title on him. There should be no doubt. He created it for himself.

    Others, like Sydney Barnes and Cecil Parkin, rebelled also. They were

    > not so much defeated as pushed aside. The establishment stronghold was not to be taken by frontal catapult fire. Indeed it was never to be taken at all; it exists now ... Jack Hobbs moved round it to a position of fresh respect for him and his kind.

    Lord Skidelsky made a telling comment about Keynes approaching his death, a phrase equally applicable to Hobbs fifteen years later:

    > ... he was respectable on his own terms, not theirs, the most satisfying kind of acceptance.

90. Compare and contrast Trueman. Hobbs was being knighted in 1953 for deeds carried out thirty, forty

GOLDEN AGES AT THE FENNER'S MARGIN

years earlier at the same time that Stanley Matthews was weaving his own legend together. Without Hobbs there could have been no Matthews. The Hobbs rebellion was constructive and complete, coming right through to affect more recent personalities like David Gower and Gary Lineker.

91. The 1962/3 abolition of the distinction between amateurs and professionals was a major step in this direction, its prospect heaving into sight as the knighthood was bestowed. Further along the line lay other steps such as Packer, the World Cup, and the re-emergence of game-fixing. Each provoked a kneejerk reaction of emotional conservatism that totally failed to locate the events' importance in the longer course of history.

92. Arlott went further and said that to a young person military manoeuvres are essentially 'make-believe', making academic points, not heroes.

93. Or The Beatles thirty years later.

94. Reeve tells us that in 1888 there were thirty brewers in Cambridge, presumably not including the colleges, who brewed their own ales. By 1903 there were 13 pubs on East Road, Sara Payne tells us, and an 'alley on the east side beyond Norfolk Street was called Brewhouse Lane'.

95. Later reborn as the Maternity Hospital.

96. If we turn from Hobbs to Keynes, there is a similarly subtle view of rebellion provided by Walter Newbold and quoted by Skidelsky (2000). When J.M.K. joined the Court of The Bank of England the left winger reacted:

> You never struck me at all as a terrible fellow ... You ... have your place on the far outside left but you are part of one team indivisible & devoted to the perpetuation of the existing order.

J.M.K. himself can have the last word for The Two Masters:

> I have run as fast as I could and am now out of breath. If practical forces catch up, what can one do about it? Certainly no help to transfer into monkish rumination.

This stoic acceptance was also the advice from Sir Walter Monckton (Surrey C.C.C.'s President) to a panic-stricken Hobbs when he tried to get him to stop 'all this' business of a knighthood. J.M.K. tries to explain why Hobbs would be so honoured (even with a knighthood) many years after his retirement. The additional clues for 1953 are the captaincy of Hutton (the first professional appointed captain of England) and the genuine feeling that England had a largely professional side that deserved to win the Ashes that year.

97. This experience encouraged J.M.K.'s sister Margaret to become closely involved in the Boys' Employment Registry and in 1911 she produced a pamphlet called *The Problem of Boy Labour in Cambridge*.

98. Facially he looks very like both Darren Cousins, the Cambridgeshire/Northamptonshire seam bowler, and also David 'Dus' Venn, the Cambridgeshire bowler of the 1970s; uncannily, the other picture resembles Venn's opening partner Matthew Gray.

99. The unattributed names refer to characters in *Mrs Dalloway*, 1925. Woolf's diary for August 1934 tells us that she was attracted by J.M.K.'s

> ... imaginative ardour about history

and that she found him 'very fertile', which later gave Moggridge half a chapter title for his major biography of J.M.K. These favourable impressions were despite the fact that J.M.K. was in considerable pain on his return after several months in the U.S. and had to have his wisdom teeth removed.

100. If the incident took place during 1927/8 it is clear that the reference was to Tyldesley; he made 520 runs in 7 innings, while England were without Hendren, Jardine, Ames, Tate, Larwood, and Duckworth in addition to Hobbs, Woolley, and Chapman. This was Woolley's first absence since July 1909.

If the incident took place during January 1923 it is clear that the reference was to Mead, who scored 181 for an even more unknown England side.

101. This is the last mention of Marshall, who died in May 1924, prompting the following exchange of letters between J.M.K. in Cambridge and Lydia in London:

> My dearest, darling L
>
> I have been touched this afternoon. I had news that my old master who made me into an economist ... could not live much longer. Lying in bed in his night cap he looked like an old sage, which is what he is ... His voice was weak but he told me how he first came to study economics, and how such study was a sort of religious work for the sake of the human race ... I held his hand hard, and then went to speak to his old wife who has given all her life to helping him do his work ...
>
> Much love from your *very fond*
>
> M.

> Your letter yesterday about your master was very nice indeed, and how we all bear relation to each other in this small wide world ...
> The society was very dull last night, all the princesses were there, but I was not sorry to leave them ... Picassos took me home.
>
> Touches to you of a very pure nature.
>
> Late, after the performance and the party, I am here alone with your face and your letter, that gives me strength, and my feelings for you grow immeasurably, passionately, I had a glass of champagne, but I feel very sad and want to run fast outstretchedly towards you.

An Article Compiled During July 1937

102. The reference to Otto Niemeyer is as ironic as Wodehouse's were to A. A. Milne (a major putter-in of the boot after Plum's broadcasts to the U.S. on German radio in 1941). It was Niemeyer who took first place in the Civil Service examinations and the only vacancy in the Treasury in 1906 while J.M.K. came second and was posted to the India Office. In addition he was infuriated to find that his worst marks were in Mathematics and Economics and prompted to write the oft-quoted line to Lytton Strachey:

> Really, knowledge seesm to be an absolute bar to success.

However, although the role of tortoise hardly seems apposite for J.M.K., it seems that the hare Otto is not destined to be as long-remembered by economists and historians as the progenitor of macroeconomics.

103. Canada (1867) and New Zealand (1907) showed their autonomy within the Empire by calling themselves Dominions; Australia (1901) a Commonwealth, and South Africa (1910) a Union. The British felt a need to redefine their status after the great support given to the U.K. during the Great War and this led to the 1926 Imperial Conference (informed by the report of the Balfour Committee), where the general term 'dominion' was brought into wider play. This was followed up by the 1931 Statute of Westminster confirming the dominions' powers of independent legislation by abrogating the Colonial Laws Validity Act of 1895. This gave rise to a textbook myth that the dominions had suddenly 'come of age' in constitutional terms, but rather it was a British adjustment to changed imperial realities. For this reason Australia felt no need to ratify the statute until 1942.

By 1931 the Great Depression made economic relations more pressing than constitutional ones, and the 1932 Ottawa Agreements attempted to broker offers of unfettered access for dominion raw materials to the U.K. in return for tariff benefits for British manufactures. In reality these were a series of bilateral deals, there being no pact of solidarity, and they represented desperate weakness in the autarchic global system of the time compared to the much less fettered interstate commerce within the federal U.S.A., Stalin's state capitalism, the Schachtian bilateral bartering in eastern Europe, and the Japanese aggrandisement of empire in Asia. After a century of British propounding of the benefits of free trade the defensive tactics of two generations of Chamberlains (rather than List's 'infant industry' argument) won through in the Import Duties Act in 1932. This could have been construed as legitimate retaliation for the U.S. Hawley-Smoot Act of 1930 which put tariffs on manufactures of up to 48 per cent, but only served to further narrow world markets.

In under a decade, following the fall of Singapore, Australia and New Zealand would be looking to the U.S. rather than the U.K. for their future security. Australia, by dint of her role as a League of Nations Mandatory Power, some rather muddled British support (against the USA's wish for 'liberation' in the U.K. colonies), and what Peter Lyon has called 'the irascibly articulate Dr Evatt', was able to punch above its weight as a smaller power in the U.N. after World War Two.

At this time in the political wilderness, Keynes held little hope for the Empire after Ottawa; a chance to create a vibrant, quasi–independent sterling area of twenty nations plus was lost by conservative gropings around tariffs. There was to be no collective talk about the level of sterling, not even a strategic recognition of the *need* for the creditor gold standard nations (USA, France) to be faced by a united and active sterling area group that was enlarging trade within itself and co-operating to keep sterling steady against the dollar.

From this point he tried to develop a policy for national self-sufficiency as all international avenues seemed closed. Many students and teachers of Economics have never really got out of this mindset, which for Keynes was a temporary expedient.

104. This was clearly demonstrated even amongst historians on 10 March 2002 in a B.B.C. Radio 4 broadcast called *The History of Kitchen Gardens*; when discussing the diary of a humble worker in the Audley End gardens the extract ended with the line:

> then out to the lawn to play cricket.

The narrator then added the flippant comment:

> presumably without telling her ladyship!

This unthinking and ridiculous equation of cricket with a game of darts over a beer is typical now of English understanding of the game's place in things. For *all* would have been needed to join in the game, and it would have been carried out right outside her ladyship's front door.

Taken often to see the old house (and the outdoor model railway) in the 1960s I had always harboured an ambition to play on the beautiful ground set between the house and the lake. By the time I did get to play there for Cambridge club Camden, the often waterlogged pitch had been moved considerably away from the lake on the far side from the house. This geographical marginalisation of the ground perhaps contributed through misunderstanding to the announcer's supposed joke.

105. See Keynes; IX (*Essays in Persuasion*), p330.

An Article Compiled During February 1946

106. Rylands was the main pillar of the Marlowe Dramatic Society in Cambridge and acting bursar of King's during the war. George Kennedy (of the Kennedy and Nightingale architectural partnership in Chelsea) was mainly responsible for squeezing the Arts Theatre project onto the site available (as well as sorting out the beloved study at Tilton, Edward Skidelsky informed me recently).

107. The received wisdom on his death was that Capra was a self-righteous, homophobic Republican with some bizarre religious foibles, but beyond the rhetoric it is recognised that he left a series of memorable and successful films.

108. To such an extent that these films are now derided as 'Capra-corn' by the cynical. This was not the critical reaction to Sir Michael Tippett's vision in *The Knot Garden* of the magic net, which gives us a philosophy similar to that of Clarence in *It's A Wonderful Life*:

> one man's life touches so many others.

Capra was more stridently self-promoting than the author of *Those Twentieth Century Blues*, and perhaps ended up inviting the more biting criticism.

109. In 1945 after demobilisation and the setting up of Liberty Films Capra had in fact bought the idea and scripts for *The Greatest Gift* off Koerner as his first post-war project, although J.M.K. was unaware of this. He started filming what became *It's A Wonderful Life* on 8 April 1946 and finished after four months. There were many more changes on the way; for example, he was unsure whether to have two characters for George Bailey, or to blend the dark side into the mild-mannered role; in the end he took the risk and Bailey as played by Jimmy Stewart is a singular, complex, all-round figure. This was Capra's favourite film which was the fruit of the most intensive work of his life, and despite garnering only fair short-term profits, it has become his most loved and iconic legacy.

110. This is almost projecting onto the monopolist (Potter) the voice of Bertholt Brecht's merchant in *The Song of Supply and Demand*:

> Don't ask me what a man is, don't ask me my advice.
> I've no idea what a man is, all that I know is its price!

111. This suggests J.M.K. would have enjoyed *Mary Poppins*. Despite the babyboomers' received wisdom that it is a turkey because of Dick Van Dyke's accent, it is *really* a Keynesian film, which is appreciated by skipping the first hour and a half. It then centres on Mr George Banks who has to

> grind, grind, grind at that grindstone

while his offspring's childhood slips away. When his son Michael says he has tuppence spare he is advised to

> frugally, thriftily, prudently

put it into a bank account to earn interest and supply funds for shipping lines, canal companies, and tea plantations to borrow and invest.

> Life's a looming battle to be faced and fought,

he tells Poppins, who tries to show she can empathise with the father's aim:

> when gazing at a graph that shows the profit's up their little cup of joy should overflow.

However, she is simultaneously pointing out to the son that

> little things can be quite important

and no one comes littler than the women on St. Paul's Cathedral steps who sells birdfeed. Michael wants to spend his tuppence feeding the birds, and Mr Banks is aghast. The older Mr Dawes, the senior partner in the bank, sums up the orthodoxy:

> Feed the birds, what have you got? Fat birds!

But Mary Poppins has the opposite opinion, that the

> saints and apostles are smiling

down on the spending of these tuppences although the immediate effect is indeed, in the words of Mr Banks, to

> waste your money on a load of ragamuffin birds.

Even in 1910 this was seen as undesirable encouragement of a pest. But, as Poppins and Keynes knew, a woman on low income would have a very high propensity to consume, and that tuppence would work through local markets many times before being leaked out of the system in hoarding, creating employment and welfare for everyone including the Banks family. Save the tuppence and what have you got? Slump.

This image had a powerful effect on those of us born in 1958 and 1959. No sooner had I noted the above analysis than David Boyle, of the New Economics Foundation, published his *The Tyranny of Numbers*, the follow-up to *Funny Money*. The piece selected for the *Observer* in January 2001 began:

> Mary Poppins was the first film I ever saw.

It is pleasing to note that his conclusion also was redolent of Keynes:

> I came away from the cinema determined to make sure that I flung my tuppence away on a little old bird woman, rather than marvelling at the strange alchemy of compound interest if I put it in a bank.

In a cinematic echo of Frank Capra's *You Can't Take It With You*, Mr Banks is converted (as he fingers the tuppence rather than a harmonica) while being fired for causing a run (further echoes from *American Madness* and *It's A Wonderful Life*).

112. Capra remained close to that Keynesian spirit Marshall, who awarded him the D.C.M. for his film work. Capra hailed Marshall's handling of the U.S. economic *volte face* in Europe during 1947 with hagiographic language, which is understandable given the scale of the change of policy:

> ... has there ever been a military general who has had so much power and scope to do good in the world before or since?

113. Between 1942 and 1945, according to Capra,

> One film was shown to the American public in theatres. By an order from Winston Churchill *all* were shown to the British public in theatres. The Russians showed *Battle of Russia* [film 4] throughout all their theatres. And in the chaotic months of occupation after the war, American Embassies played the *Why We Fight* series in enemy countries, charging ten cents for admission. The State Department has stated that these showings enriched our treasury by more than $2,500,000 – a sum six times greater than their original cost.

114. The arch-critics of the Keynesian approach are to be seen *en masse* in Critical Review, volume 3, numbers 3 and 4 (summer/fall 1989); Selgin, Horwitz, Egger, Gallaway, Vedder, and Wagner all attacked Keynesianism triumphally as the refugees/economic migrants streamed out of the GDR through Hungary and the Berlin Wall came down. Their arguments centred on the successes of the Keynesian Golden Age taking place because of free market self-adjustment and in spite of fiscal policy (not vice-versa). The next step, they said, had to be the de-politicisation of monetary control and competition in the production of money; this would make everything even better. Post-Keynesians may try to imagine the world this would produce and conclude that it wouldn't correspond to anything better than the unregulated private banks of two hundred years ago. One could once again become stranded with Wiltshire notes in London when travelling to Manchester.

Tyler Cowen, however, gave food for thought in his Critical Review piece 'Why Keynesianism Triumphed, or Could So Many Keynesians Have Been Wrong?' The six points he considers are: widespread and persistent unemployment in the Great Depression, failures of the price system, stock market volatility, Lionel Robbins's conversion, the post-war recovery, and post-war stability. His conclusions start with the assertion 'I am not a Keynesian', and its subsequent chastening starkness (combined with uncharacteristic generosity and fairness to the enemy) makes the rest of the 230-page pamphlet seem self-indulgent:

> In the light of history, many have understandably concluded that Keynesian economics was a good thing, given the political constraints which are a modern reality. The Keynesian vision grappled more effectively with the actual experiences of the Great Depression than did previous economic theories. That Keynesianism still survives and sometimes flourishes is the product of neither obvious intellectual error nor of venal statesmen and their lackeys. The task remains to construct a

more powerful defense of laissez-faire.

115. And a world where there was no George Marshall in 1947 to make a u-turn on the U.S. policy towards Europe once it was found two years into the peace the old ideas weren't working.

116. How could it be that less than two centuries later it happened again, with the Qayyum Report on match-fixing in cricket in the weeks following the 50th anniversary of the Schuman Declaration?

  In his father's 'fancy-filled' diary of 1896 this was the crucial conceptual test that arguably demarcated cricket as a non-serious model of the economy in J.M.K.'s view. He had ceased taking an active interest in what he had come to see as a childish activity. The evidence of nearly half a century later is that J.N.K. was involved in prophesy rather than fancy.

117. Paul Levy, in his book on Moore, gives us a clear impression of Keynes as worldly-wise in these matters from the highest authority (Moore himself):

  > At the end of July 1914 [Moore] spent several days with the Oliver Stracheys at Clark End near Pangbourne ... Karen Corbelle ... and Keynes were the other house guests; Moore lost the considerable sum of 16*s*. 6*d*. to Keynes at Auction Bridge. Keynes was an inveterate gambler, and perhaps this was why Moore noted that 'Keynes somehow leaves a bad taste in my mouth'.

  That betting is now a general cultural problem (no longer confined to racing as in my youth) is shown by the scale of annual gambling expenditure rises (8 per cent in 1998–9 in Australia, for example). The tied nature of much gambling reinforces its virtuous aspects in society (paying for charities, hospitals, museums, etc.) and with the decline of religious influence gambling has been able to modernise its image considerably during the last thirty years or so. Cricket only officially readmitted the practice in the 1970s, but it has had a devastating impact as the rewards to participants are greater from the betting than the fees for playing. The news of Lillee and Marsh betting at 500–1 *against themselves* during the 1981 Headingley Test was treated with extraordinary complacency by the pundits and the authorities. *Laisser faire* ruled. 2000 saw Ian Botham, who saw nothing wrong in the Aussies betting on their own defeat in 1981, claiming that the game is rotten to the core and Matthew Engel writing about cricket being in crisis. On Sky TV Mark Saggers spluttered to hold in the anger he felt about the game he loved (even when he had to share a room with me when we played for Cambridgeshire together). What the *Qayyum Report*, Vic Marks, Paul Condon, and Ashley Mallett all share beyond the squabbling over details, is that match-fixing negates cricket as a worthwhile pastime and is wrong.

118. The 1980–1 recession in the U.K. so appalled moderate conservatives like Lord Gilmour and John Harvey-Jones because they saw good, well-run firms being driven to bankruptcy by macroeconomic policy. The flows of currency into Britain from oil were not offset by increased domestic expansion to increase imports, and the floating exchange rate rose, creating a positive feedback loop of expectations, leading to further rises. The combination of exploding prices for sterling exports and depressed demand within the country decimated British industry; the betting cartel was loading the results to chilling effect.

A Second Article Compiled During February 1946

119. How ironic that when the seeds of the ideas of 1919 were about to ripen and grow a prime advocate was on the verge of death and should have been, by any rational measure of matters, in despair.

120. Reading through *The Sinews of Peace* (printed in an adoring Luxembourg city in 1947) there is fire from speeches in Fulton, Zurich, and Metz that is almost extinguished by the large quantities of wayward froth. Iron curtain? Fine, although Churchill knew the U.K.'s poverty would mean running a German policy that would goad Stalin to react badly. But Stettin to Trieste? Certainly not. A United States of Europe? He got that spectacularly and generously right. British aloofness from it, because the Indian Empire would go on until 2000? Remember that the Fulton speech ends up triumphally: 'Let no man underrate the abiding power of the British Empire and Commonwealth.' Whoops, perhaps not.

121. Moreover, the U.K. has not appreciated the achievement of peace and its longevity, nearly three times the length of the peace following the Great War.

122. The ostrichlike behaviour towards the politics of the U.S. loan is one reason why J.M.K. is less well-known in Britain than he should be; British school history tends to end in 1945. Until George Marshall persuaded the U.S. administration that White's Bretton Woods plan had indeed been too timid, and that Europe really was sinking fast in 1947, Britain's decline was destined to be rapid. It took time to persuade a free-market Republican Congress that they could justify to themselves pushing ahead with the Marshall Plan in order to contain communism in France and Italy, but it is still little understood (and was way beyond the Britain of those days) that the anti-integrationist Roosevelt would never have sanctioned the package that Truman fought for in Congress.

Yet, not least by Keynes's final efforts, an atmosphere conducive to a generous peace was achieved by 1950, just seven years after the Big Three met at Tehran. For the aid of 1948–52 entailed a supranational committee to disburse it (the O.E.E.C. with a British chairman) and with Churchill's Council of Europe coming to pass in 1949 it seemed that the dreams of the British federalists of the 1930s might be realised. The astonishing events leading up to and from the *Schuman Declaration* of 9 May 1950 were made almost unbearably poignant by the self-delusion towards the Commonwealth that allowed Britain to stay aloof from the formation of the European Coal and Steel Community.

There was an unlikely relationship between U.S. Treasury Secretary Henry Morgenthau and Sir Frederick Phillips, U.K. Treasury representative in Washington. These two got on very well thanks to a mutual aversion to garrulousness, and Keynes memorably wrote in his obituary of Phillips for *The Times* that

> ... in Geneva he could be silent in several languages.

Meredith's *The Ordeal of Richard Feverel* would have supplied him with a further epithet:

> Speech is the small change of silence.

123. American economist Richard Gardner recounted his own exchanges with Beaverbrook in Milo Keynes's *Essays*:

> Lord Beaverbrook wrote me a rather angry letter ... saying: [Beaverbrook's attitude was] 'of one who sought to reconcile his belief in the Empire with his hope that a strong Empire was the best ally the United States could have. Was I wrong?' Well, of course he was. Empire was not a viable economic or political concept for Britain after the Second World War. It took a long time for some members of the British public and political leadership to recognise the fact.

So the picture from New York's Columbia University was very clear. In view of the U.S. involvement in supporting the anti-French forces in Indochina it is likely that they had factored the swift independence of India into their expectations by the negotiations of 1941–4, and used the new arrangements to ensure that the breakdown of the empire took place peacefully through economic dismemberment rather than military insurgency.

124. Confirmed by C. F. Streit in his later editions of *Union Now*.

125. He worked on the Joint Purchasing Committee and was close to Roosevelt. His most important American protégé was the young George Ball of the Lend-Lease Administration, who took charge of European affairs for Kennedy in 1961.

126. Toynbee claimed the Law of Withdrawal and Return now applied to Britain; extrication from Empire would preface a new (unspecified) creative task. Macmillan took this to mean Europe, but had years of opposition and Eden to deal with. The latter had commented at Columbia University in 1942 that with regard to joining a continental European Federation:

> We know in our bones we cannot do it.

Spaak's retort to this was not widely reported in Britain, but Robert Rothschild later claimed he said:

> That's a funny place to have thinking.

ENDNOTES

127. Churchill indeed seemed to be in the van of European integration by inspiring the European Movement, the Council of Europe, and the Parliamentary Assembly at Strasbourg, but J.M.K. was right in so far as these were hollow victories that had limited long-term significance. The cheering crowds of Strasbourg in 1949 receded into memory, and politicians like Spaak, Monnet, Adenauer, and Schuman detached themselves from Churchill's locomotive which puffed a lot but led to a dead end. The biggest puffs were when the Assembly passed Churchill's motion for the immediate creation of a European Army in August 1950. Bevin said he could put up with a talking shop. To what extent did these experiences make the British people more sceptical about the Treaty of Rome following the collapse of the Pleven Plan and the non-federal nature of the Messina Conference??

128. A lot of 'wait and see' misjudgements by the U.K. have come from the conviction that the 'inferior' continental powers could not sustain even a good idea for long. Butler admitted as much with regard to 1950 and Messina in 1955 and the Treaty of Rome in 1957. But here is Peter Jay as late as 1975 (the year of his conversion to monetarism and the debate over the Bacon and Eltis articles in the *Sunday Times*) lulling the readers of his IEA pamphlet of December into a false sense of superiority:

> Less Hope in Western Europe;
>
> Countries like West Germany ... have the weakest political institutions and are in consequence vulnerable to even a mild degree of economic adversity. Others like Italy have the worst of both worlds. In consequence they have already slipped over the abyss and presumably must soon be dashed on the waiting rocks of political anarchy and economic deprivation.

This was the sort of stuff Thatcher's new acolytes were dishing up. Meanwhile Eltis was popularising Leijonhofvud's line that Keynesian economics was not the economics of Keynes, but came to some extraordinary conclusions, like the need to reduce the automatic stabilisers and a belief that Say was tough on inflation but Keynes hadn't a clue about it; had he read *How To Pay For The War* or *The Economic Consequences Of The Peace*? Even Friedman was in no doubt that Keynes was as hot on inflation as he was, and Hayek claimed that the last time he spoke to Keynes early in 1946 J.M.K. said that at the first sign of inflation he'd be able to get public opinion behind austerity in a trice.

129. One hopes the idea of the British Establishment being ignorant is not too shocking. Butler was the most honest in admitting quite how far this went, but the modern rash of doorstop revisionist histories of Europe is not encouraging to this editor as a History teacher, nor is the National Curriculum. Each generation's blank canvas needs to be given a fresh background of understanding, which they can pick up astonishingly quickly (although some consider that shielding pupils from complexity is an excuse for inaction). This just has not happened in the state schools of the U.K. with the European integration story.

Mazower's book can seriously (and, many might say, obscenely) compare Etienne Davignon to Albert Speer yet receive solemnly approving reviews. Norman Davies can virtually ignore a half century of integration. Even the late Hugo Young could produce a huge tome without a single index references to any of the following crucial topics; the ESPRIT project, the Bilderberg Club, Davignon, Werner, Barre, the Crocodile Club, the European Roundtable of Industrialists, Coreper, biotechnological connections of *any* sort, the Trilateral Commission, Peter Gyllenhammer, supranational, UNICE, own resources, ERDF.

These are not chosen at random, they are central parts of the E.U. project comparable in importance with Ford, Lyttelton, and Ward in the development of the Fenner's project. Nicola Fielder would not be surprised at this neglect or ignorance. In Bornschier's book she says that one representative (anonymity maintained) of the 36 on the panel of interviewees, which included Lord Cockfield and Etienne Davignon,

> did not even know what the Committee of Permanent Representatives is!

130. John Kenneth Galbraith wrote (in Milo Keynes's collection about J.M.K.) that Paul Samuelson likened his excitement at the arrival of *The General Theory* in the U.S.A. to that of

> Keats on first looking into Chapman's Homer.

GOLDEN AGES AT THE FENNER'S MARGIN

An Article Compiled During April 1946

131. Christopher Dow's masterly research clearly shows that Keynes was correct as far as the U.K. goes. The other major recessions of the early 30s, mid-70s, early–80s, and early–90s had other principal causes. Harrod says that Keynes recanted his 1920 advice, Moggridge quotes him on January 7th 1942 saying that he would have given the same advice then as before about dearer money; the two statements in their entire context are not incompatible, and this final word from 1946 serves to show how times had changed and the two biographers may not be contradicting each other.

132. This is clearest in his work on the Havana Charter, where his endorsement of the benefits from European integration seem compromised by a lack of *any* constructive ideas about how to promote it:

    ... it is premature to suppose that we know today at all how how these ends can best be served.

133. J.N.K. was in fact amplifying Marshall (biological analogies are more serviceable than mechanical ones); as economic problems grow more complex they are

    less concerned with the interaction of forces and more concerned with organic life and growth.

    So Paul Ormerod's *The Death Of Economics* (1994) is not so new after all.

134. J.M.K. seems to have been leafing through pages 40–3 of his father's *Scope and Method of Political Economy* as he constructed this rather mournful passage. Crude versions of *laisser faire* were widely accessible from George, Kingsley, or Hyndman well before J.M.K.'s *General Theory* was written. J.N.K. warned against the dogmatic creed of those who spoke of 'trades-unions ... violating economic laws' and said that prices ought to be determined by supply and demand;

    these are just ignorant prejudices (rash generalisations, fallacious arguments) that need removing.

135. Pele's unfortunate description of soccer as 'the beautiful game' came long after Douglas Jardine's superior description of cricket (made in New Zealand, 1933) as

    That beautiful, beautiful game that is battle and service and sport and art.

    The Lords Taverners c.d. celebrating cricket in music and song contains not only tracks such as Percy Pavilion's *Dolly Mixture*, Don Bradman on the piano, and Roy Harper's classic *When An Old Cricketer Leaves The Crease*, but also reprises The Cavaliers' song *It's A Beautiful Game*, first put out on 7 inch vinyl by Cherry Red (GPO 11). The other accessible c.d. version is *Bellismo – The ,l Singles Part One* (Richmond, MONDE 11 CD).

136. Reading Austin Robinson's essay in the Milo Keynes collection on J.M.K. one comes across an equally arresting sentence that carries the same sort of meaning as this comment about Watt, but conveys quite a frisson when taken in isolation:

    Keynes is still alive.